CAMBRIDGE LIBRARY

Books of enduring schola

Archaeology

The discovery of material remains from the recent or the ancient past has always been a source of fascination, but the development of archaeology as an academic discipline which interpreted such finds is relatively recent. It was the work of Winckelmann at Pompeii in the 1760s which first revealed the potential of systematic excavation to scholars and the wider public. Pioneering figures of the nineteenth century such as Schliemann, Layard and Petrie transformed archaeology from a search for ancient artifacts, by means as crude as using gunpowder to break into a tomb, to a science which drew from a wide range of disciplines - ancient languages and literature, geology, chemistry, social history - to increase our understanding of human life and society in the remote past.

Discoveries in Egypt, Ethiopia and the Peninsula of Sinai

Dr Richard Lepsius (1810–1884) was a pioneering Prussian Egyptologist considered the founder of modern Egyptology. In 1842 he was commissioned by King Frederick Wilhelm IV to lead an expedition to Egypt and Sudan to explore and record ancient Egyptian remains. The expedition included artists, surveyors and other specialists and spent three years recording monuments in Egypt, modern Sudan and the Sinai. The expedition conducted the first scientific studies of the pyramids of Giza, Abusir, Saqqara and Dashur. First published in 1852, this volume is a translation of 40 reports in the form of letters written by Lepsius to King Frederick Wilhem IV during the expedition, and translated by Kenneth R. H Mackenzie. They provide descriptions of many ancient Egyptian monuments which have since been lost or destroyed, and provide an engaging and frank account of the difficulties of supervising an archaeological expedition in Egypt at that time.

Cambridge University Press has long been a pioneer in the reissuing of out-of-print titles from its own backlist, producing digital reprints of books that are still sought after by scholars and students but could not be reprinted economically using traditional technology. The Cambridge Library Collection extends this activity to a wider range of books which are still of importance to researchers and professionals, either for the source material they contain, or as landmarks in the history of their academic discipline.

Drawing from the world-renowned collections in the Cambridge University Library, and guided by the advice of experts in each subject area, Cambridge University Press is using state-of-the-art scanning machines in its own Printing House to capture the content of each book selected for inclusion. The files are processed to give a consistently clear, crisp image, and the books finished to the high quality standard for which the Press is recognised around the world. The latest print-on-demand technology ensures that the books will remain available indefinitely, and that orders for single or multiple copies can quickly be supplied.

The Cambridge Library Collection will bring back to life books of enduring scholarly value (including out-of-copyright works originally issued by other publishers) across a wide range of disciplines in the humanities and social sciences and in science and technology.

Discoveries in Egypt, Ethiopia and the Peninsula of Sinai

In the Years 1842-1845

RICHARD LEPSIUS
EDITED BY
KENNETH R.H. MACKENZIE

CAMBRIDGE
UNIVERSITY PRESS

CAMBRIDGE UNIVERSITY PRESS

Cambridge, New York, Melbourne, Madrid, Cape Town, Singapore,
São Paolo, Delhi, Dubai, Tokyo, Mexico City

Published in the United States of America by Cambridge University Press, New York

www.cambridge.org
Information on this title: www.cambridge.org/9781108017114

© in this compilation Cambridge University Press 2010

This edition first published 1852
This digitally printed version 2010

ISBN 978-1-108-01711-4 Paperback

DISCOVERIES

IN

EGYPT, ETHIOPIA.

AND THE

PENINSULA OF SINAI.

On Stone by W.L.Walton.

Printed by Hullmandel & Walton.

MOUNT BARKAL.(NUBIA)

London, Richard Bentley, New Burlington Street 1852

DISCOVERIES

IN

EGYPT, ETHIOPIA,

AND THE

PENINSULA OF SINAI,

IN THE YEARS 1842-1845,

DURING THE MISSION

SENT OUT BY

HIS MAJESTY FREDRICK WILLIAM IV. OF PRUSSIA.

By DR. RICHARD LEPSIUS.

EDITED, WITH NOTES, BY

KENNETH R. H. MACKENZIE.

MEROE.

LONDON:

RICHARD BENTLEY, NEW BURLINGTON STREET,

Publisher in Ordinary to Her Majesty.

1852.

TO

ALEXANDER VON HUMBOLDT,

WITH

THE DEEPEST RESPECT AND GRATITUDE.

AUTHOR'S PREFACE.

THE purpose of the Scientific Expedition, sent out in 1842 by his Majesty the King, was an historical and antiquarian research into, and collection of the ancient Egyptian monuments, in the valley of the Nile, and the peninsula of Sinai. It was by royal munificence provided with the means for remaining three years; it rejoiced in the favour and interest of the highest person in the realm, as well as in the most active and kindly assistance of Alexander Von Humboldt; and under such a rare combination of fortunate circumstances, it completed its intended task as fully as could have been hoped. A "Prefatory account of the expedition, its results, and their publication," (Berlin, 1849, 4to.) was published with the first parts of the great monumental work, which is brought out at the command of his Majesty, in a manner corresponding to the importance of the treasures brought back, and contains a short abstract of the more important results of the Expedition. The work, there announced, "The Monuments of Egypt and Ethiopia," will contain more than 800 plates, of the largest size, of which half are already prepared, and 240 plates already published, will lay before the public these results, as far as concerns the sculptures, the topography, and architecture, while the accompanying text will explain them more fully.

It however, appeared necessary (without taking the purely scientific labours into account), to lay before a larger circle of readers a picture of the external events of the expedition, of the relative operations of its members, of the obstacles, and the favourable circumstances of the journey, the condition of the countries through which it passed, and their effect upon the actual design of the undertaking: finally to offer a few observations on the remarkable monuments of that most historical of all countries, as must continually recur to the well prepared traveller, and which might rouse others who have already perceived the importance of the newly founded science, to a more active interest. If, besides, it be of the greatest utility for a just understanding of these scientific labours which are gradually coming to the light, and which have been caused by the journey; that the circumstances under which the materials for them were collected, I think that the publication of the following letters requires no farther excuse, as they make no pretension to any particular literary perfection, or descriptive power, or, on the other hand, to be a strictly scientific work.

The letters are almost in the original form as they were written, sometimes as a report direct to his Majesty the King, sometimes to his Excellency, the then Minister of Instruction, Eichhorn, or to other high patrons and honoured men, as A. Von Humboldt, Bunsen, Von Olfers, Ehrenberg, and sometimes to my father, who followed my progress with the most lively interest. Several of them were immediately printed in the papers on their arrival in Europe, particularly in the *Preussische Staatszeitung*, and thence in other papers. The unessential changes mostly relate to the editing. All the additions or enlargements have been added as notes; and among these belong particularly the arguments and grounds as to the true position of Sinai, which, since then has been proved in various quarters, and again disproved, and again concurred in. The thirty-sixth letter, on the arrangement of the Egyptian Museum in Berlin, turns certainly from the subject; but we may allow the exception, as this point is not alone interesting to Berlin, but in all points the examination is worth while, where there is any resemblance to or comparison with modern art.

It is proposed to add a second part to these letters, in which several treatises, written during the expedition, or on different points relating to Egyptian art or history, will be published.

BERLIN, *2nd June*, 1852.

CONTENTS.

LETTER I.—ON BOARD THE ORIENTAL STEAMER, SEPT.
5, 1842 ... ... Page 1
Sea voyage to Alexandria.

LETTER II.—ALEXANDRIA, SEPT. 23, 1842 6
Malta.—Gobat.—Isenberg.—Krapf.—Alexandria.—Mohammed Ali.

LETTER III.—CAIRO, OCT. 16, 1842 11
Alexandria. — Pompey's Pillar. — Cleopatra's
Needle.—Collection of Werne.—Departure from
Alexandria.—Sais. — Naharîeh. — Cairo.—Helio-
polis.—The king's birth-day kept at the pyramids.
—View from the pyramid of Cheops.

LETTER IV.—AT THE FOOT OF THE GREAT PYRAMID,
JAN. 2, 1843 24
Pyramids of Gizeh.—Private tombs.—Sphinx.
—Storm of rain.—Christmas.—Life in the Camp.

LETTER V.—PYRAMIDS OF GIZEH, JAN. 17, 1843 ... 32
The hieroglyphical tablet on the pyramid of
Cheops.—Historical gain.

LETTER VI.—PYRAMIDS OF GIZEH, JAN. 28, 1843 ... 37
The oldest royal dynasties.—Tomb of Prince
Merhet. — Private tombs. — Destruction by the
Arabs.—Oldest obelisk.

LETTER VII.—SAQARA, MARCH 18, 1843 44
Pyramids of Meidûm.—Architecture of the pyra-
mids.—The Riddle of the Sphinx.—Locust.—
Comet.

LETTER VIII.—SAQARA, APRIL 13, 1843 51
H. R. H. Prince Albrecht of Prussia.—Rejoicings
in Cairo.—Return of Pilgrims.—Mulid e' Nebbi.—
Doseh.—Visit of the prince to the pyramids.—
Oldest use of the pointed arch in Cairo.—Oldest
round arch in Egypt.—Night attack at Saqâra.—
Judgment day.

LETTER IX.—CAIRO, APRIL 22, 1843 64
Situation of the fields of pyramids.—Cairo.

LETTER X.—RUINS OF THE LABYRINTH, MAY 31, 1843. 67
Departure for the Faiûm.—Camels and drome-
daries.—Lisht.—Meidûm. —Illahun. — Labyrinth.
—Arab music.—Bedouins.—Turkish khawass.

LETTER XI.—LABYRINTH, JUNE 25, 1843 78
Ruins of the Labyrinth.—Its first builders.—
Pyramid.—Lake Mœris.

LETTER XII.—LABYRINTH, JULY 18, 1843 85
Excursion through the Faiûm.—Mœris embankments.—Birqet el Qorn.—Dimeh.—Qasr Qerûn.

LETTER XIII.—CAIRO, AUGUST 14, 1843 91
Departure of Frey.—Ethiopian manuscripts.

LETTER XIV.—THEBES, OCT. 13, 1843 93
Nile passage to Upper Egypt.—Rock-cave of
Surarîeh. Tombs of the sixth dynasty in Middle
Egypt, of the twelfth at Benihassan, Sint, Ber-
sheh.—Arrival at Thebes.—Climate.—Departure.

LETTER XV.—KORUSKO, NOVEMBER 20, 1843 100
Greek inscriptions. — Benihassan. — Bersheh.
Tombs of the sixth dynasty. — El Amarna.—Siut
—Alabaster quarries of El Bosra.—Echmin (Chem-
mis).—Thebes. —El Kab (Eileithyia). — Edfu.—
Ombos.—Egyptian Canon of Proportion.—Assuan.
— Philae. — Hieroglyphic demotic inscriptions.—
Series of Ptolemies. — Entrance in Lower Nubia.
—Debôd. — Gertassi. — Kalabsheh (Talmis). —
Dendûr.—Dakkeh (Pselchis).—Korte. —Hierasy-
kaminos. — Mehendi. — Sebûa. — Korusko. —
Nubian language.

LETTER XVI.—KORUSKO, JANUARY 5, 1844 133
    Scarcity of camels.—Wadi Halfa.—Ahmed Pasha
Menekle and the new Pashas of the Sudan.

LETTER XVII.—E'DAMER, JANUARY 24, 1844 ... 137
    Nubian desert.—Roft mountains.—Wadi E'Sufr.
—Wadi Murhad. — Abâbde Arabs.— Abu Ham-
med.—Berber. —El Mechêref.—Mogran or Atbara
(Astaboras).—E'Damer.—Mandera.

LETTER XVIII.—ON THE BLUE RIVER, PROVINCE OF
    SENNAR, 13° NORTH LATITUDE, MARCH 2, 1844 155
Hagi Ibrahim.—Meroe.—Begerauie.—Pyramids.
—Bounds of the tropical climate. — Khawass.—
—Ferlini.—Age of the monuments. — Shendi.—
Ben Naga. — Naga in the desert.—Mesaurât e'
Sofra.—Tamaniât.—Chârtum.—Bahr el Abiad (the
White River). — Dinka and Shilluk. — Soba. —
Kamlîn.—Bauer.— Marble inscription. — Baobâb.
—Abu Harras.—Rahad. — Nature of the country.
—Dender.—Dilêb-palms.—Sennâr.—Abdîn.—Ro-
mâli.—Sero.—Return northward.—Wed Médineh.
—Soriba.—Sultana Nasr.—Gabre Mariam. — Re-
bâbi.—Funeral.—Military.—Emin Pasha.—Taiba.
—Messelemieh.—Kamlîn.—Soba.—Urn and in-
scription.

LETTER XIX.—CHARTUM, MARCH 21, 1844 207
    Military revolt in Wed Médineh. — Insurrec-
tion of slaves.

LETTER XX.—PYRAMIDS OF MEROE, APRIL 22, 1844 ... 211
    Tamaniât.—Qirre mountains.—Meroe.—Return
of the Turkish army from Taka.—Osman Bey.—
Prisoners from Taka.—Language of the Bishari
from Taka.—Customs of the South.—Pyramids
of Meroe. — Ethiopian inscriptions. — Name of
Meroe.

LETTER XXI.—KELI, APRIL 29, 1844 233
    Departure from Meroe.—Groups of tombs north
of Meroe.

LETTER XXII.—BARKAL, MAY 9, 1844   237
    Desert of Gilif. — Gôs Burri. — Wadi Gaqedûl.
    —Mágeqa. — Desert trees.—Wadi Abu Dôm.—
    Wadi Gazâl.—Koptic church.—Greek inscriptions.
    —Pyramids of Nuri.—Arrival at Barkal.

LETTER XXIII.—MOUNT BARKAL, MAY 28, 1844 ... 248
    Ethiopian kings. — Temple of Ramses II.—
    Napata.—Meraui.—Climate.

LETTER XXIV.—DONGOLA, JUNE 15, 1844   251
    Excursion into the district of cataracts.—Bân.—
    Departure from Barkal.—Pyramids of Tanqassí,
    Kurru, and Zûma.—Churches and fortresses of
    Bachît, Magal, Gebel Dêqa.—Old Dongola.—
    Nubian language.

LETTER XXV.—DONGOLA, JUNE 23, 1844   262
    Isle of Argo.—Kermâ and Defûfa.—Tombos.—
    Inscriptions of Tuthmosis I.—Languages of Darfur.

LETTER XXVI.—KORUSKO, AUGUST 16, 1844   264
    Fakir Fenti. — Sese. — Soleb.—Gebel Doshe.
    Sedeinga.—Amâra.—Isle of Sâi.—Sulphur-springs
    of Okmeh.—Semneh.—Elevation of the Nile, under
    Amenemha (Mœris). — Abu Simbel. — Greek in-
    scription under Psammeticus I.—Ibrîm (Primis).—
    Anibis.—Korusko.

LETTER XXVII.—PHILAE, SEPTEMBER 1, 1844   ...   271
    Wadi Kenus.—Bega language of Bishari.—
    Talmis. — Philae. — Meroitic-Ethiopian inscrip-
    tions.

LETTER XXVIII.—THEBES, QURNA, NOV. 24, 1844 ... 274
    Excavations in the Temple and Rock-tomb of
    Ramses II.—Sudan languages.—Ethiopian history
    and civilisation.

LETTER XXIX.—THEBES, QURNA, JAN. 8, 1845   ...   277
    Removal of monuments and plaster casts.

LETTER XXX.—THEBES, February 25, 1845 279
    Description of Thebes.—Temple of Karnak and its
    history.—Luqsor.—El Asasif.—Statue of Memnon.
    —Memnonium.—Temple of Ramses II.—Medînet

Habu.—The Royal Tombs.—Private tombs of the
time of Psammetichus.—Time of the Cæsars.—
Koptic convent and church.—The present Kopts.
—Revenge of the Arabs.—Dwelling in Abd el
Qurna.—Visit from travellers.

LETTER XXXI.—ON THE RED SEA, MARCH 21, 1845 ... 313
Immigrations from Qurna to Karnak.—Journey
to the Sinai peninsula.—Qenneh.—Seîd Hussên.—
Stone bridge and inscriptions of Hamamât.—Gebel
Fatireh.—Lost in the desert.—Quarries of por-
phyry at Gebel Dochân.—Gebel Zeit.

LETTER XXXII.—CONVENT OF SINAI, MARCH 24, 1845. 333
Landing in Tôr.—Gebel Hammâm.—Wadi Hebrân.—Convent.—Gebel Mûsa.—Gebel Sefsaf.

LETTER XXXIII.—ON THE RED SEA, APRIL 6, 1845 ... 338
Departure from the convent.—Wadi e' Sheikh.—
Ascension of Serbâl.—Wadi Firan.—Wadi Mokatteb. — Copper-mines of Wadi Maghâra.—Rock
inscriptions of the fourth dynasty. — Sarbut el
Châdem.—Slag-hills.—Wadi Nasb.—Harbour of
Zelimeh.—True situation of Sinai.—Monkish traditions.—Local and historical relations.—Elim near
Abu Zelimeh.—Mara in Wadi Gharandel.—Desert
of Sin.—Sinai, the Mountain of Sin.—The mountain of God.—Sustenance of the Israelites.—Raphidîm near Pharan.—Sinai-Choreb, near Raphidîm.
—Review of the Sinai question.

LETTER XXXIV.—THEBES, KARNAK, MAY 4, 1845 ... 372
Return to Thebes.—Revenge.

LETTER XXXV.—CAIRO, JULY, 10, 1845 374
Dendera. — El Amarna. — Dr. Bethmann. —
Taking down the tombs near the pyramids.

LETTER XXXVI.—CAIRO, JULY 11, 1845 376
The Egyptian Museum in Berlin.—Wall paintings.

LETTER XXXVII.—JAFFA, OCTOBER 7, 1845 389
Journey through the Delta.—San (Tanis).—
Arrival in Jaffa.

LETTER XXXVIII.—NAZARETH, NOVEMBER 9, 1845 ...   391
Jerusalem.—Nablus (Sichem).—Tabor.—Nazareth.—Lake of Tiberias.

LETTER XXXIX.—SMYRNA, DECEMBER 7, 1845   ..   394
Carmel.—Lebanon. — Berut.—Journey to Da-
mascus. — Zahleh.—Tomb of Noah.—Barada.—
Abel's tomb.—Inscriptions at Barada.—Tomb of
Seth.—Bâlbek.—Ibrahim.—Cedars of Lebanon.
—Egyptian and Assyrian Rock-sculptures at
Nahr el Kelb.

APPENDIX   420
INDEX   449

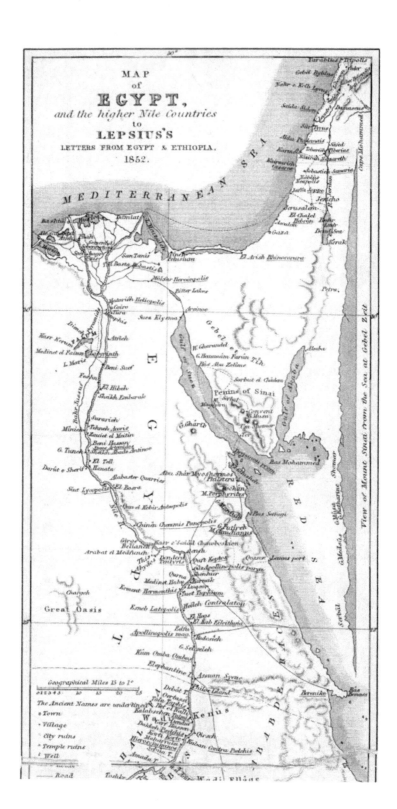

MAP
of
EGYPT,
and the higher Nile Countries
to
LEPSIUS'S
LETTERS FROM EGYPT & ETHIOPIA.
1852.

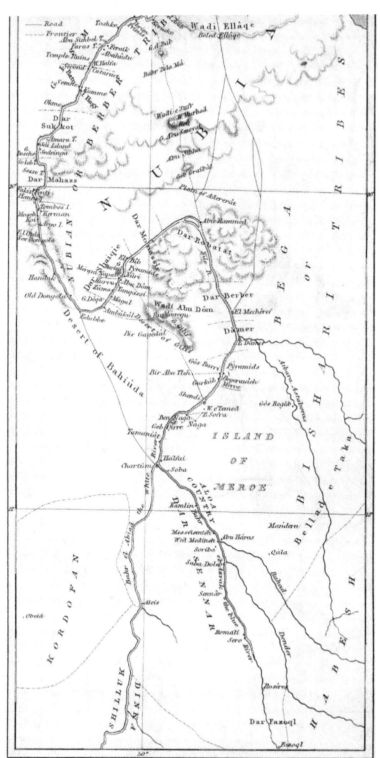

London, Richard Bentley, 1852.

T. Brooker sc.

LETTERS

FROM

EGYPT, ETHIOPIA, AND THE PENINSULA

OF SINAI.

LETTER I.

ON BOARD THE ORIENTAL STEAMER.
September 5, 1842.

ALL our endeavours were taxed to the utmost
to render our departure on the 1st of September
possible; one day's delay would have cost us a
whole month, and this month it was necessary
to gain by redoubled activity. My trip to Paris,
where I arrived in thirty hours from London, was
unavoidable; two days were all that could be
spared for the necessary purchases, letters, and
notes, after which I returned richly laden from
that city, ever so interesting and instructive to
me. In London I obtained two other pleasant
travelling companions, Bonomi and Wild, who
had readily resolved to take part in the expedition. The former, long well known as a traveller
in Egypt and Ethiopia, is not only full of practical knowledge of life in that country, but is also
a fine connoisseur of Egyptian art, and a master

in Egyptian drawing; the latter, a young genial architect, enthusiastically seeks in the Orient new threads for his rich woof of combination.

At length everything was bought, prepared, packed, and we had said farewell to all our friends. Bunsen only, with his usual kindness and untiring friendship, accompanied us to Southampton, the place of embarkation, where he spent the evening with us.

As one usually arrives at a sudden, scarce comprehensible quietude, on entering a harbour from the stormy sea, after long and mighty excitement, and yet seems to feel the earth swimming beneath one, and to hear the breakers dashing around, so did it happen to me in a contrary manner, when, from the whirl of the last days and weeks in the haven, from the immeasurable world-city, I entered on the uniform desert of the ocean, in the narrow-bounded, soon-traversed house of planks. And now there was nothing more to be provided, nothing to be hurried; our long row of packages, more than thirty in number, had vanished, box by box, into the murky hold; our sleeping-places required no preparation, as they would scarcely hold more than our persons. The want of anxiety caused for some time a new and indefinite uneasiness, a solicitude without any object of solicitude.

Among our fellow-passengers I mention only the missionary Lieder, who, a German by birth, is returning with his English wife to Cairo. There he has founded and conducted a school since 1828, under the auspices of the English Missionary Society, which is now destined exclusively for the children of the Koptic Christians. Lieder has introduced into this school the study of the Koptic tongue, and thus once more brought into honour that remarkable and most ancient language of the country, which for several centuries has been totally superseded among the people by the Arabic. The Scriptures are, however, yet extant in the Koptic tongue, and even used in the service, but they are only intoned, and no longer understood.

On the 1st of September, at 10 o'clock, we left Southampton. We had the wind against us, and therefore did not reach Falmouth for four and twenty hours, where our vessel awaited the London post, to take the letters. There we remained several hours at anchor in a charming bay, at each side of the entrance of which an old castle lies upon the heights, while the town, situated in the background, form a most picturesque group. About 3 o'clock we went to sea again; the wind took us sideways, and caused much sickness amongst the passengers. I esteem myself fortunate, that in no passage, however stormy, have I had to complain of this disagreeable condition, which has, for the unsharing spectator, a comical aspect. It is, however, remarkable, that the very same movement that cradles every child to soft slumber, and forms the charm of a sail down the river, causes, by its protracted pendulum-like motion, unconquerable suffering, prostrating the strongest heroes, without, however, bringing them into any very serious danger.

Next day we reached the Bay of Biscay, and
ploughed laboriously through the long deep waves
that rolled to us from the far-off shore. Sunday
morning, the 4th, we had a very small company
at breakfast. About 11 o'clock we assembled to
prayers, notwithstanding the continual motion.
Over the pulpit the English flag was spread, as
the most sacred cloth on board. Herr Lieder
preached, simply and well. Toward 4 o'clock we
began to see the Spanish coast, in light misty outlines. The nearer we approached it, the shorter
the waves became, as the wind blew from the
shore. The air, the heavens, and the ocean, were
incomparably beautiful. Cape Finisterre and the
neighbouring coast line came out more and more
prominently. Gradually the whole company, even
the ladies, assembled on deck. The sea smoothed
itself to a bright mirror; the whole afternoon we
kept the Spanish coast in sight. The sun set
magnificently in the sea; the evening-star was
soon followed by the whole host of heavenly stars,
and a glorious night rose above us.

Then it was that the most splendid spectacle
commenced that I have ever beheld at sea. The
ocean began to sparkle; all the combs of the
breaking waves burnt in emerald-green fire, and
from the paddles of the vessel dashed a bright
greenish-white torrent of flame, which drew behind
it, for a great distance, a broad flashing stripe
amidst the darkling waters. The sides of the
vessel and our downward-looking faces were shone
upon as if by moonbeams, and I could read print
with the greatest ease by this water-fire. When

the blazing mass, which, according to Ehrenberg's researches, is caused by infusoria, was most intense, we saw flames dancing over the waves to the shore, so that it seemed as if we were traversing a more richly-starred heaven than the one we beheld above us. I have also beheld the ocean-light in the Mediterranean, but never in such extraordinary perfection as this time: the scene was magical.

Suddenly I saw new living fire-forms among the waves, that fled radiantly from the sides of the vessel. Like two giant serpents, which, judging from the length of the vessel, must have been from sixty to eighty feet long, they went trailing along beside the ship, crossing the waves, dipping in the foam of the wheels, coming forth again, retreating, hurrying, and losing themselves at last in the distance. For a long time I could assign no cause for this phenomenon. I recollected the old and oft-told tales of monstrous sea-snakes that are seen from time to time. What I here beheld could not have resembled them more than it did. At length I thought that it might only be fishes, who, running a race with the steamer, and breaking the uniform surface of the water, caused the long streams of light behind them by their rapid motions. Still the eye was as much deceived as ever; I could discover nothing of the dark fishes, nor guess their probable size, but I contented myself at length with my supposition.

LETTER II.

MY last letter I posted on the 7th of September, at Gibraltar, where we employed the few hours allotted to us in examining the fortress. The African continent lay before us, a bright stripe on the horizon; on the rocks beneath me climbed monkeys, the only ones in Europe in a wild state, for which reason they are preserved. In Malta, where we arrived on the eleventh of September, we found the painter Frey, from Basle, whose friendship I had made at Rome. He brought me intelligence by word of mouth that he would take part in the expedition, and for that purpose he had arrived several days before from Naples. We had to wait almost three days for the Marseilles post at this place. This gave us, at all events, the opportunity to visit the curiosities of the island, particularly the Cyclopean walls discovered some years before in the neighbourhood of Lavalette, and also to make some purchases. Through Lieder I made the acquaintance of Gobat,* who until now had been the principal person at the Maltese station of the

---

* On the sudden death, soon after our departure from Palestine, of Bishop Alexander, Gobat was selected by H.M. the King of Prussia as the Protestant bishop of Jerusalem, which post he has filled with good success since 1846.

English Missionary Society, but who was now awaiting some new destination, as pecuniary circumstances had caused the Society to give up this station altogether. I had great pleasure in knowing so distinguished a person.

From Malta we were accompanied by the missionary Isenberg, who resided for a long time with Gobat in Abyssinia, and who is favourably known to philologists by his grammar of the Amharic language. Under his protection there was a young lady of Basle, Rosine Dietrich, the bride of the missionary Krapf, who has married her here, and will now return to the English missionary station at Shoa, by the next Indian steamer, with her and his colleagues, Isenberg and Mühleisen. He was married in the English chapel, and I was present as a witness at the solemnity, which was celebrated in a simple and pleasing manner.

On our arrival, on the 18th of September, we found Erbkam, Ernst Weidenbach, and Franke, who had been awaiting us for some days.

Mohammed Ali had sailed out in the fleet, as he looked anxiously forward to the arrival of Sami Bey, who was to bring him the desired reduction in tribute : instead of it he obtained the appointment of Grand Vizier.

The Swedish General Consul D'Anastasi, who manages the Prussian Consulate for our absent Consul Von Wagner, and who interests himself zealously in our behalf, presented us to-day to the Viceroy, and we have just returned from the audience. The Pasha expressed great pleasure at

the vases which I had brought him in the name
of His Majesty. Still more did he feel himself
honoured by the letter of the King, of which he
immediately had a translation prepared, reading
it very attentively through in our presence. He
signified to me his intention of giving us the reply
when we again left the country. He received and
dismissed us standing, had coffee presented, and
showed us other attentions, which were afterwards
carefully explained to me by D'Anastasi. Boghos
Bey, his confidential minister, was the only person
present, nor did he seat himself. Mohammed Ali
showed himself brisk and youthful in his motions
and conversation; no weakness was to be seen in
the countenance and flashing eye of the old man
of three-and-seventy springs. He spoke with
interest of his Nile expeditions, and assured us
that he should continue them until he had discovered the sources of the White River. To my
question concerning his museum in Cairo, he
replied that it was not yet very considerable; that
many unjust requisitions were made of him in
Europe, in desiring rapid progress in his under-
takings, for which he had first to create the foundation, that had been prepared long since with us
in Europe. I touched but slightly on our excavations, and took his permission for granted in conversation, expecting it to be soon given me in due
form.*

---

* The firman of the Viceroy, with the most unlimited permission to carry on all excavations that I should think desirable, with a recommendation addressed to the local govern-
ments to support me, was given to me before my departure from

Alexandria. All the work-people and tools that were necessary for the formation and transportation of our collection of antiquities, were demanded for wages by the Khawass given us by the government, under the authority of the firman, from the Sheikh of the next village, and nowhere refused. The monuments from the southern provinces were transported in government barks from Mount Barkal to Alexandria, and to them were added three tombs from the neighbourhood of the great Pyramid of Gizeh, which, with the assistance of the four workmen purposely sent from Berlin, were carefully taken to pieces, and embarked opposite Old Cairo. At my departure from Egypt, a written permission was given me to export the collection, and the articles were formally presented to his Majesty the King of Prussia by the Viceroy.

These peculiar favours, at a time when all private travellers, antiquarian speculators, and even diplomatists, were especially interdicted by the Egyptian government from obtaining and taking away antiquities, did not fail to gain our expedition some unfavourable opinions. We were particularly blamed for having a destructive energy, which, under the ascribed circumstances, would have taken for granted a species of peculiar barbarism among our company. For, as we did not, like many of our rivals, dig out and remove the monuments, which had mostly been hidden below the surface, in haste by night, and with bribed assistance, but at our leisure, and with the open co-operation of the authorities, as well as under the eyes of many travellers—every carelessness with respect to these monuments left behind us, of which they had formed a part, would have been the more reprehensible, the easier such carelessness was to be avoided. But on the value of the monuments, we might esteem ourselves to have a more just judgment than the greater number of the generality of travellers or collectors usually possess; and we were not in danger of allowing it to be dulled by self-interest, as we did not select the monuments for ourselves, but as the agents of our government, for the Royal Museum at Berlin, and therefore for the benefit of science and an inquiring public.

The collection, which, principally by its historical value, may be compared with the most extensive in Europe, was, immediately upon its arrival, incorporated with the royal collections, without my being placed in any official connection with it. It is already opened and accessible to the public. A careful examination of it will conduce more than anything to place the remarks of later tourists,—among whom there are even Germans, —in their true light; who have even gone so far, as in the case of a Herr Julius Braun, in the General Augsburg Journal (*Allgemeine Augsburger Zeitung*), to ascribe to us the mutilation of the gods in the temple at El Kab, done 3,000 years ago! Besides, it would show a total ignorance of present Egyptian relations, or that which gives the actual interest to the monuments of antiquity, if any one did not wish to see the as precious as unestimated and daily destroyed treasures of those lands, preserved in European museums as much as possible.

LETTER III.

CAIRO.
October 16, 1842.

WE were detained nearly fourteen days in Alexandria. The whole time went in preparations for our journey; the Pasha I saw several times more, and I found him ever favourably disposed towards our expedition. Our scientific researches were inconsiderable. We visited the Pompeian pillar, which, however, stands in no relation to Pompey, but, as the Greek inscription on the base informs us, was erected to the Emperor Diocletian by the Præfect Publius. The blocks of the foundation are partly formed of the fragments of older buildings; on one of them the throne-cartouche of the second Psammetichus was yet distinguishable.

The two obelisks, of which the one still standing is named Cleopatra's Needle, are much disintegrated on the weather side, and in parts have become quite illegible.* They were erected by Tuthmosis III. in the sixteenth century A.C.; at a later period, Ramses Miamun has inscribed

[* The mention of Cleopatra's Needle gives me an opportunity of asking whether the storm of public applause will ever wipe away the incomprehensible opinions of those who refuse to preserve this memento by bringing it, our own property, to our own Museum, and placing it under proper shelter? The authorities seem to stand as stiffly against such a course as the obelisk itself does against the sky.—K. R. H. M.]

himself; and still later, on the outermost edges, another King, who was found to be one, till now, totally unknown, and who was therefore greeted by me with great joy. I must yet mention an interesting collection of ethnographical articles and specimens of natural history of every kind which have been collected by a native Prussian, Werne,* on the second Nile expedition of the Pasha to the White River, in countries hitherto quite unknown, and have been transported to Alexandria but a few months ago. It appeared to me to be so important and so unique of its kind that I have purchased it for our museum. While we were yet there it was packed up for transport. I think it will be welcome in Berlin.

At length the *bujurldis* (passports) of the Pasha were ready, and now we made haste to quit Alexandria. We embarked the same day that I received them (on the 30th of September), on the Mahmoudîeh canal. Darkness surprised us ere we could finish our preparations. At 9 o'clock we left our hotel, in the spacious and beautiful Frank's Place, in M. D'Anastasi's two carriages; before us were the customary runners with torches. The gate was opened at the word that was given us; our packages had been transported to the bark several hours before upon camels, so that we could soon depart in the roomy vessel which I

* The diary of this Nile expedition has since been made public under the title of " Expedition to discover the Sources of the White Nile " (1840-1841), by Ferdinand Werne ; with a preface by Carl Ritter. Berlin, 1848. [The work has since been published in English, under the auspices of Mr. Bentley, in two volumes.—K. R. H. M.]

had hired in the morning. The Nile, into which
we ran at Atfeh, rolled somewhat considerable
waves, as there was a violent and unfavourable
wind. Sailing is not without danger here, particularly in the dark, as the two customary pointed
sails, like the wings of a bee, are easily blown down
at every gust; therefore I advised the sailors to
stop, which they did every night when it was
stormy.

Next day, the 2nd of October, we landed at
Sâ el Hager to visit the remains of ancient Saïs,
that city of the Psammetiche so celebrated for
its temple to Minerva. Scarcely anything exists
of it but the walls, built of bricks of Nile earth,
and the desolate ruins of the houses : there are no
remains of any stone buildings with inscriptions.
We paced the circumference of the city and took
a simple plan of the locality. In the north-
western portion of the city her Acropolis once
stood, which is still to be distinguished by higher
mounds of rubbish. We stopped the night at
Nekleh. I have the great charts of the *Description
de l'Egypte* with me, on which we could follow
almost every step of our trips. We found them,
till now, very faithful everywhere.

On the 3rd of October we landed on the western
bank, in order to see the remains of the ancient
canal of Rosetta, and afterward spent nearly the
whole of the afternoon in examining the ruins of
an old city near Naharîeh ; no walls, only rubbish-
mounds are yet visible, but we found in the
houses of the new town several inscribed stones,
mostly used for threshholds, which had originally

belonged to a temple of King Psammetichus I.
and Apries (Hophre). Next night, we stopped
on the western shore near Teirîeh, and landed
there the next morning, to seek for some ruins
situated at about an hour's distance, but from
which we obtained nothing. The Libyan desert
approaches quite close to the Nile here, for the
first time, and gave us a novel, well-to-be-
remembered prospect.

On the following morning we first perceived
the great pyramids of Memphis rising up above
the horizon: I could not turn my eyes away from
them for a long time. We were still on the
Rosetta branch; at noon we came to the so-called
Cow's Belly, where the Nile divides into its two
principal arms. Now, for the first time, could
we overlook the stately, wonderful river, resembling no other in its utmost grandeur, which rules
the lives and manners of the inhabitants of its
shores by its fertile and well-tasting waters.
Toward the beginning of October it attains its
greatest height. But this year there is an inundation like none that has been known for generations. People begin to be afraid of the dykes
bursting, which would be the second plague
brought upon Egypt in this year, after the great
cattle murrain, which down to last week had
carried off forty thousand head of cattle.

About five o'clock in the evening we arrived at
Bulaq, the port of Cairo; we rode immediately
from the harbour to the city, and prepared for a
longer residence in this place. By-the-by, that
we should say Cairo, and the French *le Caire*, is a

manifest error. The town is now never called by any name but Mas'r by the Arabs, and so also the country; it is the ancient Semetic, more euphonious for us in the dual Mis'raim. ' First, at the foundation of the present city in the tenth century, New Mas'r was distinguished from the ancient Mas'r el Atîgeh, the present Old Cairo, by the addition of El Qâhireh, *i. e.* " the Victorious." The Italians omitted the *h*, unpronounceable in their language, took the Arabic article *el* for their masculine *il*, and so considered the whole word, by its ending too, a masculine.

The holy month of the Mohammedans, the Ramadan, was just beginning, during which they take no sustenance throughout the day, nor do they drink water or " drink smoke;" and accept no visits, but begin all the business of life after sundown, and thus interchange day and night, which caused us no little trouble on account of our Arab servants. Our Khawass (the honorary guard of the Pasha that had been given us), who had missed the time for embarking at Alexandria, joined us here. As our Prussian Vice-consul was unwell, I addressed myself to the Austrian Consul, Herr Champion, to whom I had been recommended by Ehrenberg, regarding our presentations to the representative of the Pasha at this place. He interested himself for us with the greatest alacrity and zeal, and obtained us a good reception everywhere. The official visits, at which Erbkam and Bonomi mostly accompanied me, had to be made in the evening at about 8 o'clock, on account of the Ramadan. Our torch-bearers ran first,

then came, on donkeyback, first the Dragoman of
the Consul and the Khawass of the Pasha, and
lastly ourselves in stately procession. We nearly
traversed the whole town, through the Arab-filled
streets, picturesquely lighted by our firebrands, to
the citadel, where we first visited Abbas Pasha,*
a grandson of Mahomet Ali; he is the governor
of Cairo, though seldom resident. From him we
proceeded to Sherif Pasha, the lieutenant of Abbas,
and then to the war minister, Ahmet Pasha.
Everywhere we were received with great kindness.

The day after my arrival I received a diploma
as an honorary member of the Elder Egyptian
Society, of which the younger one, that had sent
me a similar invitation while in London, was a
branch. Both had meetings, but I could only
attend the sittings of one, in which an interesting
memoir by Krapf, on certain nations of Central
Africa, was read. The particulars had been given
him by a native of the Enarea country, who had
travelled into the Doko country in commercial
pursuits, and who described the people in much
the same way that Herodotus does the Libyan
dwarf-nation, after the narrations of the Nasamo-
neans, viz., as little people of the size of children of
ten or twelve years of age. One would think that
monkeys were spoken of. As the geographical
notices of the till now almost unknown Doko
country are of interest, I have had the whole
paper copied, to send it, together with the little

* Since Ibrahim Pasha's death, in 1848, viceroy of Egypt.

map that belongs to it, to our honoured friend Ritter.*

On the 13th of October we made our first trip to the ruins of Heliopolis, the Biblical On, whence Joseph took his wife Asnath, the daughter of a priest. Nothing remains of this celebrated city, which prided itself on possessing the most learned priesthood next to Thebes, but the walls, which resemble great banks of earth, and an obelisk standing upright, and perhaps in its proper position. This obelisk possesses the peculiar charm of being by far the most ancient of all known obelisks; for it was erected during the Old Empire by King Sesurtesen I., about 2,300 B.C.; the broken obelisk in the Faîum near Crodilopolis, bearing the name of the same king, being rather an obelisk-like long-drawn stele. Boghos Bey has obtained the ground on which the obelisk stands as a present, and has made a garden round it. The flowers of the garden have attracted a quantity of bees, and these could find no more commodious lodging than in the deep and sharply cut hieroglyphics of the obelisk. Within the year they have so covered the inscriptions of the four sides, that a great part has become quite illegible. It had, however, already been published, and our comparison of it pre-

* This treatise, "Report of the River Goshop, and the countries of Enarea, Caffa, and Doko, by a native of Enarea," has been translated by Ritter, read in the Geographical Society of Berlin, on the 7th of January, 1843, and printed in the monthly reports of that institution, in the fourth year, pp. 172-188.

sented few difficulties, as three sides bear the same inscription, and the fourth is only slightly varied.

Yesterday, the 15th of October, was His Majesty's birthday. I had determined on this day for our first visit to the great pyramid. There we would hold a festival in remembrance of our king and country with a few friends. We invited the Austrian Consul Champion, the Prussian Consul Bokty, our learned countryman Dr. Pruner, and MM. Lieder, Isenberg, Mühleisen, and Krapf to this party, at which, however, it is to be regretted that some were not able to assist.

The morning was indescribably beautiful, fresh, and festal. We rode in long procession through the quiet streets, and along the green alleys and gardens that are planted outside it. Almost in every place where there were well-tended plantations, we found that they had been laid out by Ibrahim Pasha. By all accounts, he appears to adorn and repair every portion of the country.

They were incomparable minutes, those, when we came forth from among the dates and acacias; the sun rising to the left behind the Moqattam Mountains, and illumining the heads of the pyramids opposite, that lay before in the plain like giant mountain crystals. All of us were enraptured by the glory and greatness of this morning scene, and solemnly impressed by it. At Old Cairo we were ferried across the Nile to the village of Gizeh, whence the larger pyramids receive the name of Háram el Gizeh. From here one may ride to the pyramids in the dry season in a direct line for an hour or little more. As, however, the inundation is now at its highest point, we were obliged to make a great circuit upon long embankments, coming almost up to Saqâra, and did not arrive at the foot of the great pyramid for five and a half hours.

The long and unexpected ride gave a relish to the simple breakfast that we immediately took in one of the tombs cut in the rock here about five thousand years ago, in order to strengthen us for the ascent. Meanwhile a spacious gaily-decked tent came down, which I had hired in Cairo. I had it pitched on the north side of the pyramid, and had the great Prussian standard, the black eagle with a golden sceptre and crown, and a blue sword, on a white ground, which had been prepared by our artists within these last few days, planted before the door of the tent.

About thirty Bedouins had assembled around us in the interval, and awaited the moment when we should commence the ascent of the pyramid, in order to assist us with their powerful brown arms to climb the steps, about three to four feet in height. Scarcely had the signal for departure been given, ere each of us was surrounded by several Bedouins, who tore us up the rough steep path to the apex like a whirlwind. A few minutes afterward our flag floated from the top of the oldest and highest of all the works of man with which we are acquainted, and we saluted the Prussian eagle with three cheers for our king. Flying toward the south, the eagle turned its crowned head homeward to the north, whence a fresh breeze was blowing, and diverting the effects of the hot rays of the noontide sun. We too, looked homeward, and each remembered, aloud, or quietly within his own heart, those whom he had left behind, loving and beloved.

Next, the prospect at our feet enchained our attention. On one side is the valley of the Nile, a wide ocean of inundated waters, which, intersected by long and serpentine embankments, broken now and then by island-like high-lying villages, and overgrown tongues of land, filled the whole plain of the vale, and reached to the opposite mountain chain of Moqattam, on the most northerly point of which the citadel of Cairo rises above the town lying beneath. On the other side, the Libyan desert, a still more wonderful ocean of sand and desolate rock-hills, boundless, colourless, soundless, animated by no beast, no plant, no trace of human presence, not even by graves ; and between both is the desecrated Necropolis, the general plan and the particular outlines of which unfolded themselves sharply and plainly, as upon a map.

What a landscape ! and with our view of it what a flood of reminiscences ! When Abraham came to Egypt for the first time, he saw these pyramids which had been built many centuries before his arrival ; in the plain before us lay ancient Memphis, the residence of those kings on whose graves we were standing ; there lived Joseph, and ruled the land under one of the mightiest and wisest Pharaohs of the New Em-

pire. Farther on, to the left of the Moqattam
Mountains, where the fertile plain borders the
eastern arm of the Nile, on the other side of
Heliopolis, distinguishable by its obelisk, begins
the fruitful country of Goshen, whence Moses
led his people forth to the Syrian wilderness.
Indeed, it would not be difficult to recognise
from our position, that ancient fig-tree, on the
way to Heliopolis, by Matarîeh, beneath the
shade of which, according to the legends of the
land, Mary rested with the Holy Child. How
many thousands of pilgrims from all nations have
sought these wonders of the world before our
days,—we, the youngest in time, and yet only
the predecessors of many thousands more who
will come after us, and behold, and climb these
pyramids, with astonishment. I will describe no
farther the thoughts and feelings that came flood-
ing in at those moments; there, at the aim and
end of the wishes of many long years, and yet at
the actual commencement of our expedition;
there, on the apex of the Pyramid of Cheops, to
which the first link of our whole monumental history is fastened immoveably, not only for Egyptian, but for universal history; there, where I
saw beneath the remarkable grave-field whence
the Moses-rod of science summons forth the
shadows of the ancient dead, and lets them pass
before us in the mirror of history, according to
rank and age, with their names and titles, with
all their peculiarities, customs, and associations.
After I had narrowly scanned the surrounding
graves, with the intention of selecting some spots

for future excavations, we descended once more to
the entrance of the pyramid, procured lights,
entered the slanting shaft with some guides, like
miners, and reached the gallery by ways I well
knew by drawings, and at the so-called King's
Chamber. Here we admired the infinitely fine
joinings of the monster blocks, and examined the
geological formation of the passages and spaces.
Then we commenced our Prussian national hymn
in the spacious saloon, the floor, walls, and ceiling
of which are built of granite, and therefore return
a sounding metal echo; and so powerful and
solemn was the harmony, that our guides afterward reported to the other Bedouins outside, that
we had selected the innermost recesses of the pyramid, in order to give forth a loud and universal
prayer. We then visited the so-called Queen's
Chamber, and then left the pyramid, reserving
the examination of the more intricate passages for
a future and longer visit.

In the mean time our orientally-decked tent
had been put in order, and a dinner prepared
within, in which Prussians only took part, with
the exception of our two English companions.
That our first toast here was "His Majesty and
the Royal family" need not be told; and no great
eloquence was necessary to render all hearts
enthusiastic in drinking it.

The rest of the day passed in gay, festal, and
hearty reminiscences and conversations, till the
time of our departure arrived. We had yet to
wait a quarter of an hour after sunset, to give
our attendants, donkey-drivers, and the rest of

our Arab suite, time to eat their frugal dinner, which they had not yet taken, despite all the heat and labour of the day, in consequence of the Ramadan. Then the bright full moon guided us in the cool still night over the sand and water ocean, through villages and plantations of date-trees, back to the city. We did not arrive there until about midnight.

LETTER IV.

AT THE FOOT OF THE GREAT PYRAMID.
January 2, 1843.

STILL here! in full activity since the 9th of
November, and perhaps for some weeks yet in
the new year! How could I have anticipated
from the accounts of previous travellers, what a
harvest we were to reap here,—here, on the
oldest stage of the chronologically definable history of mankind. It is remarkable how little this
most-frequented place of all Egypt has been
examined hitherto. But I will not quarrel with
our predecessors, since we inherit the fruits of
their inactivity. I have been obliged the rather
to restrain our curiosity to see more of this
wonder-land, as we may half solve the problem
at this place. On the best charts of former
times, two graves have peculiar designations,
beside the pyramids. Rosellini has only examined *one* grave more, and Champollion says in
his letters, " *Il y a peu à faire ici, et lorsqu'on
aura copié des scènes de la vie domestique, sculp-
tées dans un tombeau, je regagnerai nos embar-
cations!*" [There is little to be done here, and
when they have copied the scenes of domestic
life sculptured in one tomb, I shall regain our
vessels.] We have given in our exact topographical plan of the whole Necropolis forty-five
graves, with whose inmates I have become ac-

quainted by their inscriptions, and I have enumerated eighty-two in all, which seemed worthy of notice on account of their inscriptions, or some other peculiarities.* Of these but few belong to the later time; nearly all of them were erected during or shortly after the building of the great pyramid, and therefore present us with an inestimable series of dates for the knowledge of the oldest definable civilisation of the races of man. The architecture of that age, concerning which I could formerly offer only a few speculations,† now lies before me in the fullest circumstantiality. Nearly all the branches of architecture are to be found developed; sculptures of complete figures of all dimensions, in haut-relief and bas-relief, present themselves in the most astonishing variety. The style is very marked and finely executed, but it is clear that the Egyptians had not then that peculiar canon of proportion which we find universally at a later period.‡ The painting on the fine plaster is often more beautiful than could be expected, and occasionally exhibits the freshness of yesterday in perfect preservation. The subjects on the walls are usually representations of scenes from the life of departed persons, and seem mostly intended to

---

* At our departure for Upper Egypt we had examined 130 private tombs, and discovered the remains of 67 pyramids.

† See my essay, " *Sur l' Ordre des Colonnes-piliers en Egypte, et ses rapports avec le second Ordre Egyptien et la Colonne Grecque* (*avec deux planches*)," in the ninth volume of the *Annales de l'Institut de Corresp. Archéol. Rome.* 1838.

‡ See Letter XV.

place their riches, cattle, fish, boats, hunts, and servants, before the eyes of the observer. Through them we become acquainted with every particular of their private life. The numerous inscriptions describe or name these scenes, or they set forth the often widely-extended family of the departed, and all his offices and titles, so that I could almost write a Court and State Directory of the time of King Cheops, or Chephren. The most stately tombs or rock graves belonged chiefly to the princes, relations, or highest officers of those kings near whose pyramids they are situated; and not unfrequently I have found the graves of father, son, grandson, and even great-grandson; so that whole genealogies of those distinguished families, the nobility of the land fifty centuries ago, may be formed. The most beautiful of the tombs, which I have discovered among many others in the all-burying sand, belongs to a prince* of King Cheops.

I employ forty to sixty people every day in excavations and similar labours. Also before the great Sphinx I have had excavations made to bring to light the temple between its paws, and to lay open the colossal stele formed of one block of granite, eleven feet high and seven feet broad, serving as a back wall to the temple, and covered

[* The *Athenæum*, in a late review of this work, questions the word " prince," and proposes to read " son ;" now, in a subsequent letter (p. 39), Lepsius himself conjectures that this Prince Merhet was the son of Cheops, which the reviewer appears to have overlooked in his excellent remarks.—K. R. H. M.]

to about its own height with sand. It is one of
the few memorials here of the great Pharaohs of
the New Empire, after the expulsion of the
Hyksos. I have had a plaster cast taken of it.

The Egyptian winter is not always so spring-
like as one occasionally imagines in Europe. At
sunrise, when every one hurries to work, we have
already had +5° Réaumur, so that the artists
could hardly use their fingers.

Winter began with a scene that will ever
remain impressed upon my memory. I had
ridden out to the excavations, and as I observed
a great black cloud coming up, I sent an
attendant to the tents, to make them ready
against it, but soon followed him myself, as it
began to rain a little. Shortly after my arrival,
a storm began, and I therefore had the tent ropes
made fast; soon, however, there came a pouring
rain, that frightened all our Arabs, and sent
them trooping to the rock-tomb, where our
kitchen is situated. Of our party, Erbkam and
Franke were only present. Suddenly the storm
grew to a tremendous hurricane, such as I have
never seen in Europe, and hail fell upon us in
such masses, as almost to turn day into night.
I had the greatest difficulty in hunting our
Arabs out from the cavern, to bring our things
to the tombs under shelter, as we might expect
the destruction of our tents at any moment; and
it was no long time ere first our common tent
broke down, and then, as I hurried from it into
my own, to sustain it from the inside, that also
broke down above my head. When I had crept

out, I found that my things were tolerably well covered by the tents, so that I could leave them for the present, but only to run a greater risk. Our tents lie in a valley, whither the plateau of the pyramids inclines, and are sheltered from the worst winds from the north and west. Presently I saw a dashing mountain flood hurrying down upon our prostrate and sand-covered tents, like a giant serpent upon its certain prey. The principal stream rolled on to the great tent; another arm threatened mine, without quite reaching it. But everything that had been washed from our tents by the shower was torn away by the two streams, which joined behind the tents, and carried into a pool behind the Sphinx, where a great lake immediately formed, which fortunately had no outlet.

Just picture this scene to yourself! our tents, dashed down by the storm and heavy rain, lying between two mountain torrents, thrusting themselves in several places to the depth of six feet into the sand, and depositing our books, drawings, sketches, shirts, and instruments—yes, even our levers and iron crowbars; in short, every thing they could seize, in the dark, foaming, mud ocean. Besides this, ourselves wet to the skin, without hats, fastening up the weightier things, rushing after the lighter ones, wading into the lake to the waist to fish out what the sand had not yet swallowed; and all this was the work of a quarter of an hour, at the end of which the sun shone radiantly again, and announced the end of this flood by a bright and glorious rainbow.

It was difficult to see at once what we had lost,
and where we ought to begin to bring things into
order again. The two Weidenbachs and Frey had
observed the whole scene from the tombs where
they were at work, as a mighty drama of nature,
and without even dreaming of the mischances that
had happened to us, until I sent for them to assist
in preparing for the quickly-approaching night.
For several more days we fished and dug for our
things. Some things were lost, many were spoilt;
the greater part of all the things that were not
locked up inside chests or trunks bore at least
more or fewer marks of this flood. After all, there
was nothing of much importance lost; I had first
secured the great portfolios, together with my
manuscripts and books; in short, after a few days
the whole thing took the form of a remarkable
picture, leaving no unpleasant reminiscence, and
of which I should grudge my memory the loss.

Since then, we have suffered much from violent
gales, that occasionally so fills the atmosphere
with sand that it renders respiration difficult,
totally precludes painting with colours, and continually covers drawing and writing paper with a
most disagreeable, ever renewed dust. This fine
sand penetrates one's clothes, enters all boxes,
even when most closely shut, fills one's nose,
ears, hair, and is the unavoidable pepper to
every dish and drink.

January 5. On the evening of the first Christmas holiday, I surprised my companions by a
large bonfire, which I had lighted at the top of
the greatest pyramid. The flame shone magni-

ficently upon the two other pyramids, as well as on the Necropolis, and threw its light far over the dale to Cairo. That was a Christmas pyramid! I had only confided the secret to Abeken, who had arrived, with his ever merry humour and his animated and instructive conversation, upon the 10th of December. With his assistance I prepared something for the following night, in the Royal Chamber of the Great Pyramid. We planted a young palm-tree in the sarcophagus of the ancient king, and adorned it with lights and little presents that I had sent for from the city for us children of the wilderness. Saint Sylvester also must receive due honour. On New Year's eve, at midnight, there arose mighty flames from the heights of the three great pyramids, and announced, far and wide in the regions of Islâm, at their feet, the change of the Christian year.*

[* As a further illustration of this scene, but briefly passed over by the originator of it, the following observations of Mr. Gliddon will be found very interesting. " Mr. Gliddon hoped, that besides the day view, the Prussians would add their night scene of New Year's Eve, 1842, when the blaze of bonfires, lighted on the top of each of the three pyramids, cast a lurid glare on every side, bringing out the craggy peaks of the long desecrated mausolea of Memphite Pharoahs, tinting that drear wilderness of tombs with a light, emblematical of Lepsius' vindication of their inmates' memories, and leaving the shadows of funereal gloom to symbolize the fifty centuries of historic night, now broken by the hierologists :—

" ' Dark has been thy night,
Oh Egypt, but the flame
Of new-born *science* gilds thine ancient name.' "
—Gliddon's *Otia Egyptiaca* ; Lecture II. Ethnological Journal, No. VI. p. 265.—K. R. H. M.]

I consider it a proper mental diet for our company to break and interrupt our laborious, and, for the artists, very monotonous occupations, not only by the hebdomadal rest of Sunday, but also by pleasant parties of pleasure and gay festivals, as often as˙ opportunity will admit. As yet, the harmony and good humour of our society have not been disturbed by the slightest echo of discord; and they gain new strength every day, as well by the fulness of our novel impressions and the reciprocal tastes and natures of our companions, as by the obstacles and hardships of this Bedouin life.

How manifold the elements of our community are, you may perceive by the true Babel of languages in which we are ever moving. The English language is sufficiently represented by our companions, Wild and Bonomi; French and Italian serve as a medium of communication with the authorities, our chance guests, and the Levantine merchants; in Arabic we command, eat, and travel; and in very capital German we consult, chatter, sing, and live. As long as it is day we are generally each alone, and uninterruptedly at work. The morning coffee is drunk before sunrise; after sunset, dinner is served; and we breakfast while at work. Thus our artists have been already enabled to prepare a hundred great folio leaves, partly executed in lead, partly finished off in colours, for our swelling portfolios.

LETTER V.

THE inscription composed in commemoration of the birthday festival of His Majesty has become a stone tablet, after the manner of the ancient steles and proscynemata.   Here it is:—

and its contents, which, the more they assimilate with the Egyptian style, become proportionately awkward in the German, are as follows:—

" Thus speak the servants of the King, whose name is the Sun and Rock of Prussia, Lepsius the scribe, Erbkam the architect, the brothers Weidenbach the painters, Frey the painter, Franke the former, Bonomi the sculptor, Wild the architect:—Hail to the Eagle, Shelterer of the Cross, the King, the Sun and Rock of Prussia, the son of the Sun, freer of the land, Frederick William the Fourth, the Philopator, his country's father, the gracious, the favourite of wisdom and history, the guardian of the Rhine stream, chosen by Germany, the giver of life. May the highest God grant the King and his wife, the Queen Elisabeth, the life-rich one, the Philometor, her country's mother, the gracious, a fresh-springing life on earth for long, and a blessed habitation in Heaven for ever. In the year of our Saviour 1842, in the tenth month, and the fifteenth day, on the seven and fortieth birthday of His Majesty, on the pyramid of King Cheops; in the third year, the fifth month, the ninth day of the Government of His Majesty; in the year 3164 from the commencement of the Sothis period under King Menephthes."

Upon a large and expressly hewn and prepared stone, at some height, by the entrance to the Pyramid of Cheops, have we left the hieroglyphical inscription upon a space of five feet in breadth, and four feet in height, painted in with oil-colours.

It seemed good to me, that the Prussian Expedition, while it dedicated this tablet to the much-respected prince who had sent the Expedition hither, should leave some trace of its activity in this field, where it had been reserved for that enterprise to gather in the plenteous materials for the first chapter of all scientific history.

Do not imagine, however, that these are the weighty labours that have kept us so long here. It is from the advantage which we possess over former travellers that places like these have the right to detain us until we have exhausted them. We already know that the grand ruins of the Thebaïc plain cannot discover anything to us of similar interest to the Memphitic period of the Old Empire.

At some time we must of course leave off, and then always with the certainty that we leave much behind us, of the greatest interest, that has still to be won. I had already determined upon our departure some days since, when a row of tombs were discovered of a new period, a new architecture, a new style in the figures and hieroglyphics, with other titles, and, as it might have been expected, with other royal names.

Our historical gain is by no means perfected, nor is it even general. I was quite right in giving up the task of reconstructing the third dynasty after monuments, while in Europe. Nor have I yet found a single cartouche that can be safely assigned to a period previous to the fourth dynasty. The builders of the Great Pyramid seem to assert their right to form the commencement of monumental history, even if it be clear that they were not the first builders and monumental writers. We have already found some hitherto unknown cartouches and variants of others, such as :—

Keka.   Heraku.   Useskef.   Ana.

The name that I have hitherto treated as Amchura shows, in the complete and painted inscriptions, which throw not a little light upon the figurative meanings of the hieroglyphic writings, a totally different sign, to the well-known group, *amchu*, viz. :   , the pronunciation of which is yet uncertain to me.*

In the classification of the pyramids there is nothing to be altered. It cannot be doubted, after our researches, that the second pyramid really is to be assigned to Shafra (more correctly Chafra, the Chephren of Herodotus), as the first to Chufu (Cheops), and the third to Menkera (Mycerinos, Mencherinos). I think I have found the path from the valley to the second pyramid; it leads right up to its temple, by the Sphinx, but was

[* The reed; A initial, Bunsen, vol. i. p. 556, Alphabetic No. 3=A: the sickle, M Alphabetic No. 2, p. 563=M: the sieve, χ Alphabetic No. 1, p. 571=χ: unknown object, p. 571, with U, the chicken, p. 570=χU=AMCHU. This will give the unhieroglyphist an idea of the way in which hieroglyphic words are formed.—K. R. H. M.]

probably destroyed at an early period. The number of pyramids, too, is continually increasing. At Abu Roash I have found three pyramids in the place of that single one already known, and two fields of tombs; also near Zauiet el Arrian, an almost forgotten village, there once stood two pyramids, and a great field of ruins is adjoining. The careful researches and measurements of Perring, in his fine work upon the pyramids, save us much time and trouble. Therefore we could give ourselves more to the tombs and their hieroglyphical paintings, which are altogether wanting in the pyramids. But nothing is yet completed, nothing is ripe for definitive arrangement, though comprehensive views are now opened. Our portfolios begin to swell; much has been cast in gypsum; among other things, the great stele of the first year of Tuthmosis IV. between the paws of the Sphinx.

LETTER VI.

PYRAMIDS OF GIZEH.
January 28, 1843.

I HAVE ordered ten camels to come here to-morrow night, that we may depart early, before sunrise, the day after, with our already some-what extensive collection of original monuments and gypsum casts, for Cairo, where we shall deposit them until our return from the south. This will be the commencement of our move-ment toward Saqâra. A row of very recently discovered tombs, of the dynasties immediately following that of Cheops, has once retarded our departure. The fifth dynasty, which appears as an Elephantine contemporaneous dynasty in Afri-canus,* and was not at all to be expected as such here, now lies completed before us, and in general precisely as I had constructed it in Europe. The gaps have been filled up with three kings, whose names were then unknown. Also some kings, formerly hanging in mid-air, have been won for the seventh and eighth dynasties, of which we had previously no monumental names whatever. The proof of the fifth dynasty following the fourth immediately would in itself richly re-compense us for our stay of several months at this place ; and besides this, we have still much to do

[* See Bunsen's Egypt's Place in Universal History, vol. i. p. 618.—K. R. H. M.]

with structures, sculptures, and inscriptions, which, by the continually increasing certitude of the royal names, are formed into one cultivated epoch, dating about the year 4000 B.C. One can never recall these till now incredible dates too often to the memory of one's-self and others ; the more criticism is challenged, and obliged to give a serious examination to the matter, the better for the cause. Conviction will follow criticism, and then we shall arrive at the consequences that are linked with it in every branch of archæology.

With this letter you will receive a roll containing several drawings which have been copied from the tombs here. They are splendid specimens of the oldest architecture, sculpture, and painting that art-history has to show, and the most beautiful and best preserved of all those that we have found in the Necropolis. I hope we shall some day see these chambers fully erected in the New Museum at Berlin.* They would certainly be the most beautiful trophy that we could bring with us from Egypt. Their transportation would probably be attended with some difficulty ; for you may judge by the dimensions that ordinary means will not suffice to do it. I have therefore asked, in a letter addressed directly to His Majesty the King, whether it would not be possible to send a vessel next year, or at the close of the expedition, with some workpeople and tools, in order to take these

[* This has been done, and better than in any other museum in the world.—K. R. H. M.]

monuments to pieces more carefully than we can do, and bring them with the rest of the collections to Berlin.

Six of the enclosed leaves are drawings of a tomb which I myself discovered under the sand, and the paintings of which are almost as fresh and perfect as you may perceive them in the drawing.* It was the last resting-place of Prince Merhet, who, as he was a priest of Chufu (Cheops), named one of his sons Chufu-mer-nuteru, and possessed eight villages, the names of which were compounded with that of Chufu; and the position of the grave on the west side of the pyramid of Chufu, as well as perfect identity of style in the sculptures, renders it more than probable that Merhet was the son of Chufu, by which the whole representations are rendered more interesting. This prince was also " Superintendent-General of the royal buildings," and thus had the rank of Ober-hof Baurath (High Court-architect), a great and important post in these times of magnificent architecture, and which we have often found under the direction of princes and members of the royal family. It is therefore to be conjectured that he also over-

† Unfortunately the colours have now quite faded. The unequal surface of the stone had rendered it necessary to spread a thick groundwork of lime over the sculptures ere they could be painted upon; this lime has peeled off by its transportation and the moist sea air, so that only the rough sculpture is remaining. In the " Monuments of the Prussian Expedition," Part II. Plate 19—22, the colours are faithfully given, as they were preserved by the covering of sand in their original freshness.

looked the building of the Great Pyramid. Would
not this alone have justified the undertaking of
transporting to Berlin the well-joined grave-cham-
ber of this princely architect, which will otherwise be destroyed at a longer or shorter period
by the Arabs, and built into their ovens, or burnt
in their kilns ! There, at least, it would be preserved, and accessible for the admiration or
scientific ardour of the curious, as indeed European art and science teaches us to respect and
value such monuments. For its re-erection it
would require a width of 6 métres 30', a height
of 4 m. 60', and a depth of 3 m. 80'; and such a
space can certainly be reserved for it in the New
Museum.*

I must remark, in addition, that such chambers
form only a very small portion of the tomb, and
were not intended for the mummy. The tomb
of Prince Merhet is more than 70 feet long, 45
broad, and 15 high. It is massively constructed
of great blocks of freestone, with slanting outer
surfaces. The chamber only is covered with
rafters, and one, or in this case two, square
shafts lead from the flat roof through the building
into living rock, at the bottom of which, sixty
feet below, rock-chambers open at each side, in
which the sarcophagi were placed. The remains
of the reverend skull of the Cheoptic prince,
which I found in his mummy-chamber, I have

---

* On our return from the south, two other perfect tombs,
besides this one, were taken down and brought to Europe.
All three have been re-erected, with the rest of the monuments,
in the New Museum at Berlin.

carefully preserved. To my sorrow we found
but little more, because this grave, like most of
the others, has long been broken into. Originally
the entrance was closed with a stone slab. Only
the supersurfacial chamber remained open always,
and was therefore adorned with representations
and inscriptions. Thither were brought the offerings to the departed. It was dedicated to the religious belief of the dead person, and thus answered
to the temple that was built before each pyramid
for the adoration of its royal inmate. In the
same way as those temples, so these chambers
always open to the east. The shafts, like the
pyramids, lie behind to the west, because the
departed was supposed to be in the west, whither
he had gone with the setting sun to Osiris
Amente.

Finally, the seventh leaf contains two pillars
and their architrave, from the tomb of a royal
relative, who was also the prophet of four kings,
named Ptah-nefru-be·u. The grave was constructed at a later period than that of Prince
Merhet, in the fifth dynasty of Manetho.* It belongs to a whole group of tombs, the architectural
disposition and intercommunication of which are
very curious, and which I have therefore laid
quite open to the daylight, while before neither
the entrance nor anything else but the crown
of the outer wall was to be seen.

I also send you the complete plan of it,
besides that of the neighbouring graves, but only
think of bringing the architrave and the two

[* Bunsen, vol. i. p. 618.—K. R. H. M.]

finely-painted pillars of the southern space, which may be easily removed. On the architrave the legend of the departed is inscribed, who is also represented on the four sides of the pillars in full size. In front, on the north pillar, is seen the father of the dead person, Ami; on the southern one is his grandfather, Aseskef-anch. The pillars are about twelve feet in height, are slim, and are always without capitals, but with an abacus.

At the tomb of Prince Merhet I have had the whole chamber isolated, but have given up the design of taking it down for the present, as the season is not the most favourable for transporting it. I have therefore filled this grave and the other with sand, and to-morrow, on my arrival in Cairo, I shall obtain an order interdicting the removal of any of the stones of those tombs which we had opened. For it is most annoying to see great caravans of camels coming hither from the neighbouring villages, and going off in long strings loaded with slabs for building. Fortunately,—for what is not fortunate under circumstances!—the lazy Fellahs are rather attracted by the tombs of the age of the Psammetici than by those of the older dynasties, the great blocks of which are not handy enough for them. I am more seriously alarmed, however, for the tombs of the fifth and seventh dynasties, which are built of more moderately sized stones. Yesterday the robbers threw down a fine, steady, fully-inscribed pillar when our backs were turned. Their efforts to break it up seem not to have been successful. The people have become so feeble here, that, with all their mischievous indus-try, their powers are not sufficient to destroy what their mighty ancestors had raised.

Some days ago, we found, standing in its ori-ginal place in a grave of the beginning of the seventh dynasty, an obelisk of but a few feet in height, but well preserved, and bearing the name of the person to whom the tomb was erected. This form of monument, which plays so conspicuous a part in the New Empire, is thus thrown some dynasties farther back into the Old Empire than even the obelisk of Heliopolis.

LETTER VII.

SAQÂRA.
March 18, 1843.

A SHORT time ago, I made a trip, in company with Abeken and Bonomi, to the more distant pyramids of Lisht and Meidûm. The latter interested me particularly, as it has solved for me the riddle of pyramidal construction, on which I had long been employed.* It lies almost

---

* An essay " On the Construction of the Pyramids " was transmitted by me to the Royal Academy of Sciences, and printed, in accordance with a decree of the 3rd of August of the same year.—See the Monthly Report of the Academy in 1843, pp. 177—203, with three plates. [The following summary of Dr. Lepsius' discovery, obtained from various sources, may not be unacceptable to the reader. At the commencement of each reign, the rock chamber, destined for the monarch's grave, was excavated, and one course of masonry erected above it. If the king died in the first year of his reign, a casing was put upon it and a pyramid formed; but if the king did not die, another course of stone was added above and two of the same height and thickness on each side: thus in process of time the building assumed the form of a series of regular steps. These were cased over with stone, all the angles filled up, and stones placed for steps. Then, as Herodotus long since informed us (Euterpe, c. cxxv), the pyramid was finished from the top downward, by all the edges being cut away, and a perfect triangle only left.—See, in addition to Lepsius himself, Letronne, Dicuil, pp. 90—115, 1814; Athenæum, Bonomi, 16th Sept. 1843; J. W. Wild, 15th June, 1844. Wilkinson's *Materia Hieroglyphica*, Malta, 1830, p. 14; and last, though not least, Gliddon's *Otia Egyptiaca*, Lecture IV. Ethnological Journal, No. VII. p. 294.—K. R. H. M.]

in the valley of the plain, close by the Bahr
Jussuf, and is only just removed from the level
of inundation, but it towers so loftily and grandly
from the low neighbourhood that it attracts
attention from a great distance. From a casing
of rubbish that surrounds almost the half of it,
to the height of 120 feet, a square, sharp-edged
centre rises after the manner of a tower, which
lessens but little at the top, *i. e.* in an angle of
74°. At the elevation of another 100 feet there
is a platform on which, in the same angle, stands
a slenderer tower of moderate height, which again
supports the remains of a third elevation in the
middle of its flat upper side. The walls of the
principal tower are mostly polished, flat, but are
interrupted by rough bands, the reason of which
seems hardly comprehensible. On a closer examination, however, I found also within the
half-ruined building, round the foot, smoothened
walls rising at the same angle as the tower,
before which there lay other walls, following each
other like shells. At last I discovered that the
whole structure had proceeded from a little
pyramid, which had been built in steps to about
the height of 40 feet, and had then been enlarged
and raised in all directions by a stone casing of
15 to 20 feet in breadth, till at last the great
steps were filled out to a surface, and the whole
received the usual pyramidal form.

This gradual accumulation explains the monstrous size of single pyramids among so many
smaller ones. Each king commenced the construction of his pyramid at his accession; he

made it but small at first, in order to secure
himself a perfect grave even if his reign should
be but short. With the passing years of his
government, however, he enlarged it by adding
outer casings, until he thought himself near the
end of his days. If he died during the erection
of it, the outermost casing only was finished, and
thus the size of the pyramid stood ever in proportion to the length of the king's reign. Had
the other determinative relations remained the
same in the lapse of ages, one might have told off
the number of years of each monarch's reign by
the casings of the pyramids, like the annual rings
of trees.

Yet the great enigma of the bearded giant
Sphinx remains unsolved! When and by whom
was this colossus raised, and what was its signification? We must leave this question to be
decided by our future and more fortunate successors. It is almost half-buried in sand, and the
granite stele of eleven feet in height between his
paws, forming alone the back wall of a small
temple erected here, was altogether concealed;
for the immense excavations which were undertaken by Caviglia, in 1818, have long since
tracelessly disappeared. By the labour of some
sixty to eighty persons for several days, we arrived
almost at the base of the stele, which I had
immediately sketched, pressed in paper, and cast,
in order to erect it at Berlin. This stele, on
which the Sphinx itself is represented, was erected
by Tuthmosis IV., and is dated in the first years
of his government; he must therefore have found

the colossus there. We are accustomed to find
the Sphinx in Egypt used as the sign for a king,
and, indeed, usually as some particular king,
whose features it would appear to preserve, and
therefore they are always Androsphinxes, with
the solitary exception of a female Sphinx, which
represents the wife of King Horus. In hieroglyphical writings the Sphinx is named Neb, "the
Lord," and forms, among other instances, the
middle syllable of the name of King Necta-neb-us.

But what king is represented by the monster?
It stands before the second pyramid, that of
Shafra (Chephren), not directly in the axis, but
parallel with the sides of the temple lying before
it, and precisely as if the northern rock by the
Sphinx had been intended for a corresponding
sculpture; besides this, it was usual for Sphinxes,
Rams, statues, and obelisks, to be placed in pairs
before the entrances of the temples. What a
mighty impression, however, would two such
giant guardians, between which the ancient
pathway to the temple of Chephren led, have
made upon the approaching worshipper! They
would have been worthy of that age of colossal
monuments, and in right proportions to the
pyramid behind. I cannot deny that this connection would best satisfy me. What would have
induced the Thebaïc kings of the eighteenth
dynasty, the only ones of the New Empire to be
thought of, to adorn the Memphitic Necropolis
with such a world-wonder without any connection
with its surrounding objects? Add to this, that
in an almost destroyed line of the Tuthmosis stele,

King Chephren is named; a portion of his royal cartouche, unfortunately quite single, is yet preserved; it undoubtedly had some reference to the builder of the pyramid lying behind it.

But the question again arises:—If King Chephren be here represented, why does it not bear his name? On the contrary, it is named Har-em-chu, "Horus in the horizon," that is to say, the Sungod, the type of all kings, and Harmachis, in a Greek inscription found before the Sphinx. It does not seem at all unlikely to me, that upon this rests the fable of Pliny, according to which a King Amasis (Armasis?) lies interred within the Sphinx;* for in a real burial there can be no belief. Another consideration is that I have not found the representation of the Sphinx in those most ancient times of the pyramid builders; but that must not be accepted as conclusive, as the Sphinx is not often found in the inscriptions and representations of the new empire.† In short, the Œdipus for this king of all Sphinxes is yet wanting. Whoever would drain the immeasurable sand-flood which buries the tombs themselves, and lay open the base of the Sphinx, the ancient temple path, and the surrounding hills, could easily decide it.

But with the enigmas of history there are joined many riddles and wonders of nature, which

* I have spoken more fully on this subject in my " Chronology of the Egyptians," vol. i. p. 294.

† [See Bunsen's Egypt's Place in Universal History (Engl. transl.), vol. i. p. 515; Ideographics, No. 277.— K. R. H. M.]

I must not leave quite unnoticed. The newest of all, at least, I must describe.

I had descended with Abeken into a mummy pit, to open some newly-discovered sarcophagi, and was not a little astonished, upon descending, to find myself in a regular snow-drift of locusts, which, almost darkening the heavens, flew over our heads from the south-west from the desert in hundreds of thousands to the valley. I took it for a single flight, and called my companions from the tombs where they were busy, that they might see this Egyptian wonder ere it was over. But the flight continued; indeed the work-people said it had begun an hour before. Then we first observed that the whole region near and far was covered with locusts. I sent an attendant into the desert, to discover the breadth of the flock. He ran for the distance of a quarter of an hour, then returned and told us that, as far as he could see, there was no end to them. I rode home in the midst of the locust shower. At the edge of the fruitful plain they fell down in showers; and so it went on the whole day till the evening, and so the next day from morning till evening, and the third; in short, to the sixth day, indeed in weaker flights much longer. Yesterday it did seem that a storm of rain in the desert had knocked down and destroyed the last of them. The Arabs are now lighting great smoke-fires in the fields, and clattering and making loud noises all day long to preserve their crops from the unexpected invasion. It will, however, do little good. Like a new animated vegetation, these millions of winged

E

spoilers cover even the neighbouring sand-hills, so that scarcely anything is to be seen of the ground; and when they rise from one place, they immediately fall down somewhere in the neighbourhood; they are tired with their long journey, and seem to have lost all fear of their natural enemies, men, animals, smoke, and noise, in their furious wish to fill their stomachs, and in the feeling of their immense number. The most wonderful thing, in my estimation, is their flight over the naked wilderness and the instinct which has guided them from some oasis over the inhospitable desert to the fat soil of the Nile vale. Fourteen years ago, it seems, this Egyptian plague last visited Egypt with the same force. The popular idea is, that they are sent by the comet which we have observed for twelve days in the south-west, and which, as it is now no longer obscured by the rays of the moon, stretches forth its stately tail across the heavens in the hours of night. The zodiacal light, too, so seldom seen in the north, has lately been visible for several nights in succession.

At this place have I first been able to settle my account with Gizeh, and to put together the historical results of the investigation. I have every reason to rejoice at the consequences; the fourth and fifth dynasties are completed all except one king.

I have just received the rather illegible drawing of a stone in a wall at the village of Abusir, which presents a row of kings of the fourth and fifth dynasties, and, as it would seem, in chronological order. I am on the point of riding over to see the original.

LETTER VIII.

SAQÂRA.
April 13, 1843.

I hasten to inform you of an event which I should not like to be first communicated to you from other quarters, and perhaps with distorted exaggeration. Our camp was attacked and robbed a few nights since by an armed band, but none of our party have been seriously hurt, and nothing has been lost that is not to be replaced. The matter is past, and the consequences can only be favourable to us; but I must first go back a few days in my report.

On the 3rd of April, H.R.H. Prince Albrecht returned from Upper Egypt to Cairo; next day I went to town and submitted a portion of our labours to him, in which he took the more lively interest as he had already seen more of the wonder-land than we, and had only omitted to visit the pyramid fields. On his former arrival in Cairo I was absent with Abeken and Bonomi on a journey of several days' duration in the Faiûm. The Prince came just in time for some Mohammedan festivals, which I should have neglected but for his presence. On the sixth was the entrance of the solemnly-welcomed caravan of pilgrims from Mecca, and a few days later, the birthday festival of the prophet "Mulid e'Nebbi," one of the most original feasts through-

E 2

out the Orient. The principal parts fall to the share of the Derwishes, who arrange processions during the day, and in the evening exhibit their terrible dance named Sikr in the gaily-lighted tents erected among the trees of the Ezbekîeh; thirty to forty of this religious sect place themselves in a circle, and begin to move their bodies backward and forward, according to the time, first slowly, and then more violently, at last with the most cruel strains upon the nerves; at the same time they repeat their maxim rhythmically with a loud howling voice, " *Lâ ilâha ill' Allah* " (no God but Allah), gradually lowering and softening the tone until it resembles a faint snore: at length, their powers wholly exhausted, some fall down, others withdraw reelingly, and the broken circle, after a short pause, is replaced by another.

What a fearful, barbarous worship, which the astounded multitude, great and small, gentle and simple, gaze upon seriously and with stupid respect, and in which it not unfrequently takes a part! The invoked deity is manifestly much less an object of reverence than the fanatic saints who invoke him; for mad, idiotic, or other psychologically-diseased persons, are very generally looked upon as holy by the Mohammedans, and treated with great respect. It is the demoniacal, incomprehensibly-acting, and therefore fearfully-observed power of nature, that the natural man always reveres when he perceives it, because he is sensible of some connection between it and his intellectual power, without being able to command it; first in the mighty elements, then in the wondrous but obscure law-governed instincts of animals, and, at last, in the yet more overpowering exstatical, or generally abnormal mental condition of his own race. We must decidedly look upon the Egyptian animal-worship, as far as it was not the covering for deeper and more refined doctrines, as resting upon the same idea of a worship of nature;* and the reverence occasionally manifesting itself among some nations of mentally-diseased men may be regarded as a curious branch of the same feeling. Whether such conditions really exist, or whether, as with the *derwishes*, they are artificially produced and purposely fostered, is not criticised by the masses, and it is

[* The more extended our acquaintance with ancient monuments or ancient writings becomes, the more simple and human do we find their signification to be. It has been the case with Egypt, Assyria, and with the Sinaïtic inscriptions, so ably treated by the Rev. Charles Forster, and indeed with most of those monuments that occur in connexion with the ancient world, in the popular acceptation of the word. If mystery and types possess a home anywhere, it must be in India, for even in America, the picture writings are very simple and the reverse of mysterious, when properly examined, as I hope to prove one day, in an extended investigation into Mexican antiquities, upon which the labour of some years has been bestowed. Instead of seeking for such remote causes, the reader will do well to consider the simple opinion of Gliddon, in his *Otia*, Lecture VIII. Ethnological Journal, No. IX p. 395, regarding the origin of animal worship. I should not have been led to this lengthy note if I did not feel that, while the earliest tenets of worship were indeed veiled in types (the result, however, as much of accident as design), animal worship is too recent to conceal any such mysterious dogmas. I do not wish to place my notion in competition with that of Lepsius; this is a mere suggestion.—K. R. H. M.]

much the same in individual cases. In such a
presence one would feel oneself overcome by a
mysterious feeling of dread, and would not care
to express repugnance, or even to manifest it by
signs, or by a token of having even observed
anything, for fear of diverting upon oneself the
storm of brute passion.

The nine days' festival closes with a peculiar
ceremony called *doseh*, the treading, but which
I was myself prevented from witnessing. The
sheîkh of the Saadîeh-*derwishes* rides to the
cheif sheîkh of all the *derwishes* of Egypt, El
Bekri. On the way thither, a great number of
these holy folk, and others too, who fancy themselves not a whit behindhand in piety, throw
themselves flat on the ground, with their faces
downward, and so that the feet of one lie close
to the head of the next; over this living carpet,
the sheîkh rides on his horse, which is led on
each side by an attendant, in order to compel the
animal to the unnatural march. Each body
receives two treads of the horse; most of them
jump up again without hurt, but whoever suffers
serious, or, as it occasionally happens, mortal
injury, has the additional ignominy to bear, for
not having pronounced, or for not being able to
pronounce, the proper prayers and magical charms
that alone could save him.

On the 7th of April, I and Erbkam accompanied
the prince to the pyramids, and first to those of
Gizeh. The pyramid of Cheops was ascended,
and the inside visited; the beautiful tomb of
Prince Merhet I had had laid open for the

purpose of showing it. Then we left for our camp at Saqâra.

Here we heard that a barefaced robbery had been committed in Abeken's tent the night before. While he was asleep, with a light burning, after his return from Cairo, his knapsack, pistols, and a few other matters lying about, were stolen ; as the thief was departing, a noise was perceived by the guard, but the darkness precluded all pursuit.

After the prince had inspected the most beautiful tomb of Saqâra, we rode across the plain to Mitrahinneh to visit the mound of Memphis, and the half-buried colossus of Ramses Miamun (Sesostris), the face of which is almost perfectly preserved. Late at night, we arrived again in Cairo, after sixteen hours of motion, scarcely interrupted by short pauses of rest; the unusual fatigue, however, rather raised the lively taste for travelling in the prince's mind than otherwise.

The next day the mosques of the city were visited, which are partly considerable for their magnificence, and are partly of interest in the history of mediæval art on account of the earliest specimen of the general application of the pointed arch. The questions touching this characteristic architectural branch of the so-called Gothic style had employed me so much some years ago, that I could not avoid pursuing the old traces ; the pointed arch is found in the oldest mosques up to the ninth century. With the conquest of Sicily by the Arabs, this form of the arch was carried over to the island, where the next conquerors, the Normans, found it in the eleventh century, and were led to employ it much. To deny some historical connection between the Norman pointed arch of Palermo and our northern style appears to me to be impossible; the admission of such a connection would certainly render it more difficult to explain of the sporadically but not lawlessly used rows of pointed arches which occur in the cathedral of Naumburg in the eleventh century, and at Memleben already in the tenth. The theorists will not yet admit this; but I must await the confutation of the reasons.*

The Nilometer on the island of Roda, which we visited after the mosques, also contains a row of pointed arches, which belong to the original building, going back to the ninth century, as the carefully-examined Kufic inscriptions testify.

Egypt does not only lay claim to the oldest employment, and therefore probable invention, of the pointed arches, but also upon that of the circular arch.† Near the pyramids a group of tombs may be seen, the single blocks of which manifest the proper concentric way of

* See my essay " On the general employment of the Pointed Arch in Germany in the Tenth and Eleventh Centuries," as an Introduction to H. Gally Knight's Progress of Architecture from the Tenth to the Fourteenth Century under the Normans, from the English; Leipsig, 1841; and my father's treatise, " The Dome of Naumburg," by C. P. Lepsius, Leipsig, 1840 (in Puttrich's " Monuments of Architecture," II. pt. 3, 4).

[† In Catherwood's beautiful work on Central America we find that at some of the cities a peculiar arch was employed. This consisted in an arch of which the point was destroyed by laying a beam across at the top. In the Polynesian island we also find almost perfect approaches to the pointed arch.— K. R. H. M.]

cutting. They belong to the twenty-sixth Mane-
thonic dynasty of the Psammetici, *i. e.* in the
seventh and sixth centuries B.C., are therefore
of about the same antiquity as the *Cloaca maxima*
and the *Carcer Mamertinus* at Rome. We have
also found tombs with vaults of Nile bricks, that
go back as far as the era of the pyramids. Now
I deny, in contradistinction to the opinion of
others, that the brick arch, the single flat bricks
of which are only placed concentrically by the aid
of the trowel, admits of a previous knowledge of
the actual principle of the arch, and particularly
with respect to its sustaining power, of which
denial there is already proof in the fact that
before the Psammetici there is no instance of a
concentrically laid arch, but many pseudo-arches,
cut, as it were, in horizontal layers. But where
the brick arch was ancient, we may also most
naturally place the origin of the later concentric
stone arch, or at least admit of its appearing
contemporaneously in other lands.

I was about to accompany the prince the next
morning to the interesting institution of Herr
Lieder, when Erbkam unexpectedly arrived from
our camp. He reported that on the previous night,
between three and four o'clock A.M., a number of
shots were suddenly fired in the neighbourhood of
our tents, and at the same time a crowd of more
than twenty people rushed into the encampment.
Our tents stand on a small surface before the rock
tombs, which are excavated half-way up the steep
Libyan Vale-wall, and have a considerable terrace
in front, formed by the rubbish. Almost the only

way in which it was to be approached was on one
side by a gorge that passes down from above by
our tents. Thence the attack was made. It was
first directed against the tent which served as a
salon for our whole society. This soon fell down
in a mass. Then followed the other great tent
in which slept Erbkam, Frey, Ernst Weidenbach,
and Franke. This was also torn down, and
covered up its inhabitants, who had great difficulty in creeping out from among the ropes and
tent-cloths. Besides this, all the guns had been
placed in one tent together on the previous day,
at the visit of the prince, and fastened to the
centre pole, so that they were not at hand. The
guards, cowardly in the extreme, and knowing
that they had made themselves liable to punishment, even if such a thing had happened without
their being in fault, immediately fled with loud
cries in every direction, and have not yet returned. The thieves now stuck to what was
nearest at hand, rolled everything they could
lay hold of down the hill, and were soon lost
in the plains below. Their shots had evidently
been blank, for no one had been hurt by them;
but they had gained their object of rendering the
confusion greater. Only Ernst Weidenbach and
a few of our attendants were wounded in the
head or shoulders by blows from gunstocks,
bludgeons, or stones, but they were none of them
dangerous. The things stolen will have bitterly
disappointed the expectation of the thieves. The
great trunks scarcely contained anything but
European clothes and other things that no Arab

can use. A number of coloured sketches is most
to be regretted, the artistical Sunday amusement
of the talented Frey.

We are perfectly aware of the quarter whence
this attack originated. We live on the frontier
of the territory of Abusir, an Arab village long
bearing but a doubtful reputation, between Kafr-
el-Batran, at the foot of the pyramids of Gizeh and
Saqara. By Arabs (*'Arab*, pl. *'Urbán*) I mean,
according to custom, those inhabitants of the land
who have settled in the valley of the Nile, at a
late period, and have built villages with some
show of right. They distinguish themselves very
markedly, by their free origin and manlier character, from the Fellahs (*Fellah'*, pl. *Fellah'in*),
those original tillers of the soil, who, by centuries
of slavery, have been pressed down and enervated,
and who could not withstand the invading Islam.
A Bedouin (*Bedaui*, pl. *Bedauín*) is ever the free
son of the desert, hovering upon the coasts of the
inhabited lands. Along the pyramids, therefore,
there are situated a number of Arab villages. To
them belong the three places named above. The
sheîkh of Abusir, a young, handsome, and enter-
prising man, had a kind of claim, by the reason
of our camp lying on his border, to post a
number of excellently-paid guards around us. I
preferred, however, to withdraw ourselves to the
protection of the sheîkh of Saqâra, a mightier
man and more to be relied on, whom I had previously known, and to whose district the larger
portion of the scene of our labours belonged.
This determination cost the people of Abusir a

service, and us their friendship, as I had already observed for some time without troubling myself further about it. Evidently, they had now taken advantage of my absence in Cairo, with several attendants, to carry out this design. To Abusir the traces led through the plain; a little active boy, the grandson of an old Turk of the Mameluke time, the only stranger dwelling in Abusir, with whom we occasionally changed visits, seems to have served as a spy. This boy, who was often in our camp, must have carried out the first robbery, in Abukir's tent, with which he was well acquainted.

The attack was a serious matter, and a precedent for the future, if it were left unpunished. I immediately went with Herr von Wagner to Sherif Pasha, the minister, in order to discover the thieves.

In a few days the plain beneath our camp wore an animated appearance. The Mudhir (governor) of the province came, with a magnificent train, and a great flock of under-officers and servants, and pitched his varied camp at the foot of the mountain. We interchanged visits of politeness, and conversed upon the event. The Mudhir told me at once that the actual thieves would never be discovered, at least never brought to confession, as each one knew that it would cost him his neck. But the second day the sheîkhs of Saqâra and Abusir, with a number of suspected persons, were brought up to be judged. Neither confrontation nor examination succeeded in obtaining any decision, as it was expected.

The punishment was therefore summarily executed; one after the other they were shut in the stocks, with their faces down and their soles up, and pitifully beaten, often to fainting, with long whips, called kurwatch, the thongs of which are strips of hippopotamus skin. It was in vain that I represented that I really saw no reason for punishing these persons precisely, and I was still more astonished when our reverend old friend the sheîkh of Saqâra, for whose innocence I had pledged my strongest belief, was led down and laid in the dust like all the others. I expressed my surprise to the Mudhir, and protested seriously against it, but received for answer that the punishment could not be spared him, for though we had not been exactly upon his soil, yet we had received our guides from him, who had run away, and until now had not returned. With much difficulty I obtained a shortening of the proceeding, but he was already scarcely sensible, and he had to be carried to the tent, where his feet were bound up. The whole matter ended with an indemnification in money for the worth of the stolen things, which I purposely estimated at a large sum, as every loss in money remains for years in the memory of the Arab, while he forgets his thrashing, or, indeed, exults in it, when he no longer feels it. "*Nezel min e' semmá e' nebút, bárakah min Allah*," say the Arabs, *i.e.* "Down came the stick from heaven, a blessing of Allah." Even at the proportioning of the fine, the sum we had asked was so divided that the rich sheîkh of Saqâra had to pay a much

larger share than he of Abusir, a partiality in
which the request of the respected old Turk of
Abusir, from the Turkish mudhir, no doubt had
its due weight.

As soon as the money was counted out, I went
to our sheîkh of Saqâra, whose unmerited ill-
fortune seriously discomforted me, and returned
him publicly the half of his money, with the
confidential assurance that the rest should be
restored on the departure of the Mudhir. This
was so unexpected on the part of the reverend
sheikh, that he long stared at me incredu-
lously, then kissed my hands and feet, and called
me his best friend on earth,—I, who had just been
at least the indirect cause of his stately beard
having been mingled with the dust, and of his
feet being beaten in week-enduring pain. His
surprised pleasure did not, however, so much
have me for its object as the unexpected sight of
the money, that never fails in its magical effects
on the Arab.

There is in the Arab a remarkable mixture of
noble pride and low avarice, which is at first
quite incomprehensible to the European. His
free, noble carriage and imperturbable rest seem
to express nothing but a proud feeling of honour.
But against the least prospect of profit this
melts like wax in the sun, and the most debasing
usage is of no consideration when money is at
stake, but is creepingly borne. One of these two
natures appears at first to be but apparent or
delusive ; but the contradiction comes back in
every shape, in little things and great, too often

not to cause the conviction that it is characteristic of the Arab, if not of the whole east. The
Egyptians had so degenerated already in the
Roman æra, that Ammianus Marcellinus could
say of them, " *Erubescit apud eos, si quis non
infitiando tributa plurimas in corpore vibices
ostendat;*" just in the same way the Fellah
to-day points to his red weals with a contented
smile as soon as the tax-gatherer had departed,
minus a few of his desired piastres, notwithstanding his intruments of torture.

LETTER IX.

CAIRO.
April 22, 1843.

A severe cold, which has for some time stopped my usual activity, has brought me hither from our camp near Saqâra. The worst of it is, that we are obliged to postpone our journey, although we should all have liked to quit Saqâra. Certainly everything that such a place offers is of the highest importance; but its wealth almost brings us into a dilemma here. To the most important, but most difficult and time-occupying pursuits, belongs that of Erbkam, our architect. He has the great task allotted him of making the detailed plans of the desert coasts, in about the centre of which we lie. This extent of country embraces the almost unbroken chain of tomb-fields, from the pyramid of Rigah to those of Dahshûr, The single plans of the northern fields of Abu Roash, Gizeh, Zauiet el Arrian, are already completed. The sketches of Perring, useful as they are, cannot be compared with ours. Whole Necropolîs, with the pyramids belonging to them, have been discovered, partly by myself, partly by Erbkam. Some of the hitherto unknown pyramids are even now from eighty to a hundred feet in height, others are almost worn away, but were originally of considerable size, as is shown by the extent of their ground plans.

My return to Saqâra will, it is to be hoped, be the
signal of our departure.

We shall proceed by land to the Faiûm, that
province branching into the wilderness. The
season of the year is still most beautiful, and the
desert journey will no doubt be more conducive
to our health than the Nile passage, which we
formerly intended.

My health will, it is to be hoped, not long detain
me here, for with every day my impatience in-
creases to leave the living city of the Mamelukes,
for the solemn Necropolis of the ancient Pharaohs.
And yet it might give you more pleasure, perhaps,
could I picture to you, in colours or words, how it
looks from this my window.

I live on the great place of the Ezbekîeh, in
the most handsome and populous part of the city.
Formerly there was a large lake in the middle,
but it is now transformed into gardens. All
around run broad streets, parted off for riders and
walkers, and shaded by high trees. There the
whole East flits by me with its gay, manifold, and
always picturesque forms; the poor with blue or
white tucked-up dresses, the rich with long garments of the most various stuffs, with silken
kaftans, or fine clothes in delicate broken colours,
with white, red, green, or black turbans, or with
the noble but little-becoming Turkish *tarbush;*
then Greeks with their dandified *fustanellas*, or
Arabian sheîkhs in their wide, antiquely-draped
mantle: the children quite, or half, naked, with
shaven heads, from which a single lock stands
up on their bare polls like a handle; the women

F

with veiled faces, whose black-rimmed eyes glance ghostly from out the holes cut in the covering. All these and a hundred other indescribable forms go, creep, dash by on foot, on asses, mules, dromedaries, camels, horses, only not in carriages; for they were employed much more in the Pharoahic times than now. If I look upward from the street, I see on one side a prospect of magnificent mosques with their cupolas and slender minarets shooting into the air, with long rows of generally carelessly-built, but now and then richly-ornamented houses, distinguished by artistically-carved lattices, and elegant balconies; on the other side my view is bounded by green palm-trees, or leaf-wealthy sycamores and acacias. In the far back-ground at last, beyond the level roofs and their green interruptions, there come forth on the Libyan horizon the far-lighting sister-pair of the two great pyramids, sunny amidst the fine æther in sharply-broken lines. What a difference to the mongrel Alexandria, where the oriental nature of the country and the mightily progressed culture of Europe still strive for the mastery. It seems to me as if I had already penetrated to the inmost heart of the East of the present.

LETTER X.

After my return to the camp at Saqâra, I required but three days to finish our labours there. I made a last visit to the ruins of ancient Memphis, the plan of which had, meanwhile, been completed by Erbkam; a few interesting discoveries closed our examination.

On the 19th of May we at length departed with twenty camels, two dromedaries, thirteen donkies, and a horse. As I am speaking of camels and dromedaries, it may not be superfluous to remark what is here understood by those terms; for in Europe, an inaccurate, or at least negligent distinction is made between both, which is not known here. We call Camel what the French-man names *dromadaire*, and dromedary (Trampel-thier, trampling beast) what he names *chameau*. The first has one hump, the other two. Thus Dromedaries or *chameaux* could not be spoken of at all in Egypt, for there are no bi-humped animals, although they occur now and then in single-humped families. In Syria and Farther Asia, there would again be no camels or *droma-daires;* at least the single-humped animals are very rare. In fact, it is very immaterial, and taken by itself, should hardly warrant the dis-tinction of another species, whether or not the fat hump on the back is divided into two. At the present time the orientals make no distinction between them, and the ancients evidently did the same, for the single-humped animals do not carry more easily than the others, nor do they run faster, nor does the rider sit between the two humps more securely than on one, for these are as entirely built over by the saddle as the single hump. However, a great distinction is made, though not a naturalistic one, between the strong and unwieldy burthen camel, commonly called *gémel*, and the younger, more active, thoroughly-broken riding camel, which is called *heggín*, because the Mekka pilgrims (*hágg*, pl. heggâg) have a great estimation for good riding animals. An Arab takes it as ill when any one calls his slender, well-bred camel a *gémel*, as one would feel angry at having one's thorough-bred horse called a plough-horse or dray-horse. The meaning, indeed, of *dromedarius* or *camelus dromas*, κάμηλος δρομάς with the ancients, was nothing more, as the name proves, than a runner, of the lighter, more rideable race.

As the latter are far more expensive, it is often difficult to obtain even a few of the better kind of animals from the Arabs who are bound to produce them; the greater part of our company was obliged to be contented with the usual beasts of burthen; mine was, however, passable, and was at least called *heggín* by the Arabs.

I did not await the general break up of the camp, at which our Sheîkh of Saqâra and he of Mitrahinneh were present, but rode forward with

Erbkam along the desert. On the way he took the plan of a pyramid with its neighbourhood, that I had remarked on a former occasion. We have now noted in all sixty-seven pyramids, almost twice as many as are found in Perring. The topographical plans of Erbkam are indeed a treasure.

Shortly after sundown we came to the first pyramid of Lisht, where we found our camp already pitched. Next morning I had the caravan broken up early, and stayed behind with Erbkam in order to employ ourselves in the examination and surveying of the two pyramids, somewhat apart from each other, in this alone-standing tomb-field. A 2 o'clock we followed, and arrived about 7 o'clock in the evening at our tents, which were erected on the south side of the stately pyramid of Meidûm. To the pyramid of Illahûn was another short day's journey, and from hence,* through the mouth of the Faiûm, about three hours. We set out very late. I left Erbkam and Ernst Weidenbach behind in order to bring their researches on paper, and rode off with a couple of servants half an hour before the train, in order to reach the labyrinth by another and more interesting way along the Bahr Jussuf, and to fix upon a place for the encampment.

Here we are since the 31st of May, settled at the south side of the pyramid of Mœris, upon the ruins of the labyrinth. That are fully justified in employing these terms, I was quite

[* From the labyrinth and the remains of lake Mœris.— K. R. H. M.]

sure, as soon as I had surveyed the locality rapidly. I did not think that it would be so easy to determine this.

As soon as Erbkam had measured off a small plan and had committed it to paper, I had workmen got together by the Mudhir of Medînet el Faiûm, the governor of the province, trenches drawn through the ruins and excavations made in four or five places at once; one hundred and eight people were at work to-day: these I allow to encamp for the night on the north side of the pyramid, with the exception of the people of Howara, the nearest village, who return home every night. They have their foremen, and bread is brought to them; they are counted every morning, and paid every evening; each man receives a piastre, about two silver *groschens,** each child half a one, occasionally thirty paras, (forty go to a piaster) when they were very industrious. The men must each bring a hoe, and a shallow plaited basket, called *maktaf*. The children, forming by far the greater number, need only come with baskets. The maktafs are filled by the men, and carried away by the children on their heads; this is done in processions, which are kept in strict order and activity by overseers.

Their chief delight, and a considerable strengthener during their daily work, is song. They have certain simple melodies, which at a distance make an almost melancholy impression by reason of their great monotony; but near, they are hardly

[* About two-pence halfpenny English.—K. R. H. M.]

bearable, by reason of the pitiless duration of the yelling voices that often continue the same tune for hours together. Only the knowledge that by forbearance I assist so many in carrying half the burden of the day, and materially hasten their labours, has ever deterred me from meddling in this, though I am often driven from my tent in despair to seek rest for my ears in some distant sphere of activity. In the performance of the two-lined stanzas, the only change is, that the first line is sung by a single voice, the second by the whole chorus, while every fourth of a bar is marked by a clap of the hands, *e.g.*

Solo   Chorus

1.   Om - mí be - tá - kul má - ku - lí   U a-
2.   Dill   ás - sa - rí   mál u mál   Bun-
3.   Yâ - min sa - báh'   ú le-bén   U

Solo

ná bagh-bágh - tét 'a - léï   (Dill)
yál dill ebánne ú 'a - léï   (Yâ-)
sám-neh sâïh   "a - le - *t*   &c.

I.e.   1. My mother eats my dates
           And I,—I am angry.
     2. The shadow of Asser* bows it and bows it.
           The wall (*bunyân*) . . . . . .
     3. Oh joy! when the morning milk
           And butter pours over me.

Makûl, in the first line, is more properly only

---

* Evening.

"food," but it has generally become an expression for dates, as they are the principal food in the hut of the Fellah, and for some indeed is the only food. Another melody, a little more animated, is as follows :—

where the chorus exceptionally sings two notes and not one. But I hardly believe that even these chords are intentional; they run down without knowing it, for it often occurs that single voices sing the same note in different keys without in the least observing the continual discord. The power of joining voices together, in even the simplest harmony, seems to be wholly wanting in the Arab. The artistical music of the most celebrated singers and players, which inexpressibly delights even the most educated Mussulman, consists only of a hundred-wise screaming, restlessly-hurrying melody, the connecting idea of which is utterly untenable to an European ear.* And just as little are the musical

---

[* It is to be remarked that even in the " Thousand and One Nights," where occasionally æsthetic observations are to be found, there is nothing relating to music which would lead us to estimate the musical tastes of the Arabs at any higher standard than that manifested in the account of Lepsius and others.—K. R. H. M.]

instruments, when sounding together, used for any other harmonious variations than rythm produces.

In the night we have eight watchmen, who really do watch, as I often prove to myself by going a nightly round; one of them is always walking up and down upon the walls about our camp, with his gun on his shoulder; for if we have to anticipate an attack at any place, it is here; not on the part of the Arabs, but of the yet more dangerous Bedouins, who inhabit the borders of the desert in many single hordes, not living under great sheîkhs, who might be secured to our interests. On the way from Illahûn hither, we came through a Bedouin camp, the sheîkh of which must have been aware of our approach, as he mounted his horse, rode to meet us, and offered us his services in case we might require them. Some distance further, we met an old man and a girl crying aloud in despair; they threw dust in the air and heaped it upon their heads; when we had come up to them they complained bitterly to us, that just then two Bedouins had robbed them of their only buffalo; indeed, we could see the thieves on horseback in the distance, driving the animal before them into the desert. I was alone with my dragoman and my little donkey groom, 'Auad, an active, dark-brown Berber, and could render them no assistance. Such robberies are not at all rare here. A short time since, one tribe drove away one hundred and twenty camels from another, and not a single one of them has come back yet.

However, we shall probably not be molested, for the judgment of Saqâra is not forgotten, and it is known that we are particularly recommended to the authorities. They were also aware that we carried no gold and silver with us in our heavy trunks, as the Arabs had universally imagined. We are also prepared for every other attack. The most important chests are all together in my tent, and beside my bed at night I always keep a double-barrelled English gun and a brace of pistols. Every evening I clear all away, in order to be prepared for anything, and storms in particular, from which we have suffered much lately, and the violence of which cannot be conceived in Europe. Abeken's tent fell down upon him three times in the course of one day, and the last time disturbed him from sleep in a rather disagreeable manner. Thus, we are often in continual expectation for whole days and nights that the airy dwelling will fall down upon us at the next gust, and one must be accustomed to this feeling in order to go on quietly working or sleeping.

It would seem as if we were to taste of all the plagues of Egypt; our acquaintance with a flood was made at the great pyramids; then came the locusts, the young broods of which are numberless as the sands of the sea, and are eating up the green meadows and trees again, and, together with the passing cattle murrain, are almost enough to bring on a famine; after that came the attack, with a daring robbery at the beginning. The plague of fire has not quite failed. By a careless salute, Wild's tent was set on fire in Saqâra, and was partially burnt while we stood around in the bright sunlight that concealed the conflagration. Now comes the plague of mice, with which we were not formerly acquainted; in my tent they gnaw, play, and whistle, as if they had been at home here all their lives, and quite regardless of my presence. At night they have already run across my bed and face, and yesterday I started terrified from my slumbers, as I suddenly felt the sharp tooth of such a daring guest at my foot. I jumped up angrily and got a light, knocked at every chest and tent-peg, but was only hissed and whistled at anew on my lying down again. With all these annoyances, however, we are in good spirits, and, thank God, they have only threatened us as yet, made us aware of their existence, and not particularly harmed us.

I have now much lightened the labours of inspecting the attendants and administering many outward labours by having brought an excellent *khawass* from Cairo. These *khawasses*, who form a peculiar corps of officers of the Pasha, are in this country a very exclusive and important class of people. Only Turks are admitted into it, and these, by their nationality, have an inborn preponderance over every Arab. There are few nations that possess so much talent for governing as the Turks, whom we often picture to ourselves as half-barbarians, rough and uncultivated in the highest degree. On the contrary, they, nationally, have a species of aristocratic feeling. A most imperturbable quiet, cold bloodedness, reservedness, and energy of will, seem to be peculiar to every Turk, down to the lowest soldier, and they do not fail at first to make a certain impression upon the European. Among the noble Turks, who have all been subject to the most rigid etiquette from childhood, this outward carriage of apparently pre-conceived firmness, this reserved and proud politeness, moving lightly, as it were, in strict forms, is only present in the refined degree. They have an inborn contempt for everything that does not belong to their nation, and seem not to possess any feeling for the natural weight of higher mental culture and civilization which generally makes the most every-day European respected among other nations. Nothing is to be won from the Turk by kindness, consideration, demonstration, or even by irritation; he only looks upon it as weakness. The greatest reserve alone, and the most scrupulous and proud politeness toward the great, or aristocratic usage and categorical commands toward the little, succeed. A Turkish *khawass* hunts a whole village of Fellahs or Arabs before him, and makes a decided impression upon the yet prouder Bedouins. The Pasha employs this body in delicate missions and trusts throughout the country. They are the principal acting servants of the Pasha and of the governors of the provinces. Every foreign consul also has such a *khawass*, without whom he scarcely moves a step, because he is his guard of honour, the token and executive of his incontestible authority. When he rides out, the *khawass* precedes him on horseback, with a great silver staff, and drives the people and animals out of the way with words

and blows, and woe be to him that assumes
a gesture or even a look of opposition. The
Pasha occasionally gives peculiarly-recommended
strangers such a guard, with equal authority,
and thus we, on our arrival, immediately received
a *khawass*, who was, however, duly troublesome to
us during our long stay at Gizeh, and was at last
very ungraciously dismissed by me on account of
his improper pretensions. On the occasion of the
attack at Saqâra, I had another given me by Sherif
Pasha; but still he was not the sort of man we
wanted, so I have brought a third with us from
Cairo, who has answered excellently till now.
He takes the whole responsibility of the attendants off me, and manages admirably everything
that I have to negotiate with the people and
officials. In Europe I judged myself perfectly
strong enough to conduct the whole outward
affairs of the Expedition; but in this climate one
must take another standard of measure. Patience
and rest are here as necessary elements of existence as meat and drink.

LETTER XI.

LABYRINTH.
June 25, 1843.

From the Labyrinth these lines come to you; not from the doubtful, or, at least, always disputed one, of which I could form no idea from the previous and more than meagre descriptions of those who placed the Labyrinth here, but the clearly-identified Labyrinth of Mœris and the Dodecarchs. There is a mighty knot of churches still existing, and in the midst is the great square, where the Aulæ stood, covered with the remains of great monolithic pillars of granite, and others of white, hard limestone, gleaming almost like marble.

I came near to the spot with a certain fear that we should have to seek to confirm the account of the ancients by the geographical position of the place, that every form of its architectural disposition would be wiped away, and that a shapeless heap of ruins would frighten us from every attempt at investigation; instead of this, there were immediately found, on a cursory view of the districts, a number of confused spaces, as well super as subterranean, and the principal mass of the building, which occupied more than a stadium (Strabo),* was distinctly to be seen. Where

[* Lib. XVII. p. 789, ed. Parisii, 1620.—K. R. H. M.]

the French expedition had fruitlessly sought for chambers, we find literally hundreds, by and over each other, little, often very small, by larger and great, supported by diminutive pillars, with thresholds and niches, with remains of pillars and single wall slabs, connected together by corridors, so that the descriptions of Herodotus and Strabo are quite confirmed in this respect; at the same time, the idea, never coincided in by myself, of *serpentine*, cave-like windings, instead of square rooms, is definitely contradicted.

The disposition of the whole is, that three mighty clumps of buildings, of the breadth of 300 feet, surround a square 600 feet in length and 500 in width; the fourth side is bounded by the pyramid lying behind, which is 300 feet square, and therefore does not quite come up to the side wings of the great buildings. A rather modern canal, which may be pumped up, at least at this season of the year, is diagonally drawn through the ruins, cutting right through the most perfectly-preserved of the Labyrinthic rooms, and a part of the square in the centre, which was once divided into courts. Travellers have not wished to wet their feet, and so remained on this side, where the continuation of the wings of the buildings is certainly much concealed by the rubbish mounds; but even from this, the eastern bank, the chambers on the opposite side, and particularly at the southern point, where the walls rise almost 10 feet above the rubbish, and 20 above the level of the ruins, are very easy to be seen, and when viewed from the heights of the pyramid, the regular plan of the whole lies before one like a map. Erbkam has been employed since our arrival in surveying the place, and inserting in the plan every room and wall, however small; the ruins on the other side are therefore much more difficult in the execution of the plan; here it is easier, as there are fewer chambers, but therefore more difficult to be understood with respect to the original structure. The labyrinth of chambers runs along here to the south. The Aulæ lay between this and the northerly pyramid opposite, but almost all traces of them have disappeared. The dimensions of the place alone allow us to suspect that it was divided into two parts by a wall, to which the twelve Aulæ, no longer to be distinguished with certainty, adjoined on both sides, so that their entrances were turned in opposite directions, and had close before them the innumerable chambers of the Labyrinth. Who was, however, the Maros, Mendes, Imandes, who, according to the reports of the Greeks, erected the labyrinth, or rather the pyramid belonging to it, as his monument? In the Royal Lists of Manetho,* we find the builder of the labyrinth towards the end of the *twelfth* dynasty, the last of the Old Empire shortly before the irruption of the Hyksos. The fragments of the mighty pillars and architraves, that we have dug out in the great square of the

[* See Bunsen's Egypt's Place, &c. vol. i. p. 624-5, and also the comparative lists of Eratosthenes and Manetho at pp. 124, 125 of the same work. "ὃς τὸν ἐν Ἀρσινοΐτῃ λαϐύρινθον ἑαυτῷ τάφον κατεσκεύασεν."—K. R. H. M.]

Aulæ, give us the cartouches of the sixth king of this twelfth dynasty, Amenemha III.; thus is this important question answered in its historical portion.* We have also made excavations on the north side of the pyramid, because we may expect to discover the entrance there; that is, however, not yet done. We have obtained an entry into a chamber covered with piles of rubbish that lay before the pyramid, and here we have also found the name of Amenemha several times. The builder and possessor of the pyramid is therefore determined. But the account of Herodotus, that the construction of the Labyrinth was commenced two hundred years before his time by the Dodecarchs, is not yet confuted. In the ruins of the great masses of chambers surrounding the great square, we have discovered no inscriptions. Later excavations may very probably certify to us that this whole building, and also the arrangement of the twelve courts, really fall in the twenty-sixth dynasty of Manetho, so that the original temple of Amenemha was only included in this mighty erection.†

So much for the Labyrinth and its Pyramid. The historical determination of the builder of this structure is by far the most important result that we can expect here. Now something about the other wonder of this province, Lake Mœris.

The obscurity in which it was previously involved seems to be removed by a happy discovery that the

* Compare my " Chronology of the Egyptians," vol. i. pp. 262 sqq.

[† Bunsen, vol. i. pp. 640—641.—K. R. H. M.]

G

excellent Linant, the Pasha's hydraulic engineer,
has lately made. Up to this time it was only agreed
that the lake lay somewhere in the Faiûm. As
there is at the present time in this remarkable half-
oasis only a single lake, the Birqet el Qorn, lying
in its most distant part, this was of course taken
to be Lake Mœris; there appeared to be no
other solution to the question. Now its great
fame was expressly founded upon the fact that it
was artificial (Herodotus says that it was excavated), and of immense utility, filled at the
time of the overflow of the Nile, and at low water
running off again by the canal, on one side toward
the lands of the Faiûm, on the other, in its backward course, it waters the region of Memphis, and
yielding a most lucrative fishery at the double
sluices near the end of the Faiûm. Of all these
qualities, however, to the annoyance of antiqua-
rians and philologers, the Birqet el Qorn did not
possess a single one. It is not artificial, but a
natural lake, that is partly fed by the water of the
Jussuf canal; its utility is as good as non-existent;
no fishing-boat enlivens the hard and desert-circled
water mirror, as the brackish water contains scarcely
any fish, and is not even favourable to the vegetation at the shores; when the Nile is high and there
is plenty of water flowing in, it does swell, but it is
by far too deep to allow a drop of the water that
flows into it to flow out again; the whole province
must be buried beneath the floods ere this could
find a passage back again to the valley, as the
artificially-deepened rock gorge by the Bahr
Jussuf, branching from the Nile at a distance of

forty miles to the south, lies higher than the whole oase. The *niveau* of the Birqet el Qorn now lies seventy feet below the point at which the canal flows in, and can never have risen much higher.* This is proved by the ruins of ancient temples lying upon its shores. Just as little do the statements tally that inform us that on its shores were situated the Labyrinth and the metropolis Arsinoë, now Medînet el Faiûm. Linant has discovered mighty mile-long dams, of ancient solid construction, which form the boundary between the upper part of the shell-formed convex basin of the Faiûm, and the more remote and less elevated portion. According to him, these could only be intended to restrain an artificially-constructed lake, which, however, since the dams have long since been broken through, lies perfectly dry; this lake he considers to be Mœris. I must confess that the whole, after his personal information, impressed me with the idea that it was a most fortunate discovery, and one that would save us many fruitless researches; and the examination of the region has now quite solved every doubt of mine as to the accuracy of this

---

* According to Linant the difference is 22ᵐ, i.e. 70 feet Rhenish. In June, 1843, Nascimbeni, an engineer of the viceroy, visited us in our camp by the pyramid of Mœris, being at the time engaged on a new chart and levelling of the Faiûm. He had only found 2 metres fall from Illahûn to Medînet, but from thence to the Birqet el Qorn, 75 metres. I am not aware that anything has been made known regarding these widely different measures. Sir G. Wilkinson, Modern Egypt and Thebes, vol. ii. p. 346, states the lake *niveau* to be about 125 English feet below the Nile shore at Benisuef.

judgment; I consider it an immoveable fact. Linant's essay is now being printed, and I will send it as soon as it is to be got.*

Should you, however, ask me what then the name of Mœris has to do with that of Amenemha, I can only reply, nothing. The name Mœris occurs in the monuments or in Manetho; I rather imagine that here again is one of the numerous Greek misunderstandings. The Egyptians called the lake *Phiom en mere,* " the Lake of the Nile flood (Koptic, ⲙⲏⲣⲉ, *inundatio*)." The Greeks made out of *mere,* the water that formed the lake, a King Mœris, who laid out the lake, and troubled themselves no more about the real originator of it, Amenemha. At a later period, the whole province obtained the name of Ⲫⲓⲟⲙ, *Phiom,* the Lake, from which arises the present name *Faiúm.*

* *Mémoire sur le lac Mœris, présenté et lu à Société Egyptienne le 5 Juillet,* 1842, *par Linant de Bellefonds, inspecteur-général des ponts et chaussées, publié par la Société Egyptienne. Alexandrie,* 1843, 4to. See my " Chronology of the Egyptians," vol. i. p. 262 sq.

LETTER XII.

LABYRINTH.
July 18, 1843.

OUR tour in the Faiûm, this remarkable province so seldom visited by Europeans, which may be called the garden of Egypt by reason of its fertility, is now ended; and as these regions are almost as unknown as the distant Libyan oases, it may be pleasing to you to hear something more about this from me.

I set out on the 3rd of July, in company with Erbkam, Ernst Weidenbach, and Abeken; from the Labyrinth we followed the Bahr Wardâni, which traverses the eastern boundary of the desert, and marks the frontier to which the shores of Lake Mœris once extended. Now the canal is dry, and its place is taken by the still more modern Bahr Sherkîeh, which, it is said, was the work of Sultan Barquq, and leads through the middle of the Labyrinth, crosses and recrosses the Wardâni, but then keeps more inland. In three hours we arrived at the place where the monster dam of Mœris, from the middle of the Faiûm, touches the desert. It runs from there in a direct line for one and a half geographical miles to El Elâm; in the middle of this course it is interrupted by the Bahr bela-mâ, a deep river bed, which now passes through the old lake bottom, and is generally dry, but is used at

a great inundation to draw off the surplus toward
Tamîeh and into the Birqet el Qorn. This gave
us the advantage of being able to examine more
closely the dyke itself. The occasionally high-
swelling and tearing stream has not only penetrated the disturbed bed of the lake, but also
several other strata, and even the lowest, crumbling limestone, so that the water now flows during
the dryest season of the year, at sixty feet below
the now dry surface. I measured the single strata
carefully, and brought away a specimen of each.
The breadth of the embankment cannot be exactly
given, but was probably 150 feet. Its height has
probably decreased in the lapse of time. I found
1 m. 90. above the present basin, and 5 m. 60.
above the opposite surface. If we take that to
be of an equal height with the original lake
bottom (which, however, appears to have been
deeper, because the outer region was watered,
and was therefore made higher), the former height
of the embankment, its gradual declension not
being considered, would have been 5 m. 60., *i. e.*
17 feet, and the bottom of the lake would thus
have been raised by the sediment about 11 feet in
its existence of 2,000 years. But if we take for
granted that the 11 or 12 feet of black earth were
deposited in historical times, the above amounts
would be almost double. Thus it may be understood how it is that its usefulness is so much
diminished, for, by the deposit of 11 feet, the
lake lost (if we accept Linant's statement as to
its circumference) about 13,000,000,000 square
feet of water, which it could formerly contain.

Raising the dykes would not, it may be readily understood, have counteracted it, because they had already been put into the proper connection with the point of entrance of the Bahr Jussuf into the Faiûm. This may have been one of the most cogent reasons for the neglect into which Lake Mœris had been permitted to fall, and even if Linant had the Bahr Jussuf turned off much higher from the Nile than the ancient Pharaohs found it good, his daring project of restoring the lake again would not completely succeed.

In two hours and a half from this breach, we arrived by El Elâm, where the dam ends, at the remarkable ruins of the two monuments of Biahmu, which Linant considers to be the two pyramids of Mœris and his wife, mentioned by Herodotus as seen in the lake. They are built up of massive blocks; there is yet a heart existing of each of them, but not in the middle of the square rectangles, which appear as if they had been originally quite filled by them. They rose in an angle of 64°, therefore much more steeply than pyramids usually do. Their present height is only twenty-three feet, to which must be added, however, a protruding base of seven feet. A slight excavation convinced me, that the undermost layer of stone, which only reaches four feet below the present surface of the ground, is neither founded upon sand or rock, but upon Nile-earth, by which the high antiquity of this structure is much to be doubted. At least this proved that they did not stand in the Lake, which must have had a considerable bend to the north-west if it included them.

Up to this time we had ridden along the boundary of the ancient lake, and the adjoining region. This was bare and unfruitful, because the land now lies so high, that it cannot be inundated. The land, however, immediately enclosing the old lake, forms by far the most beautiful and fertile part of the Faiûm. This we now traversed, leaving the metropolis of the province, Medînet el Faiûm, with the hills of ancient Crocodilopolis, to our left, and riding by Selajîn and Fidimîn to Agamîeh, where we staid for the night. Next morning we arrived by way of Bisheh on the frontier of the uninterrupted garden land. Here we entered a new region, particularly striking by its unfertility and desolateness, which lies round the other like a girdle, and separates it from the deepest, and most distant, crescent-shaped Birqet el Qorn. About noon we reached the lake. The only bark we could possibly find here, carried us in an hour and a half over the waters, surrounded on all sides by desert, to an island in the middle of the lake, called Gezîret el Qorn. However, we found nothing remarkable upon it, not a single trace of building: towards evening we returned back again.

On the following morning, we cruized in a more northerly direction across the lake, and landed on a little peninsula on the opposite side, that rises immediately to a *plateau* of the Libyan desert, one hundred and fifty feet high, commanding the whole oasis. Thither we as-

cended and found, about an hour distant from
the shores, in the middle of the inhospitable
water and barren desert, the extended ruins of an
ancient city, which is called in earlier maps Medînet Nimrud. Of this name no one knew anything; the place was known as Diméh. Next
morning, the 7th of July, the regular plan of
these ruins, with the remains of their temple,
was made by Erbkam, who had stopped the night
here with Abeken. The temple bears no inscription, and what we found of sculptures point to
the late origin of this remarkable site. Its
purpose can only have been a military station
against Libyan incursions into the rich Faiûm.

On the 8th of July we sailed in our ship to
Qasr Qerûn, an old city at the southern end of
the lake, with a temple, in excellent preservation,
but bearing no inscriptions of recent date, the plan
of which was taken next day. Hence we pursued
the southern boundary of the oasis by Neslet, to
the ruins of Medînet Mâdi at lake Gharaq, in the
neighbourhood of which the old embankments of
Lake Mœris run down from the north, and we
arrived in our camp at the ruins of the labyrinth,
on the 11th of July. We found all well except
our Frey, whom we had left indisposed, and whose
recurring, seemingly climatic, illness gives me
some pain.

To-morrow I am thinking of going to Cairo,
with Abeken and Bonomi, to hire a bark for our
journey to the south, and to prepare everything
required by our final departure from the neighbourhood of the metropolis. We shall take four

camels with us, for the transport of the monuments gathered in the Faiûm, and go the shortest
way, by Tamiêh, which we did not touch on our
tour, and thence over the desert heights, which
divide this part of the Faiûm from the valley of
the Nile.   We shall enter this by the pyramids of
Dahshur.   Thus we expect to reach Cairo in two
days and a half.

LETTER XIII.

CAIRO.
August 14, 1843.

UNFORTUNATELY, I received, soon after our return to Cairo, such very questionable news of Frey's health, that Abeken and Bonomi have determined to go to the camp and bring him, in a litter they took with them, from the Labyrinth to Zani, on the Nile, and thence by water hither. As soon as Dr. Pruner had seen him, he declared that the only advisable course was to let him depart immediately for Europe. Disease of the liver, in the way it developed itself in him, is incurable in Egypt. So he left us yesterday at noon. May the climate of his native land soon restore the powers of a friend, equally talented as estimable, in whom we all lose much.

A few days ago I purchased from a Basque Domingo Lorda, who has stayed a long time in Abyssinia, and has since accompanied d'Abadie in several journeys, some Ethiopic Manuscripts for the Berlin Museum. He bought them, probably at an inconsiderable price, in a convent on the island of Thâna, near Gorata, a day's journey from the sources of the Blue Nile, where the inhabitants had been put to fearful distress by the locusts. One contains the history of Abyssinia from Solomon to Christ, is reported to come from Axum, and to be 500 or 600 years old! This first portion of Abyssinian history, named *Kebre Negest*, "The Fame of the Kings," is said to be far rarer than the second, *Tarik Negest*, "The History of the Kings;" but this manuscript contains at the end a list of the Ethiopian kings since Christ. The largest manuscript, with many pictures ornamented in the Byzantine style, and, according to what Lieder tells me, almost unique in its kind, contains mostly lives of Saints. In the third, the yet valid *Canones* of the church are completely preserved. I hope the purchase will be welcome to our library.*

Now, too, are our purchases for the voyage ended; a comfortable bark is hired, and will save us the great difficulties of a land journey, which is scarcely possible during the coming season of inundation.

---

* The same Domenico Lorda set out again in the same year to Abyssinia, and transmitted thence six other Abyssinian MSS. to Herr Lieder, who submitted them to me on my return to Cairo. These were also purchased for the Royal Library at my suggestion. They contain, according to the account of Herr Lorda:—

    A. *Abusher*, Almanacco perpetuo civile-ecclesiastico-storico.
    B. *Settà Neghest*, Codice dell' imperadore Eeschias.
    C. *Jaseph*, Storia civile ed ecclesiastica (?)
    D. *Beraan*, Storia civile ed ecclesiastica.
    E. *Philkisius e Marisak*, Due opere in un volume che trattano della storia civile.
    F. *Sinodus*, Dritto canonico.

LETTER XIV.

THEBES.
October 13, 1843.

On the 16th of August, I went from Cairo to the Faiûm, where our camp was broken up on the 21st. Two days later we sailed from Benisuef, sent the camels back to Cairo, and only took the donkeys with us, as it was found, upon careful consideration, that the originally-intended land journey by the foot of the mountains, far away from the river, was altogether impossible during the season of the inundation, and, on the eastern side, it was not only too difficult, but perfectly useless for us, by reason of the proximity of the desert, towards which there is nothing more to be found for our purposes. We have therefore made excursions from our bark, on foot, and with donkeys, principally to the east and some attainable mountains, though we have also visited the most important spots on the western shore.

Even on the day of our departure from Benisuef, we found, in the neighbourhood of the village of Surarîeh, a small rock temple, not mentioned by former travellers, indeed, not even by Wilkinson, which was dedicated already in the nineteenth dynasty of Menephthes, the son of Ramses Miamun,* to Hathor, the Egyptian Venus.† Farther

[* See Bunsen's Egypt's Place in Universal History, vol. i. p. 632.—K. R. H. M.]

[† Bunsen, vol. i. pp. 400-402. Het-her signifies the habitation of Horus.—K. R. H. M.]

on, lie several groups of graves, which have scarcely received any attention, although they are of peculiar interest by reason of their great antiquity. The whole of middle Egypt, to judge from the tombs preserved, flourished during the Old Empire, before the irruption of the Hyksos, not only under the twelfth dynasty,* to which period the famous tombs of Benihassan suit, and Bersheh belong, but even under the sixth dynasty† we have found extensive series of tombs, belonging to these early times, and attached to cities, of which the later Egyptian geography does not even know the names, as they were probably already destroyed by the Hyksos. In Benihassan we stayed the longest time—sixteen days; through this, the season is far advanced, and it must not be lost in our journey southward. At the next places, therefore, only notes were taken, and the most important forms in paper, so also at El Armana, Siut, at the reverend Abydos, and in the younger, but not less magnificent, almost intactly preserved, temple of Dendera. At Siut, we visited the governor of Upper Egypt, Selim Pasha, who is working an ancient alabaster quarry between Bersheh and Gauâta, discovered by the Bedouins some months ago.

The town of Siut is well built and charmingly situated, particularly if it be looked upon from the steep rocks of the western shore. The

[* Bunsen, vol. i. p. 620. Therefore, about the time of Nitocris.—K. R. H. M.]

[† Bunsen, vol. i. p. 624. Coeval with the pyramid of the Labyrinth.—K. R. H. M.]

prospect of the inundated Nile valley from these heights is the most beautiful that we have yet seen, and is very peculiar in these times of inundation in which we travel. From the foot of the abrupt rock, a small dyke, overgrown with vines, and a bridge leads to the town, which lies like an island in the boundless ocean of inundation. The gardens of Ibrahim Pasha, to the left, form another island, green and fresh with trees and bushes. The city, with its fifteen minarets, rises high upon the rubbish mounds of ancient Lyco-polis; from it a great embankment reaches to the Nile; toward the south may be seen other long dykes stretching through the waters like threads; on the other side, the Arabian moun-tains come on closely, by which the valley is bounded, and formed into an easily-overlooked picture.

Since the 6th of October we have been in Royal Thebes. Our bark touched the shore first beneath the wall of Luqsor, at the southerly point of the Thebaïc ruins. The strong current of the river has thrust itself so near to the old temple, that it is in great danger. I endeavoured to obtain a general view of the ruins of Thebes from the heights of the temple, in order to compare it with the picture I had idealised to myself, from plans and descriptions.

But the distances are too great to give a com-plete view. One looks into a wide landscape, in which the temple groups are distinguishable only to those who are acquainted with the neighbour-hood. To the north, at a short hour's distance

stand the mighty pylones of Karnak, forming
a temple city in itself, gigantic and astounding
in all its proportions. We spent the next days
in a cursory examination of it. Across the
river, at the foot of the Libyan mountains, lie
the Memnonia, once an unbroken series of palaces, which probably found their equal nowhere
in antiquity. Even now, the temples of Medînet
Hâbu, at the southern end of this row, show
themselves, with their high rubbish-mounds at a
distance, and at the northern end, an hour away
down the river, is the well-preserved temple of
Qurnah; between both lies the temple of Ramses
Miamun,* (Sesostris), already most celebrated by
the description of Diodorus. Thus the four Arab
villages, Karnak and Luqsor on the east, Qurnah
and Medînet Hâbu on the west of the river, form
a great quadrangle, each side of which measures
about half a geographical mile, and gives us some
idea of the dimensions of the most magnificent part
of ancient Thebes. How far the remainder of the
inhabited portion of the hundred-gated city extended beyond these limits to the east, north, and
south, is difficult to be discovered now, because
everything that did not remain upright in the
lapse of ages gradually disappeared under the
annually rising soil of the valley, induced by the
alluvial deposit.

No one ever asks after the weather here; for
every day is pleasant, clear, and up to the present

[* Bunsen, vol. i. pp. 624-625. Ramses is the third king in
Manetho's twelfth dynasty.—K. R. H. M.]

time not too hot. We have no red either in the morning or at night, as clouds and mists fail. But every first beam of the day calls a thousand colours forth from the naked and precipitate limestone rocks, and the brown shining desert, in opposition to the black or green-clad plain of the valley. A dawn scarcely exists, as the sun sinks directly down. The boundary between day and night is as sudden as that between meadow and desert; one step, one moment, parts the one from the other. The more refreshing, therefore, is the darkly sheen of the moon and star-bright night to the eye, dazzled by the light ocean of the day. The air is so pure and dry, that no dew falls, except in the immediate vicinity of the river, notwithstanding the sudden change at sundown. We have almost forgotten what rain is, for, as far as we are concerned, it is six months since it last rained at Saqâra. A few days ago, we were rejoicing at having discovered toward evening some light clouds in the south-western part of the sky, which reminded us of Europe. However, we are not in want of cooling, for a light wind is almost always blowing, which does not allow the heat to become too oppressive. Besides this, the water of the Nile is of a sweet taste, and can be taken in great quantities without danger.

An inestimable benefit are the earthenware water-vessels (*Qulleh*), which, formed of a fine, porous Nile earth, allow the water to continually filter through. This evaporates as soon as it comes out to the warm surface, the evaporation produces cold, as is well known, and, by this simple

H

process, the bottles are kept constantly cool, even in the warmest days. The water is therefore generally cooler than it is to be had in Europe during summer. Our food usually consists mostly of fowls; as a change, we kill a sheep from time to time. There is but little vegetable. Every meal is ended with a dish of rice, and as a desert, we have the most excellent yellow melons, or juicy red water-melons. The dates are also excellent, but are, however, not always to be obtained. I have at length agreed, to the great joy of my companions, to smoke a Turkish pipe; this keeps me for a quarter of an hour in perfect *kéf* (so the Arabs call their state of perfect rest), for as long as one "drinks" from the blue pipe with the long, easily-spilt bowl, it is impossible to leave one's place, and begin any other business. Our costume is comfortable: full trowsers of light cotton, and a wide, long blouse, with short falling sleeves. I wear, also, a broad-brimmed, grey felt hat, as a European symbol, which keeps the Arabs in proper respect. We eat, according to the custom of the country, sitting with crossed legs on cushions, round a low, round table, not a foot high. This position has become so comfortable to me, that I even write in it, sitting on my bed, with my letter case upon my knees. Above me a canopy of gauze is spread, in order to keep off the flies, these most shameless of the plagues of Egypt, during the day, and the mosquitos at night. For the rest, one does not suffer so much from insects here as in Italy. Scorpions and serpents have not bitten us yet, but there are very malicious wasps, which have often stung us.

We shall only stop here till the day after to-morrow, and then journey away to the southward without stopping. On our return, we shall give the treasures here as much time and exertion as they require. At Assuan, on the Egyptian frontier, we must unload for the first time, and send back our large bark, in which we have become quite homeish. On the other side of the cataracts we shall take two smaller barks for the continuation of our journey.

LETTER XV.

Korusko.
November 20, 1843.*

Our journey from the Faiûm through Egypt was obliged to be much hastened on account of the advanced season of the year; we have, therefore, seldom stopped at any place longer than was necessary to make a hasty survey of it, and have confined ourselves in the last three months to a careful examination of what we have, and to extending our important collection of paper impressions of the most interesting inscriptions.

We have obtained, in our rapid journey to Wadi Halsa, three or four hundred Greek inscriptions, in impressions or careful transcripts. They often confirm Letronne's acute conjectures, but not seldom correct the unavoidable mistakes incident to such an investigation as his. In the inscription from which it was, without reason, attempted to settle the situation of the city of Akoris, his conjecture ΙΣΙΔΙ ΛΟΧΙΑΔΙ is not corroborated; L'Hote has read ΜΟΧΙΑΔΙ but ΜΩΧΙΑΔΙ is to be found there, and previously ΕΡΩΕΩΕ not ΕΡΕΕΩΕ.

The dedicatory inscription of the temple of Pselchis (as the inscriptions give with Strabo,

---

* This letter, addressed to Alexander von Humboldt, has been printed in the "Preussische Staatszeitung," of the 9th of February, 1844.

instead of Pselcis) is almost as long again as
Letronne considers it, and the first line does not
end with ΚΛΕΟΡΑΤΡΑΣ, but with ΑΔΕΛΦΗΣ,
so that it should probably be supplied—

Ὑπὲρ βασιλέως Πτολεμαίου καὶ βασιλίσσης
Κλεοπάτρας τῆς ἀδελφῆς
θεῶν Εὐεργετῶν......... ;*

* The correction Ἀδελφῆς in this inscription, dated in the
thirty-fifth year of Euergetes (136 B. C.), is of importance to
some chronological determinations of that period. Letronne
(*Rec. des Inscr. vol.* i. *p.* 33 *sqq.* 56) assumed that Cleopatra III.
the niece and second wife of Euergetes II., was here mentioned. From this alone he judged that this king only added
the name of his wife, Cleopatra III., to his own in the official
documents, previous to his expulsion in the year 132 B. C.,
and therefore placed all the inscriptions, in which after the
King, both Cleopatras, the sister and the (second) wife are
named, in the period after the return of Euergetes (127—117),
e. g. the inscriptions of the obelisk of Philae (*Rec. vol.* i. *p.* 333).
In this he is followed by Franz (*Corp. Inscr. vol.* iii. *p.* 285),
who places for the same reason the inscriptions *C. I. No.* 4841,
4860, 4895, 4896, between 127 and 117 B. C., although he
was aware of my correction of the inscription of Pselchis (*C. I.
No.* 5073).

It is always remarkable that only *one* Cleopatra is mentioned
in the inscription of Pselchis, but as it is Cleopatra II., the
first wife of the king, whom he always distinguishes from his
second wife by the designation of " the sister," it is not to be
concluded that he should have expressly omitted mention of
the latter in the documents from the beginning of his second
marriage. This is confirmed in the decisive manner by two
demotic Papyri of the Royal Museum, in which *both* Cleopatras
are mentioned, although one is of the year 141 B. C., and the
other of the year 136 B. C. All the inscriptions, which,
according to Letronne (*Rec. des Inscr. tome* i. *No.* 7, 26, 27,
30, 31) and Franz (*Corp. Inscr. vol.* iii. *No.* 4841, 4860, 4895,
4896) fall between 127 and 117 B. C., for this reason, can

At the end of the second line TΩIKAI is confirmed; the title of Hermes, following in the third line, was, however, ΠΑΟΤΠΝΟΥΦΙ(ΔΙ), varying from the spelling in other subsequent inscriptions, where he is called ΠΑΥΤΝΟΥΦΙΣ. The same name is found not unfrequently hieroglyphically, and is then *Tut en Pnubs*, *i. e.* Thoth of, or lord of Πνούψ,* a city, the position of which is yet obscure. I have already encountered this Thoth in earlier temples, where he often appears besides the Thoth of Shonun, *i. e. Heliopolis magna.* In the language of the people it was pronounced Pet-Pnubs, whence Paot-Pnuphis.

The interesting problem concerning the owner of the name Εὐπάτωρ, which Letronne endeavoured to solve in a new way in connection with the inscriptions of the obelisk of Philae, seems to be determined by the hieroglyphical inscriptions, where the same circumstances occur, but lead to other conclusions.† I have discovered several very per-

---

therefore be referred with the same probability to the years between 145 and 135 B.C.

[* See Bunsen, vol. i. pp. 393—395.—K. R. H. M.]

† Compare Letronne *Recueil des Inscription Grecques de l'Egypte, tome* i. *pp.* 363 *sqq.* Ptolemaeus Eupator is not mentioned by the historians. The name was first discovered in a Greek Papyrus at Berlin, written under Soter II. in the year 105 B.C., and indeed foisted in between Philometor and Euergetes. Böckh, who published the Papyrus (1821), referred the surname of Euergetes to Soter II. and his wife, and held Eupator to be a surname of the deified Euergetes II. In the same year Champollion-Figeac treated of this papyrus, and endeavoured to prove that Eupator was that son of Philometer put to death by Euergetes II. on his accession. This view was afterwards accepted by St. Martin, Böckh, and

fect series of Ptolemies, the longest coming down
to Neos Dionysos and his wife Cleopatra, who

Letronne (*Rech. pour serv. à l'Hist. de l'Eg. p.* 124). In the
meantime the name Eupator had been found in a second papyrus of the reign of Soter II., as also in a letter of Numenius
upon the Phileusian obelisk of Herr Bankes of the time of
Euergetes II. Eupator was named in both inscriptions, but
did not stand behind, but before Philometor, and therefore
could not be his son. Letronne now conjectured (*Recueil des
Inscr. tome* i. *p.* 365) that Eupator was another surname of
Philometor. Then, however, it should have been καὶ θεοῦ
Εὐπάτορος τοῦ καὶ Φιλομήτορος, and not καὶ θεοῦ Εὐπάτορος καὶ
θεοῦ Φιλομήτορος. In a letter to Letronne of the 1st December,
1844, from Thebes, which has been printed in the *Revue
Archéol. tome* i. *pp.* 678 *sqq.*, I informed him that I had also
found in several hieroglyphical inscriptions the name Eupator, and always before Philometor. The same reasons that I
alleged against Letronne's interpretation of the Greek name
(that portion of the letter was not printed in the *Revue*),
i. e. the simple recurrence of the Θεοῦ, did also not allow
Eupator to be considered another name of Philometor in the
hieroglyphical lists. He must have been a Ptolemy recognized
for a short time as king, but not mentioned by the historians;
and as Franz (*Corp. Inscr. vol.* iii. *p.* 285) and Letronne (*Rec.
vol.* ii. *p.* 536) have recognized an elder brother of Philometor,
who died in a few months, and was therefore omitted in the
Ptolemaic canon.

The son of Philometor and his sister Cleopatra II., however,
mentioned by Justin and Josephus, in which it was formerly
thought that the Eupator of the Berlin papyrus had been
found, is particularly mentioned in the hieroglyphical inscriptions and of the other Ptolemies, in his place between Philometor
and Euergetes, and we thus learn his name, which the historians had not added. He is sometimes called Philopator, sometimes Neos Philopator, and is therefore to be referred to in the
series of reigned Ptolemies, as Philopator II. Of fourteen
hieroglyphical lists which come down to Euergetes II., seven
mention Philopator II.; in four other lists in which he might

was surnamed Tryphæna by the Egyptians, according to the hieroglyphic inscriptions.* A fact of some importance is also that in this Egyptian list of Ptolemies, the first King is never Ptolemæus Soter I. but Philadelphus. In Qurna, where Euergetes II. is adoring his ancestors, not only Philometor, the brother of Euergetes, is

have been mentioned he is passed over, and these seem all to belong to the first year of Euergetes II., his murderer, which readily explains the cause. That he does not appear in the canon is quite natural, because his reign did not extend over the change of the Egyptian year; but, as might be expected, he is named in the protocolls of the Demotic Papyrus, where those Ptolemies receiving divine honours are enumerated, and in which Young had already properly seen Eupator. In fact, he is mentioned here in all the lists known to me (five in Berlin of the years 114, 103, 103, 99, 89 B.C., and one in Turin of the year 89 B.C.) which are later than Euergetes II., as also in a Berlin papyrus of the fifty-second year of Euergetes himself (therefore in 188 B.C.). A comparison of the Demotic lists manifests that the interchange of the names Eupator and Philometor in the Greek papyrus of the year 105 B.C. (not 106, as Franz, *Corp. Inscr. p.* 285 writes), is not only a mistake of the copyist, as these and similar interchanges are also not uncommon in the Demotic papyrus. The different purposes of the hieroglyphic and demotic lists render it comprehensible, that in the former such variations were not admissible, as in the latter.

* Wilkinson (*Modern Egypt and Thebes,* vol. ii. p. 275) considers this Cleopatra Tryphæna to be the famous Cleopatra, daughter of Neos Dionysos; Champollion (*Letters d'Egypt,* p. 110) to be the wife of Philometor; but the cartouche combined with her name belong neither to Ptolemæus XIV., the elder son of Neos Dionysos, nor to Ptolomæus VI. Philometor, but to Ptolemæus XIII. Neos Dionysos or Auletes, who is always Philopator Philadelphus, on the monuments. Cleopatra Tryphæna was therefore the wife of Ptolemæus Auletes.

wanting, which may easily be accounted for, but
also Soter I., and it is an error of Rosselini, if
he look upon the king beneath Philadelphus as
Soter I. instead of Euergetes I. It seems that
the son of Lagus, although he assumed the title
of King from 305 B.C., was not recognized by
the Egytians as such, as his cartouches do not
appear upon any monument erected by him. The
rather, therefore, do I rejoice, that I have not
yet found his name once upon an inscription of
Philadelphus, as the father of Arsinoe II. But
here, it must be observed, Soter certainly has the
Royal Kings about his names, and a peculiar
cartouche; but before both cartouches, contrary
to the usual Egyptian custom, there stands no
royal title, although his daughter is called "royal
daughter," and "Queen." *

* The inscription referred to is in the rock-cave of Echmin,
and was, without doubt, first engraved under Ptolemæus Philadelphus, with double cartouches and the usual royal titles,
but without the surname of Soter; he is mentioned on a stele
in Vienna which was erected under Philopator. Here, however, he has another cartouche than at Echmin, and moreover,
in a remarkable manner, the same as that which Philippus
Aridaeus and Alexander II., under whom Ptolemæus Lagus was
Viceroy in Egypt, bore before his time. In like manner he is
named on a statue of the king in the ruins of Memphis, where
the Horus name of the king may be found, and which may
probably have been made during his reign. Finally, the Soters
are sometimes only mentioned by their surnames, at the head
of the honoured ancestors of later kings, as in the inscription
of Rosetta, and in the bilingual Decrees of Philae written

[hieroglyphs], while Soter II. is always written [hieroglyphs]

p. nuter enti nehem, which would answer to the Koptic

It is remarkable how little Champollion seems to have attended to the monuments of the Old

ⲡ.ⲛⲟⲩⲧⲉ ⲉⲧ-ⲛⲉⲅⲙ, *deus servator.* In the Demotic inscriptions, too, the first Soters are designated by *nehem,* and in the singular, by the Greek word *p. suter.*

Although it is not to be doubted that the Soters, who, according to the Demotic papyrus, had a peculiar cultus with the rest of the Ptolemies, not only in Alexandria and Ptolemais, but also in Thebes, were looked upon as the chiefs of the Ptolemaic dynasty, it is more remarkable that till now no building has been discovered which was erected under Ptolemæus Soter as king, although he continued twenty years in this capacity. To this must be added that the above-mentioned hieroplyphic lists of Ptolemies, without exception, do not begin the series with Soters, but with the Adelphi, as said at Echmin, his cartouches have no royal titles, and that in Karnak, under Euergetes II., Philadelphus is represented as King, and Soter, answering to the same period, not as king. Also in the Demotic king lists of the papyrus, the Alexandrian series passes over the Soters down to Philometor, and lets the Adelphi immediately follow Alexander the Great. The Soters have come before me at the earliest in a papyrus of the seventeenth year of Philopator (210 B.C.), the oldest in the Berlin collection; the Thebaic culters of the Ptolemies seems to have excluded the Soters altogether. Although, therefore, the beginning of the royal government in the year 305 B.C., as the Canon asserts, is an ascertained fact, and is incontestably confirmed by the hieroplyphic stele in Vienna, which has been cited for it by my friend M. Pinder (*Beitr. zur älteren Münz kunde, Band* I. p. 201) in his instructive essay " on the era of Philippus on coins," it seems to authorize another legitimate view, according to which, not Ptolemæus Lagus, but Philadelphus, the eldest king's son (if not Porphyrogenitus), was the head of the Ptolemies. Thus it may also be explained, that we find under Euergetes I. an astronomical era employed, that of the otherwise unknown Dionysius, which took its beginning from the year 285 B.C. the first of Philadelphus, while the coins of Philadelphus neither count from his own accession,

Empire. In his whole journey through Middle Egypt up to Dendera, he only found the rock graves of Benihassan worthy of remark, and these, too, he assigns to the sixteenth and seventeenth dynasty, therefore to the New Empire. He mentions Zauiet el Meitîn and Siut, but scarcely makes any remark about them.

So little has been said by others of most of the monuments of Middle Egypt, that almost everything was new to me that we found here. My astonishment was not small, when we found a series of nineteen rock tombs at Zauiet el Meitîn, which we all inscribed, gave the names of the departed, and belong to the old time of the sixth dynasty, thus almost as far back as the pyramid builders.* Five of them contain, several times repeated, the cartouche of the Macrobiote Apappus-Pepi, who is reported to have lived one hundred and sixty years, and reigned one hundred; in another, Cheops is mentioned. On one side is a single tomb, of the time of Ramses.

At Benihassan I have had a complete rocktomb perfectly copied; it will serve as a specimen of the grandiose style of architecture and art of the second flourishing time of the Old Empire, during the mighty twelfth dynasty.† I think it will cause

nor from the year 305 B.C., but from the year of the decease of Alexander the Great, or the beginning of the viceroyship of Ptolemaeus, as the beginning point of a new era. (See Pinder, p. 205).

[* Manetho in Bunsen, Egypt's Place, vol i. p. 620. Nitocris is the last of this dynasty. K. R. H. M.]

† *Denkmäler ans Ægypten und Æthiopien, Abth.* II. *Blatt.* 123-133.

some surprise among Egyptologers, when they learn
from Bunsen's work,* why I have divided the tables
of Abydos, and have referred Sesurtesen and
Amenemha, these Pharaohs, well known through
Heliopolis, the Faiûm, Benihassan, Thebes, and up
to Wadi Halfa, from the New Empire into the
Old. It must then have been a proud period for
Egypt—that is proved by these mighty tombs
alone. It is interesting, likewise, to trace in the
rich representations on the walls, which put before
our eyes the high advance of the peaceful arts, as
well as the refined luxury of the great of that
period; also the foreboding of that great misfortune
which brought Egypt, for several centuries, under
the rule of its northern enemies. In the representations of the warlike games, which form a charac-
teristically recurring feature, and take up whole
sides in some tombs, which leads to a conclusion of
their general use at that period afterwards dis-
appearing, we often find among the red or dark-
brown men, of the Egyptian and southern races,
very light-coloured people, who have, for the
most part, a totally different costume, and generally red-coloured hair on the head and beard, and
blue eyes, sometimes appearing alone, sometimes in
small divisions. They also appear in the trains of
the nobles, and are evidently of northern, probably
semitic, origin. We find victories over the Ethiopians and negroes on the monuments of those times,
and therefore need not be surprised at the recurrence of black slaves and servants. Of wars against
the northern neighbours we learn nothing; but it

[* Bunsen's Egypt's Place, vol. i. p. 45. K. R. H. M.]

seems that the immigration from the north-east was already beginning, and that many foreigners sought an asylum in fertile Egypt in return for service and other useful employments.

I have more in mind the remarkable scene in the tomb of the royal relation, Nehera-si-Numhotep, the second from the north, which places the immigration of Jacob and his family before our eyes in a most lively manner, and which would almost induce us to connect the two, if Jacob had not really entered at a far later period, and if we were not aware that such immigrations of single families could not be unfrequent. These, however, were the precursors of the Hyksos, and prepared the way for them in more than one respect. I have traced the whole representation, which is about eight feet long, and one-and-a-half high, and is very well preserved through, as it is only painted. The Royal Scribe, Nefruhotep, who conducts the company into the presence of the high officer to whom the grave belongs, is presenting him a leaf of papyrus. Upon this the sixth year of King Sesurtesen II. is mentioned, in which that family of thirty-seven persons came to Egypt. Their chief and lord was named Absha, they themselves Aama, a national designation, recurring with the light-complexioned race, often represented in the royal tombs of the nineteenth dynasty, together with three other races, and forming the four principal divisions of mankind, with which the Egyptians were acquainted. Champollion took them for Greeks when he was in Benihassan, but he was not then aware of the extreme antiquity of the monuments before him.

Wilkinson considers them prisoners, but this is confuted by their appearance with arms and lyres, with wives, children, donkeys and luggage; I hold them to be an immigrating Hyksos-family, which begs for a reception into the favoured land, and whose posterity perhaps opened the gates of Egypt to the conquering tribes of their Semetic relations.

The city to which the rich rock Necropolis of Benihassan belonged, and which is named Nus in the hieroglyphic inscriptions, must have been very considerable, and without doubt lay opposite on the left bank of the Nile, where old mounds are still existing, and were marked on the French maps. That the geography of the Greeks and Romans knows nothing of this city, Nus, as indeed was true of many other cities of the Old Empire, is not very astonishing, if it be considered that the five hundred years of Hyksos dominion intervened. The sudden fall of the Empire and of this flourishing city, at the end of the twelfth dynasty, is recognised by some in the circumstance, that of the numerous rock-tombs, only eleven bear inscriptions, and of these but three are completely finished. To these last, broad pathways led directly up from the banks of the river, which, at the steep upper end, were changed into steps.

Benihassan is, however, not the only place where works of the twelfth dynasty were found. Near Bersheh, somewhat to the south of the great plain, in which the Emperor Hadrian built, to the honour of his drowned favourite, the city of Antinoe, with its magnificently and even now partially passable streets, with hundreds of pillars, a small valley opens to the east, where we again found a series of splendidly-made rock-tombs of the twelfth dynasty,

of which the greater portion are unfortunately
injured. In the tomb of Ki-si-Tuthotep the transportation of the great colossus is represented, which
was already published by Rosellini, but without the
accompanying inscriptions; from the latter it is
certain that it was formed of limestone (the hieroglyphic word for which I first ascertained here), and
was about thirteen Egyptian ells, that is circa
twenty-one feet, in height.* In the same valley, on
the southern rock wall, there is hewn a series of still
older, but very little inscribed tombs, which, to
judge from the style of the hieroglyphics, and the
titles of the deceased, belong to the sixth dynasty.

A few hours more to the southward comes another
group of graves, also belonging to the sixth dynasty;
here King Cheops is incidentally mentioned, whose
name already appeared several times in an hieratic
inscription at Benihassan. At two other places,
between the valley of El Amarna, where the very
remarkable rock-tombs of King Bech-en-Aten is
situated, and Siut, we found graves of the sixth
dynasty, but presentiug few inscriptions. Perring,
the pyramid measurer, has, in a recent publication,
attempted to establish the strange notion, which I
found also existed in Cairo, that the monuments of
El Amarna were the work of the Hyksos: others
wished to refer them to a period anterior to that of
Menes, by reason of their certainly, but not inexplicable, peculiarities ; I had already explained them
in Europe as contemporaneous kings† of the eighteenth dynasty.

* *Denkmäler, Abth.* II. *Bl.* 134.
† [I. e., *the cartouches* of contemporaneous kings. —
K. R. H. M.]

In the rock wall behind Siut, mighty tombs gape, in which we could recognize the grand style of the twelfth dynasty already from a distance. Here too, unfortunately, much has been lately destroyed of these precious remnants, as it was found easier to break down the walls and pillars of the grottoes, than to hew out the stones from the mass.

I learnt from Selim Pasha, the Governor of Upper Egypt, who received us at Siut in the most friendly manner, that the Bedouins had some time since discovered quarries of alabaster two or three hours' journey into the eastern mountains, the proceeds of which Mahommed Ali had presented him, and from his dragoman I ascertained that there was an inscription on the rocks. I therefore determined to undertake the hot ride upon the Pasha's horses, which he had sent to El Bosra for this purpose, from El Bosra thither, in company with the two Weidenbachs, our dragoman and the *khawass*. There we found a little colony of eighteen workmen, with their families, altogether thirty-one persons, in the lonely, wild, hot rock gorge, employed in the excavation of the alabaster. Behind the tent of the overseer there were preserved, in legible, sharply-cut hieroglyphics, the names and titles of the wife, so much revered by the Egyptians, of the first Amasis, the head of the eighteenth dynasty, who expelled the Hyksos, the remains of a formerly much larger inscription. These are the first alabaster quarries, the age of which is certified by an inscription. Not far from the place were others, which were already exhausted in antiquity; from those now reopened they have extracted within the last four months more than three hundred blocks, of which the larger ones are eighty feet long and two feet thick. The Pasha informed me, through his dragoman, that on our return I should find a piece, the size and form of which I was myself to determine, of the best quality the quarry afforded, which he desired me to accept as a testimonial of his joy at our visit. The alabaster quarries discovered in this region are all situated between Bersheh and Gauâta; one would be inclined, therefore, to consider El Bosra as the ancient Alabastron, if its position could be reconciled with the account of Ptolemæus; at any rate, Alabastron has certainly nothing to do with the ruins in the valley of El Amarna, as hitherto thought, to which also the relation of Ptolemæus does not answer, and which seems to be quite different. The hieroglyphical name of these ruins recurs continually in the inscriptions.

In the rock chains of Gebel Selîn there are again very early, but little inscribed, graves of the Old Empire, apparently of the sixth dynasty.

Opposite ancient Panopolis, or Chemmis, we climbed the remarkable rock cave of the ithyphallic Pan (Chem).* It is dedicated by another contemporaneous king of the eighteenth dynasty, whose grave we have since visited in Thebes. The holy name of the city often occurs in the inscriptions,— " Dwelling-place of Chem," *i. e.* Panopolis. Whether this, however, was the origin of the popular name, Chemmis, now Echmîn, is much to be doubted. I have always found at Siut, Dendera, Abydos, and other

[* See Bunsen's Egypt's Place, vol. i. p. 373, where an account of this deity is given.—K. R. H. M.]

have cities, two distinct names, the sacred eno and the popular name; the first is taken from the principal god of the local temple, the other has nothing to do with it.* My hieroglyphical geography is extended almost with every new monument.

At Abydos we came to the first greater temple building. The last interesting tombs of the Old Empire we found at Qasr e' Saiât; they belong to the sixth dynasty. At Dendera we visited the imposing temple of Hathor, the best preserved perhaps in all Egypt.†

In Thebes we stayed for twelve over-rich, astonishing days, which were hardly sufficient to learn to find our way among the palaces, temples, and tombs, whose royal giant magnificence fills this spacious plain. In the jewel of all Egyptian buildings, in the palace of Ramses Sesostris, which this greatest of the Pharaohs erected in a manner worthy of himself and the god, to "Ammon-Ra, King of the Gods," the guardian of the royal city of Ammon, on a gently-rising terrace, calculated to overlook the wide plain on this side, and on the other side of the majestic river, we kept our beloved King's birthday with salutes and flags, with chorus singing, and with hearty toasts, that we proclaimed over a glass of pure German Rhine wine. That we thought of you with full hearts on this occasion I need not say.

[* This resembles, in fact, the system of calling parishes after the names of the Saints, to commemorate whose martyrdom the church was erected; as, for instance, the church and parish of St. Alphege, in the town of Greenwich.—K.R.H.M.]

[† See Bunsen, vol. i. p. 400, for an account of this deity. —K.R.H.M.]

When night came we first lighted a pitch kettle,
over the outer entrances between the pylones, on both
sides of which our flags were planted; then we let a
green fire flame up from the roof of the Pronaos,
which threw out the beautiful proportions of the
pillared halls, now first restored to their original
destination by us, as festal halls; "Hall of the
Panegyries," ever since thousands of years; and even
magically animated the two mighty peace thrones
of the colossi of the Memnon.

We have reserved every greater work till our
return; but to select from the inexhaustible matter
for our end, and with relation to what has already
been given in other works, will be difficult. On the
18th of October we quitted Thebes. Hermonthis
we saw *en passant*. The great hall of Esneh was
some years ago excavated by command of the Pasha,
and presented a magnificent appearance. At El
Kab, the ancient Eileithyia, we remained three
days. Still more remarkable than the different
temples of this once mighty place are its rock-
tombs, which belong chiefly to the beginning of the
War of Liberation against the Hyksos, and throw
much light upon the relation of the several dynasties of that period. Several persons of consideration
buried there bear the curious title of a male nurse
of a royal prince, expressed by the well known
group of *mena*, with the determinative of the female
breast in Coptic, ⲙⲟⲛⲓ;* the deceased is represented with the prince in his lap.

[* Bunsen, vol. i. p. 470. Egyptian Vocabulary, No. 294,
and Determinative sign, No. 58. p. 542, the author there refers

The temple of Edfu is also among the best preserved of them; it was dedicated to Horus and
Hathor, the Egyptian Venus, who is once named
here "Queen of men and women." Horus, as a
child, is represented, as all children are on the
monuments, as naked, with his finger to his lips;
I had already explained from it the name of Harpocrates, which I have now found completely represented and written as Harpe-chroti, *i. e.* "Horus the
Child."* The Romans misunderstood the Egyptian
gesture of the finger, and made of the *child* that
can not speak, the God of Silence, that *will* not
speak. The most interesting inscription, unre-
marked and unmentioned as yet by any one, is
found on the eastern outer wall of the temple, built
by Ptolemaeus Alexander I. It contains several
dates of King Darius, of Nectanebus, and the falsely
named Amyrtæus, and has reference to the lands
belonging to the temple. The glowing heat of that
day caused me to postpone the more careful examination and the paper impression of this inscription
till our return.† Gebel Silsilis is one of the richest
places in historical inscriptions, which generally
bear some reference to the mighty working of the
sandstone quarries.

At Ombos, I was greatly rejoiced to discover a

to Champollion, Grammaire, and Rosellini, Monumenti Reali,
cxlii. 1.—K. R. H. M.]

[* Bunsen (vol. i. p. 434, n. 333,) says, "The discovery of
the meaning of Harpocrates is mine; but I explained it as
Her-pe-schre (Horus the child), and adopted Lepsius's correction." In the text it is given Her-pa-χruti.—K. R. H. M.]

† *Denkmäler, Abth.* IV. *Bl.* 38, 39. A special essay is
prepared on these inscriptions.

third canon of proportions of the human body, which
is very different to the two older Egyptian canons
that I had found in many examples before. The
second canon is intimately connected with the first
and oldest of the pyramid period, of which it is only
a farther completion and different application. The
foot is the unit of both of them, which, taken six
times, makes the heighth of the upright body; but
it must be remarked, not from the sole to the crown,
but only as far as the forehead. The piece from
the roots of the hair, or the forehead to the crown,
did not come into the calculation at all, and oc-
cupies sometimes three-quarters, sometimes half,
sometimes less of another square. The difference
between the first and second canons concerns mostly
the position of the knees. In the Ptolemaic canon,
however, the division itself is altered. The body
was not divided into 18 parts, as in the second
canon, but into $21\frac{1}{4}$ parts to the forehead, or into
23 to the crown. This is the division which Diodorus gives us in the last chapter of his first book.
The middle, between forehead and sole, falls beneath the hips in all the three divisions. Thence
downward, the proportions of the second and third
canons remain the same, but those of the upper
part of the body differ exceedingly; the head is
larger, the breast falls deeper, the abdomen higher;
on the whole, the contour becomes more licenti-
tious, and give up the earlier simplicity and modesty
of the forms, in which the grand and peculiar Egyptian character consisted, for the imperfect imitation
of a misunderstood foreign style of art. The proportion of the foot to the length of the body remains,

but it is no longer the unit on which the whole calculation is based.

We were obliged to change boat at Assuan, on account of the Cataracts, and had, for the first time for six months or more, the homeish greeting of a violent shower and blustering storm, that gathered beyond the Cataracts, surmounted the granite girdle, and burst with the most thundering explosions into the valley down to Cairo, which (as we have since learnt) it deluged with water in a manner scarcely recollected before. Thus we too may say with Strabo and Champollion :—" In our time it rained in Upper Egypt." Rain is, in fact, so unusual here, that our guards remembered no similar scene, and our Turkish *Khawass*, who is intimately acquainted with the land in every respect, when we had long had our packages brought into the tents and fastened up, never laid a hand to his own things, but quietly repeated, *abaden moie*, "never rain," a word, that he had since been often obliged to hear, as he was thoroughly drenched, and caught a tremendous fever cold, that he was obliged to suffer patiently at Philae.

Philae is as charmingly situated as it is interesting for its monuments. The week spent on this holy island belongs to the most beautiful reminiscences of our journey. We were accustomed to assemble before dinner, when our scattered work was done, on the elevated temple terrace, which.rises steeply above the river on the eastern shore of the island, to observe the shades of the well-preserved temple, built of sharply-cut, dark-glowing blocks of sandstone, which grow across the river and mingle

with the black volcanic masses of rock, piled wildly
one upon another, and between which the golden-
hued sand pours into the valley like fire-floods. The
island appears to have become sacred at a late period
among the Egyptians, under the Ptolemies. Herodotus, who went up to the Cataracts in the time of
the Persians, does not mention Philae at all; it was
then inhabited by Ethiopians, who had also half
Elephantine in their possession. The oldest buildings, now to be found on the island, were erected
nearly a hundred years subsequent to the journey of
Herodotus, by King Nectanebus, the last but three
of the kings of Egyptian descent, upon the southern
point of the island. There is no trace of any earlier
buildings, not even of destroyed or built-up remains.
Inscriptions of much older date are to be found on
the great island of Bigeh close by, called hieroglyphically Senmut. It was already adorned with
Egyptian monuments during the Old Empire; for
we found there a granite statue of King Sesur-
tesem III., of the twelfth dynasty. The little rock-
islet Konossa, hieroglyphically Kenes, has also very
ancient inscriptions on the rocks, in which a new,
and hitherto quite unknown, king of the Hyksos
period is named. The hieroglyphical name of the
island of Philae has generally been read Manlak. I
have found it several times undoubtedly written
Ilak. This, with the article, becomes Philak, in
the mouths of the Greeks Philai. The sign read
"man" by Champollion also interchanges in other
groups with "i," thus the pronunciation I-lak, P-i-
lak, Memphitic Ph-i-lak is confirmed.

We have made a precious discovery in the court

of the great temple of Isis, two somewhat word-rich bilingual, *i. e.* hieroglyphical and Demotic decrees of the Egyptian priests, of which one contains the same text as the decree of the Rosetta stone. At least, I have till now compared the seven last lines, which not only correspond with the Rosetta in the contents but in the length of each individual line; the inscription must first be copied, ere I can say more about it; in any case the gain for Egyptian philology is not inconsiderable, if only a portion of the broken decree of Rosetta can be restored by it. The whole of the first part of the inscription of Rosetta, which precedes the decree, is wanting here. Instead of it, a second decree is there, which relates to the same Ptolemæus Epiphanes; in the beginning the "fortress of Alexander," *i. e.* the city of Alexandria, is mentioned, for the first time, upon any of the monuments hitherto made known. Both decrees close, like the inscription of Rosetta, with the determination to set up the inscription in hieroglyphical, Demotic, and Greek writing. But the Greek inscription is wanting, if it were not written in red and rubbed out when Ptolemy Lathyrus engraved his hieroglyphic inscriptions over earlier ones.*

* The first news of the discovery of this important inscription, which had also not been noticed by the Franco-Tuscan Expedition, made some commotion. Simultaneously with the more circumstantial account in the *Preussische Staatszeitung*, a careless English notice appeared, in which the discovery of a second specimen of the inscription of Rosetta was spoken of, and the place assigned was Meroe. Later, when M. Ampère had brought an impression of the inscription to Paris, the Academician, M. de Saulcy, contrariwise put forth an argument on the opposite side, asserting that the inscription had some

The hieroglyphic series of Ptolemies, which occurs here, again begins with Philadelphus, while it
begins with Soter in the Greek text of the Rosetta
inscription. Another very remarkable circumstance
is, that Epiphanes is here called the son of Philopator Ptolemæus, and Cleopatra is mentioned,
while according to the historical accounts the only
wife of Philopator was named Arsinoe, and is so
named in the Rosetta inscription and on other monuments. She is certainly also named Cleopatra in
one passage of Pliny ; this would have been taken
for an error of the author or a mistake of the manuscripts, if a hieroglyphic and indeed official document
did not present the interchange of names. There
is consequently no farther reason to place, as
Champollion-Figeac does, the embassy of Marcus
Atilius and Marcus Acilius from the Roman Senate
to Egypt to settle a new treaty concerning the
Queen Cleopatra mentioned by Livy, in the time
of Ptolemæus Epiphanes, instead of under Ptolemæus Philopator, as other authors inform us. We
must rather conceive, either that the wife and sister
of Philopator had both names, which would not
obviate all the difficulties, or that the project which
Appian mentions of a marriage of Philopator with

resemblance to that of Rosetta, and referred it to Ptolemæus
Philometer. I therefore took occasion to prove, in two letters
to M. Letronne (*Rev. Archéol.* vol. iv. p. 1 sqq. and p. 240 sqq.),
as also in an essay in the Transactions of the German Oriental
Society (vol. i. p. 264 sqq.), that the document in question was
prepared in the twenty-first year of Ptolemæus Epiphanes,
and contained a repetition of the Rosetta inscription, the
provisions of which were extended to Queen Cleopatra I.,
who had come to the throne in the meantime.

the Syrian Cleopatra, who afterwards became the wife of Epiphanes, was carried out after the murder of Arsinoe, without mention of it by the historians. Here naturally means are wanting to me in order to bring this point clearly out.*

The quantity of Greek inscriptions at Philae is innumerable, and Letronne will be interested to hear that I have found on the base of the second obelisk, still in its own place, of which a portion only went to England with the other obelisk, the remains of a Greek inscription written in red, and perhaps once gilt, like those lately discovered on the base in England, but which is, of course, extremely difficult to decipher. That the hieroglyphical inscriptions of the obelisks, which I myself copied in Dorsetshire, besides the Greek on the base, and subsequently published in my Egyptian Atlas, have nothing to do with the Greek inscriptions, and were also not contemporaneously set up, I have already stated in a letter to Letronne; but whether the inscription on the second base had not

* The name Cleopatra, in place of Arsinoe, in the hieroglyphic inscriptions appears to rest wholly upon an error of the scribe, which is avoided in the Demotic, for Arsinoe is here correctly mentioned. The hieroglyphic text of the inscription of Rosetta is less correct than the Demotic. [If the hieroglyphic be the *text*, then it is decidedly the Demotic that is in error. The hieroglyphic seems to have been engraven first, and in that case it would be the text. Probably, however, at this late period, Greek was the language in which the inscriptions of the time were composed, thus the question would lie not between the hieroglyphic and Demotic, *i.e.* the archaico-Egyptian (but little understood) and the modern, but between the Greek and the hieroglyphic modes of expression.—K. R. H. M.]

some connection with that of the first is still a question; the correspondence of the three known inscriptions seems certainly to be settled. The principal temple of the island was dedicated to Isis. She is named exclusively " Lady of Philek ; " Osiris was only Θεὸς σύνναος, which is peculiarly expressed in the hieroglyphics, and is only exceptionally called " Lord of Philek ;" but he was " Lord of Ph-i-uêb," *i. e.* Abaton, and Isis, who was σύνναος there, is only occasionally called " Lady of Ph-i-uêb." From this it is evident that the famous grave of Osiris was upon his own island of Phiuêb, and not on Philek. Both places are distinctly indicated as islands by their determinations. It is therefore not to be thought that the Abaton of the inscriptions and historians was a particular place on the island of Philae ; it was an island in itself. So also do Diodorus and Plutarch intimate by their expression πρὸς Φίλαις. Diodorus decidedly refers to the island with the grave of Osiris as a distinct island, which was named ἱερὸν πεδίον, " the holy field," by reason of this grave. This is a translation of Ph-i-uêb, or Ph-ih-uêb (for the h is also found expressed hieroglyphically), Koptic Ⲫ-ⲓⲁϩ-ⲟⲩⲏⲃ, Ph-iah-uêb, " the sacred field."* This consecrated place was an Abaton, and unapproachable except for the priests.

[* It is well to remark the structure of the word Ⲫ-ⲓⲁϩ-ⲟⲩⲏⲃ Ph-iah-uêb "the field of Jah, or Jao," as the Rev. Charles Forster reads the Hamyaritic name of God, in the Wady Mokatteb inscriptions. It serves as a collateral proof of the Coptic origin of the language of the inscriptions deciphered by that learned investigator. The form of the letters being similar also proves a cognate origin.—K. R. H. M.]

On the sixth of November we quitted the charming island, and commenced our Ethiopian journey. Already at Debôd, the next temple lying to the south, hieroglyphically Tabet (in Coptic perhaps ⲦⲀ ⲀⲂⲎⲦ), we found the sculptures of an Ethiopian King Arkamen, the Ergamenes of the historians, who reigned at the time of Ptolemæus Philadelphus, and stood probably in very friendly relations with Egypt. In the French work on Champollion's Expedition (I have not Rosellini's work with me) there is great confusion here. Several plates, belonging to Dakkeh, are ascribed to Debôd, and *vice versâ.* At Gertassi we collected nearly sixty Greek inscriptions. Letronne, who knew them through Gau, has perhaps already published them; I am anxious to know what he had made of the γόμοι, the priests of whom play a conspicuous part in these inscriptions, and of the new Gods Σϱούπτιχις and Πουρσεποῦνις.

With what inaccuracy the Greeks often caught up the Egyptian names is again shown by the inscriptions of Talmis, which call the same god Mandulis, which is distinctly enough in the hieroglyphic Meruli, and was the local deity of Talmis. It is remarkable that the name of Talmis, so frequently occurring in this temple, nowhere appears in the neighbouring, though certainly much more ancient, the rock temple of Bet el Ualli. Dendûr, also, had a peculiar patron, the God Petisi, who appears nowhere else, and is usually named Peshir Tenthur; Champollion's plates are here again in a strange disorder, the representations and the inscriptions being wrongly put together.

The temples of Gerf Hussên and Sebûa are peculiarly remarkable, because Ramses-Sesostris, who built them, here appears as a deity, and is adorning himself, beside Phtha and Ammon, the two chief deities of this temple. In the first, he is even once called "Ruler of the Gods."

Champollion has well remarked, that all the temples of the Ptolemies and Roman emperors in Nubia were probably only restorations of earlier sanctuaries, which were erected in the old time by the Pharaohs of the eighteenth, and nineteenth dynasties. That was the temple of Pselchis, first built by Tuthmosis III. Beside the scattered fragments of this first building, which, however, was not dedicated to Thoth, as Champollion thinks, but to Horus, and therefore underwent a later change, we have found others of Sethos I. and Menephthes: also, it appears that the earlier erection did not have its axis parallel with the river like the later one, but, like almost all other temples, had its entrances toward the river.

At the temple of Korte, the doorway only is written over with hieroglyphics of the worst style. But these few were sufficient to inform us that it was a sanctuary of Isis, here denominated "Lady of Kerte." We also found blocks rebuilt in the walls, which has escaped former travellers, belonging to an earlier temple erected by Tuthmosis III., the foundations of which may still be traced.

We gathered our last harvest of Greek inscriptions at Hierasykaminos. To this place, the Greek and Roman travellers were protected by the garrison of Pselchis; and by a fixed camp called Mehendi,

some hours southerly from Hierasykaminos, which
is not mentioned in the maps. Primis seems only to
have had a temporary garrison during the campaign
of Petronius. Mehendi—which name probably only
signifies the structure, the camp in Arabic—is the
best preserved Roman encampment that I have ever
seen. It lies upon a somewhat steep height, and
thence commands the river and a little valley extending on the south side of the camp from the
Nile, and turns the caravan road into the desert,
which comes back to the side of the river again at
Medik. The wall of the town encloses a square
running down the hill a little to the east, and
measuring one hundred and seventy-five paces from
south to north, and one hundred and twenty-five
from east to west. From the walls there rise
regularly four corner and four middle towers; of
the latter, the south and north formed also the gates,
which, for the sake of greater security, led into the
city with a bend, and not in a direct line. The
southern gate, and the whole southerly part of the
fortress, which comprehended about one hundred
and twenty houses, are excellently preserved.
Immediately behind the gate, one enters a straight
street, sixty-seven paces long, which is even now,
with but little interruption, vaulted; several narrow
by-streets lead off on both sides, and are covered,
like all the houses of the district, with vaults of
Nile bricks. The street leads to a great open place
in the middle of the city, by which lay, on the
highest point of the hill, the largest and best-built
house—no doubt belonging to the commandant—
with a semicircular niche at the eastern end. The

city walls are built of unhewn stone; the gateway
only, which has a well-turned Roman arch, is erected
of well-cut freestone, among the blocks of which
several are built in, bearing sculptures of pure
Egyptian, though late style, as a proof that there
was an Egyptian or Ethiopian sanctuary here (probably an Isis chapel) before the building of the
fortress. We discovered an Osiris head and two
Isis heads; one of which still distinctly bore the red
marks of the third canon of proportion.

The last monument we visited before our arrival
in Korusko, was the temple of Ammon in the Wadi
Sebùa (Lion's Dale); so called from the rows
of sphinxes which just peep out of the sand ocean
that fell and covered the whole temple as far as
it was exposed. Even the western portion of the
temple, hewn in the rock, is filled with sand; and
we had to summon the whole crew of our bark to
assist in obtaining an entrance into this part. We
encountered a novel and very peculiar combination of
divine and human natures in a group of four deities,
the first of whom is called " Phtha of Ramses in the
house of Ammon;" the second, " Phtha," with other
usual cognomens; the third, " Ramses in the house
of Ammon;" and the fourth, " Hathor." In another
inscription "Ammon of Ramses in the house of
Ammon" was named. It is difficult to explain this
combination.*

---

* Similar designations occur at an earlier period; thus, in
Thebes, an "Ammon of Tuthmosis (III.)" is mentioned; it
would seem to infer a newly-instituted worship of these gods
brought about by these kings. Ramses II. dedicated to the
three highest gods of Egypt (see my essay " On the Primeval

I was not less astonished to find in the front
court of the temple of Ammon a representation of
the posterity of the King Ramses-Miamun, in
number one hundred and sixty children, with their
names and titles, of which the greater part are
scarcely to be read, as they are very much destroyed,
and others are covered with rubbish, and can only
be reckoned by the space they occupy. There were
but twenty-five sons and ten daughters of this great
king previously known. The two legitimate wives
whose images appear on the monuments, he did not
have at the same time, but took the second at the
death of the first. To-day we were visited by the old,
blind, but powerful and rich, Hassan Kachef, of Derr,
who was formerly the independent regent of Lower
Nubia; he has had no less than sixty-four wives, of
which forty-two are yet remaining; twenty-nine of
his sons and seventeen daughters are yet living;
how many have died, he has probably never troubled
himself to count, but, according to the usual proportion of this country, they must have been about

Egyptian Circle of Gods," in the papers of the Berlin Academy,
1851), Ra, Phtha, and Ammon, three great rock temples, in
Lower Nubia, at Derr, Gerf Hussén, and Sebuâ, and called the
contemporaneously-founded places after these gods, this in
Greek Heliopolis, Hephaistopolis, and Diospolis. A fourth
mighty and fortified residence was founded by the same king in
Abusimbel, and was named after himself, Ramessopolis, or "The
Fortification of Ramessopolis," as he also founded two cities in
the Delta, and called them after himself. No doubt it is this
new worship, in reference to which the gods honoured there
were named Ammon of Ramses, and Phtha of Ramses. The
king was himself adored in those rock temples, particularly in
that of Abusimbel, in common with those deities.

four times the number of the living ones; therefore, about two hundred children.

Korusko is an Arab place, in the midst of the land of the Nubians, or Barâbra (plural of Bérberi), who occupy the valley of the Nile from Assuan to the other side of Dongola. This is an intelligent and honest race, of peaceable, though far from slavish disposition, of handsome stature, and with shining reddish brown skin.* The possession of Korusko by Arabs of the Ababde tribes, who inhabit the whole of the eastern desert, from Assuan down to Abu Hammed, may be accounted for by the important position of the place, as the point whence the great caravan road, leading directly to the province of Berber, departs, thus cutting off the whole western bend of the Nile.

The Arabic language, in which we could now, at any rate, order and question, and carry on a little conversation of politeness, had grown so familiar to our ear in Egypt, that the Nubian language was attractive on account of its novelty. It is divided, as far as I have yet been able to ascertain, into a northern and a southern dialect, which meet at Korusko.† The language is totally distinct in character to the Arabic, even in the primary elements, the consonantal and vocalic systems. It is much more euphonious, as it has scarcely any doubling of consonants, no harsh guttural tones, few sibilating

[* See Pickering's Races of Man and their Geographical Distribution, chap. x. The Ethiopian race, Nubians, and Barabra of the Nile, p. 211-215.—K. R. H. M.]

† A grammar and vocabulary of the Nubian language, and a translation of St. Mark into Nubian, is prepared for publication.

sounds, and many simple vowels, more distinctly separated than in Arabic, by which an effeminate mixture of vowels is also avoided. It has not the slightest connection in any part of its grammatical constitution, or in the roots, either with the Semetic languages, nor with the Egyptian, or with our own; and therefore, certainly belongs to the original African stock, unconnected with the Ethiopic-Egyptian family, though the nation may be comprehended by the ancients under the general name of Ethiopians, and though their physical race may stand in a nearer relation to them. They are not a commercial people, and therefore can only count up to twenty in their language; the higher numbers are borrowed from the Arabic, although they employ a peculiar term for one hundred, *imil.** Genders scarcely exist in the language, except in personal pronouns, standing alone; they distinguish " he " and " she," but not " he gives " and " she gives." They use suffixed inflections, as in our languages, rather than changes of accent, like the Semetic. The ordinals are formed by the termination *iti*, the plural by *ígi*; they have no dual. The union of the verb with the pronoun is both by prefix and affix, but is simple and natural; they distinguish the present tense and the preterite; the future is expressed by a particle, even for the passive they have a peculiar formation. The root of negation is " *m*," usually with the following " *n*,"

[* The following are some of the terms for one hundred among the African tribes, BIENGGA, Island of Corisco, 'Nkama, JEDAH, *Jjeje;* JGBERRA, *Obere;* KANGACOUNTRY, Sy district, *Mosulu bandi.*—K. R. H. M.]

the single affinity, probably more than accidental
with other families of language. Their original
number of roots is very limited. They have certainly distinct words for sun, moon, and stars ; but
the expressions for year, month, day, hour, they
borrow from the Arabic ; water, ocean, river, are all
signified by the same words with *essi*, yet it is
remarkable, that they designate the Nile by a
peculiar term *tossi*. For all native tamed wild
animals, they have native names, for houses, and
even all that concerns shipping, they use Arabic
terms ; the boat only they call *kub*, which has no
very apparent connection with the Arabic *mérkab*.
For date-fruit and date-tree, which have different
designations in Arabic, *bellah* and *nachele*, they have
only one word, *béti* (*feutî*) ; the sycamore-tree they
name in Arabic, but it is remarkable, that they
designate the sont-tree by the word for tree in
general. Spirit, God, slave, the ideas of relationship, the parts of the body, weapons, field
fruits, and what relates to the preparation of bread,
have Nubian names ; while the words servant,
friend, enemy, temple, to pray, to believe, to read,
are all Arabic. It is curious that they have separate words for writing and book, but not for stylus,
ink, paper, letter. The metals are all named in
Arabic, with the exception of iron. Rich are they
in Berber, poor in Arabic, and in fact they are all
rich in their poor country, to which they cling like
Switzers, and despise the Arab gold, that they
might win in Egypt, where their services, as guards
and all posts of confidence, are much sought.

We now only stay for the arrival of the camels to

begin our desert journey. Hence to Abu Hammed, an eight days' journey, we shall only find drinkable water once, and then we shall continue our camel ride for four more days to Berber. There we shall find barks, according to the arrangements of Ahmed Pasha. We must then continue on to Chartûm, in order to provision; to proceed higher up, to Abu Haras, and thence to Mandera, in the eastern desert, will scarcely be worth while, if we may believe Linant; but Ahmed Pasha has promised to send an officer to Mandera, in order to test again the reports of the native.

This report I shall send with other letters by an express messenger to Qeneh.

LETTER XVI.

WITH not a little sorrow, I announce to you that
we shall probably have to give up the second priu-
cipal object of our expedition,—our Ethiopian journey, and return northward hence. We have waited
here in vain since the 17th of November, for the
promised but never-coming camels, which are to bring
us to Berber, and there seems to be no more chance
of our getting them now than at first. What we
heard on our arrival, I am sorry to say, is confirmed;
the Arab tribes, who are the sole managers of
traffic, are dissatisfied with Mohammed Ali's reduction of the rate from 80 to 60 piastres per camel
hence to Berber; they have agreed among themselves to send no more camels hither; and no *firman*,
no promises, no threats, will obviate this evil. A
great number of trunks with munition for Chartûm,
have been lying here for ten months, and cannot be
sent on any further. We hoped for the assistance
of Ahmed Pasha Menekle,* the new Governor of
the Southern Provinces, which he has also promised
us in the most friendly and unbounded manner. The
officer who has remained with the munition, received
definite orders from him to retain the first camels
which arrived here, for our use. Notwithstanding
that, we shall scarcely attain our end. The Pasha

[* Menekle signifies "great ear."—K. R. H. M.]

himself could hardly get on further, although he
required but few camels. Some he had brought
from the north, and some he had assembled by force.
Yet he was ill-furnished enough on his departure,
and half of his animals are said to have become ill,
or perished in the desert.

On the 3rd of December, as no camels came,
although the Pasha must have passed the province
Berber, whence he was going to send us the nece ssary
number, I sent our own trustworthy and excellent
khawass, Ibrahim Aga, through nine days wilderness,
to Berber, with Mohammed Ali's *firman*. In the
meantime, we went on to Wadi Halfa to the second
cataract, visited the numerous monuments in that
neighbourhood, and returned hither in three weeks,
with a rich harvest.

It is thirty-one days this morning, since our *khawass* has departed, and some time since I received a
letter from the Mudhir of Berber, in which I learn
that the camels cannot be collected, although immediately on the arrival of our *khawass*, and the
delivery of the letter from the Mudhir of this place,
he sent out soldiers to get together the necessary
number of sixty camels. Matters are just the same
there as here. The authorities can do nothing
against the ill-will of the Arabs.

On the sudden death, by poison, of Ahmed Pasha,*
the governor of the whole Sudan, at Chartûm, who,
it is said, had for some time been meditating an
independence of Mohammed Ali, the south is divided
into five provinces, and placed under five pashas,

[* For a character of Ahmed Pasha, see Werne's White Nile,
vol. i. p. 33. The author was acquainted with him.—K. R. H. M.]

who are to be installed by Ahmed Pasha Menekle. One of them, Emir Pasha, was formerly Bey under Ahmed Pasha, at Chartûm, whom he seems to have betrayed. Three others arrived at Korusko, soon after Ahmed Pasha Menekle. Of these, the most powerful, Hassan Pasha, is gone by water to Wadi Halfa, in his province of Dongola; he was almost unattended, and required but a few camels to get on farther. The second, Mustaffa Pasha, intended for Kordofan, has seized on a trade caravan returning from Berber. The Arabs report, however, that of these tired animals, a part have already become useless before arriving at the wells, which lie at about four day's journey into the wilderness; there he found some merchants, eight of whose camels he seized; the remainder of the caravan has not arrived here, but had taken another road to Egypt for fear of being stopped again. The third, Pasha Ferhât, is waiting here, at the same time with ourselves, and tries every plan that he can think of, to procure a few camels from the north or south. But every hope of ours thus becomes fainter and fainter, as we cannot set the insignificant power of the authorities so mightily to work as he, and have not now either *khawass* or *firman* with us. Everyone, and the pashas most particularly, endeavours to comfort us from day to day; but, meantime, the winter, the only time when we can do anything in the Upper Country, elapses. To this must be added, that the Mudhir of Lower Nubia, with whom we had become friendly, has been accused to Mohammed Ali by the Nubian sheikh of his province, and had just been summoned away by the viceroy, This region has been provisionally placed under the jurisdiction of the Mudhir of Esneh, from whose lieutenant, a young, and otherwise well-disposed man, there is nothing to be obtained by us.

I have, therefore, made up my mind to the last step that is yet remaining. I will myself go to Berber with Abeken upon a few camels, and leave Erbkam with the rest of the company and all the luggage here. There I shall be able to look into the matter myself, and try what can be done, with the aid of the *khawass* (whose authority I miss here much) and the *firman*. We were received here by Ahmed Pasha Menekle in the most friendly manner, and are assured of his most strenuous co-operation by the assistance of his physician, our friend and countryman, Dr. O. Koch. Perhaps money or threats will bring us sooner or later to our end. By a mere chance, I have myself been able to secure six camels. Two more are wanting to complete our little caravan. These two, however, the lieutenant of the Mudhir cannot procure for us, even with the best desire. We have been awaiting them three days, and know not whether we shall obtain them.

LETTER XVII.

E' DAMER.
January 24, 1844.

OUR trouble has at last come to an end, though at a late period. Yesterday I arrived here with Abeken, yet two days' journey from the pyramids of Meroë, and our whole camp probably was also yesterday pitched near Abu Hammed, at the southern end of the great desert. After the last little encouraging communication from Berber, I set out on the 8th of January about noon, with Abeken, the dragoman Juffuf Sherebîeh, a cook, and 'Auad, our Nubian lad. We had eight camels, of whom two were scarcely in condition for the journey, and two donkeys. As the promised guide was not at his post, I made the camel-driver Sheikh Ahmed himself accompany us, as he would be of service in consequence of the high estimation in which he was held among the tribes of the resident Abâbde-Arabs. We had beside these, a guide, Adâr, who was sent us instead of the one promised, five camel-drivers; and soon after our departure several foot-travellers joined us, besides two people with donkeys, who took this opportunity of returning to Berber. We took with us ten water-skins, some provision of rice, maccaroni, biscuit, and cold meats, also a light tent, our coverlets to ride upon and sleep in, the most necessary linen, and a few books; to this must be added a tolerable stock of courage, which never fails me on a journey. Our friends accompanied us for some distance into the rock valley, which soon deprived us of all idea of the proximity of the shore and its friendly palms.

The dale was wild and monotonous, nothing but sandstone rock, the surfaces of which were burnt as black as coals, but turned into burning golden yellow at every crack, and every ravine, whence a number of sand-rivulets, like fire-streams from black dross, ran and filled the valleys. The guides preceded us, with simple garments thrown over their shoulders and around their hips, in their hands one or two spears of strong light wood with iron points and shaft-ends; their naked backs were covered by a round, or carved shield, with a far-reaching boss of giraffe's skin; other shields were oblong, and they are generally made of the skin of the hippopotamus, or the back skin of the crocodile. At night, and often during the day, they bound sandals under their feet, the thongs of which are not unfrequently cut out of the same piece, and being drawn between the great and second toes, surround the feet like a skate.

Sheikh Ahmed was a splendid man, still young, but high and nobly grown, with peculiarly active limbs of shining black-brown hue, an expressive countenance, a piercing, but gentle and slyly-glancing eye, and an incomparably beautiful and harmonious pronunciation, so that I liked much to have him about me, although we were always in a contention at Korusko, as he was obliged to furnish the camels and their concomitants, and through circumstances, could not or would not, procure them. Of his

activity and elasticity of limb he gave us a specimen
in the desert, by taking a tremendous run on the
sandy and most unfavourable soil, and leaped fourteen feet and a half; I measured it with his lance,
which was somewhat more than two mètres in
length. Adâr only, our under guide, dared to try
his powers after him, at my suggestion, but did not
reach the same distance by far.

We had departed on the first day early about
eleven o'clock, and rode till five, stayed for an hour
and a half, and went on till half-past twelve; then
we pitched our tent upon the hard soil, and laid
ourselves down after a twelve hours' march. The
most interesting thing after the hot active days was
the evening tea, but we were obliged to accustom
ourselves to the leathery taste of the water, which
was plainly to be perceived even through both tea
and coffee. The second day we stopped for fourteen
hours on our camels; we set out at eight, stopped
in the afternoon at four, to eat something, went on
about half-past five, and pitched for the night at
half-past twelve, after having issued from the mountains at about ten, at the rising of the moon, into a
great plain. No tree, no tuft of grass had we yet
seen, also no animals, except a few vultures and
crows feeding on the carcase of the latest fallen
camel. On the third day, after an early beginning,
we met a herd of 150 camels, bought by government, to be taken to Egypt. The Pasha is going to
import several thousand camels from Berber, in
order to obviate the consequence of the murrain of
last year; many had already come through Korusko
without our being able to avail ourselves of them, as

they are the private property of the Pasha; we could not have ridden on them, too, as they had no saddles.

The guide of the herd, whom we met, gave us the long desired intelligence that our *khawass*, Ibrahim Aga, had left Berber with a train of sixty camels, and was quite in our vicinity, but on a more westerly track. Sheikh Ahmed was sent after him, in order to bring in three good camels instead of our weak ones, and to obtain any further news from him. Next night, or at farthest in the following one, he was to rejoin us. By the Chabîr (leader) of the train, I sent a few lines to Erbkam. We stopped at half-past five, and stayed the night, in the hopes of seeing Sheikh Ahmed earlier. Towards evening we first beheld the scanty vegetation of the desert, thin greyish yellow dry stalks, hardly visible close by, but giving the ground a light greenish yellow tint in the distance, which alone drew my attention to it.

On the fourth day we ought actually to have been at the wells of brackish but, for the camels, drinkable water; but in order not to go too fast for Sheikh Ahmed, we halted at four o'clock, still about four hours' distance from the wells. At last, towards mid-day, we left the great plain Bahr Bela ma, (river without water,) which joins the two days' long mountain range of El Bab, into which we had entered from Korusko, and now neared other mountains. Till now we had had nothing but uniform sandstone rocks beneath and around us, and it was a pleasing circumstance when I perceived, from the high back of the camel, the first plutonic rock in the sand. I slipped down immediately from my saddle,

and knocked off a piece; it was a grey green stone,
of very fine texture, and without a doubt of graniti-
cal nature. The other mountains also were mostly
composed of species of porphyry and granite, with
which the red syenite, so much employed by the
ancient Egyptians, as so extensively seen at Assuan,
not unfrequently appears in broad veins. Farther
into the mountains quartz predominated, and it was
somewhat peculiar to see the snow-white flint veins
peeping at different heights from the black mountains, and flowing streamwise down into the valley,
where the white extended somewhat after the fashion
of a lake. I took small specimens, also some of the
various kinds of rock.

After we had passed, crossing a little ravine, the
little valley Bahr Hátab, (Wood River, by reason of
the wood somewhat farther in the mountains), and
another Wadi Delah, on the north side of the mountains, we came to the rock-gorge of E'Sufr, where
we expected to find rain-water, to replenish our
shrunken water-bags (*girbe* pl. *geràb*). In this high
mountain it rains in one month of the year, about
May. Then the mighty basins of granite in the valleys are filled, and hold the water for the whole year.
On this plutonic rock, there was some little vegetation
to be seen, in consequence of the rain, and because
the granite seems to contain a somewhat more fertile element than the sad brittle sand, composed
almost wholly of particles of quartz. At Wadi
Delah, which has water in the rainy season, we
came to a long-continued row of dûm-palms, the
rounded leaves and bushy growth of which makes a
less crude impression than the long slender-leaved

date-palms; the latter will not bear rain, and are therefore altogether wanting in Berber, while the dûm-palms occur at first very singly in Upper Egypt, and become more numerous, more full, and more large, the farther they reach southward. When their fruit drops off unripe and dry, the little remaining flesh round the stony centre tastes like sugar; when ripe, one may eat the yellow very woody meat, it tastes well, and some fruits had an aroma like the pine-apple. They sometimes grow to the size of the largest apples.

At four o'clock we pitched our tent, the camels were sent behind into the ravine where was the rain-water, and I and Abeken mounted our donkeys, to accompany them to these natural cisterns. Over a wild and broken path and cutting stones, we came deeper and deeper into the gorge; the first wide basins were empty, we therefore left the camels and donkeys behind, climbed up the smooth granite wall, and thus proceeded amidst these grand rocks from one basin to another; they were all empty; behind there, in the furthest ravine, the guide said there must be water, for it was never empty: but there proved to be not a single drop. We were obliged to return dry. The numerous herds which had been driven from the Sudan to Egypt in the previous year, had consumed it all. We had now only three skins of water, and therefore it was necessary to do something. Higher up the pass, there were said to be other cisterns; behind this ravine I proposed to climb the mountain with the guide, but he considered it too dangerous; we therefore turned back and rode to the camp, and at sundown the camels

had to set forth again to the northern mountains in
search of water reported to exist at an hour's distance, and they returned late, bringing with them
four skins—the water was good and tasted well.
Sheikh Ahmed, however, did not return this night
also, and we now hoped to meet him at the wells,
whither he might have hasted by a more southerly
track.

We set out on the fifth day soon after sunrise, and
entered the great mountain passes of Roft, the uniform strata of which were first in layers of slate, then
more in blocks, and afterwards very rich in quartz.
The heat of the day was more oppressive in the
mountains than in the plains, where the continual
north-wind created some degree of coolness. Except the various sorts of rock, there was nothing of
very great attractiveness. I found a great ant-hill
in the midst of the desolate waste, and looked at it
for a long time ; they were small and large shining
black ants, who carried away all the grosser earthy
particles they could manage, and left the stones for
walls ; the larger ones had heads comparatively twice
as large as the others, and did not work themselves,
but acted as overseers, by giving a push to every
little ant who did not help to carry, which drove it
forward and instigated it to labour.

It is difficult to keep up a conversation on the
clumsy camels, which cannot be kept side by side
so easily as horses or donkeys. If you have a good
dromedary (*heggîn*), and travel without luggage, or
with very little, the animal remains in trot. This is
easy and not very tiring, while it requires some time
to accustom oneself to the slouching step of the usual

burthen-camel; this, however, we managed to lighten, by occasionally mounting our donkeys, and often walked long distances early in the morning and late at night.

I return to our fifth day in the desert, on which we set forth early, about eight o'clock, from the little valley E' Sufr, where we had pitched our tent under some gum or sont-trees, and arrived at half-past twelve, after we had left the road about half an hour, and turned to the left into a wide valley, at the brackish wells of Wadi Murhad. Here we had concluded about half of our journey; we saw a few huts built of small stones and sedge, near which a couple of thin goats sought fruitlessly for some food; our black host led us into an arbour of bulrushes, where we made ourselves as comfortable as circumstances would permit.

In this valley we had for some time observed the snow-white surface of the natron on the sand, which makes the water in the valley brackish. Toward the end of the valley, where it divides into two branches, there are the standing waters, five or six feet below the surface, which have been dug out into eight wells. The furthest wells have a greenish, salt, and ill-tasting water, which, however, serves the camels very well; the three front ones, however, have brighter water, which we could have drunk very well, if it had been necessary. This is a government station usually occupied by six people; at this time four were on an excursion and only two in the place. Two ways led hence to Korusko, a western and an eastern one; Ibrahim Aga had unfortunately chosen the former, by which we had missed him, having ourselves taken the latter. Sheikh Ahmed was not to be found here; probably he had only reached our camels on the second day, and we were therefore obliged to proceed without him.

The Abâbde Arabs, with whom we had now everywhere to do, are a true and trustworthy people, from whom one has less to fear than from the cunning thievish Fellahs of Egypt. To the north-east of them are the Bishari tribes, who speak a peculiar language, and are now at bitter feud with the Abâbde, because they waylaid and murdered some Turkish soldiers two years ago in the little valley, where we stayed the night, and for which Hassan Chalif, the superior sheikh of the Abâbde, to whose care the highway between Berber and Korusko is committed, had nearly forty of the Bishari executed. With the aid of the Abâbde, too, Ismael Pasha had been able four-and-twenty years before to bring his army though the desert and seize the Sudan. Guides are only posted by government along the road by which we were coming, but not on the longer but better watered line from Berber to Assuan, which is now little used.

At half-past four we rode away from the wells, after we had examined some *hagr mektub* (written stones), for which we everywhere inquired, on some rocks in the neighbourhood, where a number of horses, camels, and other animals had been rudely scratched, at some by no means modern period, in the same manner as we had often seen in Nubia. At half-past nine we halted for the night, after we had left the mountains for an hour and a half. On the morning of the sixth day we passed the wide plain of Múndera, to which another high mountain range called Abu Sihha joins; the southern frontier of this plain, by those mountains, they call Abdêbab; the southern part of the Roft mountains behind us, Abu Senejât.

At three o'clock we left the plain, and entered the mountains again, which, like the former ranges, were of granite. Half an hour later we halted for a noontide rest. After two hours we rode on and encamped about midnight, after passing through another little plain, and the mountains of Adar Auîb into the next plain, comprehended under the same designation, which stretches to the last mountains of this desert, Gebel Graibât.

On the seventh day we set forth at the early hour of half-past seven, and came at last beyond Gebel Graibât, into a great and boundless plain, Adererât, which we did not leave until our arrival at Abu Hammed. To the south-west the little mountain El Farût, and the higher range Mograd, were in sight; in the far-east there joins another mountain to Adur Auîb, that of Abu Nugâra. South-easterly there are the other mountain chains of Bishari, the names of which were unknown to our Abâbde guides. The beginning of the plain of Adererât was quite covered for hours with beautiful pure flint, which sometimes jutted out of the sand, as rock, although the principal sort of rock continued to be black granite, which was intersected about noon by a broad vein of red granite. Early in the day a small caravan of merchants passed us at some distance.

We saw the most beautiful *mirages* very early in the day; they most minutely resemble seas and lakes, in which mountains, rocks, and everything in their vicinity, are reflected like in the clearest water. They form a remarkable contrast with the staring dry desert, and have probably deceived many a poor wanderer, as the legend goes. If one be not aware that no water is there, it is quite impossible to distinguish the appearance from the reality. A few days ago I felt quite sure that I perceived an overflowing of the Nile, or a branch near El Mechêref, and rode towards it, but only found Bahr Sheitan, "Satan's water," as the Arabs call it.

By day the caravan road cannot easily be missed, even when the sand has destroyed every trace of it; it is marked by numberless camels' skeletons, of which several are always in sight; I counted forty-one within the last half-hour before sunset, on the previous day. Of our camels, however, although they had not long rested in Korusko, and got scarcely anything to eat or drink on the way, none were lost. Mine, in whose mouth I had occasionally put a bit of biscuit, used to stretch back his long neck in the middle of the march, until it laid its head with its large tender eyes in my lap, in order to get some more.

We halted at about four o'clock in the afternoon for two hours, and then proceeded till eleven, when we pitched our camp in the great plain. The wind, however, was so violent, that it was impossible to fasten up our tents. Notwithstanding the ten iron rings which are prepared for keeping it up, it fell

three times before it was quite finished ; we, therefore, let it lie, laid our own selves down behind a
little wall, that the guide had constructed of camel
saddles as a shelter, and slept *à la belle étoile*.

On the eighth day we might have arrived at Abu
Hammed late in the evening, but we resolved to
stay the night at an hour's distance from that place,
that we might reach the Nile by day. The birds
of prey increased in the neighbourhood of the river;
we scared away thirty vultures from the fresh carcase
of a camel ; the day before I had shot a white
eagle, and some desert partridges, which were
seeking *durra* grains on the caravan road. We
only saw traces of wild beasts by the carcases; they
did not trouble us at night, as in the camp at
Korusko, where we had shot a hyæna, and several
jackals. In the afternoon we met a slave caravan.
The last encampment before reaching Abu Hammed was less windy, but our coals were exhausted,
and the servants had forgotten to gather camel's
dung for the fire ; therefore we were obliged to
drink the last brown skin-water without boiling it,
to quench our thirst. The donkeys could not be
spared any of it.

We ascended the high thrones of our camels on
the 16th of January, at half-past seven o'clock in
the morning, and looked down thence towards the
Nile. It was, however, only visible shortly before
our arrival. The stream here does not flow through
a broad valley, but runs along a bare rock-channel,
that stretches through the flat wide plain of rock.
On the other side of the river only was there any
appearance of the valley, and on an island formed

there stood a few dûm-palms. A little way from
the shores we met another train of 150 camels,
which had just left Abu Hammed. Then came an
extensive earthwork, with a few towers like fortifications, which had been erected by the great Arab
sheikh Hassan Chalif, for government stores. A
little ravine contains five huts, one of stones and
earth, another of tree trunks, two of mats, and one
of *bus* or *durra* straw; then a wider place opened,
surrounded with several poor-looking houses, one of
which was prepared for us. A brother of Hassan
Chalif, who resides here, came to receive us, led us
into the house, and offered us his services. A few
anqarêb (cane bed-places), which are much used here,
on account of the creeping vermin, were brought
in, and we established ourselves for that day and the
following night; we felt that we must give the
camels so much grace.

A great four-cornered space surrounded us, thirty
feet on every side, the walls formed of stone and
earth; a couple of trees, forked at the top, bore a
great trunk for an architrave, above which there
were again other roof-branches laid, and bound up and
covered with mats and hurdles. It reminded me
much of a primeval architecture which we had found
imitated on the rock caves of Beni-hassan; there were
the same pillars, the same network of the roof, through
which, except by the door, as at those caves, the light
only entered by one four-cornered opening in the
middle, at the top, and no windows. The door-posts
were composed of four short trunks, of which the
upper one quite resembled the lintel in the graves of
the pyramid era. We hung up a curtain before the

door, to protect us from the wind and dust; at the opposite corner, a doorway led into a space that was used as a kitchen. The day was windy, and the air unpleasantly filled with sand, so that we could scarcely get out of doors. We refreshed ourselves, however, with pure, cool Nile water, and an excellent dinner of mutton. The great desert was behind us, and we had only four days more to El Mechêref, the chief town of Berber, following the course of the river. We learned that Ahmed Pasha Menekle was in our neighbourhood, or would soon arrive, in order to make a military expedition from Dâmer, a short day's journey on the other side of El Mechêref, up the Atbara, to the province of Taka, where some of the Bishari tribes had revolted.

When we came forth the next morning, our Arabs had all anointed themselves and put on good clothes; but what more particulary surprised us was the sight of their stately white wigs, making them look quite reverend. It is a part of their "dress," to comb the hair into a high *toupé*, which is sprinkled with peculiar finely drifted butter, shining white, as if with powder. In a little while, however, when the sun is risen higher, this fat snow melts, and then the hair looks all covered with innumerable pearly dew-drops, till these, too, disappear, and run down their shoulders and neck from their dark brown hair, spreading a light upon their well-burned limbs, like antique bronze statues.

We set forward the next morning at eight o'clock, with a new camel that we had found opportunity to exchange for a tired one. The valley becomes broader and more fertile the nearer we come to the

island of Meroë; the desert itself became more
rank and wild, like steppes. The first station was
Geg, where we spent the night in an open space;
the air is very, very warm; at half-past five in the
afternoon we had 25° Reaumur. The second night
we stayed on the other side of Abu Hashîn, in the
neighbourhood of a village, which is in reality no
station, as we desired to pass the five usual stations
in four days; the third day we stopped out in the air
by a cataract of the Nile. On the fourth day from
Abu Hammed, we kept a little further away from
the river in the desert, but still within the limits of
the original valley, if I may so call a yellow earth,
which is not covered by the inundations, but is dug
out by the villagers immediately below the sand, in
order to mend their fields. We halted in the evening at the village of El Chôr, an hour from El
Mechêref, and arrived in the metropolis of the province of Berber early on the fifth day.

I sent the dragoman forward to announce us, and
to demand a house, which we received, and immediately entered upon. The Mudhir of Berber was
in Dâmer; his vakeel, or lieutenant, visited us, and
soon came Hassan Chalif, the chief Arab sheikh,
who promised us better camels to Dâmer, was rejoiced to hear good tidings of his and our friends,
Linant and Bonomi, and amused himself with our
own books of plates, in which he found portraits of
his relations and ancestors. We had scarcely arrived, ere we received intelligence that Hassan
Pasha had entered the town on another side. He
had journeyed from Korusko to his province of
Dongola, and now returned from Edabbe, on the

southern boundaries of Dongola, right through the
desert of El Mechêref, where Enrin, the new Pasha
of Chartûm, had come to meet him. The rencontre
caused some disturbance in our plans ; but we managed to travel southward on the next morning, the
22nd of January, soon after Hassan Pasha's departure, after leaving two camels, no longer wanted for
water-carrying, behind, and exchanging three others
for better ones.

We rode off towards noon, and stayed in the
evening at the last village, before the river Mogrân,
the ancient Astaboras, which we had to pass before
reaching Dâmer. It is called in the maps Atbara,
evidently a corruption of Astaboras ; but this designation seems to be applied to the upper river, from
the place of that name, and not to the lower one.
Next morning we passed the river near its *embouch-
ment*. Even here it was very narrow in its great
bed, which it entirely fills in the rainy season, while
for two months it is only prevented from disappear-
ing entirely by some stagnating water. On the other
side of the river, we landed on the island of Meroë
of Strabo, by which name the land between the
Nile and Astaboras was designated. Yet two hours
and we reached Dâmer.

The houses were too poor to take us in ; I therefore sent Jussuf to Emin Pasha, in whose province
we now were, and who had encamped, with Hassan
Pasha, on the shore of the river. He sent a *khawass* to meet us, and to invite us to dine with him.
I, however, judged it more expedient to pitch our
tent at some distance, and to change our travelling
costume. Immediately the Mudhir of Berber paid

us his visit, to ask after our wishes, and soon after
Emin Pasha sent an excellent dinner to our tent,
consisting of four well-prepared dishes, and besides
that, a lamb roasted whole upon the spit and filled
with rice, and a flat cake filled with meat.

Toward Asser (three o'clock in the afternoon) we
had our visit announced; just as we were about to
proceed to it, we heard the singing of sailors; two
boats came swimming down the stream with red
flags and crescents : it was Ahmed Pasha Menekle
returning from Chartûm.   The Pasha and the Mudhir immediately proceeded on board, and they did
not separate till late; our friend, Dr. Koch, was unfortunately not expected from Chartûm for two days.
I had received a note from Erbkam at an early
period after my arrival, in which he informed me, by
the medium of a passing *khawass*, that he had left
Korusko with Ibrahim Aga, on the 15th of January; he wrote from their first camp.   The *khawass*
had ridden with incredible swiftness from Cairo to
Berber, in fourteen days, and brought Ahmed Pasha
the desired permission to raise the government price
for the camels from Korusko to Berber, from sixty
piasters to a higher price than before, *i. e.* ninety
piasters.

January 26th. The day before yesterday we made
our visit to Ahmed Pasha, which he returned yesterday. He will do everything to facilitate our further
journey. He informed us, that he, in accordance
with his former promise, had sent an officer from
Abu Haras to Mandera, three days into the desert,
and had obtained the information from him that
great ruins were existing there. The same was told

us yesterday in a letter by Dr. Koch, and confirmed to-day by his word of mouth.   After dinner he will bring us Musa Bey, who has been there.   He also announced to us that some letters had arrived for us, and were deposited at Chartûm, and that the artist sent for from Rome had arrived at Cairo.

For our fellow-travellers a bark is prepared at El Mechêref; but I shall precede them with Abeken. Ahmed Pasha sends me word, that in an hour a courier will leave for Cairo, who shall bear these letters.

POSTSCRIPT.—The magnificent news from Mandera does not seem to be confirmed on closer inquiry. It will hardly be worth while to go thither.

LETTER XVIII.

To-day we reach the southernmost boundary of
our African journey. To-morrow we go northward
and homeward again. We shall come as far as the
neighbourhood of Sero, the frontier between the
provinces of Sennâr and Fasoql. Our time will not
admit of more stay. I have travelled from Chartûm
hither with Abeken only. We gave up the desert
journey to Mandera, the rather as the eastern regions are now unsafe by reason of the war in Taka.
I now employ the time in learning the nature of the
river, and the neighbouring country some days' journey beyond Sennâr. The journey is worth the
trouble, for the character of the whole land decidedly changes in soil, vegetation, and animals, on
passing Abu Haras, between Chartûm and Sennâr,
at the *embouchure* of the Rahad. It was necessary
for me to gain as much personal knowledge of the
whole Nile valley, as far up as possible, since the
nature of this country, so limited in its width, has
more influence than anything else upon the progress
of its history.

On the White River one cannot journey for more
than a few days to the frontier of Mohammed Ali's
conquests, without peculiar preparations and pre-
cautions. There are found the Shilluk on the
western shore, and on the eastern, the Dinka, both

native negro people, who are never the best friends
with the northern folk. The Blue River is accessible to a much higher extent, and was, and is now,
historically, of more consequence than the White,
as it is the channel of communication between the
north and Abyssinia. I should like to have proceeded into the province of Fasoql, the last under
Egyptian dominion ; but that will not tally with our
reckoning ; so we shall put a period to our southern
journey to-night.

But I return in my reports to Dâmer, where I
embarked on the 27th of January with Abeken, in
the bark of Musa Bey, Ahmed Pasha's first adju-
tant, who had kindly placed it at our disposal. We
stopped for the night at about eight o'clock in the
evening, near the island of Dal Haui. We had obtained a *khawass* from Emin Pasha, the same who
had come hither on the conquering of the country
with Ismael Pasha, who had accompanied the
Defterdar Bey to Kordofan, (or, according to his pronunciation, Kordifal), who had then journeyed with
the same on his errand of vengeance to Shendi for the
murder of Ismael, and since then had traversed the
whole Sudan in every direction for three and twenty
years. He has the most perfect map of these countries
in his head, and possesses an astounding memory for
names, bearings, and distances, so that I have based
two charts upon his remarks, which are not without
geographical interest in some parts. He has also
been to Mekka, and therefore likes to be addressed
as Haggi Ibrahim (Pilgrim Ibrahim.) In other
things, too, he has much experience, and will be

very useful to us by reason of his long and extended acquaintance with the land.

On the twenty-eighth of January, we stopped about noon at an island called Gomra, as we heard that there were ruins in the vicinity which we should like to see. We had to proceed through a flat arm of the Nile, and ride for an hour on the eastern shore to the north. There at last we found, after passing the villages of Motmár and El Akarid, between a third village, Sagâdi, and a fourth, Genna, the inconsiderable ruins of a place built of bricks, and strewn with broken tiles.

We returned but little satisfied amidst the noon-day heat, and arrived with our bark only just before sunset in Begerauîe, in the neighbourhood of which are situated the pyramids of Meroë. It is remarkable that this place is not mentioned by Cailliaud. He only speaks of the pyramids of Assur, *i.e.* Sûr, or e'Sûr. The whole plain in which the ruins of the city and the pyramids lie bears the same name; and, besides this, a portion of Begerauîe, which, probably by a slip of the pen, is called Begromi by Hoskins.

Although it was already dark, I rode with Abeken to the pyramids, which stand a short hour's ride inland, upon the slopes of the low hills that stretch along eastward. The moon alone, which was in its first quarter, sparingly lighted the plain, covered with stones, low underwood, and rushes. After a sharp ride, we came to the foot of a row of pyramids, which rose before us in the form of a crescent, as was rendered necessary by the ground. To the right joins another row of pyramids, a little retreating; a third group lies more to the south in the plains, too far off to be distinguished in the dim moonlight. I tied the bridle of my donkey round a post, and climbed up the first mound of ruins.

The single pyramids are not so exactly placed as in Egypt; yet the ante-chambers, which are here built on to the body of the structures themselves, all lie turned away from the river toward the east, doubtless for the same religious reason which actuated the Egyptians also to turn the entrance of the detached temples before their pyramids to the east, thus riverward at Gizeh and Saqâra, but the tombs toward the west.

Half looking, half feeling, I found some sculptures on the outer walls of the tomb temple, and also perceived figures and writing on the inner walls. I recollected that I had a candle-end in the wallet of my donkey; this I lighted, and examined several ante-chambers. Then immediately the forms of the Egyptian Gods—Osiris, Isis, Nephthys, Atmu, &c., came out with their names in the well-known hieroglyphics.* In the first chamber, too, I found the cartouche of a king. One of the two rings contained the signs of a great Pharaoh of the Old Empire, Sesurtesen I.; the same was assumed by two later Egyptian kings, and now encountered for the fourth time as the throne-name of an Ethiopian king. The sculptures on the other side were not ended. On the same evening, I also found royal names in another ante-chamber, but they were

[* Bunsen has given these forms and hieroglyphics at the end of the English translation of his excellent Egypt's Place, of which it is much to be regretted that the first volume only has hitherto appeared.—K. R. H. M.]

rather illegible. Both writing and representations had, in fact, suffered much. The pyramids, like those in Egypt, have lost their tops, and many are totally destroyed.

Our new *khawass*, who would not leave us in the night, had followed immediately. He knew the locality perfectly, as he had been here a long time with Ferlini, and had assisted him in the examination of the pyramids. He showed us the place in the pyramid where Ferlini, in 1834, discovered the rich treasure of gold and silver rings built in the wall.

I also discovered a case-pyramid that evening, enlarged according to the principle of the Egyptian pyramids by a later mantle of stone. According to the inscriptions and representations in the ante-chambers, these pyramids are chiefly built for kings, and a few perhaps for their wives and children. The great number of them argues for a long series of kings, and a well-grounded empire that probably lasted for a number of centuries.

The most important results of this examination by moon and candlelight was, however, not the most agreeable; I was fully convinced that I had before me here, on the most celebrated spot of ancient Ethiopia, nothing but the ruins of comparatively recent art.* Already, at an earlier

[* Had Lepsius remembered that, by the determination of this most important fact, he set at rest the half-witted theories of a race of Indo-philologic dreamers, he would have rather rejoiced at the result than have regretted. These men, of whom Higgins, Faber, and Dupuis are fine specimens, with no accurate knowledge of any of the languages they so sapiently decided on, will find their favourite Mount Meru, Meroë, Menu, Manu, &c.,

period, had I judged from the monuments of Ferlini, drawings of which I had seen in Rome, and
the originals in London, that they were certainly
produced in Ethiopia, but not in any case earlier
than the first century before the Christian era;
therefore, at about the same period to which a
few veritable Greek and Roman works belong,
which we discovered together with the Ethiopian
treasure. And I must say the same now of all the
monuments not only situated here, but upon the
whole island of Meroë, as well of all the pyramids
near Begerauîe, as of the temples of Ben Naga, of
Naga, and of the Wadi e' Sofra (Cailliaud's Me-

&c., &c., here overthrown by an evident chronological fact.
Such investigations are, however, useful for two reasons:—1.
That they collect an immense number of facts, and, in some
degree, classify them, for the benefit of the race of investigators
now arising, of whom Forster, Bunsen, Bopp, and others, are
fine examples; and 2. They show us what false scents we must
avoid in following up so intricate an inquiry as the Archæological
history of the "origenes" of mankind. Let it be understood,
however, that I do not mean to assert that men like Higgins and
Pococke are totally wrong; far from it, they are often right, but
the care which they should bestow on their researches is continually
wanting,—the critical acumen to distinguish between nonsense
and sense,—always. I can only repeat what I have said in
another place, (Buckley's Great Cities of the Ancient World,
p. 314,) in a chapter on Scandinavian and general mythology,
viz.:—That a new era is approaching in historical investigation,
and, I may add, that we must not doubt, or we may never
prove. There is plenty of time, and one fact *established* is worth
many *overthrown*, when there is nothing to replace them. The
great problem is susceptible of solution if we have only a little
faith, at any rate, to preserve, even if only *provisionally*, what
we cannot see in the full clear light, that yesterday's occurrences
are given in to-day's *Times*.—K. R. H. M.]

saurât), which we have subsequently seen. The representations and inscriptions leave not the least doubt on the subject, and it will be for ever in vain to attempt the support of the much-loved idea of an ancient Meroë, glorious and famous, the inhabitants of which were the predecessors and teachers of the Egyptians in civilisation, by referring to its monumental remains.

Yet this conviction is of no little value, and appears to throw a certain degree of light upon the historical connection of Egypt and Ethiopia, the importance of which will first be fully developed at the monuments of Barkal. There, no doubt, will be found the oldest Ethiopian memorials, although perhaps not earlier than the time of Tarhaka, who reigned contemporaneously over Egypt and Ethiopia, in the seventh century before Christ.

We rode back to the pyramids the next morning with the sunrise, and found fifteen various royal names, but some in a very bad condition.

We had just completed the survey of the two north-easterly groups of pyramids, and were riding towards the third, which lies in the plain not far from the ruins of the city, and is perhaps the oldest Necropolis, when we heard shots from the shore, and saw white sails fluttering on the river. Soon after Erbkam, the two Weidenbachs, and Franke came walking over the plain, and greeted already at a distance. We scarcely expected them so soon, and therefore the meeting was the more pleasant. We could now continue our journey to Chartûm all together.

At two o'clock in the afternoon we went off, and

M

reached Shendi at about ten the next morning.
After dinner we went on, stayed the night on the
island Hobi, and came the next morning early to
Ben Naga. Here we first visited the ruins of two
little temples, of which the west one had Typhon
columns instead of pillars, but showed no writing
on its few remains ; in the other eastern one there
were a few sculptures preserved on the low wall,
and writing on a few round pillars, but too little
that anything connected might be gathered from it.
Excavations might probably discover royal names ;
but such an attempt is only possible on our return.

Some camels were procured for the next morning, and I rode off with Abeken, Erbkam, and
Maximilian Weidenbach at nine o'clock for Naga.
So are the ruins of a city and several temples
named, which lie in the eastern wilderness, at a
distance of seven or eight hours from the Nile.
From our landing-place, near the only palm group
of the whole region, we only wanted half an hour
to the village of Ben Naga, which lies in Wadi
Teresîb. One hour eastward, down the river (for it
flows from west to east here), the ruins are situated,
where we had landed the day before, in the Wadi
el Kirbegân ; we now passed them on the left, and
rode south-east into the wilderness, sparely grown
with dry underwood, crossed the valley El Kirbegân, which stretches hither from the river, and
in which we found a camp of Abâbde Arabs.

After four and a half hours from Ben Naga, we
arrived at a solitary mountain in the wilderness,
named Buêrib. This lay between the little south-
western wadis (so they call even the most level

sinkings of the plain, when the water runs off, and
which we should scarcely call valleys) and the great
wide Wadi Auatêb, into which we now descended,
after we had passed the Buêrib at a little distance
to the left. In three and three quarter hours from
Buêrib, we came to the ruins of Naga.

The enigma which I had vainly endeavoured to
unriddle, and which neither Cailliaud nor Hoskins had
explained, as to how it was possible to build a city
and sustain it in the midst of the desert so far from
the river, was first solved in the vicinity of the
temple. The whole valley of Auatêb is still cultivated land. We found it covered far and wide with
durra stubble. The inhabitants of Shendi, Ben
Naga, Fadnie, Sélama, Metamme, thus of both sides
of the Nile, come hither to cultivate the land, and
to harvest *durra*. The tropical rain is sufficient to
fertilise the soil of this flat but extensive level, and
in ancient times it is probable that more was obtained from this region by greater care. For the
dry season there were no doubt large artificial
cisterns, like those we found at the most distant
ruins north of Naga, although without water.

The ruins lie at the end of a mountain chain
which extends for several hours, having received the
name of Gebel e' Naga, and running from north to
south ; Wadi Auatêb passes along its western side
toward the river. After an uninterrupted ride, we
arrived at about half-past five. By the way we saw
the road covered with the traces of gazelles, wild
asses, foxes, jackals, and ostriches. Lions, too,
sometimes come hither, but we saw no signs of
them.

Before the coming of night I visited the three principal temples, which all belong to a very late period, and do not admit of a single idea concerning any antiquity, which Cailliaud and Hoskins imagined they perceived. A fourth temple stand besides the three principal temples in Egyptian architecture, the well turned, and not unpleasingly selected Egyptian ornamental style of which, not only manifests the time of the universal dominion of the Romans, but also the presence of Roman builders. This has no inscriptions. Of the three others, the two southernmost are built by one and the same king; on both he is accompanied by a representation of the same queen. There is behind them yet another royal personage, bearing different names on the two temples. The name of the king has again the cartouch of Sesurtesen I. added, although he does not appear to be the same with the king at the pyramids of Sûr; and the two other persons have also old Egyptian cartouches, which might easily lead to mistakes.

The third and northern temple has suffered much, and had but little writing now, yet a king is mentioned on the door lintels, who is different from the builder of the two others.

The forms of the gods are almost Egyptian, yet there is on the southern temple a shape unknown in Egypt, with three lions' heads (perhaps there is a fourth behind) and four arms. This may be the barbarous god mentioned by Strabo, which the Meroites revered beside Herakles, Pan, and Isis.

Next morning, the 2nd of February, we visited the three temples again, took a few paper impressions, and then went our way to the third group of monuments, named Mesaurât, by Cailliaud. This is, however, a designation employed for all three groups of ruins, and which signifies "pictures," or "walls decked with pictures." The ruins of Ben Naga are called Mesaurât el Kirbegân, because they lie in the Wadi el Kirbegân ; only the southern-most group, it seems, has retained its ancient name Naga or Mesaurât e' Naga ; the third toward Shendi, called Mesaurât e' Sofra, from the mountain-crater where it lies, and which is named e' Sofra, the table.

We followed the mountain chain, Gebel e' Naga, in the valley Auatêb, for two hours in a northward direction. Then, at about half-past twelve o'clock, we passed through the first ravine, opening to the right into a more elevated valley, e'Siléha, which becoming wider behind the hills, overgrown with grass and bushes, opens (in the direction of S.S.W. to N.N.E.) after an hour and a half, to the left into the valley of Auatêb, and in front toward another smaller valley, from which it is separated by the Gebel Lagâr. This little valley it is which is called e'Sofra, from its round form ; here too lie the ruins which Hoskins saw, though he did not penetrate to Naga. At a quarter past two we arrived, and had therefore consumed not quite four hours from Naga hither. As we were going to take a rapid survey of the whole, we walked through the extensive ruins of the principal building, which Cailliaud had taken for a great school, Hoskins for a hospital ; and we perceived from the few sculptures, unaccompanied by inscriptions, that we had before us also here late monuments, probably younger than those of Sûr and Naga. Then we went to the little temple near (on the pillars of which we found riders on elephants and lions, and other strange barbaric representations), looked at the large artificial cistern, now called Wot Ma-hemût, which must have taken the place of the river during the dry season, and rode back again to Ben Naga, at four o'clock.

When we came forth from the mountains, we met great herds of wild asses, which always stopped a little in front of us, as if inviting us to chase them. They are grey or reddish grey, with a white belly, and all have a strongly marked black stripe down the back ; the tip of the tail, too, is usually black. Many are caught when young, but are not fit for carriage or riding then. The next generation is only to be employed for these purposes. Almost all the domesticated donkeys in the south, above the Ass Cataract (Shellâl homâr), in Berber, are of the race of these wild asses, and have the same colour and marks.

We pitched our tents in the rank-grown plain soon after sundown. The camel-drivers and our *khawass* were terribly afraid of the lions in this desert, until a great fire was lighted, which they carefully kept up the whole night through. When a lion lets his voice be heard in the vicinity of a caravan, sounding indeed deeply and dreadly through the whole wilderness, all the camels run away like mad, and are difficult of being secured, often not until they have suffered and done some injury. Some days ago a camel was strangled by a lion in our vicinity, although on the opposite side of the river; a man that was there saved himself on the next tree.

On the 3rd of February, we rode off again at seven o'clock, leaving the two Buêrib, the great " blue " one and the little " red " one, a good distance to the left, and came into the valley El Kirbegân shortly before nine o'clock. This we followed for half an hour riverward, seeing the Mesaurât el Kirbegân to the right; but we now stopped on the hills, until we arrived at Ben Naga, a little after eleven o'clock, and half an hour at our landing place.

After two hours we went on in our bark. With a strong contrary wind we made but little way, and saw nothing new, except a swimming hippopotamus. Next morning we landed on the western shore, opposite the village of Gôs Basabir, to inspect the ruins of an old fortress wall with towers of defence, which encircled a hill top. The place was about three hundred paces in diameter. After mid-day, we neared the Shellâl (cataracts) of Gerashâb; the higher mountains before us came nearer, and at last formed a great pool, apparently without any outlet; however, it was really close at hand, as we turned into a narrow gorge, widening into a high and wild rock valley, that we followed for almost an hour before we came into another plain on the opposite side. The Qirre granite mountains running through here, end on the eastern side of the river in a peak called the Rauiân, " the Satisfied ;" while westward, at some distance from the river, standing equally alone, is the Atshân, " the Thirsty."

On the 5th of February, we landed early at

Tamamiât, about 11 o'clock. Mohammed Said, the former treasurer of the deceased Ahmed Pasha, whose acquaintance we had made in Dâmer, had given us a letter to one of the under-officials there, containing directions to deliver to us the fragment of an inscription found at Soba. It was in the middle of a marble tablet, written on both sides with late Greek or Koptic letters. The signs, which were plainly visible, contained neither Greek nor Koptic words, only the name ⲅⲉⲱⲣⲅⲓⲟ was decipherable. The same evening we arrived at Chartûm. This name signified " elephant's trunk," and is probably derived from the narrow tongue of land between its Niles, on which the city lies.

My first visit with Abeken was to Emin Pasha, who had already reached Chartûm before us. He received us very kindly, and would not let us leave him the whole morning.

An excellent breakfast, comprising about thirty dishes, which we took with him, allowed us to make several very interesting glances into the secrets of Turkish cookery, which (as I learnt from our well-fed Pasha), in the matter of the preparation and arrangement of the dishes, like the systems of the latest French cookery, follow the rules of a more refined taste. Soon after the first dish comes lamb, roasted on the spit, which must never be wanting at any Turkish banquet. Then follow several courses of solid and liquid, sour and sweet dishes, in the order of which a certain kind of recurring change is observed, to keep the appetite alive. The *pilau* of boiled rice is always the concluding dish.

The external adjuncts to such a feast as this, are

these :—A great round plate of metal, with a plain edge of three feet in diameter, is placed on a low frame, and serves as a table, about which five or six people can repose on rugs, or cushions. The legs are hidden in the extensive folds which encircle the body. The left hand must remain invisible ; it would be very improper to expose it in any way while eating. The right hand alone is permitted to be active. There are no plates and knives or forks. The table is decked with dishes, deep and shallow, covered and uncovered ; these are continually being changed, so that but little can be eaten from each. Some, however, as roast meat, cold milks and gerkins, &c., remain longer, and are often recurred to. Before and after dinner they wash their hands. An attendant or slave kneels with a metal basin in one hand, and a piece of soap on a little saucer, on the other ; with the other hand he pours water over the hands of the washer from a metal jug ; over his arm hangs an elegantly embroidered napkin, for drying one's hand upon.

After dinner, pipes and coffee are immediately handed round, after which time one may withdraw. The Turks then take a sleep until Asser. But ere we parted from our host, he had a number of weapons, lances, bows, arrows, clubs, and a sceptre of the upper wild nations, sent to my bark, as a guest present.

We then visited our countryman, Neubauer, the apothecary of the province, who had been very unfortunate. A short while before, he had been removed from his post by the deceased Ahmed Pasha, but was now again instituted apothecary by

Ahmed Pasha Menekle, through Dr. Koch's interest. Then we went to the house of a resident Pole, named Hermanowitch, the principal physician of the province, who offered us his house in accordance with a command of the Pasha, whither we removed on the following day. It had just been repaired, and by it were a garden and court, very useful to us for the unpacking and mending of our chests and tents.

Next day the Pasha returned our visit. He came on horseback. We offered coffee, pipes, and sherbet, and showed him some pictures from Egypt, in which he took a lively interest. He is a man of tall and corpulent stature, a Circassian by birth, and therefore, like most of his countrymen, better informed than the Turks. At the house of a Syrian, Ibrahim Chêr, I saw a rich collection of all the ornithological species of the Sudan, in number about three hundred; of each twenty to thirty carefully selected specimens.

A day or two after I took a walk with Abeken and Erbkam, to the opposite side of the promontory, toward the White River, which we followed to its union with the Blue River. Its water is, in fact, whiter, and tastes less agreeably than that of the Blue, because it runs slowly through several lakes in the upper countries, the standing waters of which lakes impart to it an earthy and impure taste. I have filled several bottles with the water of the Blue and the White Nile, which I shall bring home, sealed down.

At a subsequent friendly visit of the Pasha, we met the brother of the former Sultan of Kordofan (who was himself also called Mak or Melek), and the Vizier of Sultan Nimr (Tiger), of Shendi. The latter still resides in Abyssinia, whither he fled after he had burned the conqueror of his country, Ismael Pasha, Mohammed Ali's son, and all his officers, at a nightly banquet in 1822.

We went up the White River on the 14th, but soon returned, as it has so weak a current that, by the present prevailing north wind, the way back is somewhat difficult. The shores of the White River are desolate, and the few trees, which formerly stood in the vicinity of Chartûm, are now cut down and used for building or burning. The water mass of the White River is greater than that of the Blue, and retains its direction after their union, so the Blue River is to be looked upon rather as a tributary, but the White River as the actual Nile. Their different waters may be distinguished long after their juncture.

On the 16th of February, I sent for some Dinka slaves, to inquire into their language; but they were so hard of comprehension, that I could only, with great trouble, obtain from them the names of the numbers up to one hundred, beside a few pronouns. The languages of the Dinka and the Shilluk, who live several days' journey up the White River, the former on the eastern, the latter on the western shore, are as little known in respect to their grammatical structure, as those of most of the Central African Nations; and I therefore besought the Pasha to have some sensible people found who were acquainted with their language. This was not possible at the time, but it is to be done against our return.

In the meantime our purchases and repairs were completed, and I hastened our departure as much as possible. The house of Hermanowitch remains at our disposal on our return; it is conveniently and airily built, and from my windows I could see the oldest house in the town, the pointed straw roof of which looked over the walls. These pointed thatched houses, called *Tukele*, form the peculiar style of the country, and almost the only erections more to the south. But as Chartûm is a new city, the few old huts have all disappeared except that one, and the houses are built of burnt brick.

At noon on the 17th of February we entered our barks. I sailed to the south with Abeken, up the Blue River, partly to learn its nature, partly to see the ruins of Soba, and those of Mandera; the rest of our companions, for whom there was nothing to do in the south, went northward to Meroë, to draw the monuments of that place.

Next day we landed on the eastern side, where great stacks of red burnt bricks, prepared for embarkation, informed us that we were not far off the ruins of Soba. In the whole country unburnt bricks are now made, so that all ruins of burnt bricks must belong to an earlier period. From Soba, this building material is transported in great quantities both to Chartûm and beyond it.

We landed, and had scarcely left the bushes next to the shore behind us, ere we saw the ransacked mounds of bricks, which covers a great plain, an hour in circumference; some of the larger heaps might be the

remains of the Christian churches, which are described by Selim of Assuan (by Macrizi) in the
tenth century, when Soba was yet the capital of the
empire of Alŏa, as magnificently decorated with
gold. The place was shown us where, some time
ago, a stone lion was discovered, now in the possession of Churshid Pasha, at Cairo. Nowhere could
walls or buildings be recognized, only on the southernmost and somewhat distant hill could we find
some sculptured yellow blocks of sandstone, and a
low wall ;. on another mound lay several rough slabs
of a black, slatey stone.

The country round Soba is level, as everywhere
about here, to the foot of the Abyssinian mountains,
and the soil, particularly at this season, dried up and
black ; the thicker vegetation is confined to the
river shore, farther on, there are only single trees,
now more frequent, now seldom.

I promised the sailors a sheep if we arrived early
next morning at Kamlîn ; for the wind was violent,
and allowed us to make but little way. Our ship,
too, does not go very fast, the sailors are not adroit,
and, with the present low level of the water, the
bark easily sticks in the sand-banks. We went
almost the whole night, and arrived early at eight
o'clock in Kamlîn.

The ancient place of the same name lies half an
hour further up the river, and consists but of a few
huts. The houses where we landed belong to a
number of factories instituted four years ago, in
common with the late Ahmed Pasha, by Nureddin
Effendi, a Catholic Koptic Egyptian, who has gone
over to Islâm, and which yield a rich profit.. A simple,

honest, un-Oriental German, named Bauer, has
erected a soap and brandy factory, which he himself
conducts. A sugar and indigo factory is kept by an
Arab. Bauer is the southernmost resident European that we have found in Mohammed Ali's territories, and we were glad to find so excellent a
conclusion to the long, little pleasing chain of
Europeans, generally deteriorated in civilization, who
preferred the government of Turks to their native
country.* He has an old German housekeeper
named Ursula, a funny, good-natured body, for
whom it was a no less festal occasion to see German
guests than for him. With joyful hurry she got out
what European crockery she had, and the forks that
were yet in being, and set baked chicken, vege-
tables, sausages, and excellent wheaten bread before
us; at last, too, a cherry pie of baked European
cherries (for our fruits do not grow in Egypt), in
short, a native meal, such as we had never expected
in this *ultima Thule.*

Before Bauer's house we found the most southern
Egyptian sculpture that we have seen, on a pedestal,
a seated statue of Osiris, somewhat destroyed, done
in a late style, in black granite, with the usual
attributes, about two and a half feet high, which
was discovered in Soba, and is not without interest,
as the only monument of Egyptian art from that
city.

The European furniture of Bauer's room made a
strange impression upon one here in the south among
the black population A wooden clock, made in the

* I have since heard of the decease of Herr Bauer, which
ensued in the following year.

Black Forest, ticked regularly on the wall; some half-broken European stools were ranged round the strong table, behind which a small book-shelf was put up, with a selection of German classics and histories, by the corner of a Turkish divan, which was also not wanting. Over the great table, and opposite the canopy-bed in the other corner, hung bell-pulls, leading to the kitchen. A curious Nesnas ape sometimes peeped in through the lattice by the door, and on the other side of the little court, one could see the busy Ursula in her purple, red-flowered gown, toddling backward and forward among the little, naked, black slaves, arranging this, that, and the other, with a somewhat scolding voice, and looking into the bubbling pots in the adjoining kitchen. We did not see her the whole morning, not even at the dinner, that she had prepared so well and tastily; after dinner, she first presented herself, with many curtsies, to receive our praises. She complained of the forlorn state of her cooking apparatus, and grumbled sadly at Herr Bauer for not leaving this horrid, dirty, and hot country, although he promised year after year to do it. She had accompanied him hither, had been eleven years in the country, and four at Kamlîn. Bauer intends in a year to go to Germany, and settle in Steiermark or Thüringen, with his savings, and turn farmer, like his father.

After table, the son of Nureddin Effendi sent us a complete Turkish dinner of from twelve to fifteen dishes, which we left, however, to the attendants after our European meal. We had also inspected the factories in the morning, and tasted the fine brandy (called *Marienbad*), which Bauer chiefly pre-

pares from the sugar-cane and dates. Business seemed
to be in the best order, and the unusual cleanliness
of the places, the vessels, and utensils, attest the
care with which the establishment, only worked by
slaves, is conducted. The pleasant impression that
this visit made upon us was heightened by the discovery that Bauer possessed a second piece of the
marble inscription already alluded to,* which had
been found in the ruins of Soba. He presented me
with the fragment, which was easily put together
with the other piece, although even then the inscription was not perfected. The fragment exhibits
on one side traces of twelve lines, on the other of
nine. Here, too, the writing is easy to be read, but
only the name ιλκωβ is comprehensible. It is
either a very barbarous Greek, or a peculiar language, spoken in former times at Soba. In fact,
we know from Selim that the inhabitants of Soba
possessed their sacred books in the Greek language,
but also translated them into their own.

After paying the son of Nureddin Effendi a visit,
we left with the promise to stay on our return.

From Kamlîn the shores run on at equal eleva-
tions. The character of a fluvial valley is lost. The
deposited black earth has ceased; the steep high
shores are composed of original earth and calcareous
conglomerate, which, according to Bauer, is well
capable of being burnt to lime.

On the morning of the 21st we came to a considerable bend in the river to the east; the wind
became so unfavourable through it, that our *kha-*

[* The author refers to the inscription obtained at Tamaniât
through the means of Mohammed Said. See p. 168.—K.R.H.M.]

wass landed, to impress the people of the vicinity to draw it. I went along the western shore for several hours to Arbagi, a deserted village, built of black bricks, but standing on the remains of another more ancient one, as I saw from the structures of burnt bricks. This place was once the chief centre of the trade of the Sudan, which has since turned itself to Messelemîeh. Soon after we found the two northern *baobàb* trees, which are here called *hómara*. These giant trees of creation (*andansonia digitata*) are found from here southward more and more frequently, and from Sero they belong to the usual trees of the region. One trunk which I paced round measured more than sixty feet in circumference, and certainly does not belong to the greatest of the kind, as they are here not so frequent.* At this season of the year they were leafless, and stretched their bare, death-like boughs far over the surrounding green trees, which look like low bushes beneath it. Their fruit, called *gungulês*,† I found here and there among the Arabs; they resemble pear-shaped melons, with a hairy surface. If the hard, tough shell be broken, a number of seeds are found inside, which are sur-

[* Werne, in his excellent work "Expedition to discover the sources of the White Nile," vol. i. p. 146, mentions baobàb trees of the above dimensions, and states that, near Fazoql, there is said to be one 120 feet in circumference. I cannot too strongly call attention to this most able work, in the portable form in which it has been issued by my publisher, Mr. Bentley. —K. R. H. M.]

† Russegger (Travels, vol. ii. Part II. p. 125,) found one of 95 feet in circumference. He erroneously calls the tree *ganglês;* this is *homara*, and the fruit *gungulês*.

rounded with a dry, acid, but well-tasted mass. The leaves are five-fingered.

On the 22nd of February we arrived on the western shore by a little village, where the inhabitants, mere women and children, fled through the sandy plain to the woods, from fear of our appearance, probably as they expected to be impressed for the purpose of drawing the bark. On the opposite shore lay another village, whence we saw a stately procession of finely-dressed men in Arab and Turkish dresses, and some handsomely caparisoned horses, proceed to the river. It was the Kashef and the most noble sheiks of Abu Háras, to whom we had been announced by Ahmed Pasha, as we had determined to proceed hence with camels and guides into the desert of Mandera. The horses were destined for us, and we therefore rode to the house of the Kashef, to inquire again about the antiquities of Mandera and Qala. As the desert route to the coast of the Red Sea leads hence from those places, we found several persons who had been near them. From all their tales, however, I could but find that at these two places there are only fortress-like mounds, or at most roughly built walls, as a refuge for caravans, without any buildings or hieroglyphical inscriptions. At Qala there may be some camels and horses scratched in the rock by the Arabs, or some other people, like those we had seen in the great desert at the wells of Murhad.

We therefore determine to give up this journey, and instead of it go somewhat farther up the river, in order to learn the nature of the Nile stream, its shores and inhabitants, as far as time would permit us.

At a short half-hour distance from Abu Háras we came to the mouth of the Rahad, which conveys a great quantity of water into the Nile in the rainy season, but was now almost dry, with only a little stagnant water, which may disappear altogether next month.

I left the bark as often as possible, to know as much of the shore as I could. To proceed farther inland, is impossible, from the almost impassable forests which line both shores. There stand in luxuriant magnificence the shadowy high-domed tamarind, the tower-like *hómara (baobàb)* the multi-boughed genius (sycamore), and the many species of slender gumrick sont trees. On their branches run in innumerable windings, like giant serpents, the creeping plants ; to their highest bough and down to the earth again, where they close every space between the mighty trunk in union with the low bushes. Besides this there is scarcely one thornless tree or bush in ten, by which every attempt to penetrate the thick underwood is dangerous, indeed impossible. Several of the plants —the *sittera* tree for instance—have the thorns placed in pairs, and in such a manner that one thorn is turned forward, the other back. If one should imprudently come too near the boughs, it is certain that the clothes will carry away some inevitable, and, in these wilds, imperfectly-to-be-remedied traces. In other places, the thorn trees are most elegant ; rising gracefully in the less thronged parts, like slender young birches. We distinguished two sorts of these standing mingled together, and only differing that in one the bark, extending from the trunk to the most distant twiglet, is coloured like a mass of shining red veins, while that of the other is black; on both of them the long shining white thorns and green leaves come out in strong contrast.

Of the birds, fluttering round in great numbers, I recognized not one Egyptian species. I shot many, and had them stuffed by our cook, Sirian. Among them were fine silver-grey falcons *(suqr shikl)*; birds called *gedâd el wadi*, with horns on the nose, and blue lappets on each side of the head; black and white unicorn birds *(abu tuko)*, with mighty beaks; black birds, with purple breasts *(abu labba)*; great brown and white eagles *(abu tôk)*, of which one measured six feet with extended wings; smaller brown eagles, called *hedâja*; and black ones, called *râchame*. The latter, which are more numerous toward Egypt, are the same represented in the hieroglyphics. The plover is principally found on the shore, with black crooked pricks at the joints of the wings, with the white long-legged *abu baqr* (Cow-bird), which is accustomed to sit on the backs of buffaloes and cows.

We often see great bats flying about in broad day; their long golden wings glance gleamingly through the foliage, and suddenly they hang to the boughs, head downwards, like great yellow pears, and are easily shot; they have long ears, and a curious trumpet-formed nose.

Chase was also made on the monkeys, but they are difficult to catch from their agility. One day we found a mighty tree full of monkeys. Some climbed quickly on our approach, and fled to the distant bushes; others hid themselves in the upper boughs; but some to whom both plans seemed hazardous, sprang with incredibly daring leaps from the highest branches of the tree, which was nearly a hundred feet in height, on to the little trees below, the thorny twigs of which bent low beneath their weight, without any of them falling; they gained their point, and escaped my gun.

The more south, the more crocodiles. The promontories of the islands are often covered with these animals. They usually lie in the sun, close to the edge of the water, opening their mouths and appearing to sleep, but they will not allow any one to approach them, but dive under the surface immediately, even if hit by the ball. Thus their capture is very difficult. Our *khawass*, however, struck a young one, only three feet in length, so well that it could not reach the waters. It was brought on board, where, to the horror of our Nesnas monkey, Bachit, it lived several days.

Not less impracticable than the crocodiles are the hippopotami, which we have occasionally seen in great numbers, but only with their heads above water. Once only a young Nile horse stood exposed on a sand islet, and allowed us to approach unusually near. The *khawass* shot and hit, but of course the ball did not penetrate the thick skin; then the fat animal with its shapeless head, large body, and short, elephant-like legs, broke into a highly comic gallop, in order to gain the adjacent water, where it soon disappeared. They usually only land at night, when they make terrible havoc in the durra-field and other plantations by stamping and eating. No one knew here of any hippopotamus ever being taken alive.

We did not see any lions, but their roars were heard sounding through the moonlight nights; there is something solemn in the deep sonorous voice of this royal animal.

On the 24th of February we came to a second tributary of the Nile, the Dender, which is larger than the Rahad. I went some way up it, to see what was impossible to be seen at the embouchure, whether there was yet a stream, and found that above, where the water ran in little channels, there was still a current, but very weak; in the rainy season the Dender swelled to the height of twenty feet, as its bed shows; the shores were covered with cotton-bushes, pumpkins, and other useful plants.

The heat is not inordinate; in the morning, at eight o'clock, usually 23° R.; from noon, till about five o'clock, 29°; and at eleven at night, 22°.

The evenings we spend on board, then I have the geography explained to me by our *khawass*, Hagi Ibrahim, or take some Nubians to my camels, to learn their language. I have already prepared a long vocabulary of the Nubian language. On a comparison with other lists, in Rüppell and Cailliaud, I also found in Koldági one of the languages spoken in the southernmost part of Kordofan, many similar words, which testify a narrow connection between the two languages. The Arabs call the Nubian language *lisân rotâna*, which I at first took for its actual name; it signifies, however, only a

foreign language, distinct from the Arabic. Therefore if the three Nubian dialects are spoken of, they
are not only called Rotâna Kenûs, Mahass, or Don-
qolaui, but also Rotâna Dinkaui, Shilluk, even Turki
and Franki, Turkish and Frank, *i. e.* European gib-
berish. The same error is at the bottom of the now
received designation of the Nubians as Berbers, and
their language as the Berber language; for this is
not their national name, or that of the language, as
it is generally believed, but means originally the
foreign-speaking persons, the Barbaros.*

On the 25th of February we landed near Saba
Doleb; I sought for ruins, but only found tall, well-
built cupolas of burnt brick, in the form of beehives,
and erected in quite a similar manner to the Greek
Thesauri, in horizontal layers. They are the graves
of holy Arab sheikhs of a late era ; the villagers did
not know what date to assign for their erection.
Under the cupola, in the middle of the building of
fifteen to eighteen feet in diameter, is the long
narrow grave of the saint, surrounded with larger
stones and covered with a multitude of little ones,
according to the superstition one thousand in number. I found six such domes, most of them half
dismantled, some quite ruined, but two tolerably
well preserved, and still visited ; a seventh, probably
the latest, was built of unburnt bricks.

At Wad Negûdi, a village to the west of the Nile,
we found the first dilêb-palms,† with slender naked

[* See an elaborate essay on the Berbers and their name, by
Mr. Gliddon, in the Ethnological Journal, No. X. p. 439.—
K. R. H. M.]

[† See Werne's Expedition, vol. i. p. 194, where he observes:—

trunks and little bushy crowns, like date-palms in
the distance, and dûm-palms close to it, by reason
of the leaves. The fruit is round, like that of the
dûm-palm, but larger. These trees are said to be
more frequent on the eastern tributaries; here, on
the Nile, they are found but in a very small district.
The leaves are regularly divided into fan-like folds
one under the other, and the stem has strong saw-
like notches. With such a stalk the Rais of our vessel sawed off another leaf, which I had brought to the
bark, to take with me. It is divided into sixty-nine
points, and measures five feet and a quarter from that
part of the stem where the fan begins, although it
is but young, and therefore keeps its fans quite shut
as yet. Another one, still larger, which had already
unfolded itself, we put up in the bark as a parasol, in
the shade of which we sat. The way to those palms
we had to make through the giant grass thickets,
shooting up stiffly and closely like corn, and covering
great plains. The ends of the stalks were five or
six feet above our heads, and even the tall camels,
bred in this place, could scarcely see above them.

On the 26th of February, we arrived at the village

" I do not call them *handsome* trees, because they stand there in
the green wilderness ; no, I find them really beautiful, for
there is a peculiar charm in them. They rise like double
gigantic flowers upon slender stalks, gently protruding in the
middle, and not like those defoliated date-palms, which stand
meagrely like large . cabbage-stalks. It is impossible that the
latter should delight my poor heart, full of the remembrance of
shady trees,—the oaks and the beech trees of Germany ; the.
palms near Parnassus ; the cypress on the Bosphorus, and the
chestnuts on the Asiatic Olympus." The botany of these
regions has been well treated by Werne.—K. R. H. M.]

Abu el Abás, on the eastern shore. This is the principal place of the neighbourhood, and the Kashef living here, has authority over 112 villages. I there purchased, for a few piasters, of a Turkish *khawass* a dog-ape. This is the holy ape of the ancient Egyptians, *kynokephalos*, dedicated to Thoth and the Moon, and appearing as the second of the four gods of the lower world.* It interests me to have this animal, which I have seen so innumerably represented on the monuments, about me for a time, and to observe the faithfully caught representations of its striking and usual characteristics in old Egyptian art. It is remarkable that this ape, so peculiar to Egypt in ancient times, is now only found in the south, and even there not very frequently. How many species of animals and plants, indeed manners and customs of men, with which the monuments of Egypt make us acquainted, are only to be found here in the farthest south of old Ethiopia, so that many representations, *i. e.* those of the graves of Benihassan, seem rather to picture scenes of this country than of Egypt. The *kynokephalos* has here no particular name, but only the general term *gird* (great ape). His head, hair, and colour, are not unlike those of a dog, whence his Greek appellation. Occasionally, too, he barks and

[* Bunsen in Egypt's Place in Universal History, vol. i. p. 430, refers them all to Osiris, and ranges them thus :—1. The Genius with the Hawkhead, KEBHSEN u.f. signifying "the refresher of his brothers." 2. The Jackal-head TUA-MUTF, "the adorer of his mother." 3. The Apehead, HEPI (Apis) "Osiris the devoted." 4. AMSET, God, "Osiris the devoted." The different arrangement of Lepsius is caused by his counting from right to left, while Bunsen begins from left to right.—K. R. H. M.]

growls just like a dog. He is yet young, and very good-natured, but immeasurably cleverer than Abeken's little dog and Nesnas monkey. He is very funny when he wants something good to eat, that he may see held in the hand. Then he lays his ears back, and knows how to express the greatest joy, but sits still, like a good child, and only smacks his lips like an old wine-taster. On seeing the crocodile, however, his hair ruffled up on his whole body, he cried out lamentably, and was scarcely to be held in his terror.

We arrived at the famous old metropolis of the Sudan, Sennâr, on the 27th of February, the king of which, before the conquering of the country by Ismaël Pasha, ruled as far as Wadi Halfa, and was supreme over a number of lesser tribute-paying kings. The place does not look now as if it had been so lately a royal city. Six or seven hundred pointed straw huts, (*tukele*) surround the ruins of red brick, where the palace formerly stood. The bricks are now used for the erection of a building for Soliman Pasha, who is to reside in Sennâr. It was so far finished, that the Vakil of the absent Pasha could hold his divan in it. We found him there, sitting in judgment. Many other people, Sheikhs and Turks were present; among them the Sheikh Sandalôba, the chief of the Arab merchants, and a relation of Sultana Nasr, with whom we afterwards became acquainted in her capital village Sorîba. We paid this distinguished man a visit in his house, at which honour he seemed much delighted. His chief chamber was a dark though lofty saloon, with a roof resting on two pillars and four half pillars, on to which we mounted, in order to get a view of the city.

In the meantime, an anqarêb was prepared for us in the court; mead (honey and water) was brought, and from the stable an hyæna, here called Morafil, and two young lions, of which the larger, actually the property of Soliman Pasha, was led to our bark, together with a couple of sheep, as a present from the Vakil. I had the animal tied up in the hold, and received a tear in the hand from his sharp claws, as a welcome. His body is already more than two feet long, and his voice is a most powerful tenor. Every morning now there is a tremendous row on board our not over large vessel, when we are drinking tea before the cabin early ; the monkeys jumping merrily about, and the lion is let out from the hold on deck, which is given him during the day, and we are bringing the cups and pans into safety, which he tries to reach with his already strong and inquisitive claws.

On the 29th of February we arrived at nine o'clock in Abdîn. The wind was unfavourable on the 1st of March, and we proceeded but little, so that I had plenty of time for shooting birds. Toward evening I came to a village, lying very romantically in a creek of the river, which is here broader. Many huts built of straw poked their pointed roofs into the branches of thickly-leaved trees. Narrow tortuous paths, forming a real labyrinth, led among thorns and trunks from one hut to another, in and before which the black families were lying and the children playing by a sparing light. I asked for milk, but was referred to an adjoining

Arab village, whither a man conducted me, armed
with a lance, the general weapon of the country.
By light brushwood and high grass we came to the
great herds of cattle of the Arabs, who had pitched
their mat huts about the grazing place. The Fellahs
of this region are much browner than the wandering
Arabs, although far from being negroes, and they
seem to coincide with the Nubians in race.

On the 2nd of March we anchored by an island,
near the eastern shore. At a little distance from the
landing-place, the Rais perceived a broken crocodile
egg at a spot newly dug. He dug away with his
hands, and found forty-four eggs three feet down in
the sand. They were still covered with a slimy
substance, as they had only been laid the day before
or in the past night. The crocodiles like to leave
the river in a windy night, make a hole for the eggs,
cover them up again, and the wind soon blows away
every trace. In a few months the young ones
creep out. The eggs are like great goose-eggs, but
rounded off at both ends, as the latter are only at
the large end. I had some boiled; they are eaten,
but have an unpleasant taste, so I willingly yielded
them up to the sailors, who ate them with a great
appetite.

We landed near the deserted village of Dáhela,
on the eastern shore, whence I proceeded alone
inland for three-quarters of an hour. The character
of the vegetation remains the same. The earth is
dry and level; the inconsiderable hills and dales
that occur are not original, but seem to have been
formed by the rain. My goal was a great tamarind
tree, which rose mightily amidst the low trees and

bushes, and was encircled by a number of fluttering
green and red birds, the species of which is yet
unknown to me.

I came on my way, first to a colony, by Kumr
betá Dáhela, where the inhabitants of that village
hold their *villeggiatura* ; for they stay here during
the dry months, and return to their village on the
river bank, at the beginning of the rainy season.
The last village whither I came is called Romáli, a
little above that given in the map as Sero, which
lies under the 13° N. latitude. On the hot and
tiring way back I attended a burial. Silently and
solemnly, without sound or sob, two corpses, wrapt
in white cloths, were borne along on *anqarêbs* by
several men, and laid in a grave of some feet deep
in the forest near the road. Perhaps they had
perished of the cholera-like complaint, which has
now broken out with great violence in the southern
regions.

We should have much liked to proceed to Fasoql, in the last province of Mohammed Ali, to see
the change in the character of the country beginning
at Rosêres, where so many novel forms of tropical
vegetation and animal life present themselves; but
our time was expended.

The Rais received the command to take down
the masts and sails, by which the bark at once lost
its stately appearance, and drove down the river
with the current like a wreck. Soon the pleasant
quiet of the vessel, that had seemed to fly along of
itself, was interrupted by the yelling, ill-sounding
songs of the rowers contending with the wind.

By the 4th, we were again at Sennár, and on

the 8th, at an early hour, we reached Wed Médineh. This place is almost as important as Sennâr. A regiment of soldiers lies in barracks here, with the only band in the Sudan, and two cannons. We were immediately visited by upper military scribe Seïd Hashim, one of the most important persons of the place, whom we had already known in Chartûm.

We determined to visit Sultana Nasr (Victoria) at Sorîba, an hour and a half inland, partly to learn the character of the country further from the river, and partly to get some idea of the court of an Ethiopian princess. Seïd Hashim offered us his dromedaries and donkeys for this trip, and also his own society; so we rode away that afternoon into the hot, black, but scantily treed plain, and soon accomplished the uninteresting way on the sturdy animals.

Nasr is the sister of the mightiest and richest king (*melek*) in the Sudan, Idris wed (*i. e. Welled*, son or successor of) Adlân, who is certainly under Mohammed Ali's supremacy now, but yet commands several hundred villages in the province El Fungi; his title is Mak el Qulle, King of the Qulle mountains. Adlân was one of his ancestors, after whom the whole family now calls itself; his father was the same Mohammed (wed) Adlân, who, at the time of Ismael Pasha's conquering campaign had taken most of the power of the legitimate but weak king of Sennâr, Bâdi, but who was then murdered at the instigation of Reg'eb, another pretender to the throne. When Ismael had arrived, and Reg'eb and his company had fled to the Abyssinian mountains,

King Bâdi united himself with the children and party of Mohammed Adlân, and submitted to the conqueror, who made him Sheikh of the country, had the murderers of Mohammed Adlân impaled, and gave his children, Reg'eb and Idris Adlân, great power and wealth. Nasr, their sister, also gained much consideration, which was, however, much increased, as she was allied to the legitimate royal family by her mother's side. Therefore is she called Sultâna, Queen. Her first husband was named Mohammed Sandalôba, brother of Hassan Sandalôba, whom we had visited at Sennâr. He has now been dead for a long time, but she has a daughter by him, named Dauer (Light), who married a great Sheikh, Abd-el Qader, but then parted from him, and now lives with her mother, in Sorîba. The second son of Nasr is Mohammed Defalla, the son of one of her father's viziers. He was then with Ahmed Pasha Menekle on the war march (*ghazua*, of which the French have made *razzia*) in Saka. But even when he is at home, she remains the principal person in the house, by reason of her noble birth.

Since very ancient times, a great estimation of the female sex appears to be a very general custom. It must not be forgotten how often we find reigning queens of Ethiopia mentioned, From the campaign of Petronius, Kandake is well known, a name which, according to Pliny, was bestowed on all the Ethiopian queens; according to others, always on the mother of the king. In the sculptures of Meroë, too, we occasionally find very warlike, and doubtless reigning, queens represented. According to Makrizi, the genealogies of the Beg'a, whom I consider the direct descendants of the Meroetic Ethiopians, and for the ancestors of the Bishari of the present day, were not counted by the males, but by the females, and the inheritance did not devolve upon the son of the deceased, but upon the sister or the daughter. In the same way, according to Abu Selah, the sister's son took precedence of the son among the Nubians, and Ibn Batuta reports the same custom to be existing among the Messofites, a western negro race. Even now, the court and upper minister of some southern princes are all women. Noble ladies allow their nails to grow an inch long, as a sign that they are there to command, and not to work, a custom which is found in the sculptures among the shapeless queens of Meroe.

When we arrived at Soriba, we entered the square court-yard by a particular door, running round the principal building, and thence into an open, lofty hall, the roof of which rested on four pillars, and four half pillars. The narrow beams of the roof jut out several feet beyond the simple architrave, and form the foundation of the flat roofs; the whole entrance reminded one much of the open façades of the graves of Benihassan. In the hall there was fine ebony furniture, of Indian manufacture, broad *an-qarébs*, with frames for the mosquito nets. Fine cushions were immediately brought, sherbet, coffee, and pipes handed round. The vessels were made of gold and silver. Black female slaves, in light white garments, which, fastened at the hips, are drawn up over the bosom and shoulders,—handed round the refreshments, and looked very peculiar with their plaited hair. The Queen, however, did not come;

perhaps she was ashamed of showing herself to
Christians; only a half-opened door, which soon
closed again, allowed us to perceive several women
behind, to whom we ourselves might be objects of
curiosity. I therefore let the sultana know, through
Saïd Hashim, that we were there to pay our visits,
and now hoped that we might have the pleasure of
seeing her. Upon this, the doors of strong wood
cased with metal, opened wide, and Nasr entered
with a free, dignified step. She was wrapped in
long fine-woven cloths, with coloured borders, under
which she wore wide gay trowsers of a somewhat
darker shade. Behind her came the court, eight or
nine girls in white clothes with red borders, and
elegant sandals. Nasr sat down before us, in a
friendly and unconstrained manner; only now and
then she drew her dress over her mouth and the
lower part of the face, a custom of Oriental modesty,
very general with women in Egypt, but much rarer
in this country. She replied to the greetings I offered
her through the Dragoman with a pleasant voice,
but stayed only a short time, withdrawing through
the same door.

We examined the inner parts of the house, with
the exception of her private rooms, which were in a
small building close, and mounted the roof to have
a view of the village. Then we took a walk
through the place, saw the well, in depth more than
sixty feet, and lined throughout with brick, whence
Nasr always has her water fetched, though it is warm,
and less nice than that of the Nile. Then we returned,
and were about to depart, when Nasr sent us an
invitation to remain the night in Soriba, as it was

too late to get back to Wed Médineh by day. We accepted the offer, and a banquet of boiled dishes was immediately brought, only intended, however, as preparatory to supper. The sultana, however, did not show herself again the whole evening. We remained in the hall, and slept on the same cool pillows, which had served as a divan during the day. But the next morning we were invited by her to visit her in her own rooms. She was more communicative to-day than yesterday, had European chairs brought for us, while her servants and slaves squatted on the ground about us. We told her of her namesake, the Sultana Nasr of England, and showed her her portrait on an English sovereign, which she looked at with curiosity. But she manifested little desire to see that far-off world beyond the northern water with her own eyes.

About eight o'clock we rode back to Wed Médineh. Soon after our return, Saïd Hashim received a letter from Nasr, in which she asked him confidentially whether he thought I would receive a little female slave as a guest-present. I had expressed to her, in return, that this was against the custom of our country, but that the gift would be accepted if she would choose a male slave instead, and after some little hesitation, she really sent a young slave to me, who was brought to me in the ship.

He had been the playmate of the little grandson of Nasr, the son of her daughter Dauer, and was presented to me under the name of Rehân, the Arabic name for the sweet-smelling basil. It was added, that he was from the district of Makâdi, on the Abyssinian frontier, whence the most intelligent and faithful slaves generally came. This district is under Christian dominion, and is inhabited by Christians and Mahommedans, in separate villages. The former call themselves Nazâra (Nazarenes) or Amhâra (Amharic Christians), the latter Giberta. Of these Giberta children are often stolen from their own race and from among their neighbours, and sold to Arabic slave-dealers ; for, in the interior of Abyssinia, the slave trade is strictly prohibited. This account of the lad, however, was soon found to be untrue, and was only invented to preclude the blame of offering me a Christian slave ; while, on the contrary, it would seem much more wrong to deliver me a Mahommedan. The boy first told our Christian cook, and then me, that he was of Christian parentage, had received the name Rehân here, and that his real name was Gabre Mariam, i.e. in Abyssinian, "Slave of Maria." His birth-place is near Gondar, the metropolis of Amhâra. He seems to belong to a distinguished family, for the place Bamba, which is denoted by Bruce in the vicinity of Lake Tzana, according to his story, belonged to his grandfather, and his father, who is now dead, had many flocks, which he himself had often driven to the pasturage. When he was somewhat far off his dwelling with them one day, about three or four years ago, he was stolen by mounted Bedouins, carried to the village of Waldakarel, and, afterwards sold to King Idris Adlân, who had given him to his sister Nasr. He is a handsome, but very dark-coloured boy, about eight or nine years of age, but much more advanced than a child of that age would be with us. The girls marry here

o 2

at the age of eight. He wears his hair in innumerable little plaits, which must be redone and anointed at least once a month, by a woman understanding it; his body, too, is rubbed with fat from time to time. His whole clothing consists of a great white cloth that he fastens round the hips, and throws over his shoulders. I now call him by his Christian name, and shall bring him to Europe with me.

Saïd Hashim tried his utmost to induce us to remain a few more days in Wed Médineh. On the first evening he invited us to his house with a number of the most considerable Turks, and had a number of female dancers to show us the national dances of the country, which consist chiefly in movements of the upper part of the body and the arms, as they are found on the Egyptian monuments, yet differing from the present Egyptian dances, which are made up of very ungraceful and lascivious movements and motions of the hips and legs.

An old good humoured and very comic man led the dances, singing Arabic songs having reference to persons in the room or those known to them, such as Nasr, Idris Adlân, Mak (i. e. Melek) Bâdi, and others, with a piercing but not unpleasant voice, and at the same time struck a five-stringed lyre with his left hand, beating time with the plectrum in his right. His instrument only extended to six tones of the octave. The first string to the right had the highest tone C, struck with the thumb; the next had the deepest E, then came the third with F, the fourth with A, the fifth with B. The instrument is called rabâba, the player rebâbi. This man had been instructed by an old famous rebâbi at Shendi, had made his instrument just like that of his master, also learning all his art of versification, and thus had become the black favourite bard of Wed Médineh. All his songs were composed by himself, sometimes improvised, and whoever offended himself or his patron became the target of a pasquinading song.

I sent for him the next day, and had four of his songs written down by Jussuf, one on Mohammed, son of the Mak Mesâ'd, who lives at Metammeh, one on King Nimr, who burnt Ismael Pasha, and is now living in Egypt, a third on Nasr; and, lastly, a song in praise of pretty girls.* It is impossible to give these melodies in notes. A little only, approaching our kind of music in somewise, have I written down. They are generally half recited, half sung, with wavering tones from the highest notes to the deepest tone long sustained. These are the most peculiar, but are utterly incapable of being expressed. Every verse contains four rhymes, on each of which it is easy to keep the voice, on the second more than on the first and third ; but the longest on the final line, and to this always comes one of the same deep tones, giving the song a kind of dignified progression. A certain recurrence of the melody is first observable, but is not retainable for an European ear. I bought the friendly old man's instrument, which he gave unwillingly, although I allowed him to fix the price himself, and several times a shade of sorrow passed over his expressive

* The poems contain many unusual forms and expressions, and have been composed in very free and, it seems to me, incorrect forms.

countenance when he had taken the money and laid the instrument in its place. Next day I sent for him again. He was cast down, and told me that his wife had beaten him thoroughly for parting with the instrument. It is no shame for a man to be beaten by his wife, but *vice versâ*. A beaten wife goes at once to the Kadi to complain, she generally obtains justice, and the husband is punished.

At Wed Médineh we witnessed a funeral, which seemed odd enough to us. A woman had died three days before; the first day after her decease, then the third, the seventh and later days have particular ceremonies. An hour before sunset above a hundred women and children had assembled before the house, and many more kept continually coming and cowering down beside them. Two daughters of the deceased were there, who had already strewn their highly-ornamented heads, powdered with fat in the Arab manner, with ashes, and rubbed the whole upper part of the body white with them,* so that only the eyes and mouth gleam freshly and as if inlaid from the white mask. The women wore long cloths round their hips, the young girls and children the *rahát*, a girdle of close hanging straps of leather, generally bound about the loins, with a string prettily adorned with shells and pearls, and falling halfway down the thigh. A great wooden bowl of ashes was placed there, and continually replenished. Close to the door, on both sides, crouched female musicians, who partly clapped their

[* Compare Herodotus, Euterpe, c. 85, for the ancient Egyptian mode of mourning, which is, however, not very similar to this.—K. R. H. M.]

hands in time, with yelling, ear-piercing screams, partly beat the noisy *darabúka* (a kind of hand-drum, called here in the Sudan *dalúka*), and partly struck hollow calabashes, swimming in tubs of water, with sticks. The two daughters, from eighteen to twenty years of age, and the nearest relations, began to move slowly towards the door in pairs, by a narrow lane formed in the midst of the ever-increasing mob. Then suddenly they all began to scream, to clap their hands, and to bellow forth unearthly cries, upon which the others turned round and began their horrible dance of violent jerks. With convulsively strained windings and turnings of the upper part of the body, they pushed their feet on, quite slowly and measuredly, threw their bosoms up with a sudden motion, and turned the head back over the shoulders, which they racked in every direction, and thus wound themselves forward with almost closed eyes. In this way they went down a little hill, for fifteen or sixteen paces, when they threw themselves on the ground, buried themselves in dust and ashes, and then returned to begin the same dance anew. The younger of the two daughters had a pretty slender figure, with an incredibly elastic body, and resembled an antique when standing quietly upright or lying on the ground with the head down, with her regular and soft, but immovable features and classical form, quite peaceably even during the dance. This dancing procession went on over and over again. Each of the mourners must at least have gone through it once, and the nearer the relationship the oftener it is repeated. Whoever cannot get up to the ash-tub takes ashes from the head of a neighbour to strew it on their own head. First, in this squatting assembly, some women crouch, who understand how to sob and to shed tears in quantities, which leave long black streaks on their whitened cheeks. The most prominent and disgusting feature of this scene is, however, that unrestrained passion has nothing to do with it, and that everything is done slowly, pathetically, and with evidently practised motions; children down to the ages of four or five years are put into the procession, and if they make the difficult and unnatural movements well, the mothers, cowering behind, call out *taib, taib*, to them. " Bravo, well done !" The second act of this deafening ceremony, by the continual clapping, cries, and screams, is that the whole company of dancers throw themselves upon the ground and roll down the hill ; but even this is done slowly and premeditatedly, while they draw their knees up to keep hold of their dress, poke their arms in also, and then roll away on their backs and knees. This ceremony begins an hour before sunset and continues into the middle of the night.

The whole of it causes, by its unnaturality surpassing everything else, an indescribable impression, which is rendered the more disagreeable, as one perceives throughout the empty play, the inherited and spoilt custom, and can recognize no trace of individual truth and natural feeling in the persons taking part in it. And yet the comparison with certain descriptions and representations of similar ceremonies among the ancients, teaches us to understand many things, of which, in our own life, we shall never form a proper estimate, until we have seen with our own eyes such caricatures of uncivilisation, occasionally shown to us by the Orient. Next day we visited the hospital, which we found very clean, and in good order; it contains one hundred patients, but there are only twenty-eight at the present time. Then we proceeded to the barracks, in the large court of which the exercises are gone through. The commanding officer assembled the band, and had several pieces of music played. The first was the *Parisienne*, which made a strange impression upon me in this region, as also the following pieces, which were mostly French, and known to me; they are tolerably performed. The musicians had scarcely any but European instruments, and have incorporated in their Arabic musical vocabulary our word trumpet, applying it, however, to the drum which they call *trumbéta*, while they have for the trumpet a native name, *nafir*; the great flute they call *sumára*, the little one *sufára*, and the great drum *tabli*. There were only 1,200 men of the regiment (which consists of 4,000) present, almost all negroes, who poked out their black faces, hands, and feet, from their white linen clothes, and red caps like dressed-up monkeys, only looking much more miserable and oppressed than those animals. Yet we did not suspect that in two days, these people would rebel, and go off to their mountains.

Emin Pasha was hourly expected. On the 13th, however, I received a letter from him at Meselemîeh, four or five hours hence, in which he stated that he should first come to Wed Médineh the next day, and hoped to find us still there. At the same time he informed me that the war in Taka was at an end, and that all had submitted. Some hundred natives were killed in the skirmishes; on the morning before the decisive battle, all the Sheikhs of the Taka tribes came to the Pasha to beg for mercy, which was granted them on the condition, that no fugitive should remain in the forest, which had been their chief resort. Next day he had the forest searched, and as there was nobody found, it was set on fire, and burnt down altogether. He is going on his way back through the eastern districts to Katârif, on the Abyssinian frontier, and thence to the Blue River. Scarcely had we read these news from Taka, ere the cannons at the barracks thundered forth the news of victory to the population.

In another letter, which Emin Pasha had received for me, Herr von Wagner gave me the pleasant news that our new comrade, the painter Georgi, had arrived from Italy, and had already left for Dongola, where he would await farther instructions. I shall write him to meet us at Barkal.

As we were certain by the letter to find the Pasha still in Messelemîeh, we departed thither at noon; we went by land, as the city is an hour and a half distant from the Nile.

The bark was meanwhile to follow us to the port of Messelemîeh, *i. e.* to the landing place nearest to this principal trading place of the whole Sudan. Besides Jussuf we took the *khawass* and Gabre Máriam with us, who placed himself behind me on the dromedary, where there is always a little place left for an attendant, like the dickey of a coach; he rides on the narrow back part of the animal, and holds on with his hands. The day was very hot and the ground burnt. The few birds which I saw were different from those inhabiting the banks of the river. At about half way we came to a village called Tâiba, which is only inhabited by *Fukara*, (pl. of *Fakir*). These are the literati, the holy men of the nation, a kind of priests, without exercising sacerdotal functions; they can read and write, allow no music, no dancing, no feasting, and therefore stand iu great odour of sanctity. The Sheikh of this village is the supreme Fakir of the district. Everybody believes in him as a prophet; what he has prophesied, happens. The deceased Ahmed Pasha had him locked up a month before his death; "God will punish thee," he returned in answer to the decree, and a month afterward the Pasha died. This is a very rich man, and owns several villages. We looked him up and found him in his house at dinner ; about twenty persons were seated round a colossal wooden bowl, filled with boiled durra broth and milk. The bowl was pushed before us, but it was impossible for us to partake of this meal. We conversed with the old Fakir, who replied with free, friendly, and obliging dignity, and then asked our names, and our object in travelling. Every person who entered, even our servants, approached him reverently, and touched his hand with the lips and forehead. The office of Sheikh is hereditary in his family; his son, therefore, obtains almost as much honour as himself, and thus it is explicable how, when the Sheikh is a Fakir, the whole place may become a holy village. E'Damer, on the island of Meroe, was formerly such a Fakir place. The inhabitants of Tâiba, probably of Arabic race, call themselves Arakin. There are in this neighbourhood a number of such local names, the origin of which is difficult to be assigned.

When we had smoked out our pipes, we left this assembly of holy men, and rode off. Half an hour from Messelemîeh, we came to a second village called Hellet e' Solimân. We dismounted at a house built by the deceased Mak or Melek Kambal of Halfâi, when he married the daughter of the Defalla, to whom the village belonged; now it is the property of his brother's son Mahmûd Welled Shanîsh, who is also called Melek, but is only guardian of Kambal's little son, Melek Beshîr. Thus we may see how it has fared here with the ancient honourable title of Melek (king). Mahmûd was not at home, as he had accompanied Ahmed Pasha in his campaign. However, we were entertained in his house according to the hospitable custom of the country. Carpets were spread, milk and durra bread (which does not taste ill) in thin cakes brought; besides another simple but refreshing drink, *abreq*, fermented sour durra water. Soon after Asser we arrived in Messelemîeh. Emin received us very kindly, and informed us Mohammed Ali's prime minister, Boghos Bey, whom I had visited in Alexandria, was dead, and Artim Bey, a fine diplomatist of much culture, had been appointed to his place.

We refused the Pasha's invitation to supper and night's lodging, and soon rode off to the river, where

we hoped to find our bark.   As it had not arrived,
we passed the night in the open air upon anqarebs.
The next morning, the 15th of March, we pushed
off for Kamlîn, and arrived there toward evening.
The following day we passed with our countryman,
Herr Bauer. After we had visited Nureddin Effendi
at Wad Eraue, some hours from Kamlîn, we arrived
the next day at Soba, where I immediately sent for
a vessel found in the ruins of the ancient city, and
preserved by the brother of the Sheikh.   After
waiting a long time it was brought.   It proved to
be an incense urn of bronze in open work; the
sides of the rounded vessel, about three-quarters of
a foot in height and breadth, were worked in arabesques; on the upper edge the chains had been
attached to three little hooks, of which one is
broken away, so that the most interesting part of
the whole — an inscription in tolerably large letters
running round the top, and worked *djour*, like
arabesques — is imperfect.   This is of the more
importance, as the writing is again Greek, or rather
Koptic, as on the stone tablet, but the language
neither, but without doubt the ancient language of
Soba, the metropolis of the mighty kingdom of
Aloa.   Notwithstanding its shortness, it is of more
importance than the tablet, that it also contains the
Koptic letters ⳝ (sh) and ϯ (ti), which are not to
be found in the other.   I bought the vessel for a
few piasters.   This is now the third monument of
Soba that we bring with us, for I must add that we
saw at Saïd Hashim's, in Wed Médineh, a little
Venus, of Greek workmanship, about a foot high,
which had also been found in Soba, and was pre-

sented to me by the owner. On the 19th of
March, we at length entered again the house of
M. Hermanowitch at Chartûm, at a later date, however, than our former reckoning had settled, therefore I had already announced our being later in a
letter to Erbkam from Wed Médineh.

LETTER XIX.

CHARTUM.
March 21, 1844.

HERE we first obtained more particulars concerning the military revolt at Wed Médineh, which was of the most serious nature, and we should have incurred great danger had we stopped two days longer in that city. The whole of the black soldiers have rebelled, owing to the stay of Emin Pasha. The drill-master and seven white soldiers were immediately killed, the Pasha besieged in his own house and shot at, his overtures disdained, the powder magazine seized. All the guns and ammunition fell into the hands of the negroes, who then chose six leaders, and went off on the road to Fazoql in six bodies to gain their mountain. The regiment here, in which there are at present about 1,500 blacks, was immediately disarmed, and confined to the barracks. The most serious apprehensions are entertained for the future, as Ahmed Pasha Menekle was so imprudent as to take almost all the white troops with him to Taka. For the rest, I might be glad of the flight of the blacks, as they were frightfully ill used by their Turkish masters. Still the revolt can easily put the country into disorder, and then re-act on our expedition. The blacks will, no doubt, endeavour to draw all their countrymen who meet them to their side, particularly the troops of Soliman Pasha, in Sennâr, and of Selim Pasha, in Fazoql ; the whites are far too few in number to offer any prolonged resistance. The news have just arrived that five or six hundred slaves of the deceased Ahmed Pasha at the indigo factory at Tamaniât, a little to the north of this place, have fled to the Sudan with their wives and children, and intend to join with the soldiers. The same is said to have occurred at the factory at Kamlîn, so that we are in fear for our friend Bauer, who, though not cruel like the Turks, is strict.

March 26. A report is spreading that the troops at Sennâr, and the people of Melek Idris Adlân, had overcome the negroes. The Tamaniât slaves are also said to have been pursued by the Arnauts, and killed or dragged back, while the rebellion in Kamlîn has been suppressed. Little confidence can yet be placed in these reports, as the news came to me by our *khawass* from the people of the Pasha, and a wish was particularly expressed to me, that I should spread it further, and write it in my letters to Cairo.

As we were yesterday evening walking in the large and beautiful garden of Ibrahim Chêr, in whose airy well situated house, I write this letter, we saw lofty dark sand clouds rising up like a wall on the horizon. And in the night a violent east wind has arisen and is still blowing, and folds all the trees and buildings in a disagreeable atmosphere of sand, which almost impedes respiration. I have fastened the windows and stopped the door with stones, to somewhat shelter from the first break of the storm ; nevertheless, I am obliged to keep

wiping away the covering of sand which continually
settles on the paper.

I have come back so torn and tattered from my
Sennâr hunting parties, that I have been obliged at
length to determine on adopting the Turkish costume, which I shall not be able to change very
soon. It has its advantages for the customs of this
country, particularly in sitting on carpets or low
cushions; but the flat *tarboosh* is immensely unprac-
tical under these sunny skies, and the innumerable
buttons and hooks are a daily and very troublesome
trial of patience.

March 30. We are about to leave Chartûm, as
soon as this post of the Pasha is transmitted. The
revolution is now definitely suppressed everywhere.
It would, no doubt, have had a far worse ending, if
it had not broken out some days too early in Wed
Médineh. It had already been long planned and
consulted on in secret, and was to have commenced
simultaneously in Sennâr, Wed Médineh, Kamlîn,
Chartûm, and Tamaniât, on the 19th of this
month. The precipitation at Wed Médineh, had,
however, brought the whole conspiracy into confusion, and had given Emin Pasha time to send
a courier to Chartûm, by which the imprisonment
and disarming of the negro soldiers here, was
possible, ere the news of the insurrection had come
to them. Emin Pasha, however, seems to have
been quite incapable. The victory is to be ascribed
to the courage and presence of mind of a certain
Rustan Effendi, who pursued the six hundred
negroes with one hundred and fifty determined
soldiers, mostly white, reached them near Sennâr,

P

and beat them down, after three attacks and heavy loss. More than a hundred of the fugitives surrendered, and have been led off in chains to Sennâr; the rest were killed in the fight or drowned in the river.

But at the same time the news has arrived, that an insurrection has broken out in Lower Nubia, at Kalabshe, and another village, on account of the imposts; and that therefore, both villages have been immediately razed by Hassan Pasha, who is coming to Chartûm in the place of Emin Pasha, and the inhabitants killed or hunted away.

LETTER XX.

PYRAMIDS OF MEROË.
April 22, 1844.

WE left Chartûm on the 30th of March, toward evening, and sailed half the night by moonshine.

On the next day we reached Tamaniât. Almost the whole village had disappeared, and only a single wide stretching ruin was to be seen. The slaves had laid everything in ashes on their revolt; only the walls of the factory are yet standing. As I had left the bark on foot, I was quite unprepared to come in the neighbourhood of the still smoking ruins, upon a frightful scene, in an open meadow quite covered with black mangled corpses. The greater part of the slaves, who had been recaptured, had here been shot in masses.

With sundown, we stopped near Surie Abu Ramle, at a cataract, which we could pass by night.

On the first of April we went off long before dawn, and expected to get on a good distance. With the day broke, however, a heavy storm of wind, and as the ship could not be drawn near on account of the rocky shore, we were obliged to stop after a few hours, and lie still in the annoying thick sand air. Before us lay the single mountain chain of Qirre, whence, like sentinels, rose the Ashtân (the Thirsty) to the left, the Rauiân (the Satisfied) to the right, from the plain, the former being, however, more distant from the river.

The Rauian only lay about three quarters of an hour away from our bark ; I went out with my gun, crossed the unfertile stony plain, and climbed the mountain, which is almost surrounded with water during the inundation, so that we were always told that the mount was on an island. The rock texture is a mixture of coarse and fine granite, with much quartz. On the way back we came by the village of Meláh, the huts of which lie concealed behind great mounds, formed by the excavations of the inhabitants for salt (*malh*), of which much is found in the neighbourhood. (Meláh is, therefore, the Arabic translation of Halle or Sulza.) Towards evening went farther into the mountains, and moored in a little creek. The succeeding day we also got on slowly. On the tops of the crags to the eastward, we perceived some black slaves, straying about like goats, who had probably escaped from Tamaniât, and will not long preserve their poor lives. They disappeared immediately on our *kha-wass* making the rude jest of firing into the air in their direction. I and Abeken climbed the western hills, which rose steeply from the shore to the height of two or three hundred feet. It is plainly to be seen on the rocks how high the river rises at high water, and deposits its earth. I measured thence to the present water-mirror, about eight *mètres*, and the river will yet sink a couple of feet.

From the mountain top we could see behind the last heights the wide desert which we should soon have to traverse towards Méraui. Reluctantly we quitted the picturesque mountains which had interrupted the generally even aspect of the country in so pleasant a manner.

On the morning of the 4th of April we at last reached our palm group at Ben Naga, and proceeded at once to the ruins in Wadi el Kirbegân, where we found part of a pillar and several altars in the south-western temple, newly excavated by Erbkam, upon which the same royal cartouches appeared as on those principal temples of Naga, in the wilderness. Of the three altars the middle one, hewn in very hard sandstone, was excellently preserved. On the west side the King, on the east side the Queen, were represented, with their names; on the two other sides two goddesses. There was also, on the north side, the hieroglyphic of the north engraven; and on the south side, that of the south. The two other altars showed the same representations. All three were seen in their places, and let into a smooth pavement, formed of square slabs of stone, with plaster poured over them. The means were unfortunately wanting at present for the transportation of the best of these altars, which weighed at least fifty hundred weight; I was, therefore, obliged to leave it for a particular expedition from Meroë.

On Good Friday, the 5th of April, we arrived at Shendi. We went into the spacious but very depopulated city; saw the ruins of the residence of King Nimr, in which, after a banquet he had prepared for Ismael Pasha, he had burnt him. Many houses yet bear the traces of the shots of Defterdar Bey, whom Mohammed Ali sent to avenge the death of his son. In the middle of the city stood on an artificial height the private dwelling of King Nimr, now also in ruins. Somewhat up the river, distinct from the town, lies the suburb built expressly for the military garrison. We then returned to the bark, which had moored close by the fortress-like house of Churshid Pasha, where the Commandant now resides.

The same day we reached Beg'erauîe, shortly before sundown, and immediately rode to the pyramids, where we found Erbkam and the rest all well. At Naga and Wadi Sofra they were very industrious, and the rich costume of the Kings and Gods, and the generally styleless, but ornamented representations of this Ethiopian temple look very well in the drawing, and will form a shining part of our picture-book. Here, too, much had been done, and on the cleaning out of the earth-filled ante-chambers several new things were discovered. Abeken thought he had discovered the name of Queen Kentaki (Kandake) on our first visit. It now appears that the cartouche is not written

but

which would be read Kentahebi;* it seems to me,

[* The first Cartouche is as follows :—K (the bowl with a handle, Alphabetic No. 1, (Bunsen, vol. i. p. 561); N (the water,) Alphabetic No. 1, (p. 564); TA (bag and reed), Alphabetic No. 5, (p. 568); K=KNTAK. The reeds, Alphabetic No. 3, p. 556,) occurs in the "Todtenbuch" (xxii. 63, 3,) as the sign for a noble, (Bunsen, p. 454), the heaven (p. 555) is

however, that the famous name is nevertheless meant, and the questionable sign has been interchanged by the ignorant scribes. The determinative signs ◠ ◐ prove, in any case, that it is the name of a queen. Kandake was already known as a private name. The name Ergamenes is also found, and this, too, now properly written, sometimes with a misunderstood variant.

On the following holidays, we lighted our Easter fire in the evening. Our tents lie between two groups of pyramids in a little valley, which is everywhere overgrown with dry tufts of woody grass. These were set on fire, flamed up, and threw the whirling flames up into the dark star night. It was a pretty sight to see fifty or sixty such fires burning at once, and throwing a ghostly light on the surrounding ruined pyramids of the ancient kings, and on our airy tent-pyramids rising in the foreground.

On the eighth of April, we were surprised by a stately cavalcade on horses and camels, which entered our camp. It was Osman Bey, who is now leading the army of 5,000 men back from Taka. In his company were the French military physician Peney, and the High Sheikh Ahmed Welled'Auad. The troops had encamped near Gabushîe, at an hour's distance up the river, and would pass through Begerauîe in the evening. The visit to our camp

the mark of the feminine gender, and the egg (Determinative No. 85, p. 545,) rank ;=a Queen. The second Cartouche is the same, with the exception of the variant :—the sign of festivals (Determinative No. 110 p. 547,) HBI=KNTAHBI. —K. R. H. M.]

had, however, another end ; which came to light in
the course of conversation. Osman Bey was
desirous of making his pioneers into treasure finders,
and sent some companies hither to tear down the
pyramids. The discovery of Ferlini is in everybody's head still, and had brought many a pyramid
to ruin. In Chartûm everybody was full of it; and
more than one European, and the Pasha also,
thought still to find treasures there. I endeavoured
to convince them all anew that the discovery of Ferlini was the result of pure chance, that he did not
find the gold rings in the tombs, the only place
where such a search could be made with any reason,
but in the rock, where they had been placed by the
caprice of the owner. I tried to convince Osman
Bey by the same arguments, who offered me his men
for the purpose of commencing operations under
my superintendence. Of course I refused, but
should perhaps have taken advantage of the opportunity to open the tomb-chambers, the entrance of
which would be *before* the pyramids in the natural
rock, had I not been afraid that I should arrive at
no particularly shining result, and only disappoint
the expectations of the credulous general, though
not our own. I succeeded in diverting him from
the idea ; and for the present at least, the yet existing pyramids are saved. The soldiers have left us
without making war against the pyramids.

I invited the three gentlemen to dinner with us,
at which the old Sheikh got into a mess, as he
always wanted to cut the meat with the back of
his knife, until I myself laid aside the European
instrument, and began to eat in good old Turkish

style, when all soon followed me willingly, particularly my brave dark-skinned guest, who well saw my civility. After dinner, they mounted their stately horses again, and hurried to the river.

On the 9th of April, I sent Franke and Ibrahim Aga to Ben Naga, with stone-saws, hammers, and ropes, to bring the great altar hither. I myself rode with Jussuf to Gabushié, partly to return the visit of Osman Bey—whose intention had been to give a day of rest in our neighbourhood—partly to take advantage of the presence of the respected Sheikh Ahmed, through whom I hoped to obtain barks for the transportation of our things across the river, and camels for our desert journey. The army had, however, already proceeded, and had passed the next places. I therefore rode sharply on with Jussuf, and soon came up with the 400 Arnauts, forming the rear guard. They could not, however, inform us how far Osman Bey was in advance. The Arnauts are the most feared of all the military; as the rudest and most cruel of all, who are at the same time the best used by their leaders, as they are the only volunteers and foreign mercenaries. Some months ago, they were sent by Mahommed Ali, under a peculiarly dreaded officer, to the deceased Ahmed Pasha, with the command, as it was worded, to bring the Pasha alive or dead to Cairo. His sudden death, however, naturally put a period to their errand. That officer is named Omar Aga, but is well-known throughout the country under the less flattering *sobriquet* of Tomas Aga *(commandant cochon)*, once bestowed on him by Ibrahim Pasha, and which he has since considered it an honour to bear! His own servants so called him, when we came up with his horses and baggage, and asked for their owner.

After a sharp ride of five or six hours, under a most oppressive sun, we at length reached the camp near the village of Bêida.

We had gradually gone more than half-way to Shendi, and were rejoiced to find a prospect of refreshment after the hot exhausting ride, as we prepared ourselves to remain fasting until our return in the evening, for there was nothing to be got in the intermediate villages, not even milk.

Osman Bey and Hakîm Peney were as astonished as delighted at my visit; there were immediately handed round some goblets of Suri, a drink of difficult and slow preparation from half-fermented durra, having a pleasant acid taste, and a particularly refreshing restoring flavour with sugar. After breakfast I went through the camp with Peney, the tents of which were pitched in the most various and picturesque manner on a great place, partly overgrown and wholly surrounded with trees and bushes. An Egyptian army, half black, half white, torn and tattered, returning from a thieving incursion against the poor natives, is rather a different sight to anything that comes under our notice at home. Although the terrified inhabitants of Taka, mostly innocent of the partial revolt, had already sent ambassadors to the Pasha, in order to obviate his vengeance, and did not make the slightest resistance on the nearer approach of the troops, yet several hundred defenceless men and women who would not, or could not fly, were murdered by that notorious crew of ruffians, the Arnauts; an additional number of persons, supposed to have been concerned in the rebellion, Ahmed Pasha had beheaded in front of his tent, as they were brought in. After all the conditions had been fulfilled, after the heaviest mulcts demanded of them, under every possible name, had been punctually paid, the Pasha had all the Sheikhs assembled as if for a new trial, and together with 120 more, led away in chains as prisoners. The young powerful men were condemned to the army, the women were given up to the soldiers as slaves. The Sheikhs had yet to await their punishment.

This was the glorious history of the Turkish campaign against Taka, as it was related to me by European witnesses. Twelve of the forty-one Sheikhs, who seemed as if they would not survive the fatigue of the forced march, have already been shot. The rest were shown to me. Each wore before him a club or bludgeon five or six feet in length, which ended in a fork, into which his neck was fastened. The ends of the fork were connected by a cross piece fastened by thongs. Some of them, too, had their hands tied to the handle of the fork. In this condition they continue day and night. During the march, the soldier under whose care the prisoner is placed, carries the club, and at night the greater part of them have their feet bound together. Their raven tresses were all cut off, and only the Sheikhs still retained their great plaited headdress. Most of them looked very depressed and pitiful; they had been the most respected of their tribe, and accustomed to the greatest reverence from their inferiors. Almost all of them spoke Arabic

besides their own language, and told me the tribes
to which they belonged. The most respected, however, of them all, was a Fakir, of holy repute, whose
word was considered that of a prophet throughout
the whole country. He had, by his words and
demands, brought on the whole revolution. He
was called Sheikh Musa el Fakir, and was of the
race of Mitkenâb, and his personal appearance was
that of an aged, blind, broken elder, with a few
snow-white hairs ; his body is now more like a
skeleton, he had to be raised up by others, and was
scarcely able to comprehend and answer the questions addressed to him. His little shrivelled countenance could not, under any circumstances, assume
a new expression. He stared before him fixed and
carelessly, and I wondered how such a Shemem
could have so much power over his countrymen as
to cause the revolution. But it is to be remarked,
that here, as in Egypt, all blind people stand in
peculiar odour of sanctity, and in great repute as
prophets.

After breakfast I had one of the Sheikhs, Mohammed Welled Hammed, brought into Osman's
tent, in order to ask him about his language, of
which I knew nothing. He was a sensible eloquent
man, who also employed the opportunity, which I
readily granted him, to tell his history to Osman
Bey and Sheikh Ahmed, and to declare his innocence with respect to the revolutionary movements.
He was of the tribe of Halenka, of the village
Kassala. I had the list of the forty-one Sheikhs
and their tribes given me and copied. Six tribes had
taken part in the revolt, the Mitkenâb, Halenka,

Kelûli Mohammedîn, Sobeh, Sikulâb, and Haden-duwa (plural of Henduwa).

All the tribes of Taka speak the same language, but only some also understand the Arabic. I presume that it is the same as that of the Bishari races. It has many words well put together, and is very euphonious, as the hard gutterals of the Arabic are wanting. On the other hand, however, it has a peculiar letter, which seems to stand between r, l, and d, according to its sound, a cerebral d, which, like that of the Sanskrit, is pronounced with the tongue thrown upwardly back.

The examination of the Sheikh had lasted too long to allow of a return; night would have surprised me, when it would have been impossible, especially on camel-back, to avoid the dangerous branches of the prickly trees. I therefore was content to accept the invitation to remain in the camp until moonrise; then Osman Bey was going to start in the other direction with his army. A whole sheep was roasted on the spit, which we heartily enjoyed.

From Osman Bey, who has lived sixteen years in the south, and is intimately acquainted with the land to the outermost limits of the government of Mohammed Ali, I learnt many interesting particulars of the southern provinces. In Fazoql the custom of hanging up a king who is no longer liked, is still continued, and was done upon the person of the father of a king now reigning. His relations and ministers assembled about him, and informed him that as he did not please the men and women of the country, nor the oxen, asses, hens, &c. &c. any longer, but every one hated him, it would be better for him to die. When a king once would not submit to this treatment, his own wife and mother came to him, and made him the most urgent representations, not to load himself with more ignominy, on which he met his fate. Diodorus tells just the same story of those in Ethiopia who were to die by the condemnation of the judge, and a condemned person, who intended first to save himself by flight, yet allowed himself to be strangled by his mother, who frustrated his escape, without opposition. Osman Bey first put an end to the custom in the same province, of burying old people alive, who had grown weak. A pit was dug, and at the bottom of it a horizontal passage; the body was laid in it, tightly wrapped in cloths, like that of a dead person; beside him a saucer, with merissa, fermented durra water, a pipe, and a hoe for the cultivation of land; also one or two ounces of gold, according to the riches of the person, intended for the payment of the boatman who rows him over the great river, which flows between heaven and hell. Then the entrance is filled up. Indeed, according to Osman, the whole legend of Charon, even with a Cerberus, exists there.

This usage of burying old people alive is also found, as I have subsequently heard, among the negro races of south Kordofan. There sick people, and particularly those with an infectious disease, are put to death in the same manner. The family complains to the invalid, that on account of him no one will come to them; that after all, he is miserable, and death only a gain for him; in the other world he would find his relations, and would be well and happy. Every one gives him greetings to the dead, and then they bury him as in Fazoql, or standing upright in a shaft. Besides merissa, bread, hoe and pipe, he there also receives a sword and a pair of sandals; for the dead lead a similar life beyond the grave, only with greater pleasures.

The departed are interred amidst loud lamentations, in which their deeds and good qualities are celebrated. Nothing is known there of a river and boatman of the under world, but the old Mohammedan legend is there current, of the invisible angel Asrael, or as he is here called, Osraîn. He, it is said, is commissioned by God to receive the souls of the dead, and lead the good to the place of reward, the bad to the place of punishment. He lives in a tree, el ségerat mohana (the tree of fulfilling), which has as many leaves as there are inhabitants in the world. On each leaf is a name, and when a child is born a new one grows. If any one become ill, his leaf fades, and should he be destined to die, Osraîn breaks it off.* Formerly he used to come visibly to those whom he was going to carry away, and thus put them in great terror. Since the Prophet's time, however, he has been invisible; for when he came to fetch Mohammed's soul, he told him that it was not good that by his visible appearance he

---

[* A superstition exists among the Moravian Jews to this effect. At new moon a branch is held in its light, and the name of any person pronounced. His face will appear between the horns of the moon, and should he be destined to die, the leaves will fade. This is mentioned, as well as I can remember, in Beaumont's Demonology.—K. R. H. M.],

should frighten mankind. They might then easily die of terror, before praying; for he himself, although a courageous and spirited man, was somewhat perturbed at his appearance. Therefore the Prophet begged God to make Osraîn invisible, which prayer was granted.

Of other tribes in Fazoql, Osman Bey told me, that with them the king should hold a court of justice every day under a certain tree. If he be absent three days by illness or any other reason that makes him unfit to attend to it, he is hanged: two razors are put in the noose, which cut his throat on the rope being tightened.

The meaning of another of their customs is obscure. At a certain time of the year they have a kind of carnival, at which every one does as he likes. Four ministers then carry the king from his house to an open place on an anqareb, to one leg of which a dog is tied. The whole population assemble from every quarter. Then they throw spears and stones at the dog till it dies, after which, the king is carried back to his house.

Over these and other stories and particulars regarding those races, which were also certified by the old High Sheikh Ahmed, we finished the roasted sheep in the open air, before the tent. Night had long commenced, and the camp fires near and far, with the people busy around them, sitting still or walking to and fro among the trees, was immensely picturesque and peculiar. Gradually they went out, all except the watch fires; the poor prisoners were bound more tightly, and it grew quieter in the camp.

Osman Bey is a powerful, merry, and natural man, also a strict and esteemed officer. He promised me a specimen of the discipline and good order among his soldiers,—whose outward appearance would not inspire any very favourable prejudice,— in having the reveillé beaten at an unprepared time. I slept with a military cloak about me on an anqareb in the open tent. About three o'clock I awoke, through a slight noise; Osman, who lay beside me on the ground, rose and gave the order to beat the reveillé to the nearest drummer of the principal guard. He struck some broken and quickly silent notes on his drum. These were immediately repeated at the post of the next regiment, then at the third, fourth, fifth, and succeeding encamptments; and suddenly the whole mass of 5,000 men were under arms. A soft whispering and hissing of the soldiers waking each other, and the slight crackling sound caused by the muskets, was all that could be heard. I went through the camp with Dr. Peney, who came out of the neighbouring tent, and we found there the whole army in rank and file under arms, the officers going up and down in front. When we returned and told Osman Bey of the surprising punctuality in carrying out his commands, he allowed the soldiers to disperse again, and first gave the signal for departure at four o'clock. This had a very different effect. Everything was in activity and motion; the camels let their horrid voices and pitiful bleatings be heard during the loading, the tents were taken down, and in less than half an hour the army marched off to the sound of fife and drum to the south.

I took my way in the contrary direction. The early morning and bright moonlight was very refreshing; the birds woke up with the grey dawn; a fresh wind arose, and we trotted lustily along through the alleys of prickly sont-trees. Soon after sunrise we met a stately procession of well-dressed men and servants with camels and donkeys. It was King Mahmûd Welled Shauish, whose father, the warlike Shauish, King of Shaiqie, is known from the history of the conquering campaigns of Ismael Pasha, to whom he succumbed at a late period, and at whose house at Hellet e' Solimân, near Messelemieh, we had stayed some weeks before. He had gone with Ahmed Pasha Menekle to Taka, and followed the army to Halfaï, where he now resides. At half-past nine, we again came to the pyramids, after my camel, yet young and very difficult to manage, had galloped round in a circle with me, and finally stumbling over a high mound of grass, fell down on one knee, and sent me far away over his head, fortunately without doing me any damage.

After my return I employed myself continually on the pyramids and their inscriptions, had several chambers excavated, and drew out a careful description of each pyramid. Altogether I had found nearly thirty different names of Ethiopian kings and queens. I have not as yet brought them into any chronological order, but have in the comparison of the inscriptions learned much on the kind of succession and the form of government. The King of Meroë * (which is written Meru or

[* Compare Colonel Rawlinson's Outline of Assyrian History, p. 23, where Sennacherib's invasion of Meroe is mentioned.— K. R. H. M.]

Merua in one of the southernmost pyramids) was at
the same time High Priest of Ammon: if his wife
outlived him she followed him in the government,
and the male heir of the crown only occupied a
second place by her; under other circumstances, it
seems, the son succeeded to the crown, having
already, during his father's lifetime, borne the royal
cartouche and title, and held the post of second
priest of Ammon. Thus we see here the priest
government of which Diodorus and Strabo speak,
and the precedence of the worship of Ammon already
mentioned by Herodotus.

The inscriptions on the pyramids show that at the
time of their erection the hieroglyphic system of
writing was no longer perfectly understood, and
that the hieroglyphical signs were often put there
for ornament, without any intended meaning. Even
the royal names are rendered doubtful by this, and
this prevented my recognizing for a long time the
pyramids of the three royal personages who had
built the principal temples in Naga, Ben Naga and
in Wadi Teméd, and belonged, no doubt, to the
most shining period of the Meroitic Empire. I am
now sure, that the pyramid, with antechamber
arched in the Roman style, in the wall of which
Ferlini found the treasure concealed, notwithstanding the slight change in the name, belonged to the
same mighty and warlike queen who appears in Naga
with her rich dress and her nails almost an inch
long. Ferlini's jewellery, by the circumstance that
they belonged to a known, and, it seems to me, the
greatest of all Meroitic queens, who built almost all
the preserved temples of the island, acquired a far

greater importance for the history of the Ethiopian art in which they now take a certain position. The purchase of that remarkable treasure is a considerable gain for our Museum. At that time an Ethiopian demotic character, resembling the Egyptian demotic in its letters, although with a very limited alphabet of twenty-five to thirty signs, was more generally employed and understood than the hieroglyphics. The writing is read from right to left as there, but always with a distinct division of the words by two strong points. I have already found twenty-six such demotic inscriptions, some on steles and libatory slabs, some in the antechambers of the pyramids over the figures in the processions (which are generally proceeding towards the deceased king with palm-branches), some outside on the smooth surfaces of the pyramids, and always plainly of the same date as the representations, and not added at a subsequent period. The decipherment of this writing will perhaps not be difficult on a narrower examination, and would then give us the first certain sounds of the Ethiopian language spoken here at that time, and decide its relation to the Egyptian; while the almost perfect identity of the Ethiopian and Egyptian hieroglyphics would till now give decidedly no sanction to any conclusion as to a similar identity between the two languages. On the contrary, it seems. and may be safely asserted for the later Meroitic period, that the Egyptian hieroglyphics were taken from Egypt as the sacred monumental writing, without change, but also without a full comprehension of their signification. The few continually recurring signs prove that the Ethiopian-demotic writing is purely alphabetic, which must very much lighten the labour of decipherment. The partition of the words is perhaps taken from the Roman writing. The analogy with the development of writing in Egypt, however, proceeded still farther; for next to this Ethiopian-demotic there occurs at a later period, an Ethiopian-Greek, which may be fairly compared with the Koptic, and indeed has borrowed several letters from it. It is found in the inscriptions of Soba and in some others on the walls of the temple ruins of Wadi e' Sofra. We have now therefore, as in Egypt, two doubtless successive systems of writing, which contain the actual Ethiopian popular dialect. It is customary now to call the old Abyssinian-Geez language the Ethiopic, which has no right to this denomination in an ethnographical point of view, as a Semetic language brought from Arabia, but only as a local term. A Geez inscription, which I have found in the chamber of a pyramid, has evidently been added at a later period.

I hope that by the study of the native inscriptions, and the yet living languages, some important results may be obtained. The name Ethiopian with the ancients comprehended much of very various import. The ancient population of the whole Nile valley to Chartûm, and perhaps along the Blue River, as also the tribes in the desert east of the Nile, and the Abyssinians, then probably were more broadly distinguished from the negroes than at present, and belonged to the Caucasian race; the Ethiopians of Meroë (according to Herodotus, the mother state of all the Ethiopians) were reddish-brown people, like

the Egyptians, only darker, as at the present day.
This is also proved by the monuments, on which I
have more than once found the red skin of the
kings and queens preserved.* In Egypt the women
were always painted yellow, particularly during the
Old Empire, before the Ethiopian mixture, at the
time of the Hyksos; and the Egyptian women of
the present day, who have grown pale in the harems,
incline to the same colour.† After the eighteenth
dynasty, however, red women appear, and so it is
certain the Ethiopian women were always represented. It seems that the so-called Barâbra nation
has much Ethiopian blood mixed with it, and perhaps this may be more fully shown at some time by
their language.‡ It is no doubt the ancient Nubian,
and has continued under that name in somewhat
distant south-westerly regions ; for the languages of
the Nubians in and about Kordofan are, to some
extent, evidently related to the Berber language.
That this last, which is now only spoken from

[* See Pickering's Races of Man, p. 214, on the Ethiopian
Race, and pp. 368 sqq., for further remarks on Egypt. This
excellent work is well worthy the serious attention of the
ethnologist in every way.—K. R. H. M.]

[† I may here mention that an excellent term for the red-
skinned race has been invented, though I forget by whom,
though the person was an American archeologist, viz. cinnamon-
coloured, applicable enough both to the red Mexican and the red
Egyptian. In the picture chronicles of Mexican social life and
history we also find that the women are also painted yellow, a
coincidence perhaps worthy of notice.—K. R. H. M.]

[‡ Pickering states that he first met with a mixed race of
Barâbra at Kenneh, thirty miles below the site of ancient
Thebes, but he considers the boundary of the races to be at
Silsilis. P. 212.—K. R. H. M.]

Assuan to Dar Shaiqîeh, south of Dongola, in the
Nile valley, ruled for a time in the province of
Berber, and still higher up, I have found enough
proof in the names of the localities.

Next to the ruins of Meroë are situated, along
the river, from south to north, the villages of Marûga, Danqêleh and e' Sûr, which are comprehended
in the name Begerauîeh, so that one almost always
only hears the last name. Five minutes to the north
of e' Sûr, lies the village of Qala, and ten minutes
farther, el Guês, which are both included in the
name Ghabîne. An hour down the stream are two
villages, called Marûga, already deserted before the
conquest of the country, but a little distant from
each other, and still more northward, near the Oma-
râb mountains, running to the river from the east, is
a third village, called Gebel (Mount village), only
inhabited by Fukara. Cailliaud was only acquainted
with the southernmost of the three Marûgas, lying
by the great temple ruins. The name attracted his
attention by its similarity to Meroë. The similarity
is still greater when one knows that the actual
name is Maru, as—*ga* is only the general noun termination, which is added or omitted according to
the grammar, and does not belong to the root. In
the dialect of Kenus and Dongola this ending is—
gi ; in the dialect of Mahass and Sukkôt—*ga.* When
I went through the different names of the upper
countries with one of our Berber servants, I learned
that *maro,* or *marôgi,* in the one dialect, *maru,* or
marûga, in the other, signifies " ruined mound,
ruined temple;" thus are the ruins of ancient
Syene, or those of the island Philæ, called Ma-

rôgi. Quite different from it is another Berber word, Mérua, which is also pronounced Méraui, by which all white rocks, white stones, are distinguished; for instance, a rock near Assuan, on the east side of the Nile, by the village of el Gezîret. By this it is clear that the name Marûga has nothing to do with the name Meroë, as it is not usual to call a city " Ruin-town," immediately on its foundation. On the other hand, the name Merua, Méraui (in English " white rock"), would be a very good name for a city, if the position of the place were favourable, as it is at Mount Barkal, although not here.

LETTER XXI.

KELI, OPPOSITE MEROE.

April 29, 1844.

FRANKE did not return from his expedition at Ben Naga until the 23rd. He brought the altar hither in sixteen blocks, on a bark. The stones which we shall have to take hence, a wearisome journey of six or seven days through the wilderness, are a load for about twenty camels, so that our train will be considerably greater than before. Unfortunately, we have been unable to bring away anything from Naga, in the desert, on account of the difficulty of transportation, except the already mentioned Roman inscription, and another large peculiarly carved work. There are on it some particularly curious representations ; among others, a sitting figure in front, a nimbus round the hair, the left arm raised in a right angle, and the first and middle fingers of the hand pointing upward, as the old Byzantine figures of Christ are represented. The right hand holds a long staff resting on the ground, like that of John the Baptist. This figure is wholly strange to the Egyptian representation, and is doubtlessly derived from another source, as also another often-represented deity, also represented in full front, with a richly curling beard, which one would be inclined to compare with a Jupiter or Serapis in posture and appearance. The mixture of religions at that evidently late era had

obtained exceedingly, and I should not be astonished if later researches were to show that the
Ethiopian kings included Christ and Jupiter among
their widely different classes of gods. The god with
the three or four lions' heads is probably not of
ancient origin, but taken from somewhere else.

On the 24th, we crossed the Nile in our bark, in
order to take our way to Gebel Barkal by the
desert. Camels again seemed to be difficult to
procure, but the threat that I should not call the
Sheíkh, but the government to account, by virtue of
my firman, if he would not manage to obtain the
necessary animals, worked so fast, that we could
already depart to the desert from Gôs Burri with
eighty camels.

Here, at Keli, I had again opportunity to witness
a funeral, this time for a deceased Fellah, at which
nearly two hundred people were assembled, the men
parted from the women. The men sat down opposite each other in pairs, embraced each other, laid
their heads on their shoulders, raised them again,
beat themselves, clapped their hands, and cried as
much as they could. The women lamented, sang
songs of misery, strewed themselves with ashes,
went about in procession, and threw themselves on
the ground, in a similar way to Wed Médineh, only
their dance resembled rather the violent motions of
the derwishes. The rest of the inhabitants of Keli
sat around in groups, under the shadow of the trees,
their heads down, sighing and complaining.

While we were obliged to wait for the camels, I
crossed to Begerauîeh again, to seek some ruins,
said to lie more to the north. From El Guês, I got

to the two villages of Marûga, lying not very far
from one another, in three-quarters of an hour.
A great number of grave mounds lie to the east of
the first of these, on the low heights, looking like a
group of pyramids in the distance. The elevation
runs along in a crescent-like form, and is covered
with these round hillocks of black desert-stones,
which were fifty-six in number, on my counting them
from a large one in the centre.

Five minutes farther into the desert is a second
group of similar hillocks, twenty-one in number;
but many others are scattered around on small
single plateaux. Still lower down and nearly by
the bushes, I found to the south of both groups,
another, consisting of forty graves, of which some
still clearly showed their original four-cornered
shape. The best grave had fifteen to eighteen feet
on each side; it had been, like several others, dug
up in the middle, and had filled itself with pluvial
earth, in which a tree was growing; at another
there was still a great four-cornered circumvallation
of twenty-four paces to be seen; the undermost
foundations were built of little black stones; and a
tumulus seems to have been erected inside the en-
closure, though not in the middle. Another well-
preserved stronger circumvallation had a little less
extent, but seemed to have been quite filled up
by a pyramid. Of an actual casing there was
nothing to be seen anywhere. The hillocks went
farther south into the bushes, and altogether they
might be estimated at two hundred in number.
Perhaps they continued to stretch along toward
Meroë, at the edge of the desert, whither I should

have ridden, had I not sent the boat, which I had now to find in a hurry, too far down the river. It seems from this that here was the actual burial place of Meroë, and that pyramidal, or when flat sides were wanted, tumular hillocks of stone were the usual form of the graves of private persons also at that period.

LETTER XXII.

THE desert of Gilif, which we traversed on our way hither, in order to cut off the great eastern bend of the Nile, takes its name from the principal mountain lying in the midst of it. On the maps it is confused with the desert of Bahiûda, joining it on the south-east, and through which lies the road from Chartûm to Ambukôl and Barkal. Our direction was at first due east to a well, then north-west through the Gilif mountains to the great Wadi Abû Dôm, which then conducted us in the same direction to the westerly bend of the Nile.

The general character of the country here is not that of a desert, like that between Korusko and Abu Hammed, but rather of a sandy steppe. It is almost everywhere overgrown with gesh (reed bushes), and not unusually with low trees, mostly sont-trees. The rains, which fall here at certain seasons of the year, have washed down considerable masses of earth into the levels, that might well be cultivated, and are occasionally broken by rain-streams three to four feet deep. The earth is yellow, and formed of a clayey sand. The species of rock in the soil and all the mountains, with the exception of the high Gilif chain, is sandstone. The ground is much covered with hard black blocks of the same, the road uneven and undulating.

Numerous gazelles and great white antelopes, with only one brown stripe down the spine, find a rich subsistence in these plains, which are also visited in the rainy season by herds of camels and goats.

We departed from the river on the 29th of April; yet this was only a trial of strength, as is very customary with greater caravans, like that of birds of passage, before their great migration. After two hours' journey up to Gôs Burri, lying off from the river, the guide again permitted the uneasy swarm to settle; the camel-drivers lacked provisions, a few more animals were obtained, some changed. Thus we were not in order and full readiness until the following noon. We stayed the night at Wadi Abu Hommed, where we had Gebel Omarda on the right.

The third day we left early, passed Gebel Qermâna, and came to the well Abu Ilêh, which turned our road far to the east, and detained us several hours beyond noon. Hence we crossed a broad plain in seven hours, and encamped about ten o'clock at night near Gebel Sergên. On the 2nd of May we arrived, after four hours, at a woody district to the right of Gebel Nusf, the "Mountain of the half," situated half-way between the wells of Abu Tlêh and Gaqedûl, which, in the desert, always form the hour of the desert clock.

The Arabs from the district of Gôs Burri, who guide us, are of the 'Auadîeh race; they are far more considerable than the Ababde, have a hasty indistinct utterance, and seem altogether to have little capacity. They have commingled much with the Fellahîn of the country, who here call them-

selves Qaleâb, Homerâb, and Gaalin. Shaiqîeh
Arabs also exist here, probably since the Egyptian
conquest; they have shields and spears like the
Ababde. The rich sheikh Emîn, of Gôs Burri, had
given us his brother, the Fakîr Fadl Allah, as a
guide, and his own son, Fadl Allah, as overseer of
the camels; but even the nobles of the people here
make a poor and evanescent impression in comparison
with our conductors of Korusko. The order of the
day here was this, that we generally set out about six
o'clock in the morning, and continued going on until
ten o'clock; then the caravan rested during the
noonday heat till about three, when it journeyed
again until ten or eleven o'clock at night.

The whole afternoon we rode through the extensive plain, El Gôs, probably so called from the great
sand-downs, so characteristic of this region, and
which assume, in the southern districts, a peculiar
form. They have almost all the form of a crescent,
opening toward the south-west, so that one looks
from the road into a number of amphitheatres, the
steep sand-walls of which rise ten feet with the
north wind, which blows inside, and clears away the
sand, which would otherwise rapidly fill the cavity,
from the inner field. How quickly these moveable
sand structures change their place, is shown by the
traces of the caravan road, often lost beneath high
sand-hills. Toward eight in the evening we left
the Gebel Barqugrês to the left, and stopped for
the night at a short distance from the Gilif
mountains.

On the 3rd of May we passed through the Wadi
Guâh el 'âlem, much overgrown with trees, into the

mountains, principally porphyritical, and like all
original mountains, containing more vegetation than
the sandy plains, by the longer holding of the pre-
cipitated damp and scarce rains. After three
hours we came into Wadi G'aqedûl, luxuriantly
overrun with gesh and prickly trees of every kind
—sont, somra, and serha. We here found grazing
herds of camels and goats, particularly in the neighbourhood of the water, which has also attracted
numerous birds, among them ravens and pigeons.
In the wide, deep-lying grotto, which may be 300
feet in diameter, and is enclosed by high walls of
granite, the water is said to remain three years
without requiring replenishment. It was, however,
so foul and bad smelling, that it was even despised
by my thirsty ass. The drinkable water lies farther
up the mountain, and is difficult to be obtained.

We here forsook the northerly direction, which
the wells after Gebel Nusf had obliged us to take,
and went westerly by the Gilif mountains, in Wadi
el Mehêt, crossed the dry Chôr el Ammer, whence
the way to Ambukôl branches off, and encamped at
night after ten o'clock in the Wadi el Uêr, called
by others the Wadi Abu Harôd. From this place
the Gilif mountains retreated eastward again for
some time, and only left sand-hills in the foreground,
by which we travelled on the following morning.
To the W.N.W. we saw another chain, no longer
called Gilif; a single projecting double-pointed
mountain was called Miglik. The great creek of the
Gilif chain, filled with sand-rock, is two hours' journey broad; then the way leads northward into these

mountains, which is called Gebêl el Mágeqa after
the well of Mágeqa.

Before the entrance into these mountains we
came to a place covered with heaps of stones, which
might be taken for grave tumuli, but under which
no one lies buried. When the date-merchants,
whom we encountered on the following day with
their large round wicker-baskets, come this way,
they are here asked for money by their camel-
driver. Whoever will not give them anything has
such a cenotaph raised from its stones, as a memorial of his hardheartedness. We also found a
similar place in the desert of Korusko. After nine
o'clock we got to the well; we did not however stop,
but ascended a wild valley to a considerable height,
where we encamped towards noon.

The whole road was well-wooded, and thus offered
a pleasant variety. The sont or gum trees were
scarce here; the somra was the most frequent, which
always spreads out into several strong branches on
the ground, and ends in an even crown of thin
twigs and little green leaves, so that it often resembles a regularly formed cone overturned, frequently attaining a height of fifteen feet. By it
grows the heglik, with branches all round the trunk,
and single groups of leaves and twigs like the
pear-tree. The unprickly serha, on the contrary,
has all its branches surrounded with very small
green leaflets like moss, and the tondûb has no
leaves at all, but instead of them little green zigzag growing branchlets, almost as thick as foliage,
while the sálame-bush consists of long slender

R

switches, which are beset with green leaflets and long green thorns.

After four o'clock we set out, and came down very gradually from the heights. In the Wadi Kalas there are again a number of wells, twenty-five feet deep, with very good rain-water. Here we encamped for the night, although we had only arrived there shortly after sunset. The animals were watered and the skins filled. The whole plateau is rich in trees and bushes, and is inhabited by men and animals.

Our road on the following day retained the same character, as long as we journeyed between the beautiful and wildly rising walls of porphyry. After two hours we arrived at two other springs also called Kalas, with little but good water. Hence a road leads north-eastward to the well Meroë in the Wadi Abu Dôm, probably so denominated from a white rock.

Three hours farther, passing by Gebel Abrak, we entered the great Wadi Abu Dôm, which we pursued in a W.N.W. direction. This remarkable valley runs from the Nile by Mechêref along an extended mountain chain to the village of Abu Dôm, which is situated opposite Mount Barkal, in a slanting direction. If it be considered that the upper north-east mouth of this valley, crossing the whole peninsula and its mountains, is almost opposite the confluence of the Atbara, which runs into the Nile in the same direction above Mechêref, the idea may be entertained that at one time, though not in historical times, there was here a water communication which cut off the greater part of the

eastern reach of the Nile, which now exists through
the circumstance that the rocky plateau near Abu
Hammed turns the stream southernward for a degree
and a half against its general direction. The name
of the valley is taken from the single *dóm* palms
that are found scattered up and down in it. The
mountain chain running north of the valley is distinctly different from the mountains which we had
formerly passed. With our entrance into this
valley, we lost the hard mountain soil, and the flying
sand again predominated, without, however, over-
coming the still not scarce vegetation.

After we had passed a side valley, Om Shebah,
containing well-water, in the afternoon, on the left,
we encamped at about nine o'clock for the night.
Next morning we came to the deep well, Hanik.
I stopped about noon at a second, called Om Sarale,
after the tree of the same name.

Here I left the caravan with Jussuf, to reach
Barkal by a circuit to Nuri, lying somewhat higher
up the river on this shore. After an hour and a
half, we came to the very considerable ruins of a
great Christian convent in Wadi Gazâl; so named
from the gazelles, who scrape here in the *Chor*
(valley-bed), for water in great numbers. The
church was built of white unhewn sand-stone up to
the windows, and, above them, of unburnt brick; the
walls covered with a strong coating of gypsum, and
painted inside. The vaulted apse of the tri-naved
basilica, lies as usual to the eastward, the entrance
behind the western transept to the north and
south; all the arches of the doors, windows, and
pillar niches are round. Koptic, more or less orna-

mented, crosses are frequently placed over the
door, the simplest form of which, ⊞ is easily com-
parable to the ancient Egyptian symbol of life.
The whole is a true type of all the Koptic churches
which I have seen, and I therefore add the little
ground-plan, which Erbkam took of it.

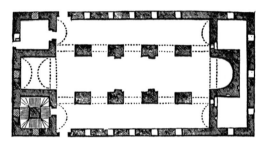

The building is about eighty feet long, and
exactly half as broad. The north wall is ruined.
The church is surrounded by a great court, the
outer walls of which, as also the numerous partly
vaulted convent cells, still well preserved, are built
of rude blocks. Before the western entrance of the
church, separated only by a little court, lies the
largest building, forty-six feet in length, probably
the house of the prior, from which a particular side
entrance led into the church. On the south side of
the convent are two church-yards ; the western one,
about forty paces from the church, contained a
number of graves, which were simply erected of
black stones collected together. Nearer to the
buildings was the eastern one, which was remarkable for a considerable number of grave-
stones, partly inscribed in Greek and partly in
Koptic, which will cause me to make a second visit
to this remarkable convent before our departure from

Barkal. I counted more than twenty inscribed
stones, of which some had of course suffered
extremely, and as many slabs of baked earth, with
inscriptions scratched upon them, almost all, however, broken to pieces. They contain the most
southern Greek inscriptions which have yet been
discovered in the Nile regions, with the exception
of the inscription of Adulis and Axum in Abyssinia ;
and though it be not doubtful that the Greek
language after the promulgation of Christianity, the
traces of which we can detect in architectural remains
farther than Soba, was used and understood by the natives in all the flourishing countries up to Abyssinia,
at least for religious purposes ; yet these epitaphs,
(among which, on a cursory examination, I could find
none in the Ethiopian,) seemed to point to immigrating Græco-Koptic inhabitants of the old convent.

I left my comrades here, who went direct to
Abu Dôm at five o'clock, and proceeded to Nuri.
Soon there gleamed towards us the blue heights of
Mount Barkal, which rises alone with steep sides and
a broad platform from the surrounding plain, and
immediately attracts attention by its peculiar shape
and situation. At six o'clock, the Nile valley lay
before us in its whole and somewhat broad extent ;
a sight long desired, after the desert, and which
excites the attention of travellers as much as the
nearing coasts after a sea-voyage.

Our road turned, however, to the right, and proceeded through the mountains, which still consist
of masses of porphyry. When we reached Barkal,
right opposite us, I observed on our left a number
of black, round, or pyramidal grave-hillocks, with

which I had been acquainted from Meroë. Probably it was the general burying-place of Napata, still the metropolis of the Ethiopian kings in the time of Herodotus, and situated on the opposite shore ; there must then have also been a considerable city on the left bank of the Nile, by which the position of the pyramids of Nuri on the same side is explained. Yet I have not been able to discover any ruined mounds answering to such a conjecture. Only behind the village of Duêm, and near Abu Dôm, I saw such, which were called Sánab, but they were not of any considerable extent. We did not come into the neighbourhood of this important group of pyramids until half-past seven, and we quartered ourselves for the night with the sheikh of the village.

Before sunrise I was already at the pyramids, of which I counted about twenty-five. They are partially statelier than those of Meroë, but built of soft sandstone, and therefore much disintegrated ; a few only have any smooth casing left. The largest exhibits the same principle of structure within which I have discovered in those of Lower Egypt ; a smaller inner pyramid was enlarged in all directions by a stone casing. At one part of the west side the smoothened surface of the innermost structure was distinctly visible within the eight foot thick, well-joined, outer mantle. Little is to be found here of ante-chambers, as at Meroë and the pyramids of Barkal ; I believe I have only found the remains of two ; the rest, if they existed, must have been quite ruined or buried in the rubbish. Some pyramids stand so close before one another,

that by their position it would be impossible for an
ante-chamber to exist, at least on the east side,
where they were to be expected. For the rest, the
pyramids are built quite massively, of free-stone ; I
could only find that the most eastern of all was
filled up with black, unhewn stones. A pyramid
with a flaw, like that of Dahhshur, is also here ;
but here the lower angle was probably originally
intended, as there the upper one, as it is too inconsiderable for a structure in steps. Although I could,
unfortunately, find no inscriptions, with the exception of one single fragment of granite, yet several
things combine to assure me that this is the elder
group, that of Barkal the younger.

I arrived at Abu Dôm after ten o'clock, where I
found my companions. The crossing of the Nile
occupied us the whole day, and we first came to
Barkal at sunset.

Georgi had, to my great joy, arrived here some
days ago from Dongola. His assistance is doubly
welcome to us, as everything must be drawn here
that is discovered. The Ethiopian residence of
King Tahraka, who also reigned in Egypt, and left
architectural remains behind him, — the same who
went forth to Palestine in Hiskias' time against
Sanharib,—is too important for us not to becom-
pletely exhausted.

LETTER XXIII.

MOUNT BARKAL.
May 28, 1844.

I EXPECT every moment the transport-boats requested of Hassan Pasha, which set out eleven days ago, and are to take up our Ethiopian treasures, and bring ourselves to Dongola. The results of our researches at this place are not without importance. On the whole, it is perfectly settled that Ethiopian art is only a later branch of the Egyptian. It does not begin under native rulers until Tahraka. The little which yet remains to us of a former age belongs to the Egyptian conquerors and their artists. It is wholly confined here, at least, to one temple, which Ramses the Great erected to Amen-Ra. Certainly the name of Amenophis III. has been found on several granite rams, as upon the London lions of Lord Prudhoe;* but there are good grounds for suspecting that these stately colossi did not originally belong to a temple here. They were transported hither at a later period from Soleb, as it would seem, probably by the Ethiopian king whose name is found engraven on the breast of the lions above mentioned, and which has, on account of the erroneous omission of a sign, been hitherto read Amen Asru, instead of Mi Amen Asru.

But I have found these rams so remarkable, chiefly on account of their inscriptions, that I have

[* Now standing for many years at the entrance of the Egyptian saloon in the British Museum.—K. R. H. M.]

resolved to take the best of them with us. The fat sheep may weigh 150 cwt. Yet he had been drawn to the shore on rollers within three hot days by ninety-two fellahs, where he awaits his embarkation. Several other monuments are to accompany us hence, the weight of which we need not fear, now we have the deserts behind us. I only mention an Ethiopian altar four feet high, with the cartouches of the king erecting it; a statue of Isis, on the back pillar of which there is an Ethiopian demotic inscription in eighteen lines, and another from Méraui; as also the peculiar monument bearing the name of Amenophis III., which was copied by Cailliaud, and taken for a foot, but in reality is the underpart of the sacred sparrow-hawk. All these monuments are of black granite.*

The city of Napata, the name of which I have often found hieroglyphically, and already on Tahraka's monuments, was doubtless situated somewhat lower down the river by the present place Méraui, where considerable mounds testify for such a conjecture. In the neighbourhood of the mountain the temples and pyramids only were situated. In the hieroglyphical inscriptions, this remarkable rock-mass bears the name of the " holy mountain,"

The God more especially venerated here was Ammon-Ra.

On the 18th of May we carried out our long-intended second visit to the Wadi Gazâl, took impressions of all the Greek and Koptic inscriptions of

---

* All these monuments are now erected in the Egyptian Museum. See the Ram and the Sparrow-hawk in the " Monuments from Egypt and Ethiopia," Part III. plate 90.

the burial-place, and took away with us what appeared yet legible.

We are now more sensible than before of the meaning of the summer-season in the torrid zone; the thermometer usually rises in the afternoon to 37° and 38° Reaumur; indeed, occasionally, above 40° in the shade. The glowing sand at my feet I often found to be 53°, and whatever is made of metal can only be touched with a cloth round it in the open air. All our drawings and papers are richly bedewed with pearly drops of perspiration. But the hot wind is the most annoying, which drives oven-heat in our faces, instead of coolness. The nights are scarcely more refreshing. The thermometer falls to 33° towards evening, and towards morning to 28°. Our only refreshment is continual Nile-baths, which, however, would be considered warm-baths in Europe. We have several times had storms with violent sand-filled hurricanes, and a few drops of rain. Yesterday a whirlwind beat down our tent, and at the same time our arbour of strong trunks and palm-branches fell upon us from its violence, while we were eating; the meal was scarcely eatable on account of the strong spice of sand. It would seem that violent gusts of wind are peculiar to this clime or country, for one often sees four or five high sand-pillars at the same time at different distances, dashing heavenward like mighty volcanoes. There are few serpents here; but a great number of scorpions, and ugly great spiders more feared by the natives than the scorpions. We therefore sleep on *anqarebs* brought from the village, on account of these malicious vermin.

LETTER XXIV.

DONGOLA.
June 15, 1844.

BEFORE our departure from Barkal, I undertook
an excursion up the Nile into the district of the cataracts, which we had cut off in our desert journey.
I also wished to learn the character of this part of the
country, the only portion of the valley of the Nile
which we had not traversed with the caravan. We
went by water to Kasinqar, and remained there the
night. From here arise wild masses of granite,
which form numerous islands in the rivers, and
stop the navigation.

With much trouble we arrived the next day, before
the camels were ready, at the island of Ishishi,
surrounded by violent and dangerous eddies. We
here found ruins of walls and buildings of brick,
sometimes of stone, both hewn and unhewn, which
leads us to the conclusion that they must have served
as fortifications to the island at different times; yet
there were no inscriptions, excepting one in a few
unintelligible signs. We did not mount our camels
at Kasinqar until after nine o'clock, and rode along
the right hand shore, between the granite rocks,
which leave but very little room for a scanty
vegetation. The eye is relieved almost wholly in
the numerous, and generally smaller islands, by
green clumps of trees and cultivated spots multi-
fariously intersected by the black crags. There is

scarcely room for larger villages among these rocks; few, indeed, could find sustenance among them. The villages consist of single and small rows of houses stretching along at a great distance, yet, bearing the same name, however, to a certain extent. The plain of Kasinqar ended with a beautiful group of palms. Then we entered the district of Kû'eh, followed by the long tract of Hamdab, to which belongs the island of Mérui or Méroë, more than a quarter of an hour in length. Here, too, the name is explained by the situation. It is very high, sometimes forty feet above the water-level; the one now among the larger islands is wholly barren and uninhabited, and excepting the black crags periodically washed by the waters, it is completely white. This is occasioned principally by the dazzling sand-drifts which cover it; but strangely enough, the rocks jutting out of the sand are also white, either from the broad veins of quartz, in the same manner as another peculiar white rock which I had seen in the province of Robatât, lying on the way, and which was called by the camel-drivers Hager Mérui, or because the weather-beaten granite here has contracted this colour. The name of the village of Méraui, near Barkal, has, perhaps, the same origin; here the white precipices, running from Méraui to the river, and which attracted my attention on our departure, have suggested the name by their colour.

On the opposite shore the Gebel Kongêli, comes near to the river, also called Gebel Mérui; from the island as well as the rushing cataract a little above the island, which has received the name of Shellâl Mérui.

At four o'clock we arrived at the ruin Hellet el
Bib, which from a distance has quite the appearance of a castle of the middle ages. It rises on
low rocks, the ridge of which traverses the court
and the building itself, so that a part of it appears
like an upper story. The whole edifice is built of
unburnt, but good and carefully-formed bricks,
cemented with a small quantity of mortar, and
covered with a coating of the same. Within are
various large and small rooms, some with half-round
niches in them and arched doorways. The walls of
the west side were fifteen feet high. The outer wall
of the court of unhewn stone, but carefully built up
to about five to eight feet, enclosed a tolerably regular
square, the side of which was about sixty-five paces
long.

This small castle, but still respectable for the neighbourhood, reminds one, by its niches and arched
doors, of the Christian architecture of former centuries, but it does not appear to have been destined
for any religious purpose. Perhaps in its prime it
belonged to the powerful and warlike tribes of the
Shaiqîeh, which, according to tradition, immigrated
from Arabia into this neighbourhood some centuries
ago. At the time of the Egyptian conquest the
country was under the dominion of three Shaiqîeh
princes; probably one of them resided here. The
surrounding country was also more favoured by nature, the shore flatter, beset with bushes, here and
there bordered by a fertile piece of land.

After I had sketched the plan of the building,
we set off at nine o'clock in the evening, by the
light of a full moon, on our way back, which we

shortened considerably by taking the road from the island of Saffi through the desert, where we passed the night, on an open sand plain, in the great granite field. About five o'clock, between moonshine and morning dawn, we were again on our way, and by nine o'clock we had reached our ship at Kasinqar.

Near this place I met with a tree quite new to me, in a little Wadi, which led to the river. It was called Bân, and does not grow anywhere but in this Wadi, which is called Chôr el Bân from it, and in another, near Méraui.* A strong white-barked stem, not unlike that of our walnut-tree, with some more stems round it, and short white branches, grew short and knotty out of the ground. The branches were now almost naked, a few only had leaves, if we can call the great bunches of switches by that name. The fruit is a long, round fluted ball, which splits into three pieces, when the five to ten black-shelled nuts (of about the size of a hazel-nut) which it contains, are ripe; the white

---

* From the pods and their contents Dr. Klotzsch recognised the *Moringa arabica Persoon* (*Hyperanthera peregrina Forskål*. It seems that this tree was only previously known from Arabia, and is natural there. The single trees near Barkal, which are not mentioned by former travellers, might have been first introduced from Arabia. This is the more probable as the immigration of those tribes of the Shaiqîeh Arabs from the Hegâz is now testified by manuscript authorities. [This tree must therefore be added to the botanical list of Pickering, who, in his Races of Man, has collected all the introduced animals and plants of Egypt, India, America, Polynesia, Southern Arabia, &c., and though the lists want classification, they are well worthy of attention.—K. R. H. M.]

sweet, though rather sharp, oily kernel is not unpleasant; but it is mostly used by the inhabitants to press oil from. The bloom of the tree is yellow, and grows in bunches.

At noon the Sheikh of Nuri came to our boat, from whom I obtained some more information as to the cataract country. There are in the province of Shaiqîeh and the adjoining one of Monassir eight especial cataracts: the first, Shelâl Gerêndid, near the island Ishishi; Shelâl Terâi, near Kû'eh; Shelâl Mérui; Shelâl Dahák, near the island Uli; Shelâl el Edermîeh, e'Kabenât, e Tanarâi, and Om Derás. From hence a rocky district stretches to El Kâb, whence the stream flows to Shelâl Mogrât, in the great reach to Berber.

There is nothing now spoken in this whole neighbourhood but Arabic; but there is still a recollection of the former Nubian population, as there are yet a number of villages distinguished from the others as Nuba villages. Above the province Dongola, the following were pointed out to me as such:—Gebel Maqál and Zûma on the right shore, and near the island Massaui, which also bears the Nubian name of Abranârti; then on the left hand Belled e' Nûba, between Debbe and Abu Dôm, Haluf or Nuri, and Bellel, opposite Gerf e' Sheikh and Kasinqar. Then the account springs over to Chôsh e' Gurûf, a little below the island of Mogrât, and towards Salame and Darmali, two villages between Mechêref and Dârmer; and finally, there is a Belled e' Nûba, north of Gôs Burri, in the province Metamme.

At last, on the 4th of June, we quitted Barkal,

after we had loaded the Ram and the other heavy monuments in two transport vessels.

We remained the first night in Abu Dôm on the left shore. I had heard of a Fakir, belonging to this place, who was said to possess manuscript notes on the tribe of Shaiqîeh Arabs. He was an intelligent, and for this country, a learned man, and I found him quite ready, not to give me the original of the few sheets he possessed, but to set to work immediately and copy them for me.

The next morning we landed first in Tanqássi, about the distance of an hour and a half from Abu Dôm, where we were to find ruins. The Fakir Daha, who belonged to the Korêsh, the tribe of the Prophet, accompanied us to the now inconsiderable mounds of bricks. We passed by his hereditary tomb, a little cupola building erected by his grandfather, which already had not only received him, but also his father and several other relations. From hence I espied some hills in the distance, which the Fakir declared to be natural. Nevertheless we rode up to them, and found, at about half an hour's distance from the river, more than twenty tolerably large pyramids, now apparently formed of nothing but black mud, but originally built of Nile bricks. Single stones lay round about, and on the east side, at some distance, there were always two little heaps of stones, which appeared to have belonged to a kind of ante-chamber, and perhaps were connected with the pyramid by brick walls. Nowhere, however, were there any hewn stones or inscriptions to be found. On the opposite shore, near Kurru, we also found a field of pyramids, but

very few ruins of towns were to be discovered.
The largest of the two most considerable pyramids,
named Quntûr, was about thirty-five feet high, and
towards the south-east were the remains of an ante-
chamber. Around these two were grouped twenty-
one smaller ones, of which four, like the largest
pyramid, were built entirely of sandstone, but are
now mostly in ruins; others consisted only of black
basalt. Finally, westward of all the ground plan of
a large apparently quite massive and consequently
completely ruined pyramid was to be seen, whose
foundation was in the rock. It appears also that
this pyramid, which by its solid architecture was
distinguished from all the surrounding ones, belonged to a royal dynasty of Napata; thus it was
easier to account for the want of city ruins here
than on the opposite side.

Three quarters of an hour down the stream on
the right, lies the little village of Zûma. Near
it, towards the mountains, rises an old fortress, with
towers of defence, called Kárat Négil, the outer
walls of which were ruined and destroyed about
fifty or sixty years ago, when the present inhabitants
of Zûma settled here. The name is derived from
that of an old king of the country, called Négil,
in whose time the surrounding land, which is now
barren, was still reached and fertilized by the
Nile.

The first discovery on the road to the fortress
was another number of pyramids, of which eight
were yet about twenty feet high; including the
ruined ones, which seemed to have been as usual
the most massive, there were altogether thirty; to

the south-west the old quarries are yet to be seen, which had furnished the materials for the pyramids.

Whilst these three pyramid fields, Tanqassi, Kurru, and Zûma, or Kárat Négil, lying so near to each other, and whose situation has been carefully paced off and marked by Erbkam, show that the neighbourhood had a numerous and flourishing population in the heathen times, we discovered in the adjoining country and more or less through the whole province of Dongala, the remains of Christian churches.

On the 7th of June we visited the three pyramids, at a little distance from each other, all on the right hand shore of the river. Two hours and a half distant from Zûma, Bachît is situated. Here the rock-wall of the desert extends to the river, and bears upon it a fortress, without doubt belonging to Christian times, with eighteen semi-circular projecting towers of defence. In the interior, under heaps of rubbish, were the ruins of a church, which appeared to have marked the centre of the fortress; it was here only sixty-three feet long, and the whole nave rested on four columns and two wall pillars, nevertheless the plan completely answered to the universal type.

The church of Magál, which is only half an hour further, must have been much larger, as we found among the ruins granite monolithic columns thirteen feet and a half high up to the divided capital of a foot and a half, and two feet in diameter; it appeared to have had five naves.

From here we arrived in an hour at Gebel Dêqa. Strong, massive walls here also surrounded a Chris-

tian fortress, which stood upon the projecting sandstone rock, and within it the ruins of several large
buildings, among which was a small church with
three naves, similar to that at Bachît.
This is the boundary of the province of Shaiqîeh
towards Dongola, the last place to the south whose
inhabitants speak Arabic. Formerly the boundary of
the Nubian population and speech extended without
doubt as far as the cataracts above Barkâl. This
appears to have caused the numerous fortresses in
this neighbourhood, and also the strong fortification
of the island of Ishishi.

The Nubians, to whom already, in the sixth century, Christianity had penetrated by way of Abyssinia, were then a powerful people, till their Christian priest-kings, in the fourteenth century, turned
to Islamism At this time the building of the
numerous churches, whose ruins we found scattered
through the whole province northwards from Wadi
Gâzâl, must have taken place.

We went the same day to Ambukôl, at the point
of the western reach of the Nile, and remained there
the night. The following day we reached Tifâr, and
again visited the ruins of a fortress, with the
remains of a church.

On the way we met Hassan Pasha's boat, which
was going to Méraui. We fired salutes, and ran
alongside each other. The Pasha inquired earnestly
about the treasures which he supposed would be in
the pyramids of Barkal, and with the greatest com-
plaisance promised us anything we desired in fur-
therance of our journey and object. After he had

immediately returned our visit, we parted, firing fresh salutes.

On the 10th of June we reached Old Dongola, the former capital of this Christian kingdom. The immense ruins of the town show little more at present than its former great extent. Upon a mountain, near which commands a delightful prospect all round, stands a mosque. An Arabic inscription, on marble, shows that this was opened on the 20th Rabî el anel, in the year 717 (1st June, 1317), after the victory of Safeddin Abdallah e' Nâsir over the infidels.

As we had discovered so few monumental remains since our departure from Barkal, to employ the leisure time which we had in our boat, I busied myself with making every possible research into and comparison with the present language and the Nubian. It offers very remarkable points in the science of language, but does not show the least similarity to the Egyptian. I consider that the whole race must have come at a late period out of the south-west into the valley of the Nile. We have now a servant from Derr, the capital of Lower Nubia, who speaks tolerably good Italian; he is alert and intelligent, and is of great service to me on account of his knowledge of the Mahass dialects. I have sometimes tormented him with questions for five or six hours in a day in the boat, as it is no small trouble to either of us to understand each other upon the forms and changes of grammar. He has, at any rate, acquired more respect for his own language, which everywhere here, when compared

with the Arabic, is reckoned bad and vulgar, and
people are ashamed of being obliged to speak it.

When we arrived yesterday, after three days'
journey from Old Dongola here, in New Dongola,
generally called El Orde (the camp) by the Arabs,
we had the great pleasure of receiving the large
packet of letters, of which we had already been
informed by Hassan Pasha on the road. Since
then we look forward with fresh courage to the last
difficult part of our journey to the south, as we
must here, alas! leave our boats, and mount the
far more uncomfortable ship of the desert. The
cataract district, now lying before us, is only to be
navigated at high water, and then not without
danger. Our richly-laden stone boat we were
obliged to submit to the dangerous trial, as land-
carriage for the Ram and the other monuments was
naturally not to be thought of.

We shall not be able to set out from here so
immediately, on account of the general reform
which must take place in our preparations for the
journey of the next five or six weeks. From our
boat with the packages we must, however, separate
ourselves, as it must seize upon the right moment
of the high water, which will not be for some
weeks.

LETTER XXV.

WE returned yesterday from a four day's trip to the next cataract, which we were able to reach with the boat. Our collection was unexpectedly rich. We have found a great number of old monuments of the time of the Pharoahs, the only ones in the whole province of Dongola, and part of them very ancient. On the island of Argo we discovered the first Egyptian sculpture of the time of the Hyksos, and near Kermân on the right hand shore, traces of an extensive city, spread wide over the plain, with an immense burying-ground adjoining, in which two large monuments were conspicuous, one of which was called Kermân (like the village), the other Defûfa. They are not pyramids, but oblong squares, the first 150 feet by 66, the second 132 feet by 66, and about 40 feet high, quite massive and strong, and built of good firm unburnt Nile bricks ; each has an out-building, resembling the ante-temple of the Pyramid. Many fragments of statues lying about, (in the best ancient style, partly covered with good hieroglyphics,) point out their great antiquity ; so that we may judge this to be the oldest important Egyptian settlement on Ethiopian ground, which was probably rendered necessary through the increase of Egyptian power towards Ethiopia, during the supremacy of the Hyksos in Egypt. Without doubt, the enormous granite bridges which we found some hours north of Kermân at the entrance of the cataract district, opposite the island Tombos on the right hand shore, were belonging to this town. The rock inscriptions contain arms of the seventeenth dynasty, and an inscription of eighteen lines bears the date of the second year of Tuthmosis I.

Here, in Dongola, I have also begun to study the Kong'âra language of Dar Fûr. A negro soldier born in that feared and warlike land, with woolly hair and thick pouting lips, whom we brought with us during the last year from Korusko to Wadi Halfa, as orderly officer, instead of the one appointed by Ibrahim Pasha, sought us out again, and was given up to me by the Pasha to assist me in my philological studies. He began well, but in half an hour I was obliged to get the Nubian to interpret for me. The Kong'âra is quite different from the Nubian, and appears to me in some points to have a strong analogy with certain South African languages.

It gave me great pleasure to see here the fortress built by Ehrenberg in 1822, it has certainly suffered from the inundations, but still serves Hassan Pasha as a dwelling. There will also remain a building in remembrance of us, as the Pasha begged Erbkam to give him the plan of a powder-tower, and to seek out a suitable spot for its erection.

LETTER XXVI.

KORUSKO.
August 17, 1844.

OUR departure from Dongola did not take place till the 2nd July. We journeyed slowly down the west side of this river; and on the same day we came to large fields of ruins, the inconsiderable remains of once flourishing cities whose names are lost. The first we found opposite Argônsene, others near Koï and Mosh. On the following day we passed near Hannîk, opposite Tombos, in the province of Máhas; here begins the Cataract district and a new Nubian dialect, which extends to Derr and Korusko. The Nile takes a northerly course till it comes to a high mountain named after a former conqueror, Ali Bersi; this we passed to the left early on the third day. It lies on the sudden turning of the river, from north-west to due east, where it is usual to avoid the greater part of the province of Máhas by a northerly desert road. We, however, followed the windings of the river, and came in the neighbourhood of old forts on the shore, to a grove of palm-trees, in whose shade we rested during the heat of mid-day. The nearest of these forts so romantically situated among the rent rocks, I find differently named upon every map, as Fakir Effendi (Cailliaud), Fakir el Bint, from *bint,* the Maiden (Hoskins), Fakir Bender, from *bender,* the metropolis (Arrowsmith); it is, however, called Fakir

Fenti in the dialect of the country, or Fakir Benti
in that of Dongola, and is so named from the palms
at their foot (*Fenti, benti,* means palms and dates).
We arrived on the 4th of July at Sêse, a mountain on which is the remains of a fortress. Our
servant Ahmed (from Derr), informed us that after
the death of every king, his successor was led to the
top of this mountain, and decked with a peculiar royal
head-dress. Such forts as Sêse, of which from the
high land we saw many both far and near, tell of a
former numerous and warlike population, which has
now almost disappeared. The ruins, lying about a
quarter of an hour to the south of Mount Sêse, are
called Sêsebi. Here stood an old temple, of which,
however, only four columns, with palm capitals, remain standing; these bear the cartouches of Sethos
I., the most southerly that we have found of this
king. In the neighbourhood of these remains, are
situated the ruins of a city, on an artificial platform,
the regular circumvallation of which is still to be
recognized.

On the 6th of July we got to Solb (Soleb), the
well-preserved and considerable temple of which
was erected by Amenophis III., to his own genius,
the divine Ra-neb-ma (Amenophis.)* The rich

---

* The literal expression is, that he has built the temple
𓏏𓈖𓏤𓊪𓇳𓏛 „ "to his image, Ra-neb-ma, living
on the earth." The word *chent* no longer exists in Koptic, but
it is always translated εἰκών, on the Rosetta stone. The temple
and the place belonging to it was also named after the king,
but according to his Horus-name, " Dwelling-place of Sha-em-
ma;" this led to the recognition of the original position of the
ram of Barkal and the lions in the British Museum.

decorations of this temple, (the same to which our ram from Barkal, and the lions of Lord Prudhoe once belonged,) furnished us with employment for nearly five days. On the 11th of July we first departed again. Scarcely an hour hence to the northward lies Gebel Dôshe; a sandstone rock projecting to the river, in which a grotto is hewn on the river side, containing sculptures of Tuthmosis III. The same evening we got to Sedeïnga, where Amenophis III. built a temple to his own wife Tü. In the midst of the picturesque heap of ruins a single pillar stands up. To the west, a great grave-field extends.

On the 13th of July we stopped at a *shôna* (so are the Government station magazines called), opposite Mount Abir or Qabir, a little below the northern point of the island of Saï. Indirectly over the river, lies the village of Amara, and in its neighbourhood, the ruins of a temple. I was not a little astonished to recognize the stout queen of Naga and Meroë and her husband, on the columns, of which six are still remaining. This temple was built by them, an important testimony of the far extending government of that Ethiopian dynasty. On the grave-field to the south of the temple, I also remarked fragments of inscriptions in the already mentioned Demotic-Ethiopian alphabet, of which I had also found some examples in the neighbourhood of Sedeïnga.

After we had paid a visit to the island of Saï, on the next day, where we had found the few remains of a temple with inscriptions of Tuthmosis III., and

Amenophis II., besides the ruins of a town and a
Koptic church,—we proceeded onward, and arrived
on the 15th of July at Dal, which forms the frontier
between the provinces of Sukkot and Batn el
hag'er (Stonebelly). At night we encamped by the
cataract of Kalfa.

Hence our way led in the neighbourhood of the
hot sulphur springs of Okmeh, whither I diverged
from the caravan with Abeken.. The road led us
from the Shôna where we parted, along the craggy
shore for above an hour, to a square tower, which
has been erected over the fountain, and called
Hammân Seïdna Solimân, after the architect. The
tower, which is nine feet thick, and has an inward
diameter of four feet, is now half full of sand and
earth ; the water rushes out of the east side of the
tower to the thickness of your wrist, and on the
other side sixteen little springs rise out of the sand
within the space of a square foot ; and here, where
the water is at the hottest, it has not quite
44° Réaumur. The taste is sulphurous, and a white
deposit lies all round the fountain on the ground.
Every year the river rises above the spring, and
indeed, above the tower, which stands at half the
elevation of the shore. The water mirror had now
risen to the height of a man, and had not yet
reached the fountain. A rude hole is dug in the
rubbish for the invalids that come hither, and is
covered with rushes to keep off the steam. Somewhat further down the river, another streamlet
comes out, which retains 40° of warmth at its
mouth in the open air. The legend goes, that
Okáshe, a friend of the prophet, was killed in a

campaign to the south; his body swam up hither and then disappeared in the rocks on the opposite shore. His grave is still pointed out .there at some distance from the river; a tree marking the spot.

On the 17th of July we encamped near the temple of Semneh. The village only consists of a few straw huts,* shaded by some date-trees; yet the many fragments in the district show that there was once a much more considerable place here. The temple is surrounded by mighty ancient works of defence, the building of which goes as far back as the Old Empire, under Sesurtesen III., a king of the twelfth dynasty.† It seems that this king first extended the bounds of the Egyptian empire to this place; indeed, he is found at a later period worshipped as a local divinity. The temple, built by Tuthmosis III., in the New Empire, is dedicated to him and the god Tetûn conjointly.

On the right shore too, near the village of Kummeh, old fortifications are found, and within them a still larger temple, already commenced by Tuthmosis II.

The most important discovery that we made here (which I only mention cursorily, as I have at the same time sent a complete account of it to Ehrenberg), is a number of short rock inscriptions, which give the highest Nile levels for a series of years, under the government of Amenemha III. (Mœris), and his immediate successors. These accounts are partly

---

[* For the straw huts down the Nile, and particularly beyond Chartûm, see Werne's White Nile, chapter i. vol. i. p. 28. —K. R. H. M.]

[† See Bunsen's Egypt's Place, vol. i. p. 624.—K. R. H. M.]

valuable historically, as they brilliantly confirm my conjecture, that the Sebekhotep immediately followed the twelfth dynasty, and are partly of peculiar interest for the geological history of the Nile, as they prove that the river rose, four thousand years ago, nearly twenty-four feet higher than at present and, therefore, must have caused quite different proportions of inundation and soil for the upper and lower country. The examination of this curious locality, with its temples and rock inscriptions, employed us for twelve days.

On the 29th of July we went from Semneh to Abke, and visited on the next day the old fortress north of that place, which is called El Kenissa, (the church,) and therefore probably contained one at some period. From the top of this fortress we had the most magnificent prospect of the principal cataracts of the whole district. Three great falls were distinguishable in the broad rocky islet valley from the smaller ones; several hundred islands passed under review to yonder black mountains. Toward the north, however, the wide plain stretched, which extend from Wadi Halfa to Philae. The gradual change in the geological construction of the rocks was plainly visible, as we descended from the last ridge of the shore crags into the great plain, from which but a few single sandstone cones arise from the bed of a dried up ocean. These are no doubt the sources of the endless sand, which, driven by the north wind into the mountains, rendered our journey to Semneh so difficult.

On the 1st of August we quitted Wadi Halfa in three barks, and passed through districts already well-known. Next morning we came to Abu Simbel, where we stopped nine days, in order to secure the rich representations of the two rock temples as complete as possible. I sought for a long time for the remarkable Greek inscription which Leake found on one of the four mighty Ramses-colossi, until I happily discovered it in the rubbish on the left leg of the second colossus from the south. I was obliged to have a great excavation made, in order to obtain a perfect impression on paper. There seem to me to be no grounds whatever not to take the inscription for that for which it proclaims itself, viz. for a memorial of the Greek mercenaries, who came hither with Psammetichus I. in pursuit of the rebellious warriors. Among the rest of the inscriptions of the colossus I find some Phœnician ones.

After we had visited rock monuments on the opposite shore, near Abahûda and Shataui, we left Abu Simbel, on the 11th of August, and next stopped on the right shore near Ibrîm, the ancient Primis, the name of which I have found written hieroglyphically PRM. On the left bank, opposite Ibrîm, lies Anîbe, in the neighbourhood of which we found and drew a solitary, but well preserved private grave of the time of the twentieth dynasty. Then we went on to Derr, where we received the richest of post-bags, which filled us all with joy.

With these treasures we hastened, by way of Amada, hither to Korusko; the charming palm groups of which had become dear to us during our long though unwilling stay last year. To-day (Sunday) we have, therefore, determined to celebrate the fortunate completion of our journey in the gayest reminiscences. Our barks lie quietly by the shore.

LETTER XXVII.

PHILAE.
September 1, 1844.

I AM only now first able to end my report from Korusko, which we quitted on the evening of the 18th of August, to sail for Sebûa. From thence to Philae the valley is called Wadi Kenûs, " the valley of Beni Kensi," a tribe often mentioned in the Arabic accounts. The upper valley from Korusko to Wadi Halfa is generally called Wadi Nuba on all the maps, a name certainly used by Burckhardt, but which must rest on an error. Neither our Nubian servant Ahmed, born at Derr, nor any of the inhabitants know this name, and even the septuagenarian Hassen Kashef, who governed the country before the Egyptian conquest, could not return any replies to my careful questions. According to their unanimous assertion, the lower district has always been called Wadi Kenûs. Then follows near Korusko the Wadi el Arab, so called by the immigrated Arabs of the desert, then Wadi Ibrim, and lastly Wadi Halfa. The government designation of the whole province between the two cataracts is, however, since the conquest Gism Halfa, the province Halfa.

In Korusko, I found a Bishâri, named 'Ali, whose intelligent and pleasing manners determined me immediately to engage him as a teacher for this important language. He accepted very willingly my invitation to accompany us, and now every leisure moment was occupied in preparing a grammar and vocabulary. He was born in the interior of the district Beled Elláqi, which is eight days distant from the Nile, and twenty from the Red Sea, and gives its name to the remarkable Wadi Elláqi, which extends without any interruption through the broad plains from the Nile to the sea. He calls the Bishári country Edbai and their language " Midáb. to Beg'auîe," the Beg'a language : this shows its identity with the language of the powerful Beg'a people, celebrated during the middle ages.

From Korusko we sailed to Sebûa, where we remained four days ; then by Dakke (Pselchis) and Kubân (Contra-Pselchis) to G'erf Hussên, with its rock temple, dedicated by Ramses to Ptah. By former travellers this place has often been called Girshe, a corruption of the name of a village lying on the eastern shore, called by the Arabians Qirsh, and by the Nubians Kish or Kishiga, and which lies in the neighbourhood of some important ruins, called Sabagûra. The 25th August we passed in the temple of Dendûr, built under the Roman empire, and the next day in Kalabsheh, the ancient Talmis, this temple also contains only the arms of Cæsar (Augustus). Talmis was for a long time the capital of the Blemyer, whose incursions into Egypt caused much trouble to the Romans. Upon one of the pillars of the outer court the interesting inscription of Silco is graven, who calls himself a βασιλίσκος Νουβάδων καὶ ὅλων τῶν Αἰθιόπων. He boasts in it of his victories over the Blemyers, whom I consider a branch of the Meroitic-Ethiopian race, the present Bishâri. The Demotic-Ethiopian inscriptions, among which is one remarkable for its length, and which perhaps is a counterpart of the Greek ones of the Nubian kings, can only be referred to the Blemyers. I discovered at the back of the temple another inscription of very late date in Greek, but so corrupted as to be perfectly unintelligible. I send it to be deciphered by Böckh.

On the 30th of August we reached Debôt, and the following day Philae, where we immediately took possession of the charming temple terrace, which, since that time, has been our head-quarters, and will be so for some time yet. The great buildings of the temple, although its earliest erection only dates as far back as Nectanebus, offer an unusually rich harvest of hieroglyphical, demotic, and Greek inscriptions, and to my astonishment I have discovered a chamber in one of the pylones, which contains only Ethiopian sculptures and inscriptions.

T

LETTER XXVIII.

WE arrived here, at the last great station of our journey, on the 4th of November, and feel much nearer to our native land. During our stay here, which is certain to run over several months, we have established ourselves in a charming rock fort, on a hill of Abd el Qurna; it is an ancient tomb, enlarged by erections of brick, whence the whole Thebaîc plain can be overlooked at one view. I should be afraid of being almost annihilated by the immense treasure of monuments, if the mighty character of the remains of this most royal city of all antiquity did not excite and retain the imagination at the highest point. While the examination of the previous numerous temples of the Ptolemaic and Roman periods had almost become, as it were, wearisome, I feel as fresh here, where the Homeric form of the mighty Pharaohs of the eighteenth and nineteenth dynasties come forth to us in all their majesty and pride, as at the beginning of my journey.

I have at once had excavations made in the celebrated temple of Ramses Miamun, situated at our feet, which have led to unexpected results. Erbkam had conducted the works with the greatest care, and his now finished ground-plan of this most beautiful building of the Pharaonic times, the tomb of Osymandyas, according to Diodorus, is the first which can be called complete, as it does not depend on arbitrary restorations, carried too far by the French, and not far enough by Wilkinson. In the filled-up rock tomb of the same Ramses, at Babel Meluk, erroneously considered incomplete by Rosellini, I have also had excavations made. Several chambers have already been found, and if fortune favours us, we shall also find the sarcophagus, though not unopened, (that the Persians have taken care of,) yet possibly less destroyed than others, as the deposit of soil on the tomb is very ancient.

During our journey thither from Korusko, I have been engaged upon the little known languages of the southern countries, beside my antiquarian pursuits. Among these three are the most extended: the Nuba language of the Nuba or Berber nation; the Kung'âra language of the negroes of Dar Fur; and the Beg'a language of the Bisharîba, inhabiting the eastern part of the Sudan. Of all three I have so perfectly formed the grammar and vocabulary, that their publication, at some period, will offer a complete view of these languages. The most important of them is the last named, because it proves itself a rich language in a grammatical point of view, and a very remarkable branch of the Caucasian family by its position in development. It is spoken by that nation which I believe I can prove to be the once flourishing one of Meroë, and which therefore has the most definite right to be called the Ethiopian people in the most strict sense of the term.

It has also been seen that there was nothing to

be found of a primitive Ethiopian civilisation, or even of an ancient Ethiopian national culture, of which the new school of learning pretends to know so much ; in fact, that we have every reason to deny its existence. Those accounts of the ancients which do not rest on totally erroneous information, only refer to the civilisation and arts of Egypt, which had fled to Ethiopia during the time of the supremacy of the Hyksos. The return of Egyptian might from Ethiopia, on the founding of the New Empire of the Egyptians, and its advance even into the depths of Asia, was transferred to the Asiatic traditions, and afterwards to the Greek, from the country of Ethiopia to the nation of Ethiopians; for no rumour of an older Egyptian empire, and its former peaceful prince had penetrated to the northern nations. I have transmitted a report to the Academy on the result of our Ethiopian journey, and I have given in it a sketch of Ethiopian history since the first conquest of the country by Sesurtesen III., in the twelfth dynasty of Maneth, till the prince of the Meroitic kingdom in the first centuries of our era, and then through the middle ages to the Bishariba of the present day, whose sheikhs we saw, in chains, pass by the ruins of their former metropolis, and the pyramids of their ancient kings.

LETTER XXIX.

THEBES, QURNA.
January 8, 1845.

WE have lately received the cheering intelligence that our colossal Ram and the other Ethiopian monuments have arrived safely at Alexandria. From here, too, we shall bring some important monuments; amongst them a beautiful sarcophagus, of fine white limestone, and partially covered with painted inscriptions, belonging to the Old Empire, the earliest era of the growing power of Thebes.* I have succeeded in making another conquest to-day, which causes me double pleasure, as I had inexpressible difficulty in attaining it, and as it has restored a monument to the day in the greatest perfection, and which will scarcely find its equal in any of the museums. In a deep shaft which has lately been excavated, a tomb-chamber has been found, full of interesting representations of kings, which we have drawn; hence a narrow passage leads deeper down into a second chamber, which is completely painted like the first. The spaces are hewn in a most crumbling rock, which falls in great pieces from the ceiling on the slightest touch; the rock-caves were therefore formed into cylindrical arches with Nile bricks, covered with stucco, and painted. On the sides of the inner door King Amenophis I. is represented on the right, and on the left his

* Monuments, Part II. Plates 245, 246.

mother, Aahmes-nufre-ari, highly reverenced even at a much later period. Both of them are painted on the stucco to the height of four feet, and preserved in the freshest colours. These figures, which took up the whole wall, I wished to remove. But for this purpose I was obliged to break through the brick walls around, and then take away the bricks behind the stucco singly with the greatest care. Thus I have to-day succeeded in the laborious work of laying down the whole of the stucco, only of the thickness of a finger, on two slabs made of planks, and cushioned with skins, linen, and paper, and bringing it out of the half-filled narrow tomb-grotto.*

Our plaster-casts, to my great joy, are again cared for. Five hundred-weight of gypsum, which M. Clot Bey has granted us from a quantity ordered from France, has lately arrived, and I have found and taken into our service an Arab, who at least knows enough of the manner of using gypsum and taking casts.

* Monuments, Part II. plate 1.

LETTER XXX.

WE have now dwelt for more than a quarter of a year, in our Thebaïc Acropolis, upon the hill Qurna, each of us busy in his own way, from morning till evening, in examining, describing, and drawing the most important monuments, taking off inscriptions on paper, and making out plans of the architecture, without being able to finish even the Lybian side, where there yet remains twelve temples, twenty-five king's tombs, fifteen tombs of royal wives or daughters, and a number, not to be counted, of graves belonging to persons of consequence, to be examined. The east side, with its six-and-twenty partly-standing churches, will also require not less time. And yet it is Thebes exactly that has been more explored than any other place by travellers and expeditions, (*vide* the Franco-Tuscan expedition), and we have only compared and supplied deficiencies in their labours, not done them afresh. We are also very far from imagining that we have exhausted the immense monumental riches to be found here. They who come after us with fresh information, and with the results of science further extended, will find new treasures in the same monuments, and obtain more instruction from them. The great end which I have always had before my eyes, and for which I have principally made my selections, has been history. When I thought I had collected the most essential information on this point, I remained satisfied.

The river here divides the valley into two unequal parts. While on the west side it flows near the steep projecting mountains of Lybia, it bounds on the east side a wide fertile plain, which extends as far as Medamôt, which lies some hours distant on the edge of the Arabian desert. On this side lies the actual city of Thebes, which appears to have formed a connection between the two temples, Karnak and Luqsor, which lie about half an hour's distance apart. Karnak lies north, and further from the Nile; Luqsor is directly washed by the waters of the river, and has very probably been in former times the harbour-quarter of the town. On the west side of the stream stood the Necropolis of Thebes, and for the preservation of the dead, all the temples, far and near, are employed,—yes, the whole population of these parts, which were later included under the name Memnonia by the Greeks, appear to have employed themselves principally with the care of the dead and their graves. The former extent of Memnonia is ascertained by the two cities, Qurna and Medînet Habu, which lie at the north and south points.

A survey of the Thebaïc monuments begins, most naturally, with the ruins of Karnak. Here lay the great imperial temple of a hundred doors, which was dedicated to Ammon-Ra, the king of the gods, and the particular god of the place, which after him was called the city of Ammon (No-Amon, Diospolis). Ap, and with the feminine article Tap, out of which the Greeks made Thebes, was an isolated temple of Ammon, and is sometimes hieroglyphically used in the singular, or still oftener in the plural (Napu) as the name of the city; from whence the Greeks, naturally, without changing the article, made use of Θῆβαι in the plural. The whole history of the Egyptian kingdom is connected with this temple, since the elevation of the city of Ammon into a metropolis of the kingdom. Every dynasty contended for the glory of having assisted in extending, beautifying, and restoring this national sanctuary.

It was founded under the first Thebaïc Imperial dynasty, the twelfth with Manetho, by its first king, the mighty Sesurtesen I., in the fourth century of the third millenium, B.C., and even now shows some fragments of the time and name of that king. During the succeeding dynasties, who sighed for several centuries under the oppression of their victorious hereditary enemies, the sanctuary doubtless stood unheeded, and nothing remains of what belongs to that period. But after Amosis, the first king of the seventeenth dynasty, had succeeded in his revolt against the Hyksos, about B.C. 1700, his two successors, Amenophis I. and Tuthmosis I., built round the remains of the most ancient sanctuary a stately temple with many chambers round the cella, and with a broad court and the propylæa belonging to it, before which Tuthmosis I. erected two obelisks. Two other pylones, with adjoining walls, were built by the same king, in a right angle with the temple, towards Luqsor. Tuthmosis III. and his sister enlarged this temple behind by a hall resting on fifty-six pillars, beside many other chambers which surrounded it on three sides, and were inclosed by a general outer wall. The next king partly did more toward the completion of the temple in front, and partly erected new independent temples in the vicinity, also built two other great pylones in a south-westerly direction before those of Tuthmosis I., so that from this side four high pylones formed the stately entrance to the principal temple.

A still more brilliant enlargement of the temple was, however, carried out in the fifteenth and fourteenth centuries, B.C., by the great Pharaohs of the nineteenth dynasties, by Sethos I., the father of Ramses Miamun, who added in the original axis of the temple the mightiest hall of pillars which was ever seen in Egypt, or, indeed, in any country. The stone roof is supported by 134 columns, covering a space of 164 feet in length and 320 in breadth. Each of the twelve middle columns is 36 feet in circumference, and is, up to the architrave, 66 feet high ; the other columns, 40 feet high, are 27 feet in circumference. It is impossible to describe the overpowering impression felt on first entering this forest of columns, and on passing from one avenue to another, and between the sometimes half, and sometimes whole-projecting grand gods and kingly statues which are sculptured on the columns. All the surfaces are ornamented with gay sculptures, partly in relief and partly in intaglio, which, however, were only completed under the successors of the founder, and mostly by his son Ramses Miamun. Before this hypostole, a large hypathrale court, of about 270 to 320 feet, was afterwards erected, with a majestic pylon, and ornamented only on the sides by pillars.

Here the great plan of the temple terminated a length of 1,170 feet, without reckoning the row of sphinxes before its exterior pylon, and without the private sanctuary which was erected by Ramses Miamun directly against the furthest wall of the temple, and in the same area, but in such a manner that the entrance to it was on the opposite side. This enlargement reckoned with it, would make the whole length nearly 2,000 feet, to the southernmost gate of the outer wall, which makes the whole place about the same breadth. The later dynasties, who found this principal temple completed on all sides, and yet could not renounce the idea of doing honour to this centre of Theban worship, began by erecting small temples on the great plain surrounded by the outer wall, and afterwards gradually enlarging these again.

The head of the twentieth dynasty, Ramses III., whose warlike deeds in Asia in the fifteenth century before Christ, were scarcely inferior to those of his renowned ancestors, Sethos I. and Ramses II., built a separate temple with a court of columns, and hypostole above two hundred feet long, which now destroys the symmetry of the outer wall of the great court, and founded at a little distance from it, a still larger sanctuary for the third person of the Theban Triad, Chensu the son of Ammon. This last was completed by the succeeding kings of his dynasty, and the priest-kings of the twenty-first dynasty, who added a stately court of columns and a pylon.

Out of the twenty-second dynasty, Sheshenk I. is known, the warrior king Shishak of the Bible, who conquered Jerusalem in 970 B.C. His Asiatic campaigns are recorded in the southern outer wall of the great temple, where, under the symbolical figures of prisoners, he lays one hundred and forty conquered cities and countries before Ammon. Among their names there is one, which, not without foundation, is thought to be the denomination of the kingdom of Judah, as also the names of several well known cities of Palestine.

The two above-mentioned priest-dynasties, which followed immediately after the dynasties of the Ramses, were no longer of Theban origin, but came from the cities of Lower Egypt. The power of the kingdom sank upon this change, and after the short twenty-three dynasties, of which there are, nevertheless, some remains yet to be found in Karnak, there appears to have been a revolution. The present lists of the historians mention only one king of the twenty-fourth dynasty who has not been discovered upon the Egyptian monuments. Under him occurred the irruption of the Ethiopians, who form the twenty-fifth dynasty. Shabak and Tahraka (So and Tirhaka of the Bible) reigned in Egypt in the beginning of the seventh century, B.C. These kings came from Ethiopia, but governed quite in the Egyptian manner. They, too, did not forget to pay their reverence to the Egyptian divine kings. Their names are found on several little temples at Karnak, and on a stately colonnade in the great outer court, which appears to have been first erected by Tahraka. The latter retired, according to history, voluntarily into Ethiopia, and left the Egyptian empire to its native rulers. The supplanted Saitic dynasty now returned to the throne, and again unfolded in the seventh and eight centuries the splendour, which in this country, so rich in resources and in outward might, was able to be displayed under an energetic and wise sceptre. That dynasty first opened Egypt for peaceful communication with foreign countries; Greeks settled among them, commerce flourished and accumulated new and immense riches, formerly alone obtained by rapine and tribute. But the excitement was only artificial, for the fresh energy of the nations had long been broken; art, too, matured luxury rather than practical worth. The last national glory soon passed away. The country could no longer withstand the coming storm of the Persians. In the year 525 B.C., it was conquered by Cambyses, and trodden down by barbarian fanaticism. Many monuments were destroyed, and no sanctuary, no wall was raised within this period; at least nothing has been preserved to our times of that era, not even of the long and mild government of Darius, of whom a temple, or only sculptures with his name alone, are found in the Oasis of Kargeh. Under Darius II., just one hundred years after the beginning of the Persian supremacy, Egypt again became independent, and we immediately find again the names of the native kings in the temples of Karnak, but after three dynasties had followed one another in rapid succession within sixty-four years, it again fell under the dominion of the Persians, who soon afterward lost it to Alexander of Macedonia, in the year 332 B.C. After that the land was obliged to accustom itself to foreign rule; it had lost its national independence, and passed from one hand to another, the last always worse than the preceding, down to the present day.

Egypt still had vivifying power enough under the Macedonians and Greeks to keep up its religion and institutions in the ancient way. The foreign princes occupied in every way the places and footsteps of the ancient Pharaohs. Karnak also bears testimony to that. We here find the names of Alexander and Philip Aridæus, who preceded the Ptolemies in the restoration of that which the Persians had destroyed. Alexander rebuilt the back, Philip the front sanctuary of the great temple; the Ptolemies added sculptures to it, restored other parts, and even erected new sanctuaries at no small cost, but of course no longer in the magnificent, classic-Egyptian style of ancient times. Even the last epoch of expiring Egypt, that of the Roman supremacy, is still represented in Karnak by a number of representations, carried out under Augustus Cæsar.

Thus this remarkable place, which in the lapse of 3,500 years had grown from the little sanctuary in the midst of the great temple, into an entire temple-city covering a surface of a quarter of a geographical mile in length, and about 2,000 feet in breadth, is also an almost unbroken thread and an interesting standard for the history of the whole New Egyptian empire, from its commencement in the Old Empire down to its fall under the Roman rule. Almost in the same proportion as the dynasties and kings are portrayed in and about the temple of Karnak, they stand forth or retire in Egyptian history.

Up the river from Karnak, where the stream, parted by the fertile island of el Gedîdeh, again unites, a second glorious memorial of the ancient city arises: the temple of Luqsor. One of the mightiest Pharaohs of the eighteenth dynasty, Amenophis III., who had only built a side temple at Karnak, adding little to the principal structure, here erected a sanctuary, made the more magnificent on account of the little he had done at Karnak, dedicated to Ammon, which the great Ramses enlarged by a second stately court toward Karnak. For, although a good half-hour distant, this temple must yet be looked upon as within the ancient and sacred bounds of the great national sanctuary. That is proved by the otherwise difficult, and inexplicable circumstance, that the entrance of the temple, although hard by the shore, is yet turned away from the river and toward Karnak, with which it was also architecturally placed in direct connection by colonnades, series of rams, and roads.

With Luqsor end the ruins on the eastern shore. The monuments of western Thebes offer a still greater variety, because here the subterranean dwellings and places of the dead are added to the superterranean structures for the living. From Qurna there once extended an unbroken series of the most magnificent temples to Medînet Habu, almost filling the narrow desert district between the Nile-steeped fertile land and the foot of the mountains. Immediately behind these temples stretches the vast Necropolis, the tombs of which lying close together like bee-cells, are hewn partly in the rock-soil of the plain, partly in the adjoining hills.

Qurna is situated on that spur of the Libyan mountains nearest to the river. In suddenly turning to the west, the mountains form a species of ravine, the outer part of which, where it is separated from the valley by low ranges of hills, is called El Asasîf. Behind it is bounded by high, steep crags, which rear their glorious stone in the noon and morning sun. These sudden precipices of the limestone mountains, so firmly and equally grown, and therefore so eminently calculated for the sculptures in the rock-tombs, seem to have arisen on the clay stratum beneath, which has withdrawn by its gradual disintegration.

In this rock-creek are the oldest graves belonging to the Old Empire. Their entrances are seen far up in the northern rocks, directly under the perpendicular wall, which ascends from the suddenly-inclined rubbish-mounds to the tops of the mountain-ridges. This outer position, and the paths bordered with low stone walls, leading steeply and straightly from the valley several hundred feet to their entrances, reminded me at once of the graves of Benihassan of the same period. They were made in the second half of the third millenium B.C., under the king of the eleventh and twelfth dynasties of Manetho, of which the former founded the might of Thebes, and erected the city into the seat of their dominion, independent of Memphis, the latter rendered it the imperial city of the whole country.

These grottos, of which some are found on the

neighbouring hills of the same, mostly descend deep into the rock in an obtuse angle, but are not painted or written; on the stone sarcophagi only were there any particular pains bestowed; these consist usually of the finest limestone, and are occasionally more than nine feet long, and are decorated and written in the careful and pure style of that period, but with a certain degree of sparingness. One of these sarcophagi we shall bring with us, as I have already once stated. It has, a few days since, been safely transported into the plain, after the long totally choked-up shaft had been excavated, and the living rock itself broken through, to obtain a shorter way out. The person to whom the grave belonged was the son of a prince, and himself bore the dynastic name Nentef, of the eleventh royal dynasty.

In the outermost corner of the same rock-creek is situated the oldest temple structure of western Thebes, which belongs to the period of the first mighty regeneration of the New Egyptian Empire. A street, above 1,600 feet long, ornamented on both sides by colossal rams and sphinxes, led from the valley in a straight line to a court, then by a flight of steps to another, the front wall of which was adorned with representations, and a colonnade, and at last by a second stair to a well-preserved granite portal, and the last temple court surrounded on both sides by decorated halls and chambers, and ended behind by a broad façade built on to the steep rock-wall. By another granite portal in the middle of this façade, we come at last into the innermost space of the temple, hewn in the rock and vaulted with stone, whence again several little niches and spaces opened to the sides and back. All these places were covered with the most beautiful paintings, gaily coloured on a grey ground, and executed in the most finished style of the period. This grand structure, beside which other now destroyed buildings once stood, seems originally to have been connected with the river by a street traversing the whole valley, and reaching the great temple of Karnak on the other side; and I doubt not that for this behoof the narrow, rockgate was artificially broken through, by which the temple road leads on its entrance into the valley. It was a Queen Numt Amen, the elder sister of Tuthmosis III., who carried out this daring design of an architectural communication between both the sides of the valley, the same who erected the largest obelisks before the temple of Karnak. She is never represented on her monuments as a woman, but in male attire; the inscriptions alone inform us of her sex. Without doubt it was then against the legitimate rule that a woman should hold the government; for that reason probably her brother, who was still a minor, appears as a co-regent. After her death, all her cartouches were turned into Tuthmosis-cartouches, the feminine expressions of the inscriptions changed, and her name was never mentioned in the later lists of the legitimate kings.

Of Tuthmosis III., who completed the work of his royal sister during his long reign, two temples still exist, both erected at the edge of the desert. The northernmost one of these is now only recog-

nisable in its foundations and in the remains of
its brick pylones; the southern one, however, near
Medînet Habu is yet well preserved, and, to judge
from some sculptures, might belong in its first plan-
ning to an earlier Tuthmosis, and was only completed
by the other. His second successor, Tuthmosis IV.,
also erected a temple, now almost disappeared.

He was followed by Amenophis III., under whose
long and glorious reign the temple of Luqsor was built.
He is represented by the two giant colossi, near Medînet Habu, pushed far forward into the fertile plain,
once standing at the gate of a mighty temple,
the remains of which, however, principally lie buried
under the harvests of the annually rising soil of the
valley. Perhaps a roadway, like that to the north,
led hence through the valley to the opposite Luqsor.
The north-eastern of the two colossi was the celebrated vocal statue, to which the Greeks attached
the pleasant legend of the handsome Memnon, who
greeted his mother Aurora every morn at sunrise,
while she, because of his early hero-death, watered
him with her dewy tears. This mythos, as Letronne has proved, was formed at a very late period ;
as the peculiar phenomena of the trembling tone, the
consequence of the cracking of little particles by the
sudden warming of the cold stone, took its rise
when the statue, already cracked, was more shattered by an earthquake in the year 27 B.C. The
occurrence of cracking and sounding stones in
the desert and in great fields of ruins is not
unfrequent in Egypt; the nature of the flint
conglomerate of which the statue is composed is
particularly inclined to it, as the innumerable

cracks, great and small, which pass in every direction through those portions of the statue inscribed at the Greek period, at that time therefore unharmed, show. It is also remarkable how many of the cracked and loose pieces sound bell-like on being struck, while others remain dead and toneless, according as their respective positions make them more or less damped. The numerous Greek and Roman inscriptions which are graven on the statue, and announce the visit of foreigners, particularly if they had been so fortunate as to hear the morning greeting, begin first under Nero, and only go down to the time of Septimius Severus, to whom is due the restoration of the originally monolithic statue. Since this re-erection of the upper portion in single block, the phenomenon of the sounding stone appears to have become less frequent and less apparent, if had not quite stopped. The mutation of the name of the still remembered Amenophis (as the inscriptions testify) into Memnon seems to have been principally induced by the name of this western side of Thebes, Memnonia, which the Greeks seem to have explained to themselves as " Palaces of Memnon," while the name, hieroglyphically *mennu*, signified " palaces " in general. At the present day the statues are called Shama and Tama by the Arabs, or together the Sanamât (not Salamât), *i. e.* " the idols."*

---

* Talamât " the greetings " are they called by earlier travellers. The proper pronunciation and meaning was first remarked to me by our intelligent old guide, Auad. The Arabs are for confounding them, as سَلَام *salâm*, *salus*, is pronounced with the

When we arrived here at the beginning of November, the whole plain, as far as we could see, was inundated, and formed a single ocean, from which the Sanamât arose more strange and lonely than from the green and accessible fields. I have a few days since measured the colossi, as also the rise of the Nile deposit on the bases of their thrones. The height of the Memnon statue, reckoned from head to foot, but without the tall headdress they once wore, was 14·28 metres, or 45½ feet, and to this the base, another block, 4·25 metres, or 13 feet 7 inches, of which about three feet was hidden by a surrounding step. Thus the statues originally stood nearly sixty feet (perhaps nearly seventy feet with the pshent) above the level of the temple. Now the level of the valley is eight feet above this soil, and the inundation sometimes rises to the upper edge of the bases, therefore fourteen feet higher than it could have done at the time of its erection, if the water was not to reach the temple. If this fact be added to our discovery at Semneh, where the mirror of the Nile had sunk

dental *sin*, صنم *s'anam*, *idolum*, with the lingual *sdd*. The plural, which is usually أصنام *as'nam*, here takes the feminine form صنمات *s'anamât*. That they were male figures had long since been indistinguishable from the battered heads. The stone of which the statues are formed is a peculiarly hard quartz brittle sandstone conglomerate, looking glazed, and with innumerable cracks. The frequent bursting of little particles of stone at sunrise, when the changes of temperature are most sudden, caused, according to my idea, the celebrated Memnon sounds, which were compared with the breaking of a violin string.

above twenty-three feet in historical times, it is
plain from that simple addition, that the Nile in the
cataracts, between here and Semneh, fell at least
thirty-seven feet deeper then than now.

The last king, too, of that great eighteenth
dynasty, Horus, had erected a temple in the neighbourhood of Medînet Habu, which, however, is
now buried in the rubbish. The fragments of a
colossal statue of the king in hard, almost marble,
limestone, the bust of which formed in the most
perfect style, weighing several hundred centenaries,
is intended for our museum, seem to indicate the
position of the former temple entrance.

Two temples of the next dynasty are preserved,
which were built by the two mightiest and most
celebrated of all the Pharaohs, Sethos I., and his
son Ramses II. The temple of the former is the
northernmost in position, and is usually denominated the temple of Qurna, as the old village of
Qurna here grew up round a Koptic church, lying
principally within the great temple courts, but was
subsequently abandoned by the inhabitants, and
changed for the rock tombs of the neighbouring
mountain spur.

Farther south, between the now quite destroyed
temples of Tuthmosis III. and IV., lies the temple
of Ramses (II.) Miamun, the most beautiful, probably, in Egypt, as to architectural design and proportions, though behind that of Karnak in grandeur
and various interest. The back part of the temple,
as also the halls of the hypostole, have disappeared,
and their original plan could only be ascertained
by long and continued excavations carefully superin-

tended by Erbkam. Round about this destroyed
part of the temples, the spacious brick saloons are
visible, which are all covered by regularly well built
cylindrical vaults, and belong to the period of the
erection of the temple. For this is unmistakeably
proved by the stamps, which were imprinted on
each brick in the royal factory, and contain the
cartouches of King Ramses. That this temple
had already attracted great attention in antiquity,
is evident from the particular description which
Diodorus Siculus gives of it after Hecatæus, under
the name of the Tomb of Osymandyas.

Immediately to the right of the temple, one of
the few industrious Fellahs has planted a little
kitchen garden, which gives us some change at our
table, and was therefore spared, as it should be,
with respect, in our excavations, which threatened
to extend thither, at the entreaty of the friendly
brown gardener, although it covers the foundation
of a small temple not previously seen, the entrance
of which I found in the first court of the Ramses
temple.

The most southern and best preserved of the
temple palaces, lies amid the ruined houses of Medînet Habu, a Koptic city, now quite deserted, but
once not inconsiderable. It was founded by Ramses
III. the first king of the twentieth dynasty, the
wealthy Rhampsinitus of Herodotus,* in the thirteenth century B.C., and it celebrates on its walls
the tremendous wars of this king by land and sea,
which might vie with those of the great Ramses.
Within the second court a great church was founded

[* Herodotus II. c.c. 121-122.—K. R. H. M.]

by the Kopts, the monolithic columns of which still lie scattered around. The back places are mostly buried in rubbish. But of very peculiar interest is the far-projected pylon-like fore-building of the temple, which contained, in four stories, one above another, the private rooms of the king. On its wall, the prince is represented in the midst of his family; however, he caresses his daughters, known as princesses by their side-locks, plays draughts with them, and receives fruits and flowers from them.

With this building closes the great series of palace-temples, known by the particular designation of Memnonia. They embrace the actual prime of the New Empire, for after Ramses III. the outward might, as well as the inward greatness of the empire declined. Of this period only, and that immediately following, do we find the tombs of the kings in the rock valleys of the mountains.

To these the entrance lies on the other side of the promontory of Qurna. Wild and desolate, the rock walls, which round themselves off to bald peaks, rise on both sides, and have their golden tops covered with coal-black stones, burnt, as it were, by the sun. The peculiarly solemn and dull character of this region always struck me the most when I rode after sunset over the unmeasureable rock rubbish which covers the earth to a great height, and is only interrupted by broad water-streams, which have formed themselves in the course of thousands of years, by the unfrequent, though not unknown storms, as experience has shown. All around, everything is dumb and dead; only now and then the hollow bark of the jackal, or the ominous cries of the night owl,

varies the sound of the active hoof of my little
donkey.

After many windings, which lead by great cir-
cuits almost immediately behind the high mountain
wall of the already described valley of Asasif, the
dale parts into two arms, of which the right one
leads up to the oldest of the tombs. Two only of
these are opened, both of the eighteenth dynasty,
the one belonging to the time of Amenophis IV. the
Memnon of the Greeks, the other to the king of
Ai, a contemporaneous king soon succeeding him,
who is not included in the monumental lists of the
legitimate kings.* The latter lies at the outer end
of the slowly rising rock ravine ; the granite sarcophagus of the king has been shattered in the little
tomb-chamber, and his name is everywhere carefully erased, to the least line, on the walls as well as
on the sarcophagus. The other lies far forward in
the vale, is of great extent, and with handsome, but
unfortunately much mutilated sculptures, through
the hands of time and mankind. Besides these two
graves, there are several others incomplete without
sculpture ; others, without doubt, are hidden under
the high mounds of rubbish, the removal of which
would take more time and means than we thought
proper to give to it after severe trials. On one
place, where I had excavations made after tolerably

* This King Ai was formerly a private individual, and took
his sacerdotal title into his royal cartouche at a later period.
He appears with his wife in the tombs of Amarna, not
unfrequently as a noble and peculiarly honoured officer of King
Amenophis IV., that puritanical sun-worshipper, who changed
his name into that of Bech-en-aten.

certain proofs, a door and chamber were certainly
discovered about ten feet below the rubbish, but
without sculptures. Yet some remains of bases
were brought to light, containing a yet unknown
royal title.

The left branch of the principal valley, which
was originally closed by an elevation of the soil, and
was first opened artificially by a prepared pathway,
at this place contains the graves of almost all the
kings of the nineteenth and twentieth dynasties.

Here usually there sinks a wide-mouthed shaft, on
one of the declivities of the hills, not very high over
the level of the valley, descending in an oblique
angle. As soon as the overhanging rock has reached
a perpendicular height of twelve to fifteen feet, the
sharply-cut door-posts at the first entrance appear
at once, provided with one or two great doors for
closing. There too, the painted sculptures usually
begin, forming a strange contrast to the sudden
visitor between the craggy rocks, and the wild
stones, by their sharp lines, shining surfaces, and
fresh living colours. Long corridors of imposing
height and width lead one still farther into the
rock mountains. In single divisions, formed by the
narrowing of the passage, and by new doors, the
paintings continue on the walls and ceiling. The
king appears adoring several gods, and addressing to
them his prayers and his excuses for his earthly
career. The peaceful employed of the beatified
spirits are portrayed on one wall, and the torments
of the wicked on the other; on the ceiling, the goddess is depicted lying along, as well as the hours of
the day and night with the influences which they

exercise on mankind, and the astrological meanings, all accompanied with explanatory inscriptions. At length we arrive in a great vaulted pillared saloon, the walls of which generally show the representations on a golden yellow ground, from which it has received the name of the Golden Saloon. This was intended for the royal sarcophagus, which stood in the middle from six to ten feet in height. But often when the king, after the tomb was completed, felt himself yet unweakened in his powers, and expected another series of years, the middle passage of this saloon was hewn in a steeper manner, as the beginning of a new one ; new corridors and chambers were produced ; sometimes the direction of the excavation was altered, until the king put a second period to the work, and the series was closed with a second hall, generally more spacious and magnificent than the first ; to this were added, if time permitted, smaller spaces at both sides, destined for particular offerings to the dead, until the last hour sounded, and the royal corpse, after its seventy days of embalment, was laid in the sarcophagus. This was then so cunningly closed, that the granite colossus had always to be broken in pieces by the later violaters of the graves, as the cover could not be lifted off.

The tombs of the princesses also, which lie altogether in a little valley behind Medînet Habu, at the southern end of Memnonia, belong without doubt to the eighteenth and twentieth dynasties, as also the most important of the numerous private tombs, which extend from the other side of Medînet Habu, over mountain and valley to the entrance of the Valley of Kings. The priests of rank, and high officers, were fond of representing in their tombs all their wealth in horses, carriages, herds, boats, and household goods, as well as their hunting-grounds, fish-ponds, gardens, and halls ; even the artificer and mechanic, busied in their different employments, are to be found on many of the walls ; on which account many of these are of higher interest to us than even the king's tombs, the representations on which are almost always carried through the whole life to the death.

Of later monuments, those of the twenty-sixth dynasty, in the seventh and sixth century before Christ, are the most remarkable. The greater number of these are in the rocky cove between Qurna and the hill Abd el Qurna, hewn out of flat surfaces, and are, for distinction, called el Asasif. The rocky plains here alone offered room for inscriptions, and these have been largely used. Already, from here, may be perceived a multitude of high gates and walls built of black bricks ; these enclose, in long squares, sunken courts, the entrances to which are high arched pylon-doors, which, from a distance, look like large Roman triumphal arches. When you enter within the walls, you look directly into the court, dug down into the rock from twelve to fifteen feet deep, which you can descend by a staircase. This uncovered court is now the largest accessible tomb, one hundred feet long and seventy-four broad ; it was excavated for a royal writer, named Petamenap. From this you go through an antechamber into a large rock-hall, with two rows of pillars, of an extent of sixty-five feet by fifty-two feet, with rooms and corridors on both sides; then through an arched entrance into a second hall with eight pillars, of about fifty-two feet by thirty-six feet; and then into a third hall with four pillars, thirty-one feet long and broad; and at last into a chamber twenty feet by twelve feet, which ends in a niche. Out of this chamber, at the end of the first row of rooms, a door leads into a very large room, and to the right into another, to a continuation of six corridors, with two stair-cases of nine steps and one of twenty-three steps, into a chamber, in which a pit forty-four feet deep, leads to another small room. This second course of rooms and passages, which run at a right angle to the first, are 172 feet long, but the first, reckoning the outer court with them, is 311 feet. From the fountain-room, another corridor leads to the right into a diagonal room, together measuring fifty-eight feet in this direction. Before the two stair-cases, in the second suite of rooms, there opens a fourth line of passages to the right, running in the same direction for 122 feet, in which, to the left, is a large square space sixty feet each way, with other rooms adjoining, the interior of which, on the four sides, is ornamented like a monstrous sarcophagus. In the middle, under this great square, rests the sarcophagus of the dead, which one, however, can only reach by means of a sunken pit of eighteen feet deep, which reaches to the fourth suite, by a horizontal passage of fifty-eight feet, to a third pit; through this to new rooms, and at last through the roof of the last to another room, containing the sarcophagus, which really lies exactly

under the centre of the above described square.
The whole surface of this private tomb is reckoned
at 21,600 feet, and with the pit-room 23,148 square
feet.* This immense work appears much more
colossal when one recollects that all the walls, pillars, and doors from top to bottom are covered
with innumerable inscriptions and representations,
which, from the carefulness, exactitude, and elegance
of the execution, throw one into ever-increasing
astonishment.

Much less important are the few remains to
be found of the later foreign dominion. Of these
there are only two small temples in the neighbourhood of Medînet Habu, erected under the Ptolemies, and a third may be mentioned, which lies to
the south, at the end of the great lake of Medînet
Habu. The oldest sculptures in this last temple
are of the time of Cæsar Augustus; but the well-
preserved cell of Antoninus Pius was already built
at that time. The outer door of this temple contains the only representation yet found of the
Emperor Otho, the discovery of which afforded an
immense pleasure to Champollion and Rosellini.
They, however, overlooked the circumstance that
on the opposite side the name of the Emperor
Galba was to be found, till then unknown in
Egypt.

So soon as the time of Strabo, ancient Thebes
was already divided into several villages, and Ger-
manicus visited it as we do, out of a desire for
knowledge, and respect for the great antiquity of
its monuments, " cognoscendæ antiquitatis," as Ta-

* The above dimensions are here taken from Wilkinson's
Modern Egypt and Thebes, vol. ii. p. 220.

citus informs us. Decius, A.D. 250, is the Emperor's
name, which I have found mentioned in hieroglyphics in all Egypt; it appears in a representation in the temple of Esneh. A century later the
holy Athanasius retired into the Theban desert,
among the Christian Hermits. The edict of Theo-
dosius against heathendom, A. D. 391, deprived the
Egyptian temples of their last authority, and favoured
that of the monks and hermits, before whom, from
that time, Egyptian Christendom bowed down.

From that time there arose in the whole country,
and soon after in the neighbourhood of the Upper
Nile, innumerable churches and convents, and the
caverns of the desert were turned into troglodyte
dwellings, for an ascetic hermit population.* The
Theban Necropolis afforded above all places con-
venience for this new requisition. The tombs of
the kings, as well as the private ones, were used as
Christian cells, and soon bore on their walls traces
of their new destination. In a tomb at Qurna,
there is still a letter from St. Athanasius, arch-
bishop of Alexandria, to the orthodox monks of
Thebes, preserved on the white stucco in handsome
uncials, but unfortunately in a very fragmentary
state. They were particularly fond of turning
ancient temples into Koptic churches or convents.

In the temple of Medînet Habu (city of Habu),
the largest church appears to have been erected.
Immense monolithic, granite columns, cover the
floor of the second court in great numbers; in order
to make room for the choir, an old Egyptian column,

[* For an excellent description of such retreats, *vide* Floss,
Quæstiones Criticæ de Macaris, cap. i. § 1. *Coloniæ Heberle*,
MDCCCL.—K. R. H. M.]

on the north side, has been removed; and from the rooms transformed into priests' cells there has been a row of doors broken in the outer wall. The adjoining convent, Dêr el Medînet, surnamed " the townley," was erected near the Ptolemic temple, behind the hill of Qurnet Murrâi. Another church stood in the temple of Old Qurna, and to it belonged most probably the convent Dêr el Bachît, which lies on the hill of Qurna. The ruins of a third convent cover the space of the temple of the Queen Numt-amen, in the corner of the valley of Asasif, and bear the name of Dêr el Bahri, the northern convent.

Such changes in these ancient palace structures ensured their being upheld, sometimes to their advantage, and sometimes to their disadvantage. Numbers of walls were either removed or broken through, in order to make room for new arrangements; on others, the heathen representations were destroyed, in order to make naked walls, or the human figures, and even the figures of animals in the inscriptions, particularly the heads, even up to the roofs were violently hacked and disfigured. Sometimes, however, the same pious, busy hands served us by preserving the ancient glory in the most complete manner; instead of tiring themselves with the hammer, they plastered them over from top to bottom with Nile earth, which afterwards was generally covered with white, in order to receive Christian pictures. In the course of time, however, this Koptic plaster crumbled away, and the ancient painting appeared again, with a brilliancy and astonishing freshness, which they would have hardly retained had they been left uncovered, and exposed to the sun and air. In the niche of an old cell I found St. Peter in old-Byzantine style, holding the keys, and pointing upwards with his finger; out of his nimbus peeped, however, from his half-fallen Christian mantle the cow-horns of the goddess Hathor, the Egyptian Venus; to her was brought originally the incense and the sacrifices of the neighbouring kings, which were now offered to the reverend apostle. Often have I assisted time with my own hand, to loosen the generally uninteresting Koptic representation on the plaster, in order to bring out the hidden magnificent sculptures of the Egyptian gods and kings, to their ancient and greater right upon our studies.

A great part of the Theban population is still Koptic on both sides of the Nile; our Christian cook Siriân was born here, and a rich Kopt, Mustafieh, who does not live far from us, brings us daily most excellent wheaten bread. But for a long time the Arabian Mahommedan population has taken the lead here, as well as in the whole country, against which the Kopts have only ancient customs to bring forward, and their knowledge of calculation, and the right of settlement in the most important financial places.

The little church in which now every Sunday the Theban Christians assemble, lies isolated in the great stony plain south of Medînet Habu. It has an Arabic cupola, and is surrounded by a court and wall. A few days since I went there, as I observed that the black turbans, which are only worn by the Kopts, were going to the chapel in greater number

than usual. They were celebrating the feast of St.
Donadeos, who founded the church. The service
was over; I met the old priest (who lived in, and
took care of the church), together with his numerous family. The spaces were covered with mats;
they showed me the divisions for the men and the
women, the little chapels ornamented with gay
carvings, the square fonts for christening, and holy
water. Upon the reading-desk lay a large old
Koptic book, with sections of the Psalms and the
Gospels, and Arabic translations of them; I asked
the old man if he could read Koptic; he answered
in the affirmative, but said his little boy could do it
better than he; his eyes had already become weak.
I now seated myself upon the mat, and the whole
swarm of big and little yellow-brown children and
grandchildren of the old priest squatted round
me. I asked the eldest boy to read to me,
and he immediately, with great fluency, began,
not to read, but to sing, i. e. to chaunt in an
awkward, grumbling tone. I interrupted him, and
requested him to read slowly in his usual voice;
this he did with great difficulty and making
many mistakes, which his younger brother sometimes corrected over his shoulder; but when I
went so far as to ask the meaning of the separate
words, he pointed coolly to the Arabic translation,
and told me that it was all there, and wanted to
read it to me; as to the single words, or the value
of the single letters over the sections, he could give
no account, and the old man also had doubtless
never understood them. I then asked them to show
me the rest of the book-treasures belonging to the

church, they were immediately brought to me, in a
large cloth, tied up by the four corners; it contained
some much-read Koptic and Arabic prayer-books.
I left a small present for the benefit of the church,
and I had already ridden some distance, when one of
the boys overtook me, and out of breath, brought
me a small holy cake of biscuit, stamped with
Koptic crosses and Greek inscriptions, which had to
be paid for by a second bakshish. These are the
Epigoni, the purest, unmixed successors of that
ancient Pharoah-people, who formerly conquered
Asia and Ethiopia, and led their prisoners from the
north and south, into the great hall of Ammon, at
Karnak, in whose wisdom Moses was educated, and
to whose priesthood the Greek sages went to
school.

"*O Aegypte, Aegypte! religionum tuarum solae
supererunt fabulæ, aeque, incredibiles posteris, solaque
supererunt verba lapidibus incisa tua pia facta nar-
rantibus, et inhabitabit Aegyptum Scythes aut Indus
aut aliquis talis, id est vicina barbaria.*" *

Now we know this *aliquis*, whom Hermes Trisme-
gistos could not name; it is the Turk, housing
now in the regions of Osiris.

At the foot of our hill towards the green plain
there stands a fine clump of sont-trees, overshadow-
ing a friendly well-built cistern; here the sheep and
goats are daily watered, and every evening and
morning the brown maidens and the veiled matrons,
in their blue draped garments, come down from
their rock-caves, and then return with a solemn step,
with their water-jugs on their heads; a lovely pic-

* Apuleii Asclepius, dialogus Hermetis Trismegisti, c. 24.

ture from the patriarchal times. But hard by this
place of the refreshing element there lies in the
middle of the fruitful field a white barren spot ; on
it two kilns are erected, on which, whenever there
is any want of material, the next blocks of the old
temples and rock-caves, with their paintings and
inscriptions, are crushed and burnt into lime for
mortar to join other blocks drawn from these handy
and inexhaustible quarries, into a stable or some
other government buildings.

On the same day on which I had visited the
Koptic church, I desired to ride thence to the village of Kôm el Birât, on the opposite side of the
great lake of Habu, now dried up. To my no small
astonishment my guide, the excellent old 'Auad,
whom I have taken into my service on account of
his immense acquaintance with the locality, declared
to me that he could not accompany me ; indeed, he
almost dreaded to mention the name of the village,
and could not be induced to tell me anything
about it, or about his strange behaviour. At home,
I first learnt through others, at a later time too
from himself, the reason of his refusal. Seven or
eight years before, a man was killed in the house of
the sheîkh of Qurna, to whose household 'Auad then
belonged, though for what cause does not appear.
In consequence of this event, the whole family of
the murdered man emigrated hence, and settled in
Kôm el Birât. Since that time the law of blood-
vengeance exists between the two houses. No
member of that family has since set foot on the soil
of Qurna, and if 'Auad, or any one else from the
house of the sheikh were to show himself in that

village, any member of the injured family would be
quite right in killing him in open day.* Such is
the ancient Arab custom.

I return from my wandering through the ruins of
the royal city, and through the changing thousands
of years, which have passed over them, to our fort
on the exposed hill of Abd el Qurna. Wilkinson
and Hay have done an eminent service to later travellers, who, like ourselves, purpose remaining a
long time in Thebes, by the restoration of these
inhabitable places. An easy broad way leads wind
ingly from the plain to a spacious court, the left side
of which towards the mountain is formed by a long
shadowy pillared row; behind this are several inhabitable rooms. At the extremity of the court
there is still a single watch-tower, whence the Prussian flag is streaming, and close by it a little house
of two stories, the lower of which I myself inhabit.
Space, too, is there for the kitchen, the servants, and
the donkeys.

Incomparably beautiful and attractive is the
boundless prospect over the Thebaic plain from the
wall of the court, low towards the inside and deep
on the outside. Here all that remains of ancient
Thebes may be seen, or still better from the battle-
ments of the tower or from the hills immediately
behind our house. Before us the magnificent ruins
of the Memnonia, from the hill of Qurna on the
left, to the high pylones towering over the black
ruins of Medînet Habu to the right, then the green
region surrounded by the broad Nile, whence on the

* When I wrote the above, I did not think that the crime
would be so soon avenged. See Letter XXXV.

right the lonely colossi of Amenophis rise ; and on the
other side of the river the temple groups of Karnak
and Luqsor, behind the plain, stretches for several
hours to the sharp little undulating outline of the
Arabian mountains, over which we see the first rays
of the sun gleaming, and pouring a wonderful flood
of colours over the valley and rocky desert. I cannot compare this ever-existing prospect with any
other in the world ; but it reminds me forcibly of
the picture, which I had for two years, from the top
of the Tarpeian rock, and which comprehended the
whole extent of ancient Rome, from the Aventine
and the Tiber beneath it to the Quirinal, and thence
over the hill to the undulating Campagna, with the
beautiful profile, so strikingly like the one here, of
the Alvan mount in the back ground.

But our glance never turns on the far-reaching
prospect without gliding down to the silver water-
way with peculiar attention, and following the
pointed sails, which may bring us letters or travellers from the north. Winter here, as everywhere
else, is a season of sociability. A week never passes
in which we do not see several guests. A visitor's
book, which I have opened here for later travellers,
and provided with a preface, was dedicated to that
use by our own signatures at the new year. Since
then more than thirty names have been entered,
although the book is only obtainable at our fort,
and will only be delivered up to our worthy
castellan 'Auad on our departure.

For Christmas we have for the third time selected
a palm, this much nicer symbol than our fir, and
decked it with little gifts and lights. Our artists,

also, celebrated the gay festival in another symbolical manner; and a Christmas manger, carried
out in a typical way, and placed at the end of the
rock-gallery, with the proper lights, was particularly
successful.

Among the travellers England, of course, was
the most fully represented; the French are less
frequent, among whom, however, I must mention
the kindly scholar Ampère, who, as he told me, is
going to remain several months in the country, in
order to improve his Egyptian studies.* But German countrymen are also not wanting, and at the
end of the year we had the pleasure of seeing the
Lic. Strauss, son of the Court Chaplain at Berlin,
enter our dwelling with his cousin Dr. Krafft.
We were just about commencing our simple Sunday
service, which I myself conduct since the departure
of our dear friend and former preacher of the wilderness, Abeken, at Philae. I immediately yielded
up to one of the two reverend gentlemen what was
much more fitting for them than for me, and, as it
happened that we had with us the sermons of both
the fathers of our dear guests, one of them was
chosen for the day. Almost at the same period,
Herr Seufferheld and Dr. Bagge, from Frankfort,

---

* I have since learnt (*Rev. Arch.*, vol. iv. p. 32,) that
M. Ampère had been expressly sent to Egypt, by the Paris
Academy, to copy the bilingual inscription at Philae, to which I
had turned attention in my Letters. See Letter XV. p. 120,
and note. Of the impression brought back to Paris, to which,
however, the beginnings of the Demotic lines, and the date of
the decree are wanting, the very diminished representation of
Demotic text is taken, which M. de Saulcy has published in the
Revue Archéologique.

visited us, and soon after our friend Dr. Schle-
dehaus, from Alexandria, and also the Austrian
painter, Herr Sattler ; and when M.M. Strauss
and Krafft visited us on their return, they met four
other guests, M.M. Tamm, Stamm, and Schwab,
and the assessor Von Rohr, of Berlin. Twelve
Germans sat at our table to-day, among them nine
Prussians.

LETTER XXXI.

UPON THE RED SEA, BETWEEN
GEBEL ZEIT AND TÔR.
Good Friday, March 21, 1845.

OUR ship lies motionless on the water, in sight of
the distant coast of Tôr, which we hoped to have
reached last night. I take pen and paper in hand,
to quiet the most dreadful impatience, which is
caused by an unbearable calm under a hot sun, in a
vessel only intended for packages.

On the 20th of February we crossed from Thebes
from the west to the east shore from Qurna to
Karnak. Here we settled ourselves in some of the
rooms of the great temple; as I hoped, however,
to travel, if possible, to the peninsula of Sinai, so I
restricted myself to the most necessary examination
of the monuments, in order to arrange the work
during my absence.

On the 3rd of March I set off. The younger
Weidenbach accompanied me, to assist me in the
necessary drawings; besides him I took with me
our interpreter Jussuf, the *khawass*, Ibrahîm Aga,
Gabre Máriam, and two more servants. We sailed
down the Nile as far as Qeneh. When it became dark
and the stars appeared, the till then lively conversation flagged, and, lying on the deck, I watched
the star Isis and the sparkling Sothis (Sirius), those
pole-stars of Egyptian chronology, as they gradually passed over our heads. Our two boatmen

were only inclined to be too musical, and shouted
out their whole treasury of songs, with an eternal
repetition, only interrupted occasionally by the short
call, *sherk*, *gharb* (east, west), which was answered
by the obedient, soft, boy's voice of our little steers-
man. Half waking, half dreaming, we glided down
the stream till toward midnight ; even the Arabian
din ceased, the stroke of the oars became weaker,
and at last our boat was left entirely to the waves.
The rising of the moon's last quarter, and the grey
dawn of day, first roused us to fresh exertion.

We arrived in good time at Qeneh, where we
were most hospitably received at the house of the
illustrious Seid Hussên. This is the important
personage through whom we send and receive all
our letters, and who has rendered himself highly
esteemed by us on this account. He and his two
sons were highly serviceable to us, by the innumerable preparations which were necessary for our hasty
departure into the desert. In the meantime, I was
delighted by the patriarchal customs which governed
this most worthy family. All business was carried
on here in the open air, as it is in all Eastern
countries, and mostly in the streets. Before each
house is a long divan, another in the room, friends
come, salute shortly, seat themselves almost unnoticed, and the business continues. To important
guests coffee is served, or the long pipe is presented ;
slaves stand round ready on the slightest sign.
Humble acquaintances kiss the hand of the master
of the house, even if they only pass by, all serious
and quiet without pathos, but with the usual sometimes long murmured salutations. Should there be

no more room on the divan, or should it be occupied
by more important persons, the new comers crouch
down on the ground beside it. Every one gets up
and goes when he likes, and what particularly struck
us, without taking leave in any way, notwithstanding
the forms of salutation are so long. The master of
the house will also leave his guests without the
slightest notice, if it be not a noble visitor, which,
when such happens, binds you often for a long time
to the uniform, and generally empty conversation.
This domestic life in the streets, which the old
Greeks and Romans used in a greater or less extent, and which is so different from our office-and-
room life, agrees with the whole Oriental character.
The appearance of each is always proper, attentive
to everything that happens, complaisant and obliging.
In good families, like this, there is, beside, a beautiful and real principle and example of family piety.
The old Hussên is above seventy, tall, with a white
beard ; yet, notwithstanding his age, is an active par-
ticipator in all that is passing, and most friendly to
everybody. The two sons are nearly fifty, and carry
on the business. They treat the old man with the
greatest respect. Both are great smokers, but they
never smoke in the presence of their father, this
would be looked upon as a want of the proper
respect due to him ; they lay the pipe down as soon
as he enters. In the evening, after supper, when
the want of the pipe would be too great a punishment, they seat themselves outside the door to
smoke ; whilst we, as guests, sit with the old man in
the room, and they only take part in the conversation through the door.

On the evening before our departure, we visited a
factory of the celebrated *qullehs* (cooling-vessels) of
which every year 200,000 are made, and also the
field whence the clay is taken used in their formation. It is only one *feddan* (160 square rods) in
size.

On the 6th of March we left Qeneh with fifteen
camels, after two days' stay. The first day we only
rode three hours, as far as the charming well Bir
Ambar, lying among the palms, which has been
supplied by Ibrahim Pasha with a domed building, for the caravans. The second encampment at
the station Leqêta, was soon reached on the following day. The old road to Kossêr from Koptos, the
present Quft, the hills of which we saw to the right
in the distance, leads first to the mountains El Qorn,
(the horns). In their vicinity we first came down into
the broad road-way of Kossêr, and reached Leqêta
after a sixteen hours' march, when the roads from
Qeneh, Quft, (Koptos), Qûs (the ancient ⲕⲱⲥ, or
Apollinopolis parva), and a fourth, leading directly
from Luqsor, all unite. Five wells give tolerable
water there; two half-formed buildings are destined
for the reception of travellers.

Here I observed a trait of Arab hospitality which
I must mention. At the parting meal in Qeneh,
a fresh draught of the well-tasted Nile-water was
handed me in a gilt goblet, elegantly ornamented
with pious passages from the Koran. The simple
yet pleasing form of the segment of a ball pleased
me, and I told old Hussên so without expecting the
answer : " The goblet is thine." As I had nothing
with me to give in return, I passed over the polite-

ness, repeatedly declining the gift, and letting the cup remain without further remark. When I went to rest at night, I found it at my bedside, but gave express orders not to pack it up the next morning. We departed, and I did not open my travelling-bag until we reached Leqêta. How astonished was I, when my first glance again fell upon the carefully-packed goblet. Gabre Máriam had closed my luggage, and he confessed, on my angry question as to how the cup had come there against my order, that he had placed it there at the particular desire of old Seid Hussên. Now I was finally beaten, and had to think of some gift for my return.

We set out the same night from Leqêta, and rode three hours forward to an old, now little used, and waterless station at the Gebel Maáuad. Our Arabs of the Ag'aïze tribe, are not so animated as the Abâbde or Bisharūn, and their camels are worse.

Beyond Gebel Maáuad, we entered the hilly sand-plain Qsûr el Benat, and then again behind another pass, the plain Reshrashi. At the end of them to the left, rises the Gebel Abu Gûeh, on which we turned our backs, and passed round the corner of a rock, on the sandstone walls of which I found the cartouches of the sun-worshipper Amenophis IV. and his queen, with the shining sun * sculptured over them. Their names were partly erased as everywhere else, although the king had not then

[* In Bunsen's list of Determinatives, No. 5. I quote his description " Disk diffusing rays of light ; light, as *sti*, a sun-beam, (sun's ray) ; *ht*, daylight ; *ubn*, to illuminate ; *mau*, to gleam ; *ui*, brilliancy ; *hai*, light ; *am*, a beam." Bunsen's Egypt's Place, vol. i. p. 537.—K. R. H. M.]

assumed the name of Bech-en-aten. Toward noon
we entered the mountain, and in three quarters of
an hour we arrived at the well Hamamât.

Here there seems to have been an ancient Koptic
colony, and the broad wall built down to the depth
of nearly eighty feet, in which a winding stair leads
to the bottom, is still ascribed by the Arabs to the
Nazâra, the Christians. The ancient quarries, our
next goal, were distant about half an hour from the
well.

In a spacious grotto, covered with Greek and
Roman inscriptions, I established my principal
quarters ; as a cursory view amply demonstrated that
we had several days' work before us. The ancient
Egyptians, who were great admirers and excellent
connoisseurs of the different sorts of stone, had here
found a layer of precious green breccia, and beside
that, fine dark-coloured veins of granite, which had
already been exhausted under the sixth dynasty in the
beginning of the thirtieth century B.C. Since that
time, numerous inscriptions have been found on the
surrounding rocks. Among these some of the Persian rule are particularly worthy of note. The hieroglyphical cartouches of Cambyses, Darius, Xerxes,
and Artaxerxes, are almost solely known from hence,
and a royal high architect of the dynasty of the
Psammetici has given his family-tree in no less than
twenty-three generations, who, without a single
exception, all occupied the same important post,
and partly in connection with considerable sacerdotal offices. At the top of the long list is an
ancestress, who must have lived seven hundred
years before the last link of the chain. A great

number of Greek proscynemata also lead us to the
conclusion that the quarries were used even in the
Greek and Roman time. We were engaged for
five days from an early hour till late in the evening in these impressions and copies, to the great
astonishment of the small caravans that passed almost
every day, as the great pilgrim-road from Upper
Egypt, and a great part of the Sudan leads through
this valley to Kossêr and Mekka.

My purpose had originally been to have gone
from Qeneh to Kossêr, and thence embark for Tôr.
But as the passage takes a long time, I was very
glad to learn at Qeneh, that there is also a way
from Hamamât through the midst of the mountains to Gebel Zeït, opposite Tôr. I therefore
determined to pursue this difficult, but more interesting and shorter way. At the same time I sent a
courier on to Kossêr, to send a ship immediately
to Gebel Zeït, to wait our arrival.

In Hamamât I had still to stand a heavy
row with the Arabs, who had suddenly taken a
decided dislike to the little-known and almost
waterless route, and who would rather have conducted us along the shore by way of Kossêr. But
as it was important for me to visit certain ancient
quarries in the depth of the mountains, I threatened
to write to the Pasha if they did not keep their word,
and made them answerable for all mischances. In
this way I brought my plan to bear, after much
hesitation. But it was nearly wrecked; for by the
negligence of our cook, who had left vinegar standing in copper pots, we were almost poisoned the
evening before our departure. However after a

wretched night, we got over it, and went off from Hamamât on the 13th of March.

We had taken six full water-pots with us for Qeneh; the camel-drivers were worse off, and were obliged to thirst a great deal. Besides our old trustworthy leader Selâm, I had brought another guide Selîm from Qeneh, who was said to know the mountainous region between Hamamât and Gebel Zeït very well, although he had only gone once over the ground twelve years before. Under his guidance we arrived in two days at Gebel Fatîreh. After much trouble and a great deal of seeking, we found the remains of the ancient colony, who had here worked a fine black and white granite. Hence, however, the conductor's ignorance became apparent in many ways. We arrived on the evening of the 15th of March at a high ridge, on the rocky ground of which we were obliged to pass the night, as no tent could be erected. The next day, Palm Sunday, we suddenly came early to a steep precipice, which sinks down to the depth of 800 feet between the two chains of the Munfieh mountains. It seemed impossible to cross the precipitous and dangerous path with a caravan. The Arabs protested in a body against every attempt to do so, and broke out into the most violent imprecations against Selím. He was now in a critical position. He was evidently unacquainted with the difficulties of the way; the passable roads lead, of course, at a great distance, either by Nech êl Delfe to the east, or by Shaib el Benât to the west. To have taken one of these

two routes would have cost us at least two more
days, and as we had lost much time at Gebel
Fatîreh, we should have come into the greater
danger of a want of water, as our provision had
been very scantily reckoned, and we had only
one well to expect between Hamamât and Gebel
Zeït, which was said to be by Gebel Dochân.
I therefore gave orders and (notwithstanding the
most violent opposition) succeeded in having all
the camels unladen at the top, and the whole of
the baggage carried down on the shoulders of the
Arabs. My own attendants had to set the example, and we all of us joined in the work. All
the boxes and packages were transported singly
from one rock to the other; this was most difficult to do with the great water-vessels, which
could only be moved by three or four men at a
time. Then the unloaded animals were carefully
led down, and lo, the daring attempt succeeded
without any misfortune or injury, under loud and
hearty invocations of the holy camel-saint Abd el
Qader. After three laborious hours everything
was completed and the animals were reloaded.

Soon, however, we were to run into a far greater
danger. I rode, as usually, before the caravan
with Maximilian* and some attendants, and left
the company to follow in my donkey's track in
the sand. Toward noon we saw to our left the
Gebel Dochân, "the smoke mountain," rising
dark blue behind the Munfieh chain; and after
some hours, when we emerged from the higher

[* Dr. Lepsius alludes to Herr Maximilian Weidenbach.—
K. R. H. M.]

Y

mountains into a hilly but more open district, we
perceived, for the first time, beyond the wide plain
and the sea behind it, the far-distant mountains of
Tôr, lying in a third quarter of the world, which
we should soon enter upon.

After three o'clock we came to two Bedouin
huts, made of mats, in which we found a woman
and a bright-eyed brown-complexioned boy, who
gave us some milk. The boy, on my question as
to whether there were any old walls in the neighbourhood, led me to a solitary granite rock, surrounded by a rough but well-laid wall ten feet in
height, about an hour distant. The square, of
which the rock formed the Acropolis, was seventy
paces long and sixty broad; the entrance from
the south had two round half-towers, the same at
the four corners, and in the middle of the three
other sides. Within spaces were divided off, in
the centre was a well of burnt bricks, but it
was now filled up.*

According to the account of our guide, we were
now in the neighbourhood of the water, which
was understood to be only half a day's journey
from our last encampment. The sun, however,
set without our having attained the desired goal.
By the sparing light of a young moon, we at last
entered a high pass, which Selîm assured us
would conduct us to the well. We ascended for
a long time between naked cliffs of granite; the
moon set, no wells were to be seen, and the guide

---

* These places were first accurately and instructively described
by Wilkinson, Journal of the Royal Geographical Society, vol. ii.
pp. 28 sqq.

confessed that he had missed the right valley.
We were obliged to return. The same occurred
in a second and third valley, to which the evidently confused guide had directed our steps,
after several changes in our route. He excused
himself on account of the uncertain light of the
moon, and was certain that he should find the
proper road at the dawn of day. Thus there was
nothing for us to do but to lie down on the hard
ground in our light and airy clothes, and seek to
obtain a fitful slumber, without food, without
water, for our bottles were long since empty, and
the little store of four biscuits per man had long
been eaten. Our only defence against the cold
north wind consisted of a few camel-saddles.
Thus we comforted ourselves, with the stars
above us and the stones beneath.

As the morning dawned we mounted again.
My donkey, who had drank his last spare
draught of water twenty-four hours before, and
who did not understand how to abstain like the
camels, refused to proceed. Selîm, however, was
in good spirits, and expected soon to be in the
right path again. We discovered camel-tracks in
great numbers. " But a little while," exclaimed
the guide, "and we shall be on the spot!" Our
hopes were again animated.

Pretty variegated granite and porphyry blocks,
which I perceived in the sand, were joyful tokens
of the proximity of the *Mons porphyrites*. In the
mean time the broad valley, into which we had
turned, got narrower and narrower, and divided
into two arms, the right one of which we took.

But this again divided, and the whole neighbourhood, according to former descriptions, showed us
that we were again on a wrong track. To give
our wearied animals some rest, I halted, and sent
out the guide alone to find the right way. We
encamped under the shadow of a cliff, hungry,
and eager for a draught of water.

Our position grew critical. I began to doubt
that our guide would succeed in discovering the
well in these uniform desolate mountain passes.
And where was our caravan? Had it found its
way to the water? If they had followed the
traces of our donkey as before, they must also
have lost their way. We waited impatiently for
Selîm; he could at any rate bring us back to the
Arab huts, which we had seen the previous day.
But one hour followed another; Selîm came not.
The sun rose higher, and robbed of the slight
shade of the rock where we had taken refuge, we
sat silently on the burning stones. We dared not
leave the spot, for fear of missing Selîm. Had
he met with an accident, or had he so forgotten
himself as only to think of his own safety, and to
leave us to our fate, as had happened some years
before to three Turks, who were never seen again,
in the same wilderness! Or was Selîm too weak
to return to us? He had almost always gone on
foot, and must have been much more exhausted
than ourselves.

From time to time we mounted the adjacent
heights and fired our muskets,—all in vain! At
last we were obliged to resign ourselves to the
melancholy certainty that we should not see our

guide again. Noon had arrived after four hours
of waiting, and also the time for departure, if the
hope of reaching the Arab huts, about six hours
distant from us, was to be accomplished. For it
would have been fool-hardy to seek any longer
for the well, as Selîm himself had not found it.
Gebel Zeït, where our ship was lying, was three
and a half days' journey from us; the Nile on the
other side of the mountain, five days' journey;
the camels had drunk nothing for four days, and
the donkey was thoroughly weakened.

We therefore set out. My companion had done
everything I had proposed ; but never have I felt
my responsibility for others, whose lives, together
with my own, were in jeopardy, so heavily as in
that hesitating resolve. It seemed foolhardy to
travel in this totally uninhabited highland, already
confused and even more put out of the way by our
nocturnal windings without a guide, according
to the stars; and yet there was nothing else to
be done.

We determined, after much consultation, to
ride back into the principal valley, which we had
entered in the morning with such hope. But the
infinite variety of the naked craggy mountains,
and the sand and rubbish-filled valley, treeless
and bushless, make so wholly uniform impressions, that no one of us would have recognised
the principal valley as the right, if the direction
and general distance of it had not told us that it
was the right one. At the end of the valley we
had again to enter the region of the hills, between
which it seemed possible to find the Arab huts

towards the south, as I had taken the bearing of
the principal peak of the Dochân from the neighbouring hill-fort. The huts were of course so
hidden, that one could ride by them at the distance of a few minutes, and not observe them ;
perhaps, too, the mats were set up in another
place. Thus we were lost in the wide burning
desert without a guide, gnawed with hunger, and
parched with thirst, and, as far as man could see,
quite abandoned to chance. In silence we journeyed on, each occupied with his own thoughts,
in the glowing noon heat, when suddenly—the
moment will never be forgotten by me !—two men
came forth from behind the rock. They rushed to
us, embraced our knees, offered us water from their
jugs, and kept continually repeating expressions of
joy and greetings, with the greatest delight.

" El hamdu l'illah"—Praised be God ! re-
sounded on all sides. We were saved !

Our caravan, whence the two Arabs came, had
as usual followed our track, and therefore like
ourselves had lost their way, but Ibrahim Aga,
soon perceiving our confusion, halted sooner, had
fires lighted in the night on all the hills, with
difficulty gathered fuel, and had almost used up
the powder. But the wind set the opposite way,
and we heard none of the signals of our distressed
comrades. Next morning they had proceeded, and
by dint of the wonderful memory of Sheikh Selâm,
who had once been here five-and-twenty years
ago, had got on the right way to the well. Yet
Ibrahim Aga encamped at a hour's distance from
it, as every trace of us was lost, and sent in great

trouble concerning our fate, Arab patrols into the mountains to find us.

How strange it was, that we should enter the great valley just in time to meet such a post! As we had come into the side valley over the mountain, no trace of our animals—who, of course, besides this could not be tracked on the stones—could lead into it; had we therefore started a few minutes later, they would certainly have passed before we were in sight, and had we come down the valley earlier, we should have turned to the right towards the huts, and gone away from the caravan far to the left.

About two o'clock, we arrived in the camp, which we entered amid shouts of joy from all present. The greatest astonishment was expressed at not finding Selîm with us; he was given up by every one. I did not, however, allow the camp to be broken up, but had the camels led to the well alone. The Arabs were again sent into the mountains to search for Selîm, and I remained quietly in my tent for the rest of the day.

Towards evening some Arabs returned from the well, and with them, loaded on a camel, Selîm. They had found him lying speechless, with open mouth, and his body swollen from intemperate draughts of water, by the edge of the well. How he had come thither, we did not immediately learn, as he answered to none of our questions. He must, however, have found his way by chance out of the mountains, or by the wonderful innate power of tracing the way peculiar to the Arab. Now he was probably speechless more by the fear of the serious consequences of the miserable trick he had played us. When he perceived that we regarded him with some pity, he soon recovered. But I did not keep him about me any more; for the remainder of the journey I took the old trustworthy Sheikh Selâm, as a guide for our advanced party, and left the other with the caravan.

Gebel Dochân, the Porphyry mountain, which had been our actual reason for coming this way, and had caused the whole undertaking, was, however, found to be far behind us. We had, as I had suspected, notwithstanding Selîm's assurances to the contrary, ridden by its foot for several hours, as we erroneously thought the well was near it. None of the caravan had seen the old quarries, and the remains of the ancient colony. Notwithstanding this, I determined to make a second attempt on the ensuing day; and in this I succeeded.

With the dawn, I set forth with Max, the Sheikh Selâm, and a young sturdy Arab. The huts had not been observed by the caravan, and lay much too far to the east for us. We therefore rode straight for the highest peak of the Dochân group. Chance decreed that we should, when in the vicinity of the ruins, meet an Abdi from those huts with some camels, for which he was seeking a grazing-place. With his assistance we arrived at our destination.

We first found the great mouth of a well, built up of rude stones, measuring twelve feet in diameter, but it was now ruined and filled up. On the

western side, were five pillars of a hall, seemingly
covered at an earlier period, a sixth was destroyed.
Three hundred paces further up the valley, on a
granite rock, projecting from the left side, a temple was built, but which was now in ruins. The
walls had been piled upon rude stones, but the
finer architectural portions well chiselled out of
red granite. A stair of twenty steps led from the
north, on the paved court, surrounded by a wall,
in the centre of which a rude altar of granite stood.
Four cells adjoined this court on the left, the most
southern of which, however, had now partially
fallen down, together with the rock foundation;
to this, as there was space on the rock, a still
smaller chamber had been added, in which a
larger, but also uninscribed altar stood. Before
these spaces in the middle of the court, there
stood, at an elevation of some feet, and grounded
with sharp blocks of granite, an Ionian portico,
consisting of four monolithic pillars, slender and
swelling, the bases and capitals of which, together
with the cornice and architrave, lay around in
pieces. The long dedicatory inscription informed
us that the temple was dedicated, in the time of
the Emperor Hadrian, to Zeus Helios Sarapis, by
the Eparch Rammius Martialis. To the left of the
wall, the ruins of the town lie on an eminence. It
was four-cornered, and, as usual, defended by
towers. In the middle there was again a well,
the principal requirement of every station, built
of burnt brick, and stuccoed. Eight rude thin
granite pillars formed the entrance to the well.

An old steep roadway leads up the adjacent

mountains, and conducts to the porphyry quarries, which, hard under the top of the mountain, gave the beautiful dark red porphyry in which so many of the monuments of the Imperial time were hewn. Its broad veins lay between another blue-white sprinkled, and an almost brick-red stone, and were worked to a considerable depth. We found five or six quarries by each other, the largest forty square paces in extent. I could nowhere find chisel holes for splitting; for the blue-stone lying next to the quarry, rubbed almost as fine as sand, seemed to indicate the employment of fire. By the town, too, I found considerable heaps of ashes.

From the quarries I climbed to the height of the mountain, which gave a splendid view of the neighbouring mountains, in the steeply-descending, first hilly, and then sandy plain, towards the sea, and beyond the blue mirror to the opposite high chain of Tôr. After taking a number of observations I descended, and was back in our camp near the Moie Messâid, after sunset.

On the 19th of March we crossed the plain to the Enned Mountains, running along the seacoast, and passing them by a cross valley. A rich fountain was here, the running water of which accompanied us for a long distance. I should take it to be the *Fons Tadmos* of Pliny, as its water has only become salt and undrinkable by the natron layer of the surface. The ruins of Abu Shâr, the ancient *Myos hormos*, or *Philoteras portus*, we left to the right, and encamped on the peninsula of Gimsheh, called by the Arabs

Kibrît, from the quantity of sulphur which is found there.

Yesterday morning we rode between the Enned Mountains and the sea-shore to the Gulf of Gebel Zeït. The ridges of Tôr, which floated milky-blue upon the watered mirror before sunrise, contrasted delicately with the heavens; first with the rising sun were its outlines lost.

After dinner we arrived at Gebel Zeït, "the oil mountain." Our ships, sent for from Kossêr, had made the passage in six days, and already awaited our arrival four days. The camels were dismissed here, and went back the same evening.

A quarter north of our anchorage lay the Zeï-tieh ; so are the five or six pits called which are excavated in the shore-sand or rock, and are filled with black-brown syrup-like earth oil. Some years ago investigations were commenced here by Em Bey, who hoped to find coals in the depths, without however, up to this time, arriving at such a result.

Last evening was calm. In the first night there arose a slight wind from the north, which we immediately used for departure. With a favourable wind we might have made the passage in a single night; but now the day is again closing, and the haven is not yet reached. The long oars, too, which are now brought into employment, scarcely bring the loaded vessel on.

The sailors of the sea are very different from those of the Nile. Their manner is far more equable, less false and less creeping. Their songs, beginning with the first stroke of the oar, consists of short broken lines, given out one by one and taken up by others, while the rest make short tones at equal intervals. The rais, on a higher seat, also rows. He is a negro, like several others among the sailors, but one of the handsomest and most powerful blacks that I have ever seen—a real Othello, when, with his athletic movements, he rolls his yellow-white eyes, shows his gleaming white teeth, and commences the song with a piercing, yelling, but practised voice, leading it for some time.

LETTER XXXII.

CONVENT OF SINAI.

Easter Monday, March 24, 1845.

WE landed on Good Friday evening, by moonlight, at Tôr. The harbour is so full of sandy that
our vessel was obliged to remain some hundred
paces from the shore. A skiff took us to land.
Here we were received by the old Greek, Nikola
Janni, who had formerly also received Ehrenberg,
Léon de Laborde, Rüppell, Isenberg, and other
well-known travellers, and who had favourable
testimonials to show of his conduct towards them.
After a long bargaining with the insolent Arabs,
who, as soon as they perceived our haste and impatience, sought every means to take advantage
of us, we set off, with as few necessaries as possible, for the land journey, early the day before
yesterday from Tôr, and let the ship go on to
Cape Abu Zelîmeh to await us there.

Cur road led in a direct northern direction
through the plain El Ge'âh, which is about five or
six hours wide, between the sea and the mountains, at the mouth of the Wadi Hebrân. But I
made an excursion on the road to the warm wells
of Gebel Hammân. These lie at the southern
end of the isolated chain of mountains, which,
beginning at Tôr, run an hour's distance to the
sea-shore. I met the caravan again by the fountain El Hai, which is pleasantly situated amongst

palm-gardens on the road. The land rises gradually from the sea-shore till behind these wells.
As soon as we had gained a complete view of the
whole plain, and the summit of the high mountain which runs down in a steep and regularly
descending chain to the end of the peninsula, I
took the bearings of all the most remarkable
points, entrances of valleys, and mountain-tops,
which the guides were able to name. About half-
past five, I arrived at the foot of the mountain.
Here already at the entrance of the valley I
remarked on the black blocks the first Sinaïtic
inscriptions. A little further we came to a
streamlet shaded by a few palms, where we encamped for the night.

Yesterday we went through the Wadi Hebrán,
which divides the Serbâl group from the chain of
mountains of Gebel Mûsa, crossed the Nakb el
Eg'âui, which forms a division between east and
west, and here turning to the south over Nakb el
Haui (the wind-saddle) we reached the convent
by sunset on Easter Sunday. We were, as all
travellers are, drawn up to the entrance in the
high fortress-wall, although there is another even
with the ground through the cloister garden, which
however is never used but from inside. The
worthy old prior of whom Robinson writes, died
in the same year at Cairo, and has been replaced
by another, Demetrios Nicodemos, who has the
rank of a bishop. As this convent is a Greek one,
instead of arriving during the Easter festival, we
came during the strict fast. But, notwithstanding
this, the lives and ways of the four priests and the

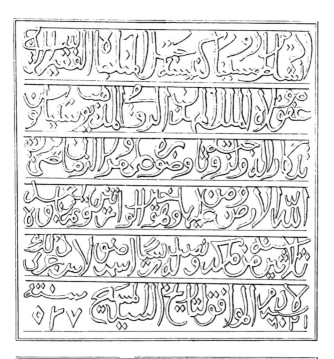

Inscriptions on the north wall of the Convent of
Mount Sinai.

twenty-one lay brothers do not make such an
edifying impression as we had hoped. A dismal
spirit of wearied indolence and ignorance lies like
a heavy cloud on their discontented countenances.
And yet these fugitives from a world of care,
living under an ever cheerful, temperate climate,
can alone of all the inhabitants of these arid
deserts stay under the dark shade of cypresses,
palms, and olive trees, besides having the care
of a library of 1,500 volumes, without in the least
degree thinking of its most beautiful destination
as an ἰατρεῖον ψυχῆς.

We have to-day been up Gebel Mûsa. It
formed, in my opinion, and also according to the
description of former travellers, the centre of the
whole chain of mountains. This, however, is not
the case. It belongs rather, as well by the plani-
metrical extent of the primitive rock, as by its
elevation, to the north-east descent. The convent lies at an exact distance, *three times nearer*
to the east than the west side of the mountain.
Gebel Katherine, which lies next to it on the south,
is higher than the almost hidden summit of Gebel
Mûsa, which is invisible to the whole neighbourhood. Beyond Mount Katherine there arise, by
degrees, higher and higher mountains, — Um
Riglên, Abu Shégere, Qettâr, &c., as far as Um
Shôman, which towers above all, and lies in the
centre between the east and west slopes of the
total elevation, and forms the north crown to the
long ridge running south along the whole peninsula. The whole way up Gebel Mûsa, with the
many points to which there are saintly legends

attached, was a walk through nature in its wildest
and most magnificent state, just as in our country
one is led through an historical, ruined castle,
where the private rooms, study, &c., of some
great king are pointed out.

After our return from Gebel Mûsa, we went up
the brow of the mountain called Hôreb, which
Robinson considers to be the true Mount Sinai,
instead of Gebel Mûsa, which has been till now
supposed to be so. We passed many hermitages
and chapels till we came to the last, situated in a
hollow in the rocks, behind which the principal
summit of Hôreb rises, rugged and grand. No
footway leads up to it. We scrambled first
through a steep cleft in the rock, then over the
southern brow of the rock itself. At half-past
five we were up just over the great plain Râha,
upon the majestic, rounded mountain-top, which
stands out so boldly from the plain. Robinson
appears first to have tried this way, and then to
have given it up, and to have ascended to the top
of Sefsâf, which is certainly higher, but lies
rather to the west, and does not stand out as the
summit we climbed, which forms an exact centre
to the plain.* Our guides all remained behind,

---

* These are the actual words of my journal as they are understood also by Ritter, p. 578. According to the printed report,
p. 8, it might appear as if Robinson had given up the attempt to
climb the whole of this mountain district; this is particularised
in the *Bibliotheca Sacra* as an inaccuracy. But I only spoke of
the top of the mountain rising in the plain in contradistinction
to the higher points lying toward the side, which Robinson has
ascended.

excepting an Arab boy, as the ascension was almost dangerous. Even this situation did not prevent the thought from rising, as to whether Moses had ever stood upon any of these mountains which are visible from the plain, if we receive the account literally. We did not ascend Gebel Katherine, as it has less to do with history than Gebel Mûsa.

LETTER XXXIII.

ON THE RED SEA.
April 6, 1845.

I SHALL employ the time of our quiet sea-voyage, which will take some days, in arranging the manifold materials collected on the peninsula, and to mark down the principal events of our journey. I will send a more copious account from Thebes.* These lines, however, will be given to Seid Hussen, at Qeneh, and be forwarded by the first opportunity.

We left the convent on the 25th of March toward evening, and went down the broad Wadi e' Shech. I chose this roundabout way, because formerly (before the wild defile, Nakb el Haui, was rendered passable) this was the only way the Israelites could go when they wanted to reach

---

* This report, sent to His Majesty, was printed, while I was still absent in 1846, under the title " *Reise des Prof. Lepsius von Theben nach der Halbinsel des Sinai vom* 4*ten März, bis zum* 14*ten April,* 1845," Berlin, with two maps, a general map of the whole peninsula, and a special map of Serbâl and Wadi Firân, which were drawn by G. Erbkam after my directions or plans. This pamphlet was not published, but was given to a few ; yet its contents have become better known by a translation into English by Charles H. Cottrell, (A Tour from Thebes to the peninsula of Sinai, &c., London, 1846); and into French by T. Pergameni, (" Voyage dans le Presq'île du Sinai, &c., lu à la Société de Géographie, séances du 21 Avril et du 21 Mai. Extrait du Bulletin de la Soc. de Géogr., Juin, 1847, Paris.")

the plain of Râha.* We remained during the night in the upper part of the valley, near the tomb of the holy Shech Sâlih, after whom the valley takes the name Wadi e' Shech. In the lower part of the valley begins the manna-rich tarfa-bushes and gradually the Sinaitic inscriptions become more numerous. Before, however, we reached the end of the valley we quitted it, and turned to the left into the Wadi Selâf, which unites further down with the Wadi e' Shech, in order to reach the foot of Serbâl by the shortest road. This immense height, towering over the mountainous landscape, we had often seen in our road when we had a clear view ; and the accounts the Arabs gave of the fertile and well-watered Wadi Firân at its foot had made me desirous to make a nearer acquaintance. I had determined to ascend the mountain, and for this reason turned into the Wadi Rim, which runs into Wadi Selâf, into which Serbâl descends. When we had ridden a little way up this valley, we came to an old stone hut, which must have been inhabited by a hermit. Soon after, we found some Arab tents, and at a little distance several sittera-trees, which we chose as a resting-place.

* The Nakb el Haui, " Windsaddle " is an exceedingly wild and narrow mountain pass, which is impassable from its shelving abysses. The road had to be made with great art along the western side, and is in many places hewn out of the rock ; on the other side, the loose soil has been paved with great flat stones. It is not to be doubted, that this daring path was made after the building of the convent, in order to have a shorter road to the town of Pharan, which before could only be reached by the wide circuit through the Wadi e' Shech.

On the 27th of March we rose early to ascend the mountain. The only way to Serbâl, Derb e'Serbâl, leads from the Wadi Firân through Wadi Aleyât up the mountain. We were obliged to go round to the south-east end of the mountain, in order to mount it behind on the south ; as it would have been far beyond our strength to have climbed up through the ridge cleft, which falls steep, and in a direct line between the two eastern summits. A quarter-hour from our resting place we came to a well, shaded by *nebek hamáda* and palms, whose fresh and pure waters were walled in for a depth of some feet. We then went over a little mountain ridge, upon which stood several stone huts, into another branch of the valley of Rim (Rim el Mehâsni), and reached in an hour and a-half the south-east corner of the mountain. From hence we followed a beaten path, which sometimes was even paved. This led us to an artificial terrace, and a wall, which appeared to be the ruins of a fallen house, and to a cool well, shaded by high rushes, a palm, and several *jassur* (of which Moses's staves were cut) ; the whole mountain being covered with *habak* and other sweet-scented herbs. Some minutes further we came to several rock caverns, which must once have served as hermits' cells; and after four hours' further journeying, we arrived at a small plain, which lay between the heights, upon which we found another house with two rooms. A way led from this level to the edge of the west side of the mountain, which at first steep and rugged, then in soft broad slopes, sinks to the sandy plain el Ge'ah. It

opened to me here a glorious prospect over the sea
to the opposite coast, and the Egyptian mountains
which bound it. From here the mountain path
suddenly sank by the rugged precipice into a wild
deep mountain hollow, around which the five
summits of Serbâl unite in a half circle, and form
a towering crown. In the middle of this hollow,
called Wadi Si'qelji, lie the ruins of an old convent, to which the mountain path leads, but
which unfortunately we could not visit for want
of time.*

I then went back across the level, and began
first to ascend the southern Serbâl summit. When
I had nearly reached the steep height, I thought
that the second summit appeared to be somewhat
higher. I hurried down again to seek a road to
this. We passed a small water-fall, and were
obliged to go almost all round the hollow before
we succeeded in ascending the north-east side.
Here, to my astonishment, I found between the
two points into which the summit is split, a
fruitful little plain, well covered with bushes and
herbs, from which I first ascended one point and
then the other, and with the assistance of my
experienced guides, and the compass, I took the

---

* It seems that this convent has not been visited by any
recent traveller. Burckhardt, who calls it Siggillye, did not
descend, but heard that it was well-built and spacious, and
provided with a good well, (Trav. in Syria, p. 610). More
accurate information concerning this convent in the Serbâl gorge
is very desirable, as it belongs probably to one of the oldest,
or, at least, the most considerable of the peninsula, as the artistic
and elaborately prepared rock-road thence to the town of Pharan
amply shows.

bearings of all the principal points which could
be seen around. I could distinguish quite plainly
that beyond Gebel Mûsa the mountains rose
higher and higher, and that the distant Um
Shômar towered over all. We did not begin to
return till towards four o'clock. The long round
by which we mounted we were obliged to avoid
on our return, in order not to be in the dark. We
determined, therefore, to make our way down the
steep rock cleft, which led in a straight line
to our camp in the Wadi Rim, and like the
chamois to spring from block to block ; and we
got down this impassable road, (the most difficult
and fatiguing that I ever went in my whole life,)
in about two hours and a-half with trembling
knees to our tent.

On the following day we went on farther, and
reached, through the Wadi Selâf and the lower
end of the Wadi e'Shech, the Wadi Firân, this
most precious jewel of the peninsula, with its
palms and tarfa woods, by the side of a lovely
bubbling stream, which flows on, winding through
bushes and flowers, as far as the old convent-
mountains of the city of Pharan, the present
Firân. Everything that we had seen, till then, and
that we afterwards saw on our way, was a naked
stony desert, in comparison with this fruitful
well-wooded and well-watered oasis. For the
first time since we left the valley of the Nile, did
we tread again on the soft black earth, obliged
to put out of our way the overhanging bushy
branches with our arms, and did we hear the
singing birds twittering in the foliage. There

where the broad Wadi Aleyât descends from
Serbâl into the Wadi Firân, and widens the valley
into a wide level, rises the rocky hill Hererât, on
the top of which lie the ruins of an old convent.
At the foot of this hill stood once a stately church,
built of well-hewn sand-stone blocks, the remains
of which have been used in building the city lying
on the opposite slope.

I went the same evening up the Wadi Aleyât,
and passed innumerable rock inscriptions, till I
came to a spring surrounded by palms and *nebek*,
from whence I enjoyed the full view of the
majestic mountain chain. Distinguished from all
the other mountains, and united in one mass, rises
the Serbâl, first in a gentle slope, and then in
steep rugged precipices, to a height of 6,000 feet
above the sea. Incomparable was the view, when
the valleys and lower mountains around were
already wrapped in the shades of night, and the
summit of the mountain, still above the colourless
grey, rose like a fiery cloud, glowing in the setting
sun. The next morning I repeated my visit to
Wadi Aleyât, and finished the plan of this remarkable district, the land points of which I had
already laid out from the top of the Serbâl.

The most fertile part of Wadi Firân is enclosed between two hills, which rise from the
middle of the level in the valley ; of these, the
upper one is called El Buêb, the lower one at the
end of the Wadi Aleyât, Meharret or Hererât.
In olden times, it appears that this valley must
have been enclosed, and the rushing water which
flowed from all sides, even from Gebel Mûsa, into

this hollow, uniting, must have formed a lake. Such a supposition alone appears to account for the extraordinary deposit of earth, which here to a height of from eighty to a hundred feet, lies along the valley walls; and it is, without doubt, this singular situation of Firân, as the lowest point of a large mountainous tract, which causes the uncommon wealth of waters which is now met with. Immediately behind the convent hill, we found the narrow valley bed as stony and barren as the higher valleys, although the stream flowed on for another half-hour by our side. The powerful rush of the water here caused no more earth deposit. Not till the next large turning of the valley, called El Héssue, did we see any palms. Here the stream disappeared in a cleft in the rock, and the more suddenly, as it had broken out behind the Buêb, and we saw no more of it. After five hours' journey, we left the valley of Firân, which here turns to the left towards the sea, and we went out of the mountains into a flat sandstone country. The high mountains turned next back towards the north, and enclosed in a great bow the hilly, sandy landscape which we crossed. We came to the Wadi Mokatteb, the "written valley," which takes its name from the inscriptions which are found here in many places.

It is easily seen that it is those rocks, shaded from the noonday sun, which invited the travellers passing to Firân to engrave their names and short maxims upon the soft stone. We took impressions in paper of all the inscriptions that we could reach, or copied with the pen such as were not suited for impression. We found these inscriptions singly, at the most various, and often very far distant places in the peninsula; and, on the whole, had no doubt that they had been engraven by the inhabitants of the land in the first centuries before and after Christ. Occasionally I found them graven over older Greek names, and Christian crosses are not unfrequently combined in them. These inscriptions are usually called Sinaitic, and not unaptly, if the whole of the peninsula of Sinai is so meant as the place where they are found. But it is worthy of remark that at Gebel Mûsa, which is generally considered to be Mount Sinai, there are but a few single and short inscriptions of this kind, in the same manner, as by a careful survey they might be found in any of these places; but their actual centre was rather Pharan, at the foot of Serbâl.*

On the 31st of March we again reached the mountains turning eastward, and entered by Wadi Qeneh, the little branching Wadi Maghâra, in which sandstone and primary stone bound each other. Here we found, high upon the northern cliff, the remarkable Egyptian rock-steles belonging to the earliest monuments of Egyptian antiquity with which we are acquainted.† Already, under

[* I must here draw the reader's earnest attention to an interesting work, (to be more completely alluded to in the sequel,) lately published by the Rev. Charles Forster. The One Primeval Language. Part I. The Voice of Israel from the Rocks of Sinai.—K. R. H. M.]

† Monuments, Part II., plates 2, 116, 137, 140, 152, III., 28.

the fourth dynasty of Manetho, the same which erected the great pyramids of Gizeh, 4,000 B.C., copper mines had been discovered in this desert, which were worked by a colony. The peninsula was then already inhabited by Asiatic, probably Semetic races ; therefore do we often see in those rock sculptures, the triumphs of Pharaoh over the enemies of Egypt. Almost all the inscriptions belong to the Old Empire ; only one was found of the co-regency of King Tuthmosis III. and his sister.

I wished to get from hence by the shortest way to the second place on the peninsula Sarbut el Châdem. But there was no direct road over the high mountains to the descent on the north-east side. So we were obliged to return to Wadi Mokatteb, and going a long way round to the south-east through Wadi Sittere and Wadi Sîch, to avoid the mountain. When we came out of the valley, we had before us the wide-spreading plain, which includes the whole northern part of the peninsula, and which consists entirely of sandstone. This falls, however, towards the south, into a double descent, so that the view appears, at a great distance, to be bounded by two lofty mountain walls, of the same height. The next southern descent, called E' Tîh, leads down to a wide sandy valley-plain, Debbet e' Ramleh, while the near side of the sandstone rocks appears to reach the height of the immense plain.

Upon one of the projecting terraces in this broad valley, which we had to climb with great fatigue, lie the monuments of Sarbut el Châdem, most astonishing even to one prepared for the sight of them. The most ancient representation here carried us back into the Old Empire, but only into the last dynasty of the same, the twelfth of Manetho. At this time, under Amenemhra III. there was a little grotto hewn out of the rock, and furnished with an ante-chamber. Outside it high steles were erected at different distances without any particular order, the most distant of which was about a quarter of an hour away on the highest point of the *plateau*. Under the New Empire, Tuthmosis III. had enlarged the building towards the west, and added a small pylon, and an outer court. The later kings built a long row of rooms in the same direction, one before the other, occasionally, as it appears, for the purpose of preserving the steles within from the weather; particularly from the sharp, and often sand-filled winds, which had all through eaten up the ancient undefended steles. The youngest stele bears the cartouches of the last king of the nineteenth dynasty. Since that time, or soon after, the place was deserted by the Egyptians.

The divinity who was mostly revered here in the New Empire, was Hathor,* with the designation, also found in Wadi Maghâra, " Mistress of Mafkat," *i. e.*, " the copper country ; " for *mafka*, signified " copper," in the hieroglyphical, as well as in the Koptic language. Therefore, no doubt copper was also obtained here. This was confirmed by a peculiar appearance, which strangely enough

[* Bunsen, vol. i. p. 400, and see Lepsius, Ueber den Ersten Aegyptischen Götterkreis, p. 30.—K. R. H. M.]

has not been observed by any earlier travellers. East and west of the temple are to be seen great slag-hills, which, from their black colour, form a strange contrast to the soil of the neighbourhood. These artificial mounds, the principal of which is 256 paces long, and from 60 to 120 paces broad, situated on the tongue of the terrace projecting into the valley, are covered with a massive crest of slag from four to five feet thick, and thence to their feet from twelve to fifteen feet, sprinkled with single blocks of the same material. The land shows that the mines could not have been in the immediate neighbourhood, but the old and still visible paths which lead into the mountain no doubt point them out. Unfortunately we had not time for it. It seems, therefore, that this free point was chosen only for smelting, on account of the sharp, and as the Arabs assure us, almost incessant draught of air.

On the 3rd of April we rode further, and visited the Wadi Nasb, in which we also found traces of ancient smelting-places; and the following day towards evening, we reached our ship, which had been waiting for us in the harbour of Abu Zelimeh for several days.

Here we found to our great astonishment, four German apprentices, among them two Prussian Schlesians from the vicinity of Neisse. They had come from Cairo, in order to visit Mount Sinai; they had arrived happily as far as Suez, and there had waited in vain for a ship, and at last, like real modern crusaders, had set off alone on the road, in order to carry out their bold purpose. They had been assured, doubtless not in good German, that the way was short, and not to be mistaken, and that there was no want of water. In this good belief, their pilgrim-flasks filled to the brim, they set off into the desert; but the footsteps of the children of Israel were obliterated, and no pillar of a cloud went on before them. On the third day they had lost their way, their bread was gone, they had missed the wells, they had been several times stopped by Arabs, and only not robbed, because they possessed nothing worth stealing; and they would certainly have perished in the waste, if they had not from the mountains, at some hours' distance, perceived our ship lying by the strand, and fortunately reached it before our arrival. Upon my inquiry as to the trade which they had intended to bring to perfection by this journey into the East, and if they expected to find employment among the monks on Mount Sinai, as they had brought no money with them, I was informed, that one was a carpenter, who hoped to make himself very useful there; unfortunately I was obliged to tell him that he would have to cope with a lay brother; another was a shoemaker, the third was a stocking-weaver, and the fourth owned, after some hesitation, that he was a woman's tailor. Nothing else could be done but to take these extraordinary people in the ship with us, although the sailors looked at them ascantly, on account of the want of water. I had them set on shore at Tôr, and took care that they should be accompanied from thence to the convent.

Besides occupying myself with the wonderful Egyptian monuments of this land of copper, and the so-named Sinaitic inscriptions, I busied myself with examining the geographical questions relating to the sojourn of the Israelites on the peninsula. I think I have obtained, with reference to these ocurrences, a result, which, although it differs in essential points from the general acceptation, if I have judged rightly, will form an important feature in the historical and geographical events of the Old Testament.* I will here merely briefly mention a few of the principal points, and will write more fully from Thebes.

It appeared very doubtful to me when I was in the convent at Gebel Mûsa,† whether it was the holy mountain on which the Commandments were given or not. Since I have seen Serbâl, and Wadi Firân, at its foot, and a great part of the rest of the country, I feel quite convinced that we must recognise Sinai in Mount Serbâl.

The present monkish tradition has no worth in an impartial research. This every one must know, who has occupied himself seriously with such things. If, even in Jerusalem they are, for the most

[* From its great length, I have found it necessary to reserve this note until the Appendix, Note A., where the reader will find it.—K. R. H. M.]

† On this point I find all the most important voices unanimous. Robinson, in particular, has the merit of having done away with many old prejudices of this kind. But Burckhardt had already allowed himself to be so little influenced in his judgment by the authority of tradition, that he did not hesitate to find a reason for the erection of the convent of Sinai on Gebel Mûsa on strategetical grounds. (Trav. in Syr. p. 609.)

part, not of the slightest value, unless they be
supported from the original source, how much less
are they worth on the Sinai peninsula, where they
relate to questions much more distant, both as
to time and place! During the long space of time
between the giving the Commandments and the first
Christian centuries, Sinai is only once mentioned
in a later historical occurrence, as the " Mountain of God, Horeb," upon which Elias appeared.
It would indeed be extremely wonderful, if during
this lapse of time the tradition had not been interrupted, and if also during that time the population
had so changed on the peninsula, that we cannot
point out a single place mentioned in the Old Testament with any certainty, and even the Greeks
and the Romans were not acquainted with these
old designations.* We must therefore return to
the Mosaic accounts, in order to prove the truth of
the present acceptation.

To this we must also add, that the general relative geographical position of the localities of the
peninsula have not essentially altered since the
time of Moses. They who take refuge in a contrary opinion, may undoubtedly prove everything,
and for that very reason they prove nothing. It
is therefore very important to keep the historical
relations of the different periods before our eyes,
because these were certainly likely to cause
changes in different places.

* The name Firân, formerly Pharan, is certainly the same as
the Biblical Paran ; but it is equally sure that this name had
shifted its application in the locality. All other comparisons of
names are totally unsatisfactory.

Hence it cannot be denied, that the fertile and
well-watered Wadi Firân, at all times, and therefore also at the time of Moses, was the most important, and most frequented centre of the whole
peninsula, by reason of its unparalleled fertility,
and of its inexhaustible bubbling fountains. That
this wonderful oasis was then, as now, in the middle of the eternally naked desert, the whole character of the land proves. On the other side it is not
less true, that the environs of the present convent
on Gebel Mûsa were formerly, (notwithstanding
the spare streamlets, which there spring from the
earth, but only moisten the neighbouring soil),
just as barren as all the other parts of that mountain waste; that the draw-wells* dug out of the
rocks at first supplied water sufficient for the use
of the inhabitants of the convent; and that an artificial irrigation of more than a thousand years'
duration, with the most careful employment of
every means of culture, rendered possible the
small plantations now found there.† In olden
times there was not the slightest reason for rendering this desert habitable by art, so much the
rather as it lay apart from all the connecting roads

* One of the two wells seems to go back to the time of the
building of the convent; it is the smaller one of the two. The
deep, principal well, which gives the most and the best water,
seems to have been first sunk in 1760, by order of an English
Lord. (*Ritter*, p. 610.)

† Burckhardt also expressly observes, that there is no good
pasturage in the neighbourhood of the convent, where the rather
more numerous little fountains would almost allow us to consider
the soil to be moisture. See Bartlett's impression in a subsequent
place.

of the peninsula, and formed a true mountain hollow, to which there was only one entrance, through the Wadi e' Shech. In contra-distinction to this, there is one point of the peninsula, which, long before Moses, and also during his time, was of great consequence, but now it is no longer so. This is the harbour of Abu Zelîmeh. Here roads led from the three different mines, which are yet known to us, Wadi Maghâra, Sarbut el Châdem, and Wadi Nasb. No landing-place lay more conveniently for the union of Egypt with these colonies; it was, according to the account of our sailors, the best harbour on the whole coast, not even excepting Tôr. Here also the Egyptians must have taken much pains in making a plentiful supply of water. As neither the sandy sea-coast, nor the valleys leading to it afforded any, so they had, without doubt, dug wells at the next place which promised water beneath the ground. Such a place was found at the lower entrance of the Wadi Shebêkeh (with others Taibeh, where there still stand a number of palms, and many other trees, and consequently the ground is damp, although there is no well to be found).* This would there-

---

* So the Arabs unanimously assured us, see also Burckhardt, p. 625, and Ritter, p. 769. Lord Lindsay here found "a small wood of tarfa trees, in which blackbirds were singing, and farther on some palm plantations." It was at the same outlet of the valley " where Seetzen first had the pleasure of gathering much manna off the tarfa bushes and eating it ; here he found the ripe fruits of the wild caper bush, which were eatable like fruit."

fore be the most proper place to dig for water,
and make a well. Now there is no difference of
opinion that near Abu Zelîmeh the encampment by
the Red Sea was made, which is mentioned in the
fourth Book of Moses as behind Elim. In the
second Book this account is omitted, and only
the twelve wells and seventy palm-trees named.
How natural, indeed unavoidable, then, is the
conclusion, that this well and palms of Elim,
towards which the harbour of Abu Zelîmeh led,
perhaps about an hour's distance from the valley,
and for this reason, in the account of the encampment of Elim by the sea, given in the second
Book, from the watering-place of apparently the
same name. According to the present, and also
according to Robinson's acceptation, the twelve
wells of Elim were situated in Wadi Gharandel,
according to the latest reckoning,* from eight to
nine hours—a long day's journey distant from the
harbour, thus for the supply of this important
place, quite useless. It is not easy to perceive
what, in Wadi Gharandel, where still, at this
present time, the brackish water of the whole district is somewhat more plentiful than elsewhere,
could exactly have suggested the plan of these
twelve wells. To this must be added that it is
necessary to put the next preceding station, Mara,
to an inconsiderable well, only an hour and a half
or two hours from Wadi Gharandel, while the
next station is considered to be eight hours
distant. It appears to me not to be doubted, that
the first three journeys into the desert led to

[* Note B, Appendix.—K. R. H. M.]

Wadi Gharandel, that is Mara; the fourth to the harbour station, Abu Zelîmeh, *i. e.* Elim. Now first, would the continuation be understandable? "And they set forth from Elim and came into the desert of Sin, *which lies between Elim and Sinai.*" At Wadi Gharandel also, the boundaries of two districts were as geographically incomprehensible as they are natural at Abu Zelîmeh. The harbour, with its small commodious plain, between Nochol-rock and Gebel Hammâm Faraûn,* forms with these two prominent mountains really the most important geographical portion of the whole coast. The northern high plain, regularly sloping towards the sea, was called the desert of Sûr; the southern, rising higher, and soon losing itself in the mountain lands of the primitive rocks, is called the desert of Sin. The remark, that the latter lay between Elim and Sinai, would have no sense, if it were not also said that the desert of Sin extends itself to Sinai, or further. The next departure, then, from the desert of Sin to Raphidîm, must not be understood that they had left the desert;

---

* Originally, both these hot springs seem not to have been called Hammân Faraûn from Pharaoh, but Farân from Pharan. For Edrisi calls the place Faran Ahrun and Istachri Taran, which should doubtless be Faran (Cf. Ritter, *Asien*, Bd. VIII. S. 170 ff.). Macrizi also calls the place Birkit Faran (Ritter, *Sinaihalbinsel, p.* 64.) Probably the harbour region of Pharan was called after the city, though it was somewhat distant; and the legend, so very inapposite here, concerning Pharaoh's ruin, only connected itself with Faraûn by a confusion with Faran. It is curious that the Arab writers, of whom Macrizi was certainly there, speak of Faran as of a coast town!

on the contrary, they remained in it till they came to Sinai, whose name "Sini," that is "the Mountain of Sin," plainly derived its name from the district, and on this account could not be visited without the other. This also is confirmed by the account of the manna, which was given to the Israelites in the desert of Sin; for this is first found in the valleys near Fîrân, and grows as little about the sandy sea coasts as it does in the higher regions of Gebel Mûsa.*

Let us place here the preliminary question, which of the two mountains, Serbâl or Gebel Mûsa, was so situated as to be especially pointed out as Sini, the " Sinaïtic mountain of the desert of Sin ;"—the answer cannot for a moment be doubted. Gebel Mûsa, which is scarcely visible from any side, and is almost hidden and " secret,"† neither from its height, nor its form, situation, or anyother distinction, presented anything that could have caused either the native races or the Egyptian hermits to point it out as the " mountain of Sin ;" whilst Serbâl, which attracts the eye from all sides and from a great distance, which domi-

---

* The part of the sandy coast, considered by Robinson to be the desert of Sin, has no tarfa bush, much less manna. Concerning the regions where manna is found, Cf. Ritter, p. 665 sqq. That Eusebius also considers the wilderness of Sin to extend to Sinai, is already mentioned. [Σίν, ἔρημος ἡ μετάξυ παρατείνουσα τῆς Ἐρυθρᾶς Θαλάσσης καὶ τῆς ἐρήμου Σίνα.]

† Robinson, vol. i. p. 173, 196. To Wilson's particular argument of the extensive prospect from Gebel Mûsa is to be objected, that, from a point very inconsiderably higher than the plain, many places can be seen, from which the elevation itself would not appear very considerable.

nates over the whole of the primary rocks, not
only by its outward appearance, but also on
account of Wadi Firân situated at its foot, ever
the centre-point for the wide straggling inhabitants of the country, and the goal of all travellers,
may claim the designation of the " mountain of
Sin." If, however, any one would wish to conclude from the departure from the desert of Sin to
Raphidîm, that only the broad coast south of Abu
Zelîmeh, which the Israelites must have passed,
was called the desert of Sin, (which is the opinion
of Robinson,*); still Serbâl, which adjoins and
commands this district, and from here is accessible over the ancient convent of Si'gelji, would
claim the designation as the mountain of Sin from
the boatmen of the Red Sea ; while Gebel Mûsa,
which lies directly on the opposite eastern side of
the great chain of mountains, could not possibly
have taken the name of Sin from the western
desert of that name, nor can it offer a suggestion
for such a statement, as that the desert of Sin lies
between Abu Zelîmeh and Gebel Mûsa. It is
also reasonable to believe, that the whole of the
primitive rocks, (that is, the whole of the peninsula
south of Abu Zelîmeh), was called the " desert of
Sin," and consequently that Gebel Mûsa was
included in it. This even does not necessarily
exclude the belief that Serbâl, as the best known,
the nearest, and as a much more important mountain to the Egyptian colonists than the southern
mountains could be, would not have been distinguished by that name ; whilst in the southern

* See Robinson, vol. i. pp. 118, 196.

principal chain not even Um Shômar as the
highest centre-point,—not the completely subordi-
nate Gebel Mûsa,—still less the isolated rock
Sefsâf, which Robinson considers the one, would
have had such a distinguished designation.
All that has been said here relative to Sinai as
the " mountain of the desert of Sin," may now
be applied to the further question, as to which
of the two mountains, Serbâl and Gebel Mûsa,
possessed such properties that it should already,
before the great event of the giving the Commandments, have been regarded as a " holy mountain,"
as a " mountain of God," by the native races of
the peninsula.* For Moses already drove the
sheep of Jethro behind the desert from Midian, to
the " mountain of God in Choreb ;" and Aaron
came to meet him on his return from Egypt to
the " mountain of God." If we hold to the
belief that the necessary centre of the Sinaïtic
population at that time was the Oasis Firân, so
does there appear every probability that that race
had founded a sanctuary, a universal place of
worship in the neighbourhood, at the foot, or
much more naturally at the summit, of the mountain which rose from that valley.† Moreover,

* Ewald, History of the People of Israel, vol. ii. p. 86, also
considers that Sinai " was already looked upon as an oracular
place and divine seat before Moses." Ritter considers it
insupportable.

† This is confirmed at the present day by Rüppell, who
considers Gebel Katharine to be Sinai. He relates in his voyage
to Abyssinia, vol. i. p. 127, the following about his ascent of
Mount Serbâl in 1831 :—" At the top of Serbâl, the Bedouins
have placed little circles of stones in a circle, and other stones are

this was the particular spot fixed for that meeting
of Moses, who came out of Midian, and Aaron,
who came out of Egypt.   There was no occasion,
in so desert and unpopulated a country, to seek out
for any particularly private and remote mountain-
corner for such a meeting.   From this it appears that the Sinaïtic inscriptions, which as has been already said, are princi-
pally to be found on the way to Wadi Firân, and
in the Wadi Aleyât leading up to Serbâl, seem to
point out that in much later times, long pilgrimages, to celebrate religious festivals, must have
been undertaken to this place.*

laid from it down the steep declivity like steps, to render the
ascent more easy; when we came to that circle *my guide took off*
his sandals, and approached it with religious reverence, he then
said a prayer inside, and afterward told me that he had already
sacrificed two sheep here as *thank-offerings,* the one at the
birth of a son, the other on regaining his health.   The mountain
of *Serbâl has been held for such superstitions in the highest*
respect by the Arabs of the vicinity, from time immemorial;
and it must once have been somewhat holy to the Christians, as
in the valley to the south-west there lie the ruins of a great
convent and many little hermits' cells.   In any case, the wild,
craggy rocks of Serbâl, and the *isolated position of this mountain*
is much more remarkable and grand than any other group of
mountains in Arabia Petræa, and it was peculiarly adapted for
the goal of religious pilgrimages.   The highest point of the
mount, or the second rock from the west, and on which the
Arabs usually sacrifice, is, according to my barometrical ob-
servation, 6,342 French feet above the level of the sea."
    * See the excellent treatise of Tuch (Einundzwanzig
Sinaitische Inschriften, Leipzig, 1849.)   This scholar endeavours
to prove, by the deciphered names of the pilgrims, that the
authors of the inscriptions were native pagan Arabs, and went
to Serbâl for religious festivals; according to him, these pil-

Let us now turn immediately to the principal
point, which, for those who keep the general circumstances of the passage of the Israelites before
them, must be the most conclusive. It is not to
be denied that when Moses determined to lead
this great multitude into the peninsula, the first
problem he had to solve by his wisdom and knowledge of the land, was the means of supporting
them. For at whatever number we may reckon
the wanderers, who, according to Robinson,
amounted to two millions, (which, according to
Lane, is the present population of all Egypt,) they
were most undoubtedly an immense multitude,
who suddenly and without any provision of food,
were to be sustained in the desert. How is it
then possible to suppose, that Moses would not
have immediately fixed upon the most fertile, best
watered, and shortest road, instead of a distant
mountain-corner, which would have been impossible even for (I mention a large number purposely) 2,000 wanderers, with what belonged to
them, to provide with food and water. Moses
would have done wrong to have depended on
miracles from God, as these happen only when
human wisdom and human thought are at an end.

grimages ended, at latest, in the course of the third century.
Here it may also be mentioned, that the name itself of Serbâl,
which Rödiger, (in Wellsted's Travels in Arabia, vol. ii. page
the last), doubtlessly correctly derived from سرب serb, palmarum
copia, and Baal, " palm grove (φοινίκων) of Baal," points to a
heathen origin. [However much M. Tuch may reproduce the
notion of Beer, he cannot set aside its confutation in Forster's
Primeval Language, Part I. pp. 8-38.—K. R. H. M.]

On reflection upon this undeniable proof
against the hitherto supposed situation of Sinai,
it appears to me that the idea will be changed,
and that every close historical examination of
these wonderful events must destroy it, even if
grounds should also be brought forward against
our acceptation of it. We will now continue the
narrative. From Elim Moses reached Raphidîm
in three days' journey. The new school are generally agreed that the caravan from Abu Zelîmeh
did not again return to the eastern sand-plain
E'Raml, through the same Wadi Shebêkeh, or
Saibeh, by which they descended, but took the
usual caravan road which leads to Wadi Firân.
How then would Moses have chosen the dry and
much longer upper way, or even the great and
still more dry round-about way along the sea-
coast, by Tôr and Wadi Hebrân, instead of immediately turning into the valleys of the primitive
rocks, both less dry, and rich with manna.

He must also come to Wadi Firân—no third
way was possible. This is the cogent reason
why (with the exception of Robinson)* almost all
without a dissentient voice, have placed Raphî-
dim after Firân. It seems impossible that this
oasis, if it had been traversed, should not once
have been named. Already Josephus,† Eusebius,

---

* Vol. i. p. 198.

† I thought to be able to conclude this indirectly from his
narrative, (Antiq. III. 2.) It now appears to me that nothing
can be elicited, as to his opinion, from it, for which reason the
name should be omitted above. In itself it is still probable that
he held the same opinion as Eusebius and Jerome.

Jerome,* and, as it appears, every other author and traveller † place Raphidîm after the city Pharan. No spot in the whole country could have been of so much value, as these fruitful gardens of Pharan, to the native races, threatened by Moses. It is then very easy to be conceived that Moses, just here in Raphidîm, should have been attacked by the Amalekites, who would

---

* Eusebius, περὶ τῶν τοπικῶν ὀνομ., etc. s.v. Ῥαφιδίμ, τόπος τῆς ἐρήμου παρὰ τὸ Χωρὴβ ὄρος, ἐν ᾧ ἐυ τῆς πέτρας ἐρρύησε τὰ ὕδατα καὶ ἐκλήθη ὁ τόπος πειρασμός ἔνθα καὶ πολεμεῖ Ἰησοῦς τὸν Ἀμαλὴκ ἐγγὺς Φαράν. Hieron. de situ et nomin., etc. s.v. Raphidim, locus in deserto juxta montem Choreb, in quo de petra fluxere aquæ, cognominatusque est tentatio, ubi et Jesus adversus Amalec dimicat *prope Pharan.* [Here again the authorities resolve themselves into one, as the reader knows that, after all, Jerome was only the translator of Eusebius, and would therefore, of course, agree with him. The Doctor does not appear to have thought of this.—K. R. H. M.]

† Of the older authors there is yet Cosmas Indicopleustes (A.D. 535) to be particularly mentioned, (Topogr. Christ, Lib V. in the *Coll. Nov. Patred. Montfaucon,* tom. II. fol. 195,) Ἔιτα πάλιν παρενέ βαλον εἰς Ῥαφιδὶν εἰς τὴν νῦν λεγομένην Φαράν, also Antoninus Placentinus, who is placed about 600, while the learned Papebroch, who has edited his *Itinerarium* in the *Acta S.S.,* May, vol. ii. p. 10-18, places him in the eleventh or twelfth century, came, as he says, *in civitatem* (which can only be Pharan) *in qua pugnavit Moyses cum Amalech : ubi est altare positum super lapides illos quos posuerunt Moyse orante."* The city is surrounded with a brick wall, and " *valde, sterilis,"* for which Tuch (Sinait. Incr. p. 38) proposes to read "*fertilis."* When Pharan is called an Amalekite city by Macrizi, (History of the Kopts, translated by Wüstenfeld, p. 116), this can only point to the same conclusion that Moses was attacked near Pharan by the Amalekites, to whom the territory belonged. Ritter is particularly to be mentioned among the new school.

lose their most valuable possessions. He drove them back, and then only could Moses say that he had possession of the peninsula. His first goal was attained. What could tempt him to go further?

It is also written in plain words, that the people were arrived at the Mountain of God, the Mountain of the Law. As it says, that after the victory near Raphidîm, Jethro, Moses's father-in-law, heard of all that had happened. " And then came Jethro, and Moses's sons, and his wife to Moses in the desert, where he was encamped at the Mountain of God;" and also the Lord had already spoken to Moses, " See I will stand before you upon a rock in Choreb, and you shall strike the rock, and water shall flow forth, that the people may drink;" words which could only refer to the wonderful fountain of Firân, as it has long since appeared to me.* That Moses really encamped here in Raphidîm, is further proved, as he now, by the advice of Jethro, organised the till now disorderly multitude, in order to be able to govern it.† He chose the most able men and set them over thousands, over hundreds, over fifties, and over tens; these became judges respecting the smaller occurrences, while he reserved only the most important to himself.

This proves clearly that the journey was over, and that the time of rest was come.

This certainly appears to be contradicted in the

---

* See the passage of Cosmas, in a former note.

† The name Raphidîm itself, " the resting-places," indicates that the place was intended for a longer rest.

beginning of the next chapter.* " In the third
month,† when the children of Israel were gone
forth out of the land of Egypt, the same day
came they into the wilderness of Sinai. For they
were departed from Raphidîm, and were come to
the desert of Sinai, and had pitched in the wilderness, and then Israel encamped before the Mount,
and Moses went up unto God, and the Lord called
to him out of the mountain," &c.

According to this there is a journey between
Raphidîm and Sinai. This decides in favour of
the tradition, which believes the Mountain of the
Law to have been found beyond Firân, in the Gebel
Mûsa. It will not, however, be guessed that, by
this acceptation, it will fall into a much greater
contradiction with the text. Furthermore the
words speak of nothing more than one day's
journey ;‡ also, not in the fourth book, where,
nevertheless, between Elim and Raphidîm, not
only Alus and Daphka, but also the Red Sea,
although this lay by Elim, are particularly mentioned. From Firân to Gebel Mûsa was, at least,
two long days' journey, if not more. Then, however, " the Mountain of God" has already been
mentioned in Raphidîm ; likewise it has been

---

* Exodus, xix. 1—3.

† See Note C, in the Appendix.

‡ Therefore Robinson and others, who admit no hiatus in the
resting stations, place Raphidîm beyond Firân, and do not
admit that the latter is named at all, or place Alus there.
What is contrary to this, and has already been made use of by
Ritter, is already mentioned above. On the contrary, Ritter, to
get over the difficulty, considers our present text to be imperfect
(p. 742).

named a rock in Choreb, and it is impossible to
understand any other to be the "Mountain of
God," but the "Mountain of God, Choreb," to
which Moses drove the sheep of Jethro.
We should thus understand, that there were
two "Mountains of God," the one, "The Mountain of God Choreb," in Raphidîm, which might
be Serbâl, and one "The Mountain of God Sinai,"
upon which the Commandments were given, which
might be Gebel Mûsa.* This acceptation would,
however, not only be scarcely credible, but would
contradict itself most positively by the fact, that
the Mountain of God, Choreb, where Moses was
called, already before was designated as the
Mountain of the Law ;* (2, 3, 1, 12,) and further
the general name of "God's Mountain," which so
often appears, without any other name (2, 4, 27,
18, 5, 24, 13, 4, 10, 33,) could only be used if
there were but one such mountain ; and finally,
that the name Sinai, or Mount Sinai, and Choreb,
or Mount Choreb, continue to be used in the very
same signification as the Mountain of the Law.

This visible difficulty has also formerly been
felt.† Josephus (*Ant.* 3, 2, 3,) helped himself out

---

* To this conclusion, which appears to me the most doubtful,
of any, Ritter feels himself driven. The tradition of the present
day is different, that Horeb and Sinai are two mountains in
close juxtaposition, but also distinctly divided.

† The three possibilities of getting quit of this difficulty have
been tried by Robinson, Ritter, and Josephus. The first places
Raphidîm in the neighbourhood of Gebel Mûsa ; the second sees
an omission between Raphidîm and Sinai, and accepts *two* divine
mountains ; the third transposes the passage, and does not
mention Horeb at all, but only Sinai.

of it, by putting the supposed beginning of the nineteenth chapter, from its present place to before the visit of Jethro ; so that Moses did not receive his family in Raphidîm, but in Sinai. By this two difficulties would certainly be overcome ; one, that there was only one Mountain of God, and the other, that the organisation of the people did not take place during the journey. He also surrenders after some consideration, the statement that the rock, which Moses struck, lay in Choreb.

The new school have, however, set forth the opinion that either Sinai was the general name of the whole range of mountains, and Choreb that of the one mountain where the law was given, or contrarywise, that Choreb signified the wider designation, and Sinai the single mountain,* while the monkish tradition gave the names to two mountains lying close together.†   A comparison of the

* Cf. the comparison and discussion of both opinions in Robinson, vol. i. pp. 197, sqq. All those places where exactly the same is said of Horeb as of Sinai, and no idea of a larger extent of region is admissible, speak against the view of the latter that Horeb is the denomination of the mountain-range or country, and Sinai the name of the particular mount. A Desert of Horeb is never spoken of, as are the deserts of Sur, Sin, Paran, and others. For a contrary view one could cite Acts, vii. 30, compared with Exodus, iii. 1. [The former passage is " And when forty years were expired, then appeared unto him *in the wilderness of Mount Sinai,* an angel," &c. ; the other runs thus, " He led the flock to the backside of the desert, and came *to the mountain of God, even to Horeb.*"— K. R. H. M.]

† This view is already to be found in the *Itinerarium* of Antoninus, who finds the convent *between* Sinai and Horeb.

individual places does not appear to me to admit
of either of these views; my opinion leans much
more to that of the indiscriminate use of the two
names Choreb and Sinai, and that both point
out one and the same mountain, and the neighbourhood.* Perhaps Choreb might be the particular local Amalekite name, and Sinai a name
derived from its situation in the desert of Sin.
As to what concerns the departure from Raphidîm, it must appear very probable to many, that

The present monkish tradition that the rock on the plain of
Râha is Horeb is already known. The arbitrariness of such
views are self-evident. Yet the latter opinion is taken up by
Gesenius, (Thesaur. p. 517), Wiener, and others.

* St. Jerome already says expressly the same thing, in adding
to the words of Eusebius, *s.v.* Choreb :—" Mihi autem videtur,
quod *duplici nomine idem mons nunc* SINA, *nunc* CHOREB
vocetur." Josephus already evidently took both mountains to
be one, as he everywhere substitutes *Sinai* where *Choreb* occurs
in the Bible ; so also does the author of Acts (vii. 30) ; and likewise Syncellus (*Chron.* p. 190), who says of Elias :—ἐπορεύετο ἐν
Χωρὴβ τῷ ὄρει ἤτοι Σιναίῳ. [The adjective termination of
Σιναίῳ shows that Syncellus meant that Choreb was part of the
Sinaitic range. Otherwise, he would have employed the Hebraic
termination.—K. R. H. M.] Of late scholars, Ewald presents
the same opinion concerning the identity of the two mounts.
He says, (Gesch. des V. Isr., vol. ii. p. 84) :—" The two
names Sinai and Horeb do not change, because they denoted two
peaks of the same mountain, lying close together, but the name
Sinai is plainly older, which is also used by Deborah, (Judges v.
5), while the name Horeb is not to be found previous to the
time of Numbers (cf. Exod. iii. 1, xvii. 6, xxxiii. 6), but
then becomes very frequent, as is proved by Deuteronomy,
and the passages, 1 Kings viii. 9, xix. 8, Mal. xii. 22, Psalm
cvi. 19, while it does not mean anything to the contrary,
when quite recent writers, for the sake of showing their acquaintance with ancient literature, re-introduce the original name of
Sinai !

those words, which so completely interrupt the
natural continuity of the events, have been purposely displaced either by Josephus, or before
him did not originally belong here, but were
placed at the beginning of the giving the Commandments, when this (as without doubt, it
frequently happened) was taken distinctly from
all that went before, or came after.* The want
of connection, since the arrival at Sinai, is mentioned before the departure from Raphidîm,
and the expression so difficult of explanation,
" and the same day," while by other statements
of time, a particular day is meant, would support
the supposition.† Those, however, to whom this
acceptation may appear too bold, as it does not
agree with the original comprehension of the
subject, may understand the new departure as a
slight misarrangement of the encampment, as we
must already consider that of the departure from
Elim to the coast of the Red Sea. This change
happened either while they advanced from El
Hessue, where the sea was first seen, to Firân,
from Firân into the upper part of the Wadi Aleyât,
where the camp could spread out, far round the
foot of the mountain.‡
Such a comprehension will alone content those
who strive to represent the whole course of events

---

* If we omit the two verses xix. 12, the narrative in xix. 3
continues quite naturally that of xviii. 27 ; " and Moses let his
father-in-law depart ; so he went his way into his own land.
And Moses went up unto God, and the Lord called unto him
out of the mountain," &c.
[† See Note C. Appendix.]
[‡ See Note A. Appendix.]

in their essential and necessary points. They will
not be able to prevent the conviction, that Serbâl,
on account of the oasis at its foot, must have been
the aim and centre of the new immigrating population, and that to be fenced in in a mountain-hollow, like the plain at Gebel Mûsa, where the multitude could find no water, no fruit, or manna-
bearing trees, and where they were cut off from
all connection with the other part of the peninsula more than anywhere else, could never possibly have been the intention of the wise and
learned man of God. It must be acknowledged that
the distinguishing Sinai as the principal mountain
of the desert of Sin, and the sanctity that it possessed, not only among the Israelites, but also
among the native-born races of the country, very
decidedly point out Serbâl ; further, that the Ra-
phîdim, with the well of Moses of Choreb, which
was defended by the Amalekites, undoubtedly lay
in the Wadi Firân, that consequently also the
mountain of God, Choreb, where Moses was called,
and the mountain of God, near Raphidîm, where
Moses was visited by Jethro, and organized the
people, could be no other than Serbâl, from which
finally, it also appears, that if we do not admit of
two mountains of God, the Mountain of the Law
lay near Raphidîm, and in Serbâl must be recognised, and not in Gebel Mûsa.

In conclusion, let us once more see how
far the present tradition agrees with our result;
this goes back as far as the founding of the convent by Justinian in the sixth century.* This was

[* Note D, Appendix.]

2 B

by no means the first church of the peninsula. At a much earlier period, we find a bishopric in the city of Pharan, at the foot of Serbâl.* This was the first Christian centre-point of the peninsula, and the church founded by Justinian was for a long time dependent upon it. It is a question whether the tradition, which sees Sinai in the present Gebel Mûsa can be referred to a time prior to Justinian.† For solitary hermits this district is particularly adapted, and exactly for the same reason it would be unfitted for a great civilized and commanding people, who would exhaust all its resources, as it is in a retired spot, distant from all the frequented and connecting roads; but nevertheless, by reason of its situation in the high mountains, it affords sufficient nourishment for the moderate necessities of the solitary scattered monks. The gradually increasing hermit-population might then have attracted the attention of the Byzantine emperor to this very spot, and at that time dying tradition, by these means have revived and fixed for the time to come.‡

[* Note E, Appendix.]
[† Note F, Appendix.]
‡ Ritter (p. 31), where he mentions that Sinai appears almost simultaneously, as Serbâl, with the Egyptian Cosmas, and as Gebel Mûsa with the Byzantine Procopius, broaches another conjecture, which I shall here quote :—" Was there, perhaps," says he, " a different tradition or party opinion prevailing in Constantinople and Alexandria on this point among the convents and the monks, which might have arisen from a jealousy to vindicate the more sacred character of one or other of the places? It is curious that at the same time such

What I have said about the situation of Elim,
Raphidîm, and of the Mount Choreb or Sinai,
fails certainly in scholarlike proof, which I also
shall not be able to send from Thebes; this
can only be drawn with any advantage from the
course of the earliest traditions before Justinian,
which, even if they should coincide in every point
with these of the present time, nevertheless would
determine nothing positively. It appears to me
that these questions must remain ever undecided,
since the elements which stood at my command,
that is to say, the Mosaic account itself, the examination of the situations and the knowledge of
the historical circumstances of that time, were
not considered sufficient for their solution. Only
a contemporary examination of these three most
essential sides of the researches will allow a correct picture to be obtained of the whole story;
while the attempt to give the same authority,
without any difference, to each single point of the
representation now lying before us, will necessarily lead us into the road of false criticism, which
always sacrifices the understanding of the one to
the understanding of the whole.

different views of the question should exist among the most
learned theologians of their time."

LETTER XXXV.

ON the 6th of April we had quitted Tôr, where we stopped one night. We landed every night on the shell and coral-rich African coast during our far voyage, until, on the 10th, we reached Kossêr, where the brave Seïd Mahommed from Qeneh was awaiting us, in order to provide us with camels for our return to Thebes. In four days we passed along the broad Rossaffa road over the mountains by Hamamât, and arrived at our head-quarters in Thebes on the 14th.

We found everything in the most desirable order and activity, only our old, faithful castellan 'Auad came to meet me with head bound up, and greeted me with a weak voice. He had but just escaped from death's door. I already mentioned, in a former letter, that he and all the rest of the house of the Sheikh at Qurna had incurred a blood-guiltiness which was not yet avenged. The family of the murdered man, at Kôm el Birâh, had, shortly after our departure, seized the opportunity, when 'Auad and a relation were returning home from Luqsor, to surprise the two unsuspecting wayfarers. They thought more of 'Auad's companion than himself, and therefore called to the latter to depart; but as he would not do it, but defended his comrade lustily, he received an almost fatal blow on the head with a sharp weapon, which stretched him fainting on the ground ; the other was murdered, and thrown into the Nile, as an expiation for the seven years' guilt. Since then there has been peace between the families.

A more extended report on our Sinai journey, to which I have added two maps of the peninsula, was carried out by Erbkam after my plans. Now I have the heavy closing of my account with Thebes before me, which, however, I hope to complete in ten to twelve days.

LETTER XXXVI.

OUR first halting-place after leaving Thebes, on the 16th of April, was Dendera, the magnificent temple of which is the last northward, and, although it is only of a late, almost merely Roman period, it furnished much matter for our portfolios and note-books. There we employed nine whole days on the remarkable rock-tombs of Amarna, of the government of Amenophis IV., that royal puritan, who persecuted all the gods of Egypt, and would only admit the worship of the sun's disk.

When we came into the neighbourhood of Benisuef, we saw a stately steamer belonging to Ibrahim Pasha hurrying toward us. We hoisted our flag, and immediately, in answer to our greeting, there appeared the red Turkish flag with the crescent on board the steamer. Then it altered its course, and bore right down for us.

We were eager for the news that was coming. A boat was lowered, and made itself fast to us. How joyfully was I surprised to recognise in the fair-complexioned Frank that came up to us, my old university friend Dr. Bethmann, who had come across from Italy to accompany me home by way of Palestine and Constantinople. Ali

Bey, Ibrahim Pasha's right hand, who was steaming to Upper Egypt, had kindly taken him in his ship, and was sorry, as he told me, to lose the pleasant travelling companion, who had become quite dear to him during their short acquaintance.

His presence, and his interest and assistance, are now of the more value to me, as the rest of my companions have left me here alone. They departed hence yesterday. How gladly should I have accompanied them, as to-day the third anniversary of my departure from Berlin has already come round ; but the taking down of the pyramid tombs yet keeps me back. The four workmen, who were sent me from Berlin as assistants, have arrived ; they are strong young men, and I took them immediately with me to the Pyramids. We ensconced ourselves in a conveniently situated grave ; a field-smithy and a scaffolding for the crane was erected, and the work was quickly commenced.

The difficulties of the whole matter lie, however, rather in the petty jealousies that surround us here on every side, and in the various diplomatic influences which not unfrequently make even Mohammed Ali's direct orders illusory. It therefore also appeared imperatively necessary to Herr von Wagner, that I should not leave Egypt under any circumstances, until the end of the taking down and shipping of the monuments, and so I shall have to remain patiently here for some weeks longer.

LETTER XXXVII.

CAIRO.
July 11, 1845.

ALLOW me now briefly to add some thoughts which have occupied me much of late.* I have never lost sight of your desire to decorate the New Museum in a manner appropriate to its contents. I hope very much that it is still your intention to do so. I have heard with great pleasure of the arrangement of the Egyptian halls through Herr Hertel, and have heard from him that the decorations of the walls are yet *in suspenso.* So favourable an opportunity will scarcely again present itself, to have all the materials at hand at the first establishment of a museum for the creation of a true whole in every respect, and to offer to the public so many novel and important things in the plan, materials, and arrangements, as at the establishment of the Egyptian Museum. You have already, if I remember right, mentioned to me that you purpose to erect an *historical* museum, as, indeed, the object and the idea of all should be,

---

* This letter, which is here printed word for word, was addressed to the General-Director der K. Preuss. Museen, Herr Geh. Legations-Rath von Olfers. Perhaps its publication may serve at the same time to spread abroad a just respect for the principles on which the Egyptian Museum, that part of one of the most grand and newest creations of Berlin first accessible to the public, has been erected and decorated.

but yet exists nowhere. It is, however, attainable to some extent in an Egyptian museum, which can only be approached by others at a vast distance, even under the most favourable circumstances, as with no other people are the dates for each single monument so simple and certain as here, and no other collection is extended over so long a period (more than 3,000 years). I therefore take for granted, generally, that you desire to arrange the principal saloons, as far as it is possible, in historical succession, and to place in juxtaposition, as it were, whatever belong to the Old, the New, and to the Græco-Roman Empire, at any rate, in such a manner that each larger space should have a definite historical character. This has always been before my eyes also in their collection, although I do not at all believe that this principle should be pedantically carried into every particular. Of the casts which you will probably desire to embody in the collection of casts, it would be very desirable, for the sake of completeness, to have some duplicates in the Egyptian saloon.

But what makes me write you on such matters already from hence, is the reflection that you are perhaps already so far advanced, or soon will be, that you will feel desirous of coming to some resolution as to the architectural and artistical decoration of the saloons, for which some remarks from me might not be quite unacceptable to you.

For the Egyptian saloon you will certainly

choose an Egyptian style of architecture, and one
carried out in every way, for which, according to
what I understand from Hertel, there is yet plenty
of time; for I think that, in order to produce a
general harmonious impression, the different styles
peculiar to the different periods, particularly orders
of pillars, must be retained in their historical order,
and in their rich glory of colours.

The coloured wall-paintings cannot be omitted.
Every temple, every grave, every palace-wall was
covered by the Egyptians from top to bottom
with painted sculptures or pictures. The first
question is, in what style these pictures should
be carried out. They can now either be free
compositions in the Greek style, or strictly Egyptian representations, but avoiding Egyptian per-
spective; therefore a kind of translation, after the
manner of the wall-frieze in the *Musée Charles X.*
or, finally, they could be exact copies of pure Egyptian representations drawn by us and only employed in such places where necessity requires it.
As to the first style, I really think that such a
man as Cornelius would be able to gain something
grand and beautiful, even from such a task, if he
were inclined to enter upon so foreign a field;
but then the public would probably take a
great deal more interest in the painter than in the
representations from a history yet so strange to
him.

The second style* might perhaps be worthy of

[* This might, not without some reason, be considered to
assimilate with the style of painting which has lately made its
appearance in England as a school—I refer to the pre-Raphaelite,

trial, which, in a single instance, might also succeed, and then certainly would not be without
interest. Still I am quite convinced that such
hybrid representations in a long series would not
satisfy the necessary requirements, because they
would take for granted a perfection in two art-
languages, and would also certainly displease the
public. All the attempts I have hitherto met
with, at different times, in this style have, according to my own feelings, totally failed, and become
ridiculous in the eyes of artists, although, as I
said before, I do not believe that such an attempt
might not succeed once, with careful selection of
the subjects. To me, it therefore seems that the
third, but least assuming style, alone remains; but
it unites so many advantages that I well believe
it will gain your approval.

As to the subjects of the representations, there
can scarcely be a doubt, They must represent
the culminating point of Egyptian history, civilisation, and art, in a characteristic manner, and I
myself was astonished at the wealth of most
appropriate situations, which immediately present
themselves if we pass in review what yet lies
before us of Egyptian history. In order to give
you a cursory idea of it, I will communicate the

which, whatever its own intrinsic merits may be,—and those, I
suspect, are very few,—will at least have one good effect, that
of calling the attention of English painters to the individualities
in their paintings, and obviating the slurring sketchy style so
prevalent at the present time, the upholders of which, after all,
are the persons who condemn the pre-Raphaelites. The remarks
of Dr. Lepsius will therefore apply to this new school of
painting.—K. R. H. M.]

single points which I wrote down while I was yet in doubt whether one or other of the two first styles of representation might not be employed. Of course, a much more extended commentary would be necessary for this than I can now present; but a merely preliminary view is all that is required now. The names enclosed in brackets show where the materials for single compositions would be found.

ANTE-HISTORICAL.

Elevation of the God HORUS to the divine throne of OSIRIS (Dendera). As a contrast to the last number.

OLD EMPIRE.

Dyn. I. Departure of MENES from This, the city of Osiris.

Founding of MEMPHIS, the city of Phthah, by Menes.

Dyn. IV. Building of the Pyramids under CHEOPS and CHEPHREN.

Dyn. VI. Union of the two crowns of Upper and Lower Egypt under the hundred years of the reign of APAPPUS.

Dyn. XII. Temple of Ammon at THEBES, the city of Ammon, founded by Sesurtesen I. in the twelfth dynasty.

Immigrating HYKSOS (Benihassan).

LABYRINTH and LAKE MŒRIS, works of AMENEMHA III. in the twelfth dynasty.

Dyn. XIII. Shortly afterwards the IRRUPTION of the HYKSOS into Lower Egypt.

Expulsion of the Egyptian rulers into Ethiopia.

Supremacy of the Hyksos.

NEW EMPIRE.

Dyn. XVII.—XVIII. AMENOPHIS I. and the black Queen Aahmesnefruari.

TUTHMOSIS III. expels the HYKSOS from Abaris.

JERUSALEM founded by them.

AMENOPHIS III. Memnon and the vocal statue.

Persecution of the Egyptian gods and introduction of sun-worship under Bech-en-Aten (Amarna).

King HORUS the avenger.

Dyn. XIX. SETHOS I. (Sethosis, Sesostris) Conquest of CANAAN (Karnak). Joseph and his brethren.

RAMSES II. the Great, Miamun; war with the Cheta (Ramesseum.)*

The (brick-making) Israelites (Thebes) built Pithom and Ramses under Ramses II.†

Colonisation of GREECE from Egypt.

MENEPHTHES. DEPARTURE of the ISRAEL-ITES to Sinai. MOSES before Pharoah. Beginning of the new SIRIUS PERIOD, 1322, B.C.

[* The Cheta are generally considered to be the Hittites.— K. R. H. M.]

[† Exodus, i. 11.—K. R. H. M.]

Dyn. XX. RAMSES III. Battle from Medînet Habu.

Dyn. XXI. SHESHENK I. (Shishak) takes JERUSALEM (Thebes).

Dyn. XXV. SABAKO the Ethiopian, rules in Egypt.

Dyn. XXVI. PSAMMETICHUS the Philhellene elevates the arts. Departure of the war-caste to Ethiopia.

Dyn. XXVII. CAMBYSES rages, and destroys temples and statues.

Dyn. XXX. NECTANEBUS (Philæ).

ALEXANDER, son of Ammon, conquers Egypt; builds Alexandria.

Ptolemæus PHILADELPHUS founds the library.

CLEOPATRA and CÆSARION (Dendera).

CHRIST near Heliopolis.

So large the selection would, of course, not be, if we had only to do with existing paintings. The Old Empire would then first begin with the fourth dynasty, and the Hyksos period would be entirely wanting, because nothing is preserved of an earlier date to the former, and nothing remains of the latter.

But, on the other hand, Egyptian art could be represented more fully, and each painting would have a scientific interest. I had preliminarily made the following selection, which, however, by reason of our great riches in 1,300 drawings, could be enlarged and enlarged in every way.

MYTHOLOGY.

1. The greater and the lesser gods. First and second Divine dynasty.

2. OSIRIS undertakes the government of the Lower World, (Karnak).

HORUS that of the Upper (Dendera).

3. Divine Triad of THIS and ABYDOS: OSIRIS, ISIS, HORUS.

4. Divine Triad of MEMPHIS: PHTHA, PACHT, IMHOTEP.

5. Divine Triad of THEBES: AMMON-RA, MUT, CHENSU.

OLD EMPIRE.

King CHUFU (Cheops), beheading enemies (Peninsula of Sinai). Domestic Scene of the fourth and fifth dynasty (Gizeh and Saqâra).

APAPPUS unites the two crowns (Road to Kossêr).

SESURTESEN I., of the twelfth dynasty, conquers the Ethiopians (Florence). Domestic scenes of the peaceful prince of the twelfth dynasty. Asiatic attendants, forerunners of the Hyksos; wrestlers, games, hunting, &c. (Benihassan). Colossus drawn by men (Bersheh).

Immigrating, fugitive Hyksos (Benihassan).

NEW EMPIRE.

Working of the quarries of Memphis (Tura).

AMENOPHIS I. and AAHMESNEFRUARI. (Thebes).

TUTHMOSIS III. and his sister (Thebes; Rome).

TUTHMOSIS III. Tribute. Erection of Obelisks (Thebes.)

AMENOPHIS III. (Memnon) and his queen Tii before Ammon Ra (Thebes).

Progress of an Ethiopian Queen to Egypt under AMEN-TUANCH (Thebes.)

AMENOPHIS IV. (Bech-en-aten) the SUN-WOR-SHIPPER.

His procession in chariots with the queen and four princesses, in the Sun-temple of Amarna (Grottoes of Amarna).

A favourite carried on the shoulders of the people before Amenophis IV. Presentations of wreaths of honour throughout the whole of the royal family.

HORUS running to Ammon (Karnak).

SETHOS I. makes war against Canaan (Karnak).

RAMSES II. War against the Asiatic Cheta (Ramesseum).

The same in the Tree of Life (Ramesseum).

The same triumphing; procession of kings (Ramesseum).

RAMSES III. Battle with the Robu (Medînet Habu.)

The same among his daughters playing with them (Medînet Habu.)

RAMSES XII. Magnificent Procession of Ammon (Quarna).

PISHEM the priest-king (Karnak).

SHESHENK I. (Shishak) leads the prisoners of Palestine before Ammon (Karnak); King of JUDAH.

SABAKO the Ethiopian (Thebes).

TAHRAKA the Ethiopian (Barkal)

PSAMMETICHUS. Amasis (Thebes).

NECTANEBUS (Thebes).

ALEXANDER. PHILIP ARIDÆUS (Thebes).

PTOLEMÆUS PHILADELPHUS (Thebes).

CLEOPATRA and CÆSARION (Dendera).

Crowning of CÆSAR AUGUSTUS (Philæ).

Ethiopian matters from MEROE.

This, or a similar selection of representations, as large as the number of wall divisions will allow, carried out in the strictly classical Egyptian style, and with the rich mass of colours of the original, would give, better than anything else could, an idea to the spectator of Egyptian art on a large scale; the matter would present itself for his decision, and their study would assimilate well with the small and single original monuments. For except the graves that we are now taking down, and which offer only the simplest things, no monument is large enough to give an idea of Egyptian temples and wall-paintings in general, in which a grandeur and a power of composition are often to be found, and a feeling for general harmony of arrangement and division of the whole, which will highly astonish the attentive. Such a selection of the most beautiful and most characteristic in large, easily examined pictures, would perhaps, conduce more than anything else, to procure a larger public for Egyptological science, and, at the same time, produce the inestimable advantage of obviating all malicious criticisms of the paintings as modern compositions; for every

2 c

hasty critic could be referred to the originals, the
highly important place of which, in the early
history of the human race, cannot be taken from
them by any peevish feuilletonist. Each would
be told, that he must first study the originals, ere
he dare venture on pronouncing upon the faithful
copies; for if our young artists of three years'
practice are employed, I am sure that little can
be objected to their works with reference to
classicality of style. The novelty of the thought,
and the large and complete effect, could certainly
not fail to produce considerable impression on the
learned and unlearned public, and clever men,
and above all his Majesty, would at once be
satisfied with the arrangement, without thinking
of the execution. To this would finally be added the
proportionately very unexpensive execution, from
the extreme simplicity of the draught and painting, as all the cost of artistical composition has
already been borne by the ancient Egyptians
themselves.

The painting must begin, according to the
Egyptian custom, at a certain height (which is
also convenient for our purpose), and must rest
upon a high band running underneath, the colour
of which must resemble simple wood or stone.
The high walls must also be divided into several
sections one above another, and in the frieze, the
whole series of the Egyptian Pharaohs, or even only
their cartouches must be depicted. The ceilings
in the ante-chambers could be blue with golden
stars, the usual manner of denoting the Egyptian
heaven, and in the historical saloons, the long rows

of wide-winged vultures, the symbol of victory, with which most of the ceilings of the temples and palaces are ornamented in an incomparably magnificent manner. Finally, a certain profusion of hieroglyphical inscriptions might not be wanting, as they are so intimately connected with all the Egyptian representations, and make a splendid effect in gay colours. For the doors and middle stripes of the ceilings, modern hieroglyphical inscriptions might easily be composed, which would refer, after the ancient Egyptian manner, to the munificence of the king, to the place and time, and to the aim of the buildings. How glorious would be the two Egyptian orders of columns in their simplicity and rich colours in the midst of all!

For the ante-rooms, at last, another idea might be realized. One could here paint on the walls views of the present Egyptian localities, in order to give the person coming in, some idea of the country, and of the condition of the buildings whence the antiquities around him were taken. These views might also be historically arranged, according to the principal place of the different epochs; yet that historical knowledge would here have to be taken for granted, which we are now seeking to diffuse. Therefore a geographical arrangement would probably be the most agreeable to the purpose, and should probably comprehend views of Alexandria, Cairo, the Pyramids of Gizeh, Siut, Benihassan, Abydos, Karnak, Qurna, Cataracts of Assuan, Korusko, Wadi Halfa, Sedeïnga, Semneh, Dongola, Barkal, Meroe, Chartûm,

Sennâr, and Sarbut el Châdem, in Arabia Petræa.

Beside all this, there might be a very rich,
highly-interesting, and at the same time useful
selection of articles and occupations of private
life in the other spaces, all copied from the larger
originals, by which in an equally inviting as certain manner, the comprehension of the collected
antiquities relating to domestic life, can be made
more easy in every way.

LETTER XXXVII.

JAFFA.
October 7, 1845.

THE taking down the tombs proceeded quickly; but as was to be expected, the transport and embarkment caused our greatest hindrance. Also the exportation of the whole of the monuments required a particular permission from the Viceroy. I set off, consequently, on the 29th August to Alexandria, in order to take leave of Mohammed Ali, and to obtain at the same time an official termination to our mission.

The Pasha received me in his former friendly manner, and immediately gave the necessary commands for the exportation of the collection, which, in a special writing which was handed to me, he presented to his Majesty our King. As soon as these preparations were concluded I returned to Cairo; found there the last orders about the transport of the monuments to Alexandria, and then, on the 25th September, departed with Bethmann for Damietta. I visited, on this journey, several ruins of cities in the eastern Delta, such as those of Atrib (Athribis), Samanud (Sebennytos), Behbet el Hager (Iseum); but, excepting the rubbish mounds of Nile earth, and fragments of bricks, which point out the historical situation, we found only a few blocks, which lay scattered about the old temples. Only in San,

the anciently renowned Tamis, to which I made
an excursion from Damietta across the Lake of
Menzaleh, are the wall-foundations of a temple of
Ramses II., and a number, namely about twelve
or fourteen, small granite obelisks of the same
king, some whole and some in fragments.

On the 1st of October we went from Damietta
to the Rheda of Ezbe, and sailed the following
morning to the Syrian coast. We had contrary
winds almost the whole way, cruised about for a
whole day on the picturesque and rocky shores of
Askalon, and only yesterday landed on the holy
land of the strand of Joppa.

LETTER XXXVIII.

NAZARETH.

November 9, 1845.

M Y last letter of the 26th of October from Jerusalem, I am sorry to say, you will not receive, as the courier (of Dr. Schulz, our consul), to whom I had given it, with five others, was attacked by robbers on the road to Berut, near Cesarea, much ill-used, and robbed of all his despatches, together with the little money he had with him. The want of order in this country is very great. The Turkish authorities, to whom the country has been again given up by Christian bravery, are lazy, malicious, and weak at the same time, whilst Ibrahim Pasha at least knew how to maintain order and security as far as his government extended.

In Jerusalem we remained nearly three weeks, which I passed in obtaining a knowledge of the religious circumstances of the present time, every day becoming more important, and partly in some antiquarian, topographical researches. The great affability and communicativeness of the Bishop Alexander, who overtook us, with Abeken of Jaffa, and the learned industry of Dr. Schulz, with whom I had been intimate since our mutual stay in Paris, in the years 1834 and 1835, have greatly assisted me in rendering these delightfnl days both important and instructive. An excursion to Jericho, to Jordon, and the Dead Sea, and back over San Saba formed an interesting episode. My copious diary of the whole time was, however, contained in the lost letter, which will never appear again, and which I can now but imperfectly replace.

On the 4th November we left the Holy City. On account of the war, now becoming serious, which the Pasha of Jerusalem was carrying on with Hebron, we had some difficulty in procuring mules and horses. The first night beyond Jerusalem we passed under the tents in Bîreh. On the second day we went through Bethin (Bethel), 'Ain el Haramîeh (the Robbers' Well), Selûn (Silo), to Nablûs (Sichem, Neapolis), and ascended the same evening the Garizim, the holy mountain of the Samaritans, the small remains of whom (about seventy men or 150 souls) we made ourselves acquainted with the next day. They are still abhorred by the Jews, and have also as little in common with the Christians and the Mahommedans.

We saw from the Garizim the naked rocky level, surrounded by some old walls, where these Sámari still offer yearly, as in former times, their sheep to their God. The next morning, after we had visited the house of prayer of the Samaritans, in which we were shown the ancient Samaritan handwriting of the Pentateuch, as well as Jacob's well and the vine-covered grave of Joseph, we rode on, accompanied by an armed servant of Soliman Bey, in whose house we had lodged, to Sebastîeh (Sebaste, the ancient Samaria) where

we saw the ruins of a beautiful old church, of the
time of the crusaders, which is said to be built
over the grave of John the Baptist. The night we
passed in the well-wooded Gennîn (Egennin).
From thence our road led through the wide fertile yet nevertheless deserted plain of Jesreel
(Esdraelon), across the great battle-field of Palestine, to Zerîn, and to the beautiful Ain Gu-
lût (Goliath's spring), where Naboth's vineyard
lay, and Ahab's whole family were murdered, then
over the Gebel Dah'i, the little Herman, behind
which arose Tabor (Gebel e' Tûr) which, on
account of its magnificent cupola form and its
open situation, distinguished itself, and enchained
our eyes, till we road again into the mountains
to the lovely Nazareth, amphi-theatrically situated
in a mountain-hollow.   Early yesterday we made
an excursion from here over Mount Tabor, to
Tiberias, to the Lake of Genezaret, and have just
returned.   There also we were obliged, against
my will, to take with us armed Arabs as body-
guards, and, in fact, we met, particularly in the
neighbourhood of the woody beautiful Tabor,
many vagabond Bedouins, in their picturesque
gay costume, watching on the roads or riding
across the fields right up to us, whom I should
not have liked to have met alone.

LETTER XXXIX.

SMYRNA.

December 7, 1845.

FROM Nazareth we went down the plain of
Jesreel to Mount Carmel, where we passed the
night in the stately newly-built convent. The
next morning we ascended from thence the mountain which commands the sea, with its fragrant
shores, and down to Haipha (Hepha), sailed
across the creek to Acca (Ako, Ptolemais), and
rode then along the coast upon the wet sand, with
the continued view of the accompanying mountains, through Sur (Tyrus) and Saida (Sidon) to
Berut (Berytos), where we were received most
cordially by the Prussian Consul General, Herr
von Wildenbruch.

On the 13th of November we set off from Berut
to Damascus. I left Gabre Mariam at the Herr
von Wildenbruch's, and took only my faithful
Berber Ibrahim and a *khawass* back with me.
Behind the nearest sand-hills to Berut, the road
leads immediately up the flowery and richly-
wooded and watered mountains, which we crossed
about the frontier, between the territories of the
Drusen and the Maronites. We ascended the
whole day, sometimes upon incredibly bad rocky
roads, and remained one night on this side the
mountain brow; this we reached only the next
morning, and had now a wide view over the

fertile plains of Leontes, which divides Libanon
and Anti-lebanon, and, with the exception of the
interruption of Gebel e' Shech (Hermon) and its
branches, which are pushed in between, forms a
continued broad immense fissure along the whole
of the valley of Jordan to the Dead Sea, to the
Gulf of Akaba and the Red Sea. We descended
to Mekseh, breakfasted on one of its flat roofs,
and were to have cut across from here south-
eastward through the valley to Megdel and Aithi ;
but we preferred taking a round northward to
Zachleh, which is one of the largest and most
flourishing towns of Christian Libanon. On the
road we met with a party of soldiers, who were
escorting several thousand muskets upon donkeys,
which they had the day before taken from the
inhabitants of Zachleh. The disarming of the
whole of Libanon by Sheikh Effendi had commenced from the south with great partiality, as
is well known, against the unhappy Christians,
who were shamefully sacrificed by a merciless
policy. In order to disarm the strong and influential Zachleh, it had been invested with 200
men of the regular troops, of whom we found
some still stationed there, and an innumerable
multitude of Bedouins, whose assistance they
would make use of, in cases of necessity, against
the Christians encamped in the valley of
Beqâ'a ; these last, however, were already gone.
We inquired, in the still agitated city, after the
Bishop Theophilus, who was described to us as
having been a heroic and powerful champion in
the battle; unfortunately he was gone to Berut.

After we left there, we met on the road a German
Catholic priest, who accompanied us to the frontier Mo'allaqa, and related to us many cruelties
committed by the Turks, here, as every where
else, on the tormented inhabitants. Some hundreds of guns more than were in the whole place,
had been demanded, and the old Sheikhs who had
to collect them, bastinadoed so long, till the
inhabitants bought them with great trouble and
at a high price in the camp of the Turks themselves.

From Zachleh we went to Kerak, in order to
visit the grave of Noah. We found a long narrow
building of well-united free-stone, and near it a
small cupola building, surrounded with a few trees,
from whence we had a beautiful view over the
plain, and disclosed Anti-libanon. I saw through
a window hung with votive rags, in an arched
space, a bricked-up tomb, in the usual oriental
form, but I was not a little surprised, upon looking through all the windows the whole length of
the building, always to see the continuation of
the same tomb, which appeared neither to have
beginning nor end. At last the door-keeper came,
and I convinced myself, with astonishment, that
the tomb was forty ells long, according to exact
measurement 31m. 77′, thus something more
than forty common Egyptian ells.* This allows
us to suppose that the measure of Noah's body

---

* It must be from some error that Burckhardt (Travels in
Syria, p. 5) only allows the grave of Noah a length of ten feet,
although the same number recurs in Schubert (*Reise in das
Morgenland*, Bd. III., p. 340). It is well known how con-

was in proportion to his life, of a thousand years long.

From Kerak we at last turned to the right, into the plain towards Tel Emdieh, then to the left into a valley, which led us straight to the north, and by sunset we came to El'Ain, a small village by a well, which lies at the end of the valley, at a tolerable height above the great plain. On account of the round to Zachleh and Kerak, we were somewhat behind our days' reckoning, and for this reason, much to the disappointment of our mule drivers, we determined to go on further to Zebedêni, which is situated on the eastern declivity of Anti-libanon, two hours from here. As none of our people had gone this journey through the mountains, we took a guide with us, who conducted us soon out of our valley, which passed between the outer mountains and the principal ridge northward, up a tremendously steep, laborious, and endless rockway. The moon rose, the hours passed, and yet the desired Zebedêni was not reached. At length we stood at the steep verge of another valley, into which we had to climb on foot laboriously, leading the horses, for a whole hour, until we arrived at

tinually the number forty is used by the Hebrews as an indefinite number. The same seems to have been peculiar to *all Semitic* nations, at least, it may be pointed out frequently, and at all times with the Phœnicians and Arabs; the numeral word for four and forty itself points, in these languages, to the general idea of multitude. Cf. my Treatise on Philological Comparison ("*Sprachvergleichende Abhandlungen,*") Berlin, 1836, pp. 104, 139, and the "Chronology of the Egyptians," vol. i. p. 15.

Zebedêni after a six hours' march. Every one
here lay in the deepest sleep; we had to knock at
several houses, to ask the way to the convent,
where we hoped to find shelter. At last it was
found that there was certainly a church in the
place, but no room to take us in, in the adjoining
convent. We therefore quartered ourselves
in the last house, which after much knock-
ing was opened to us. It contained only one
large room, which was, however, large enough for
us and our servants, and the numerous family of
men, women, and children, had withdrawn into
one corner. But the people were friendly and
kind, got their *bakshish* next morning, and let us
go with the invitation to repeat our visit upon our
return. We now journeyed down the beautiful
fertile valley of Zebedêni to the south, until we
turned eastward again in an hour and a half into
the steep rock pass, where the running brook by
which we had hitherto travelled, swelled into a
little river named Bárada, which forces itself a
passage in incomparably beautiful and picturesque
cascades through the luxuriant green to the great
plain of Damascus. For several hours we rode
along its steep banks, and sometimes along its
bed until we came to a high arch, which served as
a bridge from the left to the right shore. Here
the road went up the mountain, and we found in
the continuation of the steep rock-wall we had
just quitted, a number of ancient rock tombs.
Soon after the wild gorge opened into a broader
valley, in which the dashing river serpentines on

more easily, passing several friendly lying villages
in its course. Up to this place it had broken
through a mountain ridge running due north and
south, in an easterly direction, and whence it now
flowed through a gateway formed of rock. Two
single crags stood forth to the eastward like
mighty pylones, of which the southern one bore
upon its crown of several thousand feet in height,
a little tomb, surrounded with some trees. This
place is revered as the grave of Abel Hebbi
Habíl, who, according to tradition, was buried
here. The elevation is hardly to be climbed;
so it seemed from this side at least. We, therefore, did not seek to ascertain whether the youth
Habel had also had a grave of forty ells in length
built for him. At the foot of the rock, the ancient
town of Abila had been situated, the name of
which had probably given rise to the story.

We now left for some hours the charming valley
of Bárada, and rode over naked rocky *plateaux*,
until we descended to it again near Gedîden, and
took a short rest on its shore in the shadow of
high platanes and glistening larches. At length
we again quitted the river, which had grown
fuller and more violent from the many streamlets
running into it, climbed a high mountain, and
stood suddenly in sight of the boundless plain,
which, stopped by no mountains to the east, lay
before us like a single great garden, with innumerable thick-leaved green trees, cut through by roads
and water. Directly at our feet, in the middle of
this garden, lay glorious Damascus, with its
cupolas, minarets, and terraces. We knew that

we had to expect one of the most renowned views
in the world.   Nevertheless we were astonished,
and found our expectations surpassed by the
magnificent picture, which, as if by a magic
stroke, unfolded itself before us, after the lovely,
but narrow valleys, which alternated with the
naked rock wildernesses.   We remained at least
an hour on this spot, which has been distinguished
by the stately erection of a cupola resting on
four open columns, called Qubbet e' Nasr, "the
Cupola of Victory."

Damascus is one of the most holy and most celebrated cities of the East.   The prophet Mahommed
considered it thrice blessed, because the angels
spread their wings over it, and he, on perceiving the beautiful view, did not conquer it, as to
man but one paradise was promised, and he was
to find his in heaven.   In the Koran God swears
by the fig and the olive, that is, by Damascus and
Jerusalem, and the Arabian geographers call it
"the mole on the cheek of the world,"—"the
plumage of the bird of paradise," — "the neck-
lace of beauty;" in the titles of the sultans,
"the paradise-scented Dimishk."*   According
to the saying of the eastern Christians, Adam was
made here out of the red earth; and the neighbouring mountain Kassiûm the legend points out
as the place where Cain murdered Abel.

The Bárada, which we had followed from its
first spring, runs somewhat south of Damascus
into the great plain, then turns to the left to-

* See V. Hammer, History of the Osman Empire, part II.
p. 482.

wards the town, which it traversed in seven arms,
and then runs into a lake. It was the golden-
streamed Chrysorrhoas of the ancients, the celebrated Farfar of the eastern poets. It is this
stream which causes the whole of this paradise ;
and through it this ancient city, which was known
even to Abraham, and conquered by David, has
had its importance secured. Formerly Damascus
was the centre of Arabian literature and learning, and it is said that a disciple of the prophet
gave instruction in the Koran to 1,6ʳ0 believers
at the same time (according to the Lancastrian
method) in the great mosque of the Ommiades.
The town appeared to us, at first, not to respond.
to its glorious environs. Tolerably wide but bare
streets received us, with low houses, plaster walls,
in which were little doors, and hardly any windows. There were none of the beautiful wood-
carvings or stone ornaments to be seen either by
the doors or at the corners. Only some mosques
and wells which we passed formed an exception ;
and the many single trees in the streets and
squares gave a pleasing appearance. As we came
more into the interior of the city, the almost
massive bazaars and the full shops; the richness of
heaped-up fruit of all sorts ; the gay crowd
of large and small in the numerous costumes ;
and the never-ending turnings from one street
into another ;—everything forced upon us the
idea that we were in a large and rich oriental
city. We rode to the Prussian Consul's, but he
was lying ill of a fever. We then went further
to a newly-established hotel. Here, also, as well

as at the consul's, we entered by a narrow door in
an unsightly outer wall into a little dark court,
and from thence into a low, crooked passage.
Then, however, there opened before us a beautiful, spacious court, surrounded by stately,
shining marble walls, in the middle of which was
a fountain, overshadowed by lofty trees. At the
further end was an arched niche, whose vaulted
top was twenty-five feet high. To this one
we mounted a few marble steps, and then found
ourself in a hall not large, but rather lofty, which
opened into the court, and along the inner walls
had comfortable divans. To the left, near this
niche, was a dining-room; on the right we mounted
a staircase to the upper rooms, where we lived.
These were wainscotted all round, and the walls
and ceiling were decked with gay painting, gild-
ing, and silvering. We afterwards saw several
more of the best houses in Damascus, which all
from outside appeared almost miserable, but in-
ternally displayed an oriental magnificence that
was to be found nowhere else in this most
charming country. And in this manner they
sometimes build at the present time, at least,
if we may judge by some of the small palaces,
which have only been built within the last ten or
twenty years. There reigns here a profusion of
the use of marble and other valuable stone in
these courts, halls, and rooms, such as we only
find in royal palaces in our own country. The
beautiful open halls, which are always built with
a high arch in front, are found sometimes on two
or three sides of the court, and have very often a

small fountain, as well as the great one, which
never fails to stand in the middle of the court,
generally overshadowed by trees, which grow out
of the middle of the marble slabs.

The next day we spent entirely in looking
through the city, and particularly the large bazars
in which are spread out beautiful stuffs, worked
with gold and silver, magnificent arms, and other
oriental articles of luxury. We visited the great
Khan, with its nine splendid domed chambers ;
it is a kind of exchange for the most distinguished
tradespeople ; then the grand mosque of the
Ommiades, which is kept with the utmost sanctity, and whose hall of pillars is 550 feet long, and
150 feet broad. It was formerly a Christian
church, which must also have been built on the
foundations of a Romish Temple of Juno. We
were not allowed to enter, only to look in at the
numerous open doors, and were even prevented by
a fanatical Mussulman from going upon the roof
of a neighbouring house, so that we were obliged
to put it off till the next day. We were also
shown a splendid plane-tree, thirty-five feet in
circumference, which is in the middle of a street,
near a well, called after an old Sheikh Ali, who
is said to have planted the tree ; we went also into
the inviting coffee-house on the cool side of the
stream. The next day we rode to the south gate
of the city, called Bab Allah, towards which leads
a perfectly straight street, more than an hour long,
between magnificent shops, mosques, work-shops,
and other buildings, which merits its name of
"the street called Straight" (ἡ ῥύμη ἡ καλουμένη

εὐθεῖα), in which Saul lived when he was converted by Ananias.—(Acts ix. 11.)

On the road we stopped at the little cupola building which is usually supposed to be the tomb of Saladin, but is really only a little betort raised to his honour by Sultan Selim. The real tomb is twelve hours south of Damascus, near a place called Gibba, according to a Sheikh, whom we met here. From Bal Allah, the " Gate of God," through which the pilgrims to Jerusalem and Mekka go, we rode round the town, to the left, through the pleasant orchards of olives, poplars, mulberry, and giant-sized apricot trees; the latter produce the most delicious apricots, which are dried, and under the name of Mishmish are sent all over the world. We then came to the burying ground of the Jews, where they were just letting down a body into the grave, and according to their custom here were calling out the praises of the dead. Not far from there lies the Christian burial-ground, in the neighbourhood of which the place is pointed out where Saul was thrown to the earth by the heavenly vision. From thence our way lay over a little bridge to the town wall, in which they showed us, near a gate which is now bricked up, the window through which Paul was let down. We continued along the wall till we came to a beautiful Roman gate, with three entrances, the *Porta Orientalis*, through which we came to the house of Ananias, and the cave in the rock, which is now turned into a chapel. Then we rode through fruit and olive gardens to a neighbouring village Gôba, where Elisha crowned

Hazael king of Syria, and Elijah was fed by ravens in the cave.

We visited also the tomb of the great Arabian mystic, the renowned Sheikhs Mohieddin el Arabi, on our road from Damascus, in Salhîeh, which is situated near, and we thought also of his master the Sheiks Shedeli, who discovered how to make a drink of coffee, and used to keep his pupils awake with it. In Palestine we wandered about the tombs of Abraham, Isaac, and Jacob ; Rebecca, Leah, and Rachel ; of Joseph, David, Solomon, and the Prophets ; of Christ, his parents and his disciples. Here we came to the tombs of Noah and Abel, and soon also to Seth's ; we trode the fields of the paradise of the first human pair. What a singular feeling it is to travel in a country where legends can be occupied on such subjects !

We remained the first night after our departure in Sûk el Bárada, at the foot of Nebbi Habîl. From thence we went again over the ancient arched bridge, which, as well as most of the buildings of this country, were built by the Empress Helena ; and this time we examined more nearly the tombs in the rocks, to which we had to arrive by a very difficult path, through an old aqueduct hewn out of the rock. Some of these tombs were singularly planned and appeared to be very ancient ; further on, followed several of the Greek period, with bas-reliefs and gables, and some steles in the rock, on which we could still decypher some Greek words. From here, not far up the river, we found an immense Roman work, the great old (though now forsaken) road, hewn for a considerable distance out of the solid rock. On the flat, high, side-wall were two Roman inscriptions, each in dupli-cate. The longest ran thus :—

IMPerator CAESar Marcus AVRELius AN-TONINVS | AVGustus ARMENIACVS ET IM-Perator CAESar Lucius AVRELius VERVS AVGustus AR | MENIACVS VIAM FLVMINIS | VI ABRVPTAM INTERCISO | MONTE RESTIVERVNT PER | IVIium VERVM LE-Gatum PRo PRaetore PROVINCiæ | SYRiae ET AMICVM SVVM | IMPENDIIS ABILENO-RVM. The other was :—PRO SALVTE IMPe-ratoris AUGusti ANTONI | NI ET VERI Marcus VO | LVSIVS MAXIMVS (centurio) LEGionis XVI. Flaviæ Firmae QVI OPERI | IN STITIT Voto Suscepto.* Since then the rock has been, without doubt, undermined and broken up for the second time by the current, (probably very violent in the spring-time of the year,) as close by the second copy of the two inscriptions, the rock-road breaks off into a steep. Towards four o'clock we had ascended the Antilibanon, and we then again went to Nebbi Shît, which is Seth, in the great plain of the Leontes. We immediately went to search for the tomb of Nebbi Shît, and were not a little astonished at finding here, as well as at Nebbi Noëh, a solid ancient Ambian building, with a small cupola adjoining, and within a grave forty ells long. It was wider than that of Noah, because on both sides along the whole length of the grave three steps led up to the height of the tomb,

* Cf. Krafft, the Topography of Jerusalem, Bonn, 1846, and Plate II. No. 33.

which were wanting in the other. It is quite apparent that tradition, by giving such an uncommon measure to the bodies of these two patriarchs, intended to represent them as antediluvian men; and the number forty, which is so frequently used both in the Old and New Testament as an indefinite holy number, has, as is seen here, not lost this signification among the Arabians.

The same evening we rode two hours further, to Britân, and arrived before sunrise next morning, at Bâlbek, the ancient Heliopolis, with its famous ruins of the temple of the sun. I stopped next by the old stone bridge, by which the road passed, and measured there a building block, which was not quite loosened from the rock, of 67 feet in length, 14 feet in breadth, and 13 feet 5 inches thick. Of such blocks, or of somewhat smaller ones, consist several walls of the ruins of the temple and Bâlbek. A block that I measured on the spot, and in its place, without particularly choosing it, was 65 feet 4 inches, by 12 feet 3 inches, and 9 feet 9 inches. The ruins are, in fact, immense; the style of the architecture, in all its ornamental parts, is however heavy, overloaded, and partly of a very barbarous taste.

To Bâlbek there hangs a very sad recollection. As I approached the straggling houses of the village, which is very near the ruins of the ancient temple, my faithful servant, Ibrahim, who had arrived here before us, came to meet me with the joyful intelligence, that Abeken, from whom we had separated in Jerusalem, had just reached the village. I found him, indeed,

in the next house to the worthy bishop, Athana-
sins; hardly, however, had we greeted each
other, when they came to tell me that Ibrahim
was dying outside in the street. I found him
almost on the same spot where he had met me in
so friendly a manner, stretched out, the death-
rattle in his throat, and his eyes already fixed.
A priest, from the next convent, endeavoured to
assist him, but in vain; he died in a few minutes
before my eyes. A fever produced by being
exposed to the weather, seemed to have given
him his death-blow. He was a man of sterling
worth, and an inborn noble nature, such as is not
often found among the Arabs. I had taken him
with me, in my journey to Nubia, from Assuan;
he desired, from his own impulse and attachment,
to accompany me to Europe, and would have been
exceedingly useful to me in my labours on the
Sudan languages, on account of his knowledge of
the Nubian dialects. I wished to place a stone
over the spot where he was buried, at the foot of
Antilibanon, on the slope of the hill near a tree;
but no stone-mason could be found. For this
reason I sent one from Berut, with this inscription :—IBRAHIMO HASSAN SYENE ORI-
VNDO SERVO BENE MERENTI P. R. LEP-
SIVS. D. XXI. NOVEMB. MDCCCXLV.

This news made a deep impression upon Gabre
Mariam, when I told it him at Berut; he wept
bitterly, for they had been very good friends.

Before we left Bâlbek, the bishop advised us
to take another road than that which we had
intended to take, as the news had come that the

other side of Libanon was in a very disturbed
state, and that the population was in insurrection.
However, as the whole country was in commotion, and as we had never met with any difficulty
on that account, we cared but little about it, and
remarked to him that we were only going through
the Christian districts, whose inhabitants would
be friendly to us. We quitted Bâlbek a little
before sunset, and crossed the narrow plain, in
order to pass the night in Dêr el Ahmar, the
" red convent," and the next day, with renewed
strength, to ascend Libanon almost to its highest
point. During our whole journey through Palestine and Syria, we had, till now, been favoured
with the most beautiful weather. From day to
day, according to the calculations of other seasons, we might expect continued rains, and,
nevertheless, we had only once been wet through,
on our return from the Dead Sea to Jerusalem.
The broad plain, Begân, which we crossed now a
second time, is after the rains, at this season, not
passable ; and the numerous mountain - streams
of the well-watered Libanon, are generally so
swollen, that, on account of the want of bridges,
they can only be crossed with great danger. This
evening the sky was clouded over, in a threatening manner, the darkness of the night was
impenetrable, and at last, when we had just
perceived some lights in the distance, at Dêr el
Ahmar, we lost our way upon a desert, full of
clefts, and the ground broken and rough. At last
hardly were we arrived when a heavy rain poured
down. We shared again a large room with a

whole Christian peasant family, and passed one
of the most unquiet of nights.

Among the women and children, who appeared
to be ill, there was a constant groaning and
fretting. In a short time the continued rain
penetrated the roof and dropped upon the beds;
persons were sent up to heap fresh sand upon it,
and to roll it with heavy pieces of stone pillars,
(kept upon every house ready for this purpose,)
which, however, sent so much lime and dirt
down upon us, that we were obliged to beg that
the operation might be discontinued. In a little
shed near the door, lay a dog with a numerous
progeny, whose bed must have also been wet, as
they began to whine and yelp most piteously.
Finally, our host was with repeated and much
noise knocked up, in order to procure a horse for
a soldier, who was carrying letters on further in
haste for the Pasha. Consequently, during the
whole night we could gain no rest; and if the
Arabian proverb says, that the king of the fleas
holds his court in the holy city of the Jews, I
have every reason to suppose that he has removed
his residence from there (where we laid com-
fortably) to this place.

Towards morning the rain had ceased, and
had turned into a thick fog, which forming
together into thick clouds, appeared sometimes to
be cut by the prominent mountains of the lofty
Libanon, and sometimes with its phantom-like
play, with the light of the morning sun occasionally breaking through upon the nearer and
farther woody hills and mountain-tops, perfectly
delighted us. When we came to the first height,

which is divided from the principal chain by a
shallow valley, we had suddenly an indescribably
beautiful and astonishing view over the whole
of the mountain range of Libanon, which rose up
before us, its whole length and down a considerable distance, covered with fresh shining snow ;
a true Alpine country in its most magnificent
features, which towers majestically over this land
blessed with eternal spring, but now so shamefully oppressed by its Turkish enemies. I enjoyed
most fully this uncommon sight, which aroused
in my heart a true native joy, and I tried to retain within me this clear pure light. Before me I
drove my little Egyptian horse, who had lost his
rider at Bâlbek, and who carried on his back the
small possessions he had left ; I thought then,
how I had rejoiced a few days before, at the idea
of the good Ibrahim's astonishment, when he
should traverse with us the snowy region of
Libanon. The ass did not appear to be much
pleased with the snow-heaps that we had to ride
through; he often stood quite astonished in the
middle of the snow, and no doubt took it all for
salt, the white soft fields of which he had already
known by the Red Sea and elsewhere. We rode
zigzag along the immensely steep precipice seven
to eight thousand feet high, which is here not
rocky, but covered with earth, and terminates in
a sharp brow. " El humdu l'illah !" cried the old
guide, when we had reached the top ; and, "Salâm,
salâm," sounded in chorus. We had reached
almost the highest point of Libanon, but the view
over land and sea was unfortunately hidden from

us by clouds and fog, although the blue sky was above our heads. After a short ride down from the top, our guide showed us at our feet, in a large level inlet of the mountains, the ancient and renowned forest of cedars, out of which King Hiram sent the great stems to Solomon to build the temple ; it appeared from above as small as a garden. It had been considered for a length of time as the remains of this forest, till, in later times, in a northern part of Libanon, other forests of cedars have been discovered. We soon lost sight of the cedars as we descended lower into the clouds, which cut off all view from us. Suddenly the dark shadows of these giant trees appeared in close rows before us, out of the great masses of fog, like spirits of the mountains. We rode to the chapel of the hermit, who has usually a good glass of Libanon wine to put before a stranger, but we found it shut up ; just then the clouds broke into a regular straight-down rain, from which the needle-like roofs of the proud cedars afforded us but little shelter. I found a cedar-apple hanging low enough for me to break off, and to carry with me as a token of remembrance. Some of these stems are forty feet in circumference, and ninety feet high ; and as it is supposed that a cedar of a hundred years old will only be half a foot in diameter, so must these be reckoned three thousand years old, which would reach back to the time of Solomon. The rain increased, and we had yet several thousand feet to descend to the nearest village, Bsherreh. The lower we came, the more slippery and dangerous became the narrow, sometimes rocky, sometimes soft, footway, which leads along the steep precipice over a yawning abyss down to the right. At a bend in a corner of a rock, we at last caught sight of our desired night-quarters, the rich, pleasant, and large village of Bsherreh, which gives its name to the whole district, and is well known on account of its strong and influential, but wild and ungovernable, and often cruel inhabitants.

The rain had abated; the white houses with their flat roofs, the number of silver poplars, plane-trees, and cedars, which rose up among them either singly or in rows, formed one above another a semi-circle on a hill projecting from the right hand precipice, and appeared, as they shone with the rain-drops, as if they were just out of a fresh bath. Nothing was moving in the village; it appeared as if everything was dead in it; I rode on along a narrow path by the wall of a vineyard, with our old guide, before the rest. Suddenly, at a bend of the road, a strong voice called to us, and as I looked over the vineyard-terrace, of about the height of a man, I saw to my great surprise, twenty guns pointed towards me and the guide. The guide let the bridle of his horse fall, and raised his hands towards heaven, and cried out to the people. I immediately threw back the hood of my cloak, to show the people my European hat, and to prove to them who we were. When they saw that there were but few of us, and that we made no attempt to defend ourselves, they came in hundreds from behind the trees, surrounded us, and for a long time would not believe

that we were not disguised soldiers. Some threw
sticks down upon our horses from the terraces,
while I was endeavouring to explain who we
were to those nearest to me. Others understood
the mistake sooner, and came down to the street,
and took hold of the bridle of my horse. At last,
a boy of about fourteen, with a frank countenance, a beautiful forehead, and red fresh cheeks,
pressed through the crowd, and called out in
Italian that we should not fear, it was all a mistake, we were their friends, and we had only to
ride and dismount at his brother's house. Some
violent people accompanied us still, and cried out
to us from the walls with the most angry gestures ;
while the great crowd were already satisfied, and
raised a deafening shout of joy, fired their guns
into the air, and led us in triumph to the village.

In Bsherreh, which contains from 1,200 to
1,500 inhabitants, all were on foot ; they pressed
and pushed each other, in order to kiss our hands
or clothes. The women began their piercing cries ;
clapped their hands, and danced ; my brave boy
remained still by my side, and so, at last, we got
step by step through the thick crowd, who now
saluted us as friends, and reached the house of the
sheikh, of whom my guide was a younger brother.
We were led up the stone steps, across the hall,
into the roomy chamber where we were to lodge.

I passed almost the whole evening with the
sheikh of the village, Jûsef Hanna Dâhir, a full-
grown young man with a serious, gentle countenance, which invited confidence. His father had
been killed in battle under Ibrahim Pasha, who

will be considered yet as a saint here, if the present detestation of the Turk continues much longer. Sheikh Jûsef was the eldest son of this numerous and old family, in which the office of sheikh is hereditary. He related to me with full openness, tranquillity, and judgment, everything that was passing among them ; how they had determined to deliver up their arms, which were demanded, but had altered this determination when they had heard of the shameful acts which had been perpetrated by the Turkish soldiery in the southern districts. Now they had the number of thirty-four villages united, and all sworn in their churches, not to give up their arms, but to use them against the dogs of Turks. When I asked him if, since the death of their common leader, Emir Beshir, they had any prospect of being able to defend themselves against a disciplined army, he reckoned up in Bsherreh alone 3,000, and in the whole united district 13,000 combatants, as much as the whole Turkish military force in the country; besides these, they had their mountains, their snow, and rain, their defiles, and hiding-places, which would render all the cavalry and cannon of the Turks useless. Added to this, said I, a friendly consul in Berut, who will mediate to prevent the worst. This has, as I learned afterwards, happened ; the French General-Consul, Bourré, has negotiated in their favour with the Pasha.

But I fear that all has been too late, and that over my good host in Bsherreh the storm of war has already burst, and they will not be more

merciful to them and their children, than they
were to their less powerful neighbours.

I rejoiced much on that evening to be able to
render a service to the young Sheikh, whose quiet
dignity had so much prepossessed me, in dressing
and binding up a wound, better than was possible
with the means they had, and I supplied him with
linen and lint. He told me that we could not
go the next day, as he must prepare a feast for us,
roast a sheep, and show us that he was our friend ;
I however refused the kindly-meant invitation.

The next morning, we took a servant of the
Sheikh with us to the next village, Ehden, which
we found in great commotion, but not inimically
disposed toward us. Sentinels had been posted
at different places, and the gay population, in
their dazzling red and yellow costume, who were
stationed on the hills around the village, appeared
from a distance like a flowery meadow among the
green trees ; they surrounded us, asked us questions, and appeared to have different opinions
about us. A young Amazon ran from some distance to me, raised her finger in a threatening
manner, and reproached us that we Franks did not
openly and efficiently assist them.

We here took leave of our companion from
Bsherreh ; instead of him, a man upon a noble
spirited horse attached himself to us, unasked ;
he saluted us politely, and at a certain distance
kept us in sight. In about two hours, near a flat
inclination, we saw a troop of armed people in a
field, who had planted the blood-red flag, and
who, far over the plain, preached war and resist-

ance. The patrol came up to us, and positively refused to let us proceed. Not till after a long negotiation, through a golden bribe, and by the mediation of our companion, who proved to be the Sheikh of a neibouring village, did we obtain a free passage; but the whole troop accompanied us to the foot of the mountain. When we passed the next village, Zehêra, our companion the Sheikh was obliged to use serious threats in order to pass us safely over the frontier of the armed district; he then accompanied us along another valley, to a turn in the rock, saluted us shortly, and rode quickly back into the mountains. We had now only a few hours' journey to Tripolis, where we arrived soon after sunset, and passed the grave-looking Turkish guards, who might have been somewhat roused from their stupid carelessness by the prospect of a desperate battle with the brave mountaineers.

We remained in Tripolis, now called Tarablûs, in a Latin convent, now only inhabited and pro·tected by two monks. They told us that a short time before, the Christians of Libanon came to them, to desire their spiritual intercession, where-upon they did not hesitate to exhibit the holy sacrament for three days, on their account. Un-fortunately the Maronites have less scarcity of these spiritual prayers and good wishes than of the more material provisions of bread and gunpowder, of which the Turks cut off their supplies.

The next day we visited the Prussian-American Consul, who lives in a pleasant house, of the oriental style, and then went to the bazaar. Passing

2 E

over a beautiful old bridge in the middle of the
town, we met a division of Turkish cavalry on
their way to Libanon, in their gay, tawdry, dirty
costumes, with their lances, ten feet long, ornamented with black ostrich feathers, and the little
war-drums in full work going before. About
noon we left this place just at the same time that
the new Turkish general from Berut was passing
the same gate, out of which we rode. On our
road we met the division of troops which had been
ordered from Zachleh here. We now travelled
along the sea-shore, and almost the whole day
we heard the thunder of the cannon in the mountains.

We passed the night in a Khân on this side the
mountain Râs e' Shekâb, named by the ancients
Θεοῦ πρόσωπον, doubtless because to those who
come from the north, the Black Mountain, which
here projects into the sea, takes quite the form of
a bust. The following day we came to the ancient Byblus (Gebêl), and then crossed the river
Adonis, which still at times, after violent rains,
weeping over the wounded darling of Aphrodite,
becomes blood-red. Beyond Gûneh, almost at the
sea, partly indeed in it, we reached Nahr el Kelb,
the ancient Lycus, on whose southern side upon the
rock which projects into the sea, are sculptured
the famous bas-reliefs of Ramses-Sesostris, and of
a later Assyrian king.*   Notwithstanding our

* The king represented here is explained by Rawlinson (a
Commentary on the Cuneiform Inscriptions of Babylonia and
Assyria, London, 1850, p. 70,) to be the son of the builder of
Khorsabad, Bel-Adonim-Sha. The same king is found on the

sharp riding we did not arrive at the table-rock
till a little after sunset, and we passed the night
at a Khân at the further side. The next morning I examined the sculpture
more closely, (by which passes the ancient, artifi-
cially constructed road, now broken up,) and I rejoiced over some essential discoveries, as I found
it would be possible to decypher a date in the
hieroglyphical inscriptions. Among the three
Egyptian representations, which all bear the cartouches of Ramses II., the middle one is dedicated to the highest god of the Egyptians, to Ra,
(Helios), the southernmost to the Theban or
Upper-Egyptian Ammon, and the northern one
to the Memphite, or Lower-Egyptian Phtha.
To the same gods, this Ramses had also dedicated the three celebrated rock-temples in Nubia,
Gerf Hussên, Sebûa and Derr ; no doubt because
he believed them to be the three principal re-
presenters of Egypt. On the middle stele the
inscription begins under the representation with
the date of the 2nd Choiak, of the fourth year
of the reign of King Ramses. The Ammon's stele,
on the contrary, was of the second, or (if the two
marks were bound together at the top) of the
tenth year's date; under any circumstances, of some
other date than the middle stele,—whence it might

uildings of Kuyunjik, Nebbi Yûnas, and Mossul, according to
Layard, (Nineveh, vol. ii. p. 142, 144,) who, (p. 400), con-
jectures that the momument from Cyprus, now in the Berlin
Museum, also belongs to him. (Cf. Bonomi, Nineveh and its
Palaces, London, 1852, p. 127.)

be concluded that all three representations referred to different campaigns.

We also did not leave unvisited the tomb of St.
George, and the church dedicated to him, near
Nahr el Kelb ; and as we were going to Berut in
the evening, we turned our steps towards the well
where the dragon which he killed used to drink.
Thus on the 26th of November we concluded
our excursion to, and over Libanon, this justly
celebrated mountain, on account of its rich mass
of historical reminiscences and rare natural beau-
ties, of which the poet says, that " it bears winter
on its head, spring on its shoulders, autumn in its
lap, but that summer slumbers at its feet by the
Mediterranean."

APPENDIX.

NOTE A.

(Letter XXXIII., p. 350.)

SINCE Procopius, in the sixth century, tradition had evermore exclusively decided the Gebel Mûsa to be the Mount of the Law, without doubt on account of the church founded at its foot by Justinian. I am unacquainted with any late travellers or scholars who have doubted the truth of this. Burckhardt, also, does not do this, although he conjectured, from the numerous inscriptions at Serbâl, that that mountain had once been erroneously taken for Sinai by the pilgrims. The words of this illustrious traveller (Trav. in Syria, p. 609) are as follows :—
" It will be recollected that *no inscriptions are found either on the mountain of Moses or on Mount St. Catherine ;* and that those which are found in the Ledja valley, at the foot of Djebel Catherine, are not to be traced above the rock, from which the water is said to have issued, and appear only to be the work of pilgrims who visited that rock. From these circumstances, *I am persuaded that Mount Serbal was at one period the chief place of pilgrimage in the peninsula ;' and that it was then considered the mountain where Moses received the Tables of the Law ; though I am equally convinced, from a perusal of the Scriptures, that the Israelites encamped in the Upper Sinai,* and that either Djebel Mousa or Mount St. Catherine is the real Horeb. It is not at all impossible that the proximity of Serbal to Egypt may at one period have caused that mountain to be the Horeb of the pilgrims, and that the establishment of *the convent* in its present situation, *which was probably chosen from motives of security, may have led to the transferring of that honour to Djebel Mousa.* At present neither the monks of Mount Sinai nor those of Cairo consider Mount Serbal as the scene of any of

the events of sacred history; nor have the Bedouins any tradition among them respecting it, but it is possible, that if the Byzantine writers were thoroughly examined, some mention might be found of this mountain, which I believe was never before visited by any European traveller."

At a later period, the excellent travels of E. Robinson form a decided epoch in our acquaintance with the peninsula, as well as with Palestine. With reference to the position of Sinai, he mentions, for the first time, the favourable vicinity of the great plain of Râha to the north of Gebel Mûsa, on which the camp of the people of Israel would have had plenty of room (Palestine, vol. i. pp. 144, sqq.). In defining the position of the actual Mount of the Law, he departs from the previous tradition, and endeavours to prove that Moses had not ascended the Gebel Mûsa, but the mountain ridge rising over the plain from the south, which is now called Horeb by the monks, and the highest peak of which is named Sefsâf (vol. i. p. 176). Unfortunately, he has not visited Wadi Firân and the adjoining Serbâl. In a later essay (Bibl. Sacra, vol. iv. No. XXII. May, 1849, pp. 381, sqq.) the learned author returns to the question in respect of my hypothesis, with which he had become acquainted, and opposes to it his already published arguments for Gebel Sefsâf. He comprehends this under three points, which he particularizes from the Mosaic history, and which must therefore also be mentioned here: — " 1. A mountain-summit, overlooking the place where the people stood. 2. Space sufficient, adjacent to the mountain, for so large a multitude to stand and behold the phenomena on the summit. 3. The relation between this space where the people stood and the base of the mountain must be such, that they could approach and stand at the nether part of the mount; that they could also touch it, and that further bounds could appropriately be set around the mount, lest they should go up into it, or touch the border of it." The first of these three points would militate rather against Gebel Mûsa than Serbâl. Robinson says that the latter is excluded by the second and third points. As to the second, I will only call to mind that the encampment of the children of Israel is not otherwise described than at all their earlier stations. If, therefore, the idea of a camp was to be carried out so exclusively as that

writers should be solicitous about *space* for the occupation of so
large a people, it would be necessary to find a plain of Râha for
all former stations, particularly at Raphidîm (which, according to
almost general belief, was situated at the foot of Serbâl). As there
was a somewhat lengthy stay at that place, Moses was visited
by Jethro, and by his advice divided the whole people into divisions of ten men each, and organized them methodically ; from
which we must conclude that there was a certain local position
for all. Whoever thinks of a mass of two millions, — therefore
about the number of the inhabitants of London or the whole of
modern Egypt—encamped in tents (of which they would have
required one for each ten persons, therefore 200,000), as in a
well-ordered military camp, to him even the plain of Râha would
appear much too small ; but whoever allows that but a proportionately small number could group themselves round the principal quarter of Moses, and that all the rest would seek the
shady places and caves of the rocks, he will be able to understand the camp of Wadi Firân as easily as at any other place.
Wadi Firân also offers—even if we only think of its most fruitful portion, which must have been the most inviting for repose
—down as far as El Hessue, in connection with the broad Wadi
Aleyât, just as much extent, and, at any rate, a far more inhabitable space for a connected camp than the plain of Râha.
Indeed, if minute particulars allow of any deductions, such position of the camp would make it more understandable, why the
people were led out of the camp toward God to the foot of the
mountain in Wadi Aleyât. The command not to ascend the
mountain, which is given more expressly in the words that no
one was to touch the ends of the mount, suits any mountain that
rises before the eye, and is closed in by bushes. Just behind the
bushes is the end of the mountain. Robinson refers to my own
map of Serbâl as to this last point, and also the description of
the Wadi Aleyât by Bartlett (Forty Days in the Desert, pp.
54-59). But it would be difficult to prove, from my sketch-
map, that the people could not stretch out at the foot of the
mountain ; and Bartlett seems also to be of my opinion. As this
traveller, so well known by his excellently-illustrated, and as
sensible as interesting, descriptions of countries, is just one of
those few who have seen those localities with reference to the

question agitated by me, without previously formed opinions, the
citation of the place referred to by Robinson would be more
fitting here, and the rather as I cannot bring forward the principal points of the argument in a better manner. I may remark
that italicised passages are mine, the wide words the author's
own :—

He says (p. 55) : "If we endeavour to reconcile ourselves
to the received but *questionable system*, which seeks to accom-
modate the miraculous with the natural, *i t i s i m p o s s i b l e*,
I think, *not to close with the reasoning advanced in favour of
the Serbal.* There can be no doubt that Moses was personally
well acquainted with the peninsula, and had even probably
dwelt in the vicinity of Wadi Feiran during his banishment from
Egypt, but even common report as to the present day, would
point to this favoured locality *a s t h e o n l y f i t s p o t* in the
whole range of the Desert for the supply, either *with water or
such provisions as the country afforded,* of the Israelitish host :
on this ground, alone, then, he would be led irresistibly to fix
upon it, when meditating a long sojourn for the purpose of com-
piling the law. This consideration derives additional force when
we consider the supply of wood, and other articles, requisite for
the construction of the tabernacles, and which can only be found
readily at Wadi Feiran, and of its being also, in all probability,
from early times, a place visited by trading caravans. But if
Moses were even unacquainted previously with the resources of
the place, he must have passed it on his way from the sea-coast
through the interior of the mountains ; and *it is inconceivable
that he should have refused to avail himself of its singular
advantages for his purpose,* or that the host would have con-
sented, without a murmur, to quit, after so much privation, this
fertile and well-watered oasis for new perils in the barren desert ;
or that he should, humanly speaking, have been able either to
compel them to do so, or afterwards to fix them in the *inhospit-·
able unsheltered position of the monkish Mount Sinai, with the
fertile Feiran but one day's long march in their rear.* Supplies of *wood,* and perhaps of *water, must, in that case, have been
brought, of necessity, from the very spot they had but just abandoned.* We must suppose that the *Amalekites* would oppose the
onward march of the Israelites, *where they alone had a fertile*

territory worthy of being disputed, and from which Moses must, of necessity, have sought to expel them. If it be so, then in this vicinity and no other we must look for Rephidim, from whence the Mount of God was at a very short distance. We seem thus to have *a combination of circumstances which are met with nowhere else*, to certify that it was here that Moses halted for the great work he had in view, and that the scene of the law-giving is here before our eyes in its wild and lonely majesty. The principal objection to this is on the following ground, that there is no open space in the immediate neighbourhood of the Serbal suitable for the *encampment* of the vast multitude, and from which they could *all of them at once* have had a view of the mountain, as is the case at the plain Er Rahah, at Mount Sinai, where Robinson supposes, principally for that reason, the law to have been given. But *is this objection conclusive?* We read, indeed, that Israel 'camped *before the mount*' and that 'the Lord came down in sight of all the people' moreover, that bounds were set to prevent the people from breaking through and violating even the precints of the holy solitude. Although *these* conditions are more *literally* fulfilled at Er Rahah, yet, if we understood them as couched in general terms, *they apply, perhaps, well enough, to the vicinity of the Serbal.* A glance at the view, and a reference to this small rough map [here follows a sketch of the plan] will show the reader that the main encampment of the host must have been in Wadi Feiran itself, from which the summit of the Serbal is only here and there visible, and that it is by the lateral Wadi Aleyal that the base of the mountain itself by a walk of about an hour is to be reached. It certainly struck me, in passing up this valley, as a very unfit, if not impracticable, spot for the encampment of any great number of people, *if they were all in tents ;* though well supplied with pure water, the ground is rugged, and rocky, towards the base of the mountain awfully so ; but still *it is quite possible that a certain number might have established themselves there, as the Arabs do at present,* while, as on other occasions, the principal masses were distributed in the surrounding valleys. I do not know that there is any adequate ground for believing, as Robinson does, that because the people were warned not to invade the seclusion of the mount, and a guard was placed to prevent them from doing so, that *t h e r e f o r e   t h e   e n c a m p - m e n t   i t s e l f* pressed closely on its borders. Curiosity might possibly enough lead many to attempt this even from a distance, to say nothing of those already *supposed to be located* in the Wadi Aleyat, near the base of the mountain, to whom the injunction would more especially apply. Those, however, who press closely the literal sense of one or two passages, should bear in mind all the difficulties previously cited, and the *absolute destitution of verdure, cultivation, running streams, and even of abundant springs, which characterise the fearfully barren vicinity of the monkish Sinai*, where there is indeed room and verge enough for encampment, *but no resources whatever.* If we take up the ground of a *continual and miraculous provision for all the wants of two millions of people*, doubtless they may have been subsisted there as well as in any other place ; *otherwise it seems incredible* that *Moses* should ever have abandoned a spot, offering such *unique advantages as Feiran*, to select instead *the most dreary and sterile spot in its neighbourhood.*"

This was the clearly felt, and unhesitatingly expressed impression that the companionship of those places with the Biblical narrative made upon a man, who yet finally remains in doubt, whether, notwithstanding all the cited grounds, it would not be better to follow the other " systems," according to which the whole is regarded as an uninterrupted wonder from beginning to end, if it indeed be not so called in the Bible (see p. 19 of Bartlett's work), in which case all the researches into the human probability of that great historical event become meaningless. The author then proceeds to some specialities, which he only mentions as such, in which he departs from my feeling, as he places the attack of the Amalekites farther down the valley towards El Hessue. The many ways in which such specialities can be explained, only point out the fact to us, that the general bearing of the most important circumstances of the question can alone produce positive conviction, and that where those are concerned the objections arising from the petty variations must recede.

Soon after Robinson, in 1843, Dr. John Wilson travelled through Palestine and the Petraïc peninsula, and published his comprehensive work on the subject (" The Lands of the

Bible," 2 vols., Edinburgh, 1847). Though he does not approach in the most remote degree the high position of his learned predecessor, I cannot but coincide in some remarks which he throws out against Robinson's hypothesis, that the Sefsâf is the Mount of the Law (vol. i. pp. 222, sqq.). He again shows its connection with the tradition of Gebel Mûsa. In Serbâl, on the contrary, he believes he identifies the Mount Paran of the Bible (p. 199), an idea which could only be entertained if the name of Mount Paran was found to be another denomination of Sinai, and the latter be also identified with Serbâl. At the conclusion of the second volume (pp. 764, sqq.), the author adds a note, in which he defends himself from my contrary opinion concerning the position of Sinai. The most important reasons, however, which I have everywhere placed in the foreground, he does not at all touch upon, but only enlarges on specialities, some of which could easily be confuted, and the rest not bearing on the principal question. He places Daphka, not even mentioned in the principal history, and, therefore, certainly less considerable, in Wadi Firân, and Raphidîm, "the resting places," in the bare sandy Wadi e'Sheikh, because there is *no* water there. But in that case, to use his own weapons, where is the fountain of Moses? "Few in the kingdom of Great Britain, at least," says the author, "will be disposed to substitute the Wadi Feiran, with clear running water, for Rephidim, where there was no water for the people to drink." I believe he does his countrymen wrong, if he considers them to diverge so generally from the almost univoce traditions, and to consider the feelings of learned fathers of the church, who place Raphidîm in Firân, and take the fountain there for the Fountain of Moses, as a rationalistic explanation of it; and, besides H. Bartlett, several others of his countrymen, among whom I particularise Mr. Hogg (see below for a notice of his essay), the Rev. Dr. Croly, and the author of the Pictorial Bible, have expressly declared in favour of my opinion. If he mean to say I had overlooked the fact that the wilderness of Sin, and the wilderness of Sinai, signified two different things, I will refer him to p. 47 of my work, where the contrary is distinctly stated. The words, "out of the wilderness of Sin," I have also not left unnoticed (p. 39), as little as it was done by Eusebius and St. Jerome, who also allow the wilderness of Sin to stretch as far as that of Sinai. The strife with Amalek, as it is related in Exodus, gives the impression of a general and stubborn fight; that the principal attack in front was supported by an attack in the rear, as it is added in Deuteronomy xxv. 18, is not contradicted; the double attack, too, seems to be alluded to there in the words קָרְדָ בַּדֶּרֶךְ רַיְזַבֵּב ἀντέστη σοι ἐν τῇ ὁδῷ, καὶ ἔκοψέ σου τὴν οὐραγίαν.* Near Elim twelve springs עֵיבֹת not wells, are named; but this does not change the matter here, as twelve running springs, like those in Wadi Firân, cannot be thought of, but as the author (vol. i., p. 175) himself remarks, only standing ground waters, which must be dug out, and, therefore, in fact, wells. The great number of these is alone important, from which the size of the place can be calculated. The Sheikh Abu Zelîmeh I was well acquainted with, but that would not hinder a connection of the word with the place, although I do not lay the slightest stress on such coincidences.

The author does not bring forth other grounds, which he believes would militate against my opinion; these may, perhaps, have touched the principal points of the whole question, which were still unconfuted. Perhaps the author may now find it necessary to add them with respect to the investigations of a countryman of his, Mr. John Hogg, who took up the inquiry first in the *Gentleman's Magazine*, March, 1847, and then in the transactions of the Royal Society of Literature, second series, vol. iii. pp. 183—236 (read May, 1847, January, 1848); subsequently extending it considerably under the title of " Remarks and Additional Views on Dr. Lepsius's proofs that Mount Serbal is the true Mount Sinai; or the Wilderness of Sin; on the Manna of the Israelites; and on the Sinaitic Inscriptions." This learned writer collates the earliest traditions, and seeks to prove from them that, before the time of Justinian, they referred to Serbâl, and not to Gebel Mûsa. Indeed he seems to have succeeded, and we shall return to the question hereafter.

Since that time the comprehensive and masterly work of my honoured friend Carl Ritter : *Vergleichende Erdkunde der Sinai-Halbinsel, von Palästina und Syrien, erster Band*, Berlin,

[* Hesych. οὐραγίαν, τὴν ὄπισθεν ἀκολουθοῦσαν στρατίαν.—K.R.H.M.]

1848—(Comparative Geology of the peninsula of Sinai, of Palestine, and Syria, volume one),—has appeared. The exhausting use and employ of all sources from the oldest down to the most recent, for an as grandly conceived, as circumstantially executed, general picture of the peninsula in its geographical relations and in the relative history of its population, has also not left the question under discussion, in which history and geography are in closer connection than in any other, unillustrated. Sinai is for the peninsula what Jerusalem is to Palestine, and it is ascertained that the building of the church at Gebel Mûsa, in the sixth century, brought about by the belief that it was founded at the place where the Law was given, caused the historical centre of the peninsula,—which formerly was undoubtedly identical with the city of Pharan and its palm-forest, as the natural geographical centre,—to be parted from it, and removed several days' journey further south ; just as certain must the determination of the question, whether a *first* or *second* parting of the historical and geographical centre could be of considerable influence in the exposition of the earliest history of the peninsula, and could even exercise some influence on the future tone, not only of Sinaitic literature, but even on some of the relations of the place itself, which not unfrequently subject, to some extent, the destinations of the continually increasing number of travellers. Ritter's work, of course, had at once to choose one of the two opinions. And, naturally, after the final examination of the considerable previous works, the new opinion which first stepped forth against the view undoubted for a thousand years, and accepted by all the later travellers, in an incidental form, in a necessarily imperfect report of a journey, could make the less demand for preference, as it was not critically examined in any way, nor taken into consideration by later travellers. I know how to value the equally careful as impartial recognizing examination which Ritter has given in his work to the grounds in favour of Serbâl being Sinai.

This he does at pp. 736 seq. Here he at once rebuts the opinion, that the tradition of the convent on Gebel Mûsa, only known to us since the sixth century, can decide anything ; " the tradition of the still more ancient convent of Serbâl, and the Serbâl-city of Wadi Firân, it might be said, was just as much

existing, and has only been lost, as far as we are concerned."
Therefore, other grounds taken from nature and history ought to
vouch for it. Then he brings up the opinion of Robinson, who
places Raphidîm in the upper part of the Wadi e' Sheikh, but
forcibly instances against it, that it would then have been visited
and mentioned on the continuation of the journey, and in another
place just as appositely, that one cannot, in that case, understand
how the people could have grumbled about water, only one day's
journey beyond the well-watered Firân, while this is easily explained on the long way from Elim to the vicinity of Firân.
Ritter therefore takes, with me and the old tradition, the curious
brook of Firân to be the fountain of Moses. He only objects
that, if Moses struck the fountain from out of the rocks, it must
have been at the beginning, not at the end of the present
rivulet, and he therefore places Raphidîm in the uppermost part
of the Wadi Firân, the fertility of which could not have existed
before the fountain was made. As to the situation of the Mount
of the Law, he declines at present to pledge himself to any
distinct decision. "We see," he says, "already in the almost
contemporaneous historians, Jerome (Procopius?) and Cosmas,
the variation of opinion concerning these localities, *of which no
one appears definitely settled before another, even in the latest
double views by according and sufficient grounds, to us at least.*
As both these modes of explanation of a text so obscure in
topographical matters, as a but imperfectly known locality, can
only use *hypothetical probabilities,* as briefly for a more certain
explanation ; so let it be permitted to state *our hypothetical view*
on this probably never-to-be quite settled matter."

This is to the effect that *the* "Mountain of God," where
Moses was encamped, when he was visited by Jethro in Raphidîm, "*could not in any case be the convent Mount of Sinai,*
(*i. e. Gebel Mûsa,*) although this is so named at a subsequent
period, as that of the true God, *from which one was then in every
case far distant, but might indeed* be a denomination of the high,
much nearer *Serbâl,* as one was yet in camp at Raphidîm." He,
too, perceives an *interruption of the connection* at the beginning
of the nineteenth chapter with the previous chapters, but seeks for
the cause in *a chasm* in the text, while I would rather perceive
a short *interpolation.* In this chasm falls the departure of the

people from the valley of Firân for the upper Sheikh valley and to that of Gebel Mûsa, the true Sinai. This was first simply " the mountain," (Exodus, xix. 2,) and only obtained the name of a " Mountain of God," *after* the giving of the law (which, however, is already contradicted by the next following verse, xix. 3), while Serbâl might have received the denomination of " Mountain of God " from a heathen idol there worshipped.

" Both mountains, the Mount of God (Serbâl) in Raphidîm, and the Mount in the desert of Sinai, are therefore just as various in name, as they are separated by the last journeys between both camps." The general features of nature round about Gebel Mûsa, he considers more fitting for a longer stay of the people on account of the greater security, coolness, and the Alp-like pasture land. Only the name Horeb, already comprehended in Raphidîm, could be an objection, yet there seems to him to be no sufficient grounds existing, why this name, already considered as a general term by Robinson, Hengstenberg, and others, should not be extended to the outer ranges of Serbâl.

The acceptation of *two* mountains of God, Serbâl and Gebel Mûsa, is, as far I can tell, here attempted for the first time. It is certainly, the *necessary, only not yet enounced consequence, for all those who place Raphidîm in Firân.* In this there seems to me to lie an evident proof with reference to the critical examination of the text, that both mountains are again to be found in *Serbâl.* The greater security of the plain of Râha would not be very high for a " harnessed " (Exodus xvi. 18,) host of 600,000 men, after they had taken a firm footing, and Serbâl would also have always offered a safe place of retreat. The cold in the lofty mountains, causing water to freeze (Ritter, p. 445—630) in February in the convent (5,000 feet above the sea), according to Rüppell and Robinson, would alone have made an open camp on the plain of Râha impossible during the winter, for a population accustomed to the Egyptian climate, to the vegetation of those districts, which is certainly differently described by the different travellers; the thought there is no doubt of the Israelites having at one period been there, may partially have induced several to accept more shrubs in the neighbourhood than they actually saw at the time, partly there, no question that the season of the year may make some difference;

I therefore willingly observe, that I visited the peninsula at about the same season of the year in which, according to the Mosaic account, the Israelites came thither.

Finally, Ritter has again spoken upon the Sinai question in a more popular essay : " The Sinaitic Peninsula, and the Route of the People of Israel to Sinai," in the *Evangelischen Kalender*, for 1852, edited by F. Piper, pp. 31, sqq. Here, too, he places Raphidîm in Firân, and perceived the mountain of God at Raphidîm, in Serbâl. Against the identity of Serbâl and Sinai, he brings these two chief objections. As it has now been perfectly settled that the so-called Sinaitic inscriptions are of heathen origin, and prove Serbâl, to which they chiefly point as the " centre of an ancient worship," this remarkable mountain could not be " a mountain of Jehovah, if it were already a sacred mountain of the idolaters " (p. 51). And further on (p. 52) :—
" The holy mountain of Israel did not lie in the territory of Amalek, like Serbâl, but in the east and south parts of the territory of Midian," for it is expressly said in Exodus (iv. 19) :—
" And the LORD said unto Moses, *in Midian*, Go, return into Egypt," in order that they should sacrifice to him on these mountains, Horeb and Sinai, in Midian (Exodus iii. 1—12)."
Of these two points, however, the first seems to me a very important argument *for* Serbâl-Sinai. Serbâl was also a holy mountain for the tribes in the peninsula at a later period, as it is not called " Idol Mountain," *before* the giving of the Law, but " Mountain of God" (Exodus iii. 1, iv. 27, xviii. 5), just as it was *after* the giving of the Law (Exodus xxiv. 13 ; 1 Kings xix. 8), and a subsequent appropriation of the mountain to a heathen worship is much less remarkable. No reason is to be found, however, in the fact, that when the Lord spoke to Moses he lived in Midian with Jethro, to warrant the placing of the mountain of the Law in Midian, for that it nowhere said. We only know, that Raphidîm, where Jethro visited Moses from Midian, lay in the territory of the Amalekites, as they here made the attack. Eusebius, who (*s. v.* 'Ραφιδίμ) expressly refers Raphidîm and Choreb to Pharan, says (*s. v.* χωρήβ) that this mountain of God lay in *Madian*. Also in *Itinerar. Antonini*, c. 40, Pharan is placed in *Madian*.
Would that these observations, in which I believe I have

touched upon almost all the more important grounds of their esteemed author, may prove to him, how high a value I set upon each of his opinions, as those of a more competent judge in this field of research than any other. Ritter's long, well-known tact for the truth in such questions would have caused me to have less faith in my own view than all the grounds he produces, which are generally to be confuted, as it appears, if I had not in *this* case the advantage of a personal inspection of the localities, unprejudiced by any former opinion, which could make it less independent of former writers, than it is possible for him to have.

NOTE B.

(Letter XXXIII. p. 354.)

Robinson gives the distances from Ayûn Mûsa to the crossing point of Wadi Shebêkeh, and Wadi Taibeh (vol. iii. Part II. p. 804); these correspond tolerably well with Burckhardt (pp. 624, 625), who continues the distances up to Wadi Firân ; these last, if we take his round across Dhafari into consideration, are confirmed by my own. The calculation in Robinson (p. 196), however, does not comprehend the four or five hours' longer way round from the convent, through Wadi e' Sheikh ; for Burckhardt went over the Nakb el Haui in eleven hours to Firân, while we required sixteen, subtracting the little way through the Ktesse valley. From this the distances are thus proportioned :—From Ayûn Mûsa to Ain Hawârah, eighteen hours and thirty-five minutes ; thence to Wadi Gharandel, two hours, thirty minutes (not an hour and a half to two hours, as it is calculated in the text, from the camp of Robinson) ; to the end of the valley, near Abu Zelîmeh, seven hours, twelve minutes ; thence to the sea, one hour ; to Wadi Shellâl four hours, fifteen minutes ; to Firân, thirteen hours, forty-five minutes ; to the convent, sixteen hours. The camp in the Wilderness of Sin, Robinson cannot refer more to the south than to the end of the Wadi Shellâl ; because the people, according to him, here left the Wilderness of Sin, as necessarily Alus falls with him beyond Firân. On the other hand, according to my opinion, the camp at the sea is not only not different from that at the entrance of

2 F

the valley near Abu Zelîmeh, but the Wilderness of Sin of Exodus, which reached to Sinai, and ended with Raphidîm, is also the same with the two stations, Daphka and Alus, in Numbers, and therefore should have no more been mentioned at the latter place as particular camp stations than the Red Sea. The Wilderness of Sin comprehended, accordingly, like the Wilderness of Sur, three days' journey. The stations and their distances may be thus reckoned :—

According to Robinson :—

I.	6	hours	12	minutes	three stations from Ayûn
II.	6	„	12	„	Mûsa to Ain Hawârah =
III.	6	„	12	„	Marah.
IV.	2	„	30	„	to Wadi Gharandel = Elim.
V.	8	„	12	„	to the sea.
VI.	4	„	15	„	to Wadi Shellâh, = Desert of Sin.
VII.	7	„	—	„	two stations to Firân = Daphka
VIII.	7	„	—	„	and Alus.
IX.	8	„	—	„	two stations to the plain of Râha
X.	8	„	—	„	= Raphidîm and Sinai.

According to my researches :—

I.	7	hours	—	minutes	three stations to Wadi Gharandel = Marah.
II.	7	„	—	„	andel = Marah.
III.	7	„	—	„	
IV.	7	„	12	„	to the end of the valley near Abu Zelîmeh = Elim.
V.	6	„	—	„	three stations to Firân, i.e. by
VI.	6	„	—	„	Daphka and Alus to Raphidîm
VII.	6	„	—	„	at Sinai.

That the last stations are somewhat shorter than the first, may be understood from the greater difficulties of the way. Why had the people murmured, so near to the twelve springs of Elim? How could the particularly long journey of more than eight hours from Elim to the sea have passed without being mentioned? And how could the day's journey have become continually longer in the high mountains and heavy ground?

NOTE C.

(Letter XXXIII. p 364.)

The commentators on this passage take the words בַּחֹדֶשׁ
תַּשְׁלִישִׁי "In the third month," as if it were written: "On
the first day of the third month," and thus make the succeeding
words, " on this day," also relate to the *first* day of the month.
Vide Gesenius, *Thesaur.* p. 404, b. : — " *tertiis calendis post
exitum*," and p. 449, b. :—*tertio novilunio*, i.e. *calendis mensis
tertii.* Ewald, *Gesch. des v. Israels*, vol. ii. p. 189 :—" *The day
(?) of the third month (which is, however, of the new moon,
therefore the first day)*." But the Seventy did not understand it
thus, in any case, as they translate :—" τοῦ δὲ μηνὸς τοῦ τρίτου τῇ
ἡμέρᾳ ταύτῃ." The Jewish tradition seems also not to have
taken its meaning thus, as the Jews celebrated the Giving of the
Law, which, according to Exodus, xix. 11, 15, occurred on the third
day after their arrival, upon the fifth or sixth day of the third
month, together with that on the fiftieth day after the harvest-
feast (Leviticus, xxiii. 15, 16), subsequent to the Exode, according to which the arrival at Sinai must fall on the *third* day of the
third month. It is not to be understood how חֹדֶשׁ without any
suffix should be used for " new-moon day," though it has lost
that analogical meaning in all the different places, and only signifies *month*, even in such places where the " day of the new moon"
is intended (such as Exodus xl. 2, 17 ; Numbers i. 1 ; xxxiii.
38), where it is particularly added בְּאֶחָד לַחֹדֶשׁ " on the first
(day) of the month," against which passages like Numbers, ix.
1, and xx. 1, cannot be produced, because there is as little ground
to understand the *first* of the month, as in Exodus xix. 1, and
the Seventy do not translate ἐν ἡμέρᾳ μιᾷ, or νουμηνίᾳ, as in the
other passages, but only as the simple sense of the words is :—
" ἐν τῷ μηνὶ τῷ πρώτῳ. There would only thus remain one passage, xix. 1, from which one might conclude such an ambiguous use
of חֹדֶשׁ, because here certainly the following words, " on *this*
day," point to a certain single day which is not, however, now
to be guessed from our text. But this, in my opinion, is no
unimportant reason for supposing a transposition or a later interpolation of these two verses. The latter idea is also accepted by
Ewald, as he (*Gesch. v. Isr.* vol. i. p. 75) refers the narrative

xix. 3, 24, to the oldest source, but not the two first verses. It
has been already mentioned that Josephus (*Ant.* iii. 2, 5), who
also does not understand the words as referring to the *first*
day of the months, transposes the passage, and, indeed, *to the
same place* whither I, without knowing it, had placed it in my
former report (p. 48), i.e. *immediately after the battle* of the
Amalekites, to which "this day" most naturally refers. If this
be true, the original text also expressed that the Israelites were
not only by Horeb but by Sinai, near Raphidîm in Wadi Firân,
where they fought the battle, *i.e.* that both the holy mountains
are one, and that Moses received the visit of Jethro first at Sinai;
and, as it would seem, in natural course of events, first organized
his people at Sinai, with which, however, it is also said, that
Sinai, or Horeb, was no other mountain than Serbâl.

Granted that we have in this way understood the original
connection, no naming of the month would be necessary; this
was probably added at the isolation of the succeeding section,
referring to the giving of the law. Under these circumstances,
there would only be three exact dates for the whole journey.
The people departs from Ramses on the fifteenth day of the
first month in the first year; it proceeds from Elim, half the
distance, and just one month, on the fifteenth day of the second
month of the first year. The resting days at the stations are
unknown; but if it be taken for granted that the people proceeded without staying, it came to Raphidîm on the third day
from Elim, obtained the water on the fourth, and was attacked
by Amalek, fought on the fifth until after sunset to the beginning of the sixth day, and on the same day (for the Hebrew day
began at sundown) encamped at Sinai. This would have occurred on the twentieth day of the second month in the first
year. Now, as the departure from Sinai took place on the
twentieth day of the second month of the second year, the stay
at Sinai would have been exactly *one year*. This coincidence
was probably originally just as accidental as the lapse of exactly
one month between the first departure from Ramses and the
second from Elim.

NOTE D.

(Letter XXXIII. p. 369.)

There are yet two marble inscriptions in the wall of the convent towards the garden referring to the founding of the place, one Greek and one Arabic. Burckhardt (Trav. p. 545) says:— "An Arabic inscription *over the gate*, in modern characters, says that Justinian built the convent in the thirtieth year of his reign, as a memorial of himself and his wife Theodora. It is curious to find a passage of the Koran introduced into this inscription ; it was probably done by a Moslem sculptor, without the knowledge of the monks." Certainly the Arabic inscription is over the little door leading into the garden. But if Burckhardt saw it here, it is not to be understood how he did not see the Greek inscription beside it, with a similar border and covering. Robinson did not see either (vol. i. p. 205). Ricci had copied the Greek inscription, and it has been printed and translated by Letronne in *Journ. des Savans*, 1836, p. 538, with a few little variations. But another copy, which had escaped Letronne, had been published in 1823 by Sir F. Henniker (Notes during a Visit to Egypt, &c. pp. 235, 236), which is, however, very inaccurate, though it attempts to give even the manner of writing. The Arabic inscription has not, as far as I am aware, been made known at all. I have taken impressions in paper of both, and publish them here faithfully. The Greek is as follows :—

Ἐκ βάθρων ἀνηγέρϑη τὸ ἱερὸν τοῦτο μοναστήριον τοῦ Σιναίου ὄρους, ἔνϑα ἐλάλησεν ὁ Θεὸς τῷ Μωυσῇ, παρὰ τοῦ ταπεινοῦ βασιλέως Ῥωμαίων Ἰουστινιανοῦ πρὸς ἀΐδιον μνημόσυνον αὐτοῦ καὶ τῆς συζύγου τοῦ Θεοδώρας· ἔλαβε τέλος μετὰ τὸ τριακοστὸν ἔτος τῆς βασιλείας τοῦ, καὶ κατέστησεν ἐν αὐτῷ ἡγούμενον ὀνόματι Δουλᾶ ἐν ἔτει ἀπὸ μὲν Ἀδὰμ ,ϛκα', ἀπὸ δὲ Χριστοῦ φκζ'.

"This holy monastery was erected on Mount Sinai, where God spake unto Moses, by the humble king of the Romans, Justinian, unto the everlasting remembrance of himself and of his wife Theodora. It received its completion in the thirtieth year of his reign, and he set a governor over it, Dulas by name, in the year from Adam, 6021, and from Christ, 527."

Letronne read ἐν ᾧ πρῶτον instead of ἔνϑα, and κατέστησε τὸν

instead of κατέστησεν in the seventh line. The characters are those of the twelfth or thirteenth century. As the Emperor Justinian reigned from 527—565, it is judged by the writer that the decree for the erection of the convent and the placing of the abbot Dulas falls in the first year of the government of the emperor, although the completion of the building is first placed in the thirtieth year of the same, *i. e.* A.D. 556. The year of the world 6021 answers to A.D. 527, according to the Alexandrian era of Pandorus and Anianus.*

The Arabic inscription is thus:—

انشا دير طور سينا و كنيسة جَبل المناجاة الفقير لله الراجي

عفو مولاه الملك المهذب الرومي المذهب يوستيانوس تذكارا له

ولزوجته ثاوضوره علي مرور الزمان حتي يرث الله الارض و من

عليها وهو خير الوارثين وتم بناوه بعد ثلاثين سنة من ملكه ونصب

له ريسًا اسمه ضولس جري ذلل سنة ٦٠٢١ لادم الموافق لتاريخ

السيد المسيح سنة ١٥٢٧

"The convent of the Tôr (mountain) Sinai, and the church of the conference, the pious king Justianus (instead of Justinianus), of Greek confession, yearning after God, and hoping for the summons of his Lord, for a memorial of himself and his wife Theodora against the passing of time, that God may inherit the earth and what is upon it, for *he is the best of inheritors.* And the erection was ended after thirty years of his government. And he set over it a chief, named Dhulas. And this took place after Adam 6021, which agrees with the year 527 of the era of the Lord Christ."

The characters of the inscription certify, according to the information of the Consul, Dr. Wetzstein, who has kindly undertaken the copying and translation of the inscription, that they are not of a date previous to 550 of the Mahommedan era, which, therefore, brings us back to the time in which the Greek inscription was made. The passage of the Koran, mentioned already by Burckhardt, is in Surât, xxi., v. 18.

[* See Bunsen, Egypt's Place, vol. i. p. 209—K. R. H. M.]

In the same wall, but much higher up, over a far greater door, now bricked up, at a place behind which the kitchen is now lying, another great stone is let in, the ornament of which might lead to the supposition that there is another old inscription there. Unfortunately, it was impossible to have a ladder brought thither, to examine the stone more carefully. May a later traveller succeed in this!

NOTE E.

(Letter XXXIII. p. 370.)

The history of the palm-wood of Pharan forms the centre-point of the history of the whole peninsula. The accounts of the Greeks and Romans give a new proof of this, though their geographical determinations have, for the most part, been incorrectly apprehended. Thus the Poseidion of Artemidorus, Diodorus, and Strabo, is generally put at the extremity of the peninsula now called Râs Mahommed, even by Gosselin, Letronne, and Groskura, who had certainly perceived the incorrect gloss of the manuscripts of Strabo (p. 776 : τοῦ ['Ελανίτου] μυχοῦ). As the Poseidion lay *within* (ἐνδοτέρω) the Gulf of Suez, and as the *western* coast of the peninsula is described, this altar of Poseidion necessarily lay either at Râs Abu Zelîmeh, the haven of Faran, or at Râs G'ehân, where there was a more southerly and shorter communication by Wadi Dhaghadeh with Wadi Firân. That the Palm-grove (Φοινικών) of that author is not to be found by Tôr, but in the Wâdi Firân, has already been rightly seen by Tuch, (*Sinait. Inschr.*, p. 35), although he still places the Poseidion at Râs Mahommed (p. 37). It was the Serb Bâl—the palm-grove of Baal—from which the mountain first obtained its name. It appears that at an earlier date the name of Faran was used with particular reference to the haven near Abu Zelîmeh, and a Pharanitic colony at the place of ancient Elim, in the neighbourhood of the present Gebel Hammân Faraûn, still called Farân by the Arabic historians; while the grove itself was yet called Serb Bâl by the inhabitants. Probably, also, it was here where Aristo landed under Ptolemæus Philadelphus, and founded the Poseidion.

By Artemidorus (in Strabo, p. 776), and Diodorus (III. 42), Μαρανῖται are mentioned, for which Gosselin, Ritter, Tuch, and others, propose to read Φαρανῖται. But as the Maranites lived on the *eastern* coast of the peninsula, and are reported to have been entirely destroyed by the Garindœans, I can find no support for this conjecture. The gorge Pharan, mentioned by Josephus in Judæa (*Bel. Iud.* iv. 9, 4), has no connection with anything here. The name of the Pharanites on the *west coast* of the peninsula first occurs in Pliny (H. N. xxxvii., 40), for there is no reason to consider the *Pharanitis gens*, which he places in Arabia Petræa, to be other than the *Pharanitai* of Ptolemy. That the northern station Phara (*circa* ten hours west of Aila) on the table of Peutinger, has nothing to do with the Pharanitic palmgrove, has been placed beyond doubt by Ritter, (p. 147 sq.).

Ptolemy, in the third century, is the first who mentions a *place* called Pharan (κώμη φαράν); yet the grounds and the connection of *his* calculations so very different from the true relations of the peninsula, had remained obscure, so that the single comparison were useless. His construction of the peninsula is immediately intelligible, if it be considered that he has evidently taken the obtuse coast-angle at Râs Gehân,—whither he put Cape Pharan according to his latitudes, instead of Hammân Farûn,— for the most southern point of the peninsula, whence the more remote coast again runs up to the north-east. By this the peninsula becomes 50′ too short, although the longitude of his promontory agrees with that of the right one. The real point (Râs Mohammed) now answers to the place whither he places the round of the Elanitic Gulf (ἐπιστροφὴ τοῦ Ἐλανίτου κόλπου). The whole Elanitic Gulf (Gulf of Akaba) shrinks with him to a little angle (μυχός) of 15′, as everything is pushed up too much to the north. The coast, from "the term" up to Οννη answers in fact to that from Râs Furtak (Diodorus's or Artemidorus's ἀκρωτήριον τῆς ἠπείρου, before which the island of Phoke lay) to 'Aïn Uneh and the Elanitic Gulf, the northern end of which (ἐπιστροφή) he placed at 66° longitude, 29° latitude,*

[* It may be as well to remark that the calculations of longitude here and on the map are made from the island of Feroe, on the west coast of Africa, and not from Greenwich.—K. R. H. M.]

now takes the form of the gulf, the undermost point of which is now denoted by 'Aïn Uneh. The ocean angle of Pharan (μυχὸς κατὰ Φαράν) he imagines to extend from Cape Faran (ἀκρωτήριον Φαράν) to the inland city of the same name, like the angle of Elana, and the inner angle of Heroonpolis to the north of Arsinoe. From the same construction of the peninsula it came that the Rhainthenians, who were placed along the same coast by Tôr (even now called 'Ραιθοῦ) below the Pharanites, had now to be placed on the coast turned towards Arabia (παρὰ τὴν ὀρεινὴν τῆς Εὐδαίμονος 'Αραβίας), therefore on the oriental and not the occidental coast of the peninsula ; and finally, the primary mountain-chain (ὄρη μέλανα) extending from Faray to Râs Mohammed to Judæa, therefore to the N.E. instead of the S.E.

From all this it is clear that the place Pharan of Ptolemy is identical with the recognised Pharan in the Wadi Firân, and the Φοινικῶν of Artemidorus and Strabo. And it is less to be doubted that also the Pharan of Eusebius (s. v. 'Ραφιδίμ) and Jerome, which is expressly (s. v. φαράν) called a city (πόλις, oppidum), and is placed at the distance of three days' journey from Aila,—was the city in Wadi Firân, although by a confusion with the Biblical desert of Paran it is added, that the Israelites had returned by this Pharan on their return from Sinai (c. f. Ritter, p. 740).

According to the treatise of the monk Ammonius (*Illustr. Chr. Martyr. lecti triumphi-ed. Combefis, Paris,* 1660,—whose history, undoubtedly fictitious, refers to A.D. 370, but can in no case be used as a historical authority for that time, but seems to rest on some passages of the romance of Nilus, and to have been written for a like praiseworthy purpose,—the city of Pharan was converted to *Christianity* in the middle of the fourth century, by the monk Moses, a native of the city. By Nilus, placed at about 390, but concerning whose era and writings much uncertainty exists, a Christian council (βουλή) of the city of Pharan is mentioned (Nili app. quædam, 1539, 4to.) Soon after, from the first half of the fifth century, Le Quien, but certainly from sources of very different value (*Oriens. Christ.,* vol. iii., p. 571), cites a series of bishops of Pharan, who can be followed up into the middle of the twelfth century (*vide Reland, Palæst,* vol. ii., p. 220). The monks of the mountains were all subjected to these bishops.

As to what concerns the founding of the present convent at
Gebel Mûsa, it is certainly ascribed to the twelfth or thirteenth
year of the Emperor Justinian, as in the inscriptions, by Saïd
ben Batrik (Eutychius), who wrote about 932-953 (d'Herbelôt,
s. v.), but he is contradicted by the much more trustworthy,
and here particularly important testimony of Procopius, the contemporary of Justinian, in the most express manner. He says,
in his particular treatise on the buildings founded by Justinian
(*Procop. ed. Diod.* vol. iii. *de œdif. Just.* p. 326), that the emperor built a *church* to the Mother of God, "not on the top of
the mountain, but *a good piece below* it" (παρὰ πολὺ ἔνερθεν,
which, according to the locality, can only mean on the platform
half way down the mountain, where the chapel of Elias now
stands). Separated from it, he also found at the foot of the
mountain (ἐς τοῦ ὄρους πρόποδα) a very strong castle (φρούριον),
with a good garrison, in order to prevent the incursions of the
Saracens from the peninsula to Palestine. As Procopius just
before and after, as in the whole treatise, makes a careful distinction between convents and churches, and military posts, it is
evident, that according to him, Justinian did not found the
convent with its church. Probably, however, the military fort
was at a later period used as a convent, and built up anew.
And the church above, built by Justinian, was not dedicated,
like the present one, to St. Katherine (*vide Le Quien,* vol. iii.
p. 1306), but to Maria. What Eutychius (cited first by
Robinson, though placed by him somewhat too early in the tenth
century) relates, as well regarding the founding of the convent
as in direct contradiction to Procopius, concerning a church on
the *top of the mountain,* is therefore no more worthy of credence
than the conversation between the emperor and the architect.
As little should the convents of Râyeh (near Tôr) and Kolzum
(a *bishop* of Clysma, named Poemen, was present already at
the Constantinopolitan council of 460 ; *vide Acta Concil. ed.
Harduin,* vol. ii. p. 696, 786), be ascribed to Justinian, on the
authority of Ben Batrik, as in such a case Procopius would undoubtedly have spoken of it. Pharan is not mentioned by Procopius. On the other hand, however, he informs us of the important fact (*de bell. Pers.* 1, 19, 164, *de œdif.* 5, 8), that the
Saracen prince, Abocharagos, reigning there, presented the em-

peror Justinian with a great palm-grove (φοινικῶνα), situated in the middle of the land (ἐν τῇ μεσογαίᾳ). On a more careful examination of that narrative, there can remain scarcely a doubt, that the palm-grove of Pharan is intended here, not the place on the sea called φοινίκων κώμη by Ptolemy (vi. 7, 3), or a palm-grove quite unknown to us, also situate in the middle of a desolate waterless wilderness. According to Ammonius and Nilus, the whole population of Pharan was at that time Christian, and a *church* was certainly distinguished there ; thus the present of Abocharagos, whom Justinian himself made phy- larch of the Palestinian Saracens, is more easily comprehensible. Without doubt the founding of the fort in the higher mountains, for the guard against these Saracens, stood in connection with this.

Next to Procopius, Cosmas Indicopleustes is by far the most trustworthy source for that time. He was not only a contemporary of Justinian, but describes (about 540) what he had himself *seen* in the peninsula.* This work is the only larger geography preserved from that age, and his unpretending narrative everywhere bears the character of uncoloured truthfulness. It is more remarkable, that he neither mentions a convent, nor indeed the localities round Gebel Mûsa, but only Pharan, although he had the route of the Israelites particularly in view.

That Antoninus Placentinus, who is considered by others to be St. Anthony martyr, in his *Itinerarum* (*Acta Sanctor*, May, vol. ii. p. x-xviii.), which is referred by Ritter to about six hundred, again speaks of a convent at the Thornbush (Procopius does not mention the Thornbush), between Horeb and Sinai ; therefore, as the place of the present convent seems to lead us back to the opinion so decidedly expressed by the learned Papebrook, who first published the Itinerary, that this so learnedly defended, yet very doubtful, history belongs first to the eleventh or twelfth century. In any circumstances it would be desirable to submit the writings of Ammonius, Nilus, Antoninus, and some other of

[* To the Rev. Charles Forster it would appear we are indebted for the detection of the record of the visit of Cosmas, which, according to his read- ing, runs thus : — " μνησ τηθ ? Κοσμάν του' ν Τεβδ . . ναυτιου." " Remember Cosmas, the voyager to Tibet." See that gentleman's excellent Primeval Language, Part I. p. 4. The Greek, as the author observes, is *very* corrupt.—K. R. H. M.]

the productions of the first centuries of Christianity, to a more searching and connected criticism than has yet been done. The earliest bishop of Mount Sinai referable to is found in the eleventh century; this is Bishop Jorius, who died in 1033 (*Le Quien*, vol. iii. p. 754). The *Phronimus episc. Synnaii* (*Acta Concil. ed. Harduin*, vol. iii. p. 53), or *Synai tunorum*, p. 206), signed at the second Constantinopolitan Council (*a.* 553), and the *Constantinus ep. Synai* (*Harduin*, vol. v. p. 927), named at the fourth council (*a.* 870), have been referred hither incorrectly (Ritter, *Abhand. der Berl. Akad,* 1824, p. 216, *Peninsula of Sinai*, p. 26), as they belong to Synaus or Synnaus in Phrygia.

NOTE F.

(Letter XXXIII. p. 370.)

That, indeed, an uninterrupted and certain tradition, concerning the position of Sinai in the peninsula, has been preserved to Christian times, must be most decidedly questioned. The name Choreb, or Sinai, seems to have been taken, at a very early period, for the whole of the mountain region of the peninsula, which was generally considered one mountain at a distance. No one took any interest in fixing the name to any geographical idea, until the time of the Christian hermits there. We only read of Elias, that he fled to the " Mountain of God, Choreb," and there went into that cave (1 Kings, xiii. 9), (for it is taken for granted as known) in which the Lord had already (Exod. xxiii. 22) appeared unto Moses. The native races of Arabs gradually moved, so that of the Biblical names none remained in its place. The Greeks and Romans knew only *one place* in the whole peninsula, the *palm-grove of Pharan,* just because this place and its port were alone of any importance, since the mines of the wilderness had been deserted. Also, for the Christian hermits—for which that mountain wild, even without reference to the sacred reminiscences of the place—must have seemed the most fitted of any region, as it provided them with the more necessary sustenance with the greatest solitude. Firan must have been the earliest centre-point; therefore, we also find here the oldest church of the peninsula. When they gradually commenced to seek more definitely for Scripture localities, they had no further materials for its discovery than we possess, with far less power to use these materials properly, as every sharp criticism to examine the passages of Scripture then lay very far off. The name Sinai was indefinitely taken for the whole mountain; if one looked round for any particular peak, that of *Serbâl* would instantly present itself. To that, everything which we read in the first centuries about it in trustworthy writings points, to which, however, the treatise of the monk Ammonius certainly does not belong, in the estimation of any one who examines it more narrowly, and the excellent Romany, of Nilus, is very doubtful. What Josephus (Aut. iii. 5) says of Sinai (τὸ Σιναῖον), agrees very well with Serbâl, but not at all with Gebel Mûsa, as Hogg has already shown. According to Eusebius, Choreb and Raphidîm lay *near Pharan* (ἐγγὺς Φαράν), and Sinai beside Choreb (παράκειται τῷ ὄρει Σινᾶ.) Jerome (s. v. *Choreb*) considers both mountains to be one, which he also places *by Pharan*, and, therefore, recognises in *Serbâl*. Also, the narrative of Nilus, concerning the Saracen attack at Sinai, either does not belong to the time in which it is dated (c. 400), or refers to Serbâl; for often (pp. 38—46) a *church* (ἐκκλησία) is mentioned, which did not then exist on Gebel Mûsa, and Nilus goes down, in the same night in which the murdered people were buried, *to Pharan*, which could not have been done from Gebel Mûsa. Cosmas Indicopleustes, finally, who travelled in the peninsula about the year 535, just before the building of the church by Justinian, goes from Raithu, i. e. Tor, which he takes for Elim, although he finds but *few palms* there (the plantations at that place are therefore younger) by the present Wadi Hebrân to Raphidîm, which is now called Pharan. Here he was at the end of his Sinai journey. Hence Moses went with the elders "to the Mountain Choreb," i. e. Sinai, which was distant from Pharan about 6,000 paces (one and a half miles), and struck the water from the rock; here was the ark of the covenant built and the law given, by which the Israelites obtained writing, and had time to learn it at their leisure, from which the numerous rock inscriptions come which are still found in that wilderness, particularly at Serbâl. (Εἶτα πάλιν παρενέβαλον εἰς ʹΡαφιδῖν,

446　APPENDIX.

εἰς τὴν νῦν καλουμένην Φαράν· καὶ διψευσάντων αὐτῶν, πορεύεται κατὰ πρόσταξιν Θεοῦ ὁ Μωϋσῆς μετὰ τῶν πρεσβυτέρων καὶ ἡ ῥαβδὸς ἐν τῇ χειρὶ αὐτοῦ, εἰς Χωρὴβ τὸ ὄρος, τουτέστιν ἐν τῷ Σιναίῳ, ἐγγὺς ὄντι τῆς Φαρὰν ὡς ἀπὸ μιλίων ἕξ. (Burckhardt [*Trav. in Syr.* p. 611] required when he descended Serbâl, from its foot to west Faran, 2½ hours,) καὶ ἐκεῖ πατάξαντος τὴν πέτραν, ἐῤῥύησεν ὕδατα πολλὰ καὶ ἔπιεν ὁ λαός. Λοιπὸν κατεληλυθότος αὐτοῦ ἐκ τοῦ ὄρους προστάττεται ὑπὸ τοῦ Θεοῦ ποιεῖν τὴν σκηνήν, etc. *Topograph. Christ. lib. V.* in the *Coll. nova patr. ed. B. de Montfaucon tom.* ii. *p.* 195 *sqq.*

This testimony of the unpretending traveller is just as clear as it is certain and unsuspicious. In the beginning of the sixth century there was thus the belief after this eye-witness that the law was given on Serbâl. Cosmas is in so little doubt about it, that he does not mention the southern mountain at all. We must also conclude that the monks had extended themselves over the whole mountain, and particularly over the guarded region about the Gebel Mûsa. That among the monks of the place another opinion arose, according to which Moses turned south-ward, instead of northward, from the height of Wadi Hebrân (for, to take Elim for Raithu remained the decided opinion, as preserved by the convent there) is not at all to be wondered ; such confusions are very frequent in Christian topography. But how narrowly Horeb and Sinai, Raphidîm and the Mount of the Law, are connected together, is again shown in the fact, that with Sinai the rock of water went southward. The monks did not allow themselves to be hindered, by the verses in the beginning of the nineteenth chapter, from transporting that rock of Raphidîm, and consequently Raphidîm itself, as also the thorn-bush of Horeb, to Gebel Mûsa, their new Sinai ; there it is yet shown, for the astonishment of travellers in Wadi Lega (Robinson, vol. i. p. 184). Thus in this point the unlearned monkish notion that Raphidîm was near Sinai came closer to the truth than the new criticism.

The Legate of Justinian now found it necessary to erect his castle in that safe position, and to build a church there, for the hermits living in the neighbourhood. That this alone was suf-ficient to draw many new hermits thither, and to found a new belief as to the position of the Mountain of the Law, if this were not already there, is quite comprehensible. But as to how the two opinions in the next following centuries came together, we have no certain testimony whatever. Under any circumstances, one would have to take care, if, after the founding of Pharan, the mountain Sinai is often mentioned, to understand by it the Gebel Mûsa. As a rule, the whole range of mountains in the peninsula is intended by it. When, for example, already in the year 536, therefore probably before the building of the church, at the *Concilium sub Mema*, at Constantinople, a *Theonas presbyter et legatus S. montis Sinai et deserti Raitha et S. ecclesiæ Pharan* (Θεωνᾶς ἐλεῷ Θεοῦ πρεσβύτερος καὶ ἀποκρισιάριος τοῦ ἁγίου ὄρους Σινᾶ καὶ τῆς ἐρήμου 'Ραιθοῦ καὶ τῆς κατὰ Φαράν ἁγίας ἐκκλησίας. *Harduin*, vol. ii. p. 1281) is signed, the Church of Pharan would probably be first named as undoubtedly the most important centre and bishop's seat, if the monks all around the vicinity were not looked upon as the more important, and therefore put first. Le Quien (vol. iii. p. 735) mentions the *Episcopi Pharan sive montis Sinai* in one series, and as the earliest with the latter title the above-mentioned Bishop Jorius (†1033). Since then, and even since Eutychius (c. 940), the denomination of the single mountain of Gebel Mûsa as Sinai is certainly undoubted.

INDEX

OF

GEOGRAPHICAL NAMES.

A.

ABAHUDA, 270.
Abaton, 123.
Abdebab, 146.
Abd el Qurna, 274, 309.
Abdîn, 187.
Abke, 269.
Abu Dôm, 247, 256.
Abu el Abás, 185.
Abu Hammed, 132, 137, 146, 148.
Abu Haras, 132, 178.
Abu Hashîn, 151.
Abu Nugara, 146.
Abu Roash, 35, 64.
Abu Shar, 330.
Abu Simbel, 270.
Abu Tleh, 238.
Abu Zelîmeh, 333, 348.
Abydos, 94, 114.
Acca, 349.
Adererât, 146.
Agamîeh, 88.
'Ain el Haramîeh, 392.
Aithi, 395.

Akoris, 100.
Alabastron, 113.
Alexandria, 7, 11, 389.
Amâra, 266.
Amarna, 94, 111, 113, 374.
Ambukôl, 259.
Anîve, 274.
Antinoe, 110.
Arbagi, 177.
Argo Island, 262.
Argôusene, 264.
Asasîf, 297.
Assuan, 99, 118.
Assur, 157.
Astaboras, 152.
Atbara, 152.
Atfeh, 13.
Athirib (Athribis), 389.
Axum, 91.

B.

Bachît, 258.
Bahîuda, Desert of, 237.
Bahr bela mâ, 85, 140.
Bahr Jussuf, 82, 87.

2 G

Bahr Sherkieh, 85,
Bahr Wardani, 85,
Bâlbek, 407.
Barkal, 245,
Begerauteh, 156, 160.
Behbet el hager (Iseum), 389.
Belled e' Nûba, 255,
Bellel, 255,
Benihassan, 94, 107, 110,
Benissuef, 93, 374.
Ben Naga, 160, 162, 165, 213, 217.
Bersheh, 94, 110, 113.
Berut, 394,
Beth el Walli, 124,
Bethin, 392,
Biahmu, 87,
Bigeh, 119,
Bireh, 392,
Birqet el Qorn, 82, 83, 86, 88.
Bisheh, 88,
Blue River, 172,
Britân, 407.
Bsherreh, 414,
Bulaq, 14.
Byblus, 418.

C.

Cairo, 14, 51, 89, 91,
Carmel, 394.
Chartûm, 133, 134, 168, 206, 207, 211.
Chemmis, 113.
Chôreb, or Hôreb, 336, 351.
Chôr el Ammer, 240.
Chôsh e' Gurûf, 255
Crôcodilopolis, 88

D.

Dáhela, 188,
Dahshûr, 64, 90,
Dakkeh, 124.
Dal Hani, island, 156,
Damascus, 400.
Dâmer, 137, 152, 156,
Damietta, 389,
Danqêleh, 231,
Darmali, 255.
Debbet e' Ramleh, 346,
Debôd, 124,
Dendera, 94, 107, 114, 374,
Dendûr, 124.
Dêr el ahmar, 409,
Dêr el bachît, 304,
Dêr el bahri, 304,
Dêr el medinet, 304,
Derr, 264.
Dimeh, 89.
Dongola (Old), 251,
Dongola (New), 261,

E.

Echmim, 113,
Edfu, 116.
Eileithyia, 115,
El 'Ain, 397.
El Bosra, 112, 113,
El Chôr, 151.
El Elâm, 85, 87,
Elephantine, 119,
El Gôs, 239,
El Guês, 231, 234,
El Hessue, 368,
Elim, 351.
El Kab, 115,

Esneh, 115.
E' Sûr, 131.

F.

Fadnie, 163.
Faiûm, 69, 88, 90.
Fidimin, 88.

G.

Gabushîe, 217.
Gauâta, 99, 113.
Gebel, 231.
Gebel Adar Auîb, 146.
Gebel Ashtân, 167.
Gebel Abrak, 142.
Gebel Abu Sheqere, 335.
Gebel Barqugrês, 239.
Gebel Buêrib, 162.
Gebel Dochân, 321, 328.
Gebel el Bâb, 140.
Gebel Enned, 331.
Gebel e' Tih, 346.
Gebel Farût, 146.
Gebel Fatireh, 320.
Gebel Graîbât, 146.
Gebel Hammâm, 333, 355.
Gebel Katherin, 335.
Gebel Lagár, 165.
Gebel Maqàl, 255.
Gebel Mograb, 146.
Gebel Mûsa, 334.
Gebel e' Naga, 163, 165.
Gebel Rauiân, 167.
Gebel Roft, 143, 146.
Gebel Sefsâf, 336.

Gebel Selîn, 113.
Gebel Abu Sengât, 146.
Gebel Sergên, 238.
Gebel Abu Sibha, 146.
Gebel Silsilis, 116.
Gebel Um Shômar, 335, 342.
Gebel Zeit, 313, 319, 331.
Ge'ah, 333.
Gedideh, 287.
Geg, 151.
Genna, 157.
Gennin, 393.
Gerashâb, 167.
Gerf e' Shech, 255.
Gerf Hussên, 125.
Gertassi, 124.
Gezîret el Qorn, 88.
Ghadine, 231.
Gharag, Lake, 89.
Gibraltar, 6.
Gilif, Desert. 237.
Gizeh, 18.
Gôba, 404.
Gomra, Island, 157.
Gôs Basabir, 167.
Gôs Burri, 234, 238.
Goshen, 21.

H.

Haipha, 394.
Haluf, 255.
Hannik, 264.
Hamamât, 318.
Hamdab, 252.
Heliopolis, 17.
Hellet el Bib, 253.
Hellet e' Soliman, 204.

Hermonthis, 115.
Hieras Kaminos, 125.
Hobi, Island, 162.
Hôreb (Choreb), 336, 351.
Howara, 76.

I.

Ibrim, 270.
Jericho, 392.
Jerusalem, 391.
Illahûn, 69.
Ishishi, Island, 251.

K.

Kalabsheh, 272.
Kamlin, 173, 176.
Karnak, 280.
Kasinqar, 251, 255.
Keli, 233, 234.
Kerak, 396.
Kermân, 393.
Koi, 264.
Kôm el Birât, 308.
Konosso, 119.
Korte, 125.
Korusko, 100, 127, 129.
Kossêr, 319.
Kûeh, 252.
Kummeh, 268.
Kurru, 256.

L.

Labyrinth, 67, 78.
Libanon, 410.
Lisht, 44, 69.

Luqsor, 95, 96, 287.
Lycopolis, 95.

M.

Mágeqa, 241.
Mandera, 132, 172.
Malta, 7.
Mara, 354.
Marûga, 231, 232, 235.
Massani, 255.
Matarieh, 21.
Mechêref, 147, 154.
Medînet el Fairûn, 83, 88.
Medînet Habu, 96, 291, 294.
Medînet Mâdi, 89.
Medînet Nimrud, 89.
Megdel, 395.
Mehendi, 126.
Meidum, 44, 69.
Mekseh, 395.
Memphis, 19, 54, 67.
Melâh, 212.
Méraui, 232, 249.
Meroe, 152, 157, 161, 213, 226, 232, 252.
Mesaurât, 165.
Mesaurât el Kirbegân, 165, 167.
Mesaurât e' Raga, 165.
Mesaurat e' Sofra, 165.
Messaid Fountain, 330.
Metamme, 163.
Mitrahinneh, 55.
Mogrân, 152.
Moeris, Lake, 69, 82.
Mosh, 264.
Mundera, 146.
Myos hormos, 330.

N.

Nablûs, 392.
Naga, 160, 162, 165, 233.
Naharîeh, 13.
Nahr el Kelb, 418.
Nakb el egaui, 334.
Nakb el haui, 338.
Napata, 246, 249.
Nazareth, 391.
Nebbi Shît, 406.
Nekleh, 13.
Nesleh, 89.
Noah's Grave, 396.
Nuri, 243, 245.

O.

Okmeh, 267.
Ombos, 116.

P.

Panopolis, 113.
Pharân, 342.
Philæ, 95, 118, 122.
Philotera, 330.
Pompey's Pillar, 11.
Primis, 126.
Pselchis, 100, 125.
PYRAMIDS OF
Abu Roash, 25.
Abusir, 51.
Dahshûr, 64.
Gizeh, 18, 32.
Howara (labyrinth), 67,
78.
Illahûn, 69.
Lisht, 44, 69.
Merdûm, 44, 69.

Pyramids of—continued.
Memphis, 14, 67.
Méroe, 157, 226.
Saqâra, 44.
Zauiet el Arrian, 35.

Q.

Qala, 178, 231.
Qasr e' Salat, 114.
Qasr Qerûn, 89.
Qeneh, 313, 316, 372.
Qirre Mountains, 167.
Qirsh, 272.
Qurna, 96, 104, 270, 294.

R.

Râha, plain, 339.
Raphidîm, 355.
Rigah, 64.
Roda, 36.
Româli, 189.
Rosetta, 120.

S.

Saba Doleb, 183.
Sabagûra, 272.
Sâ el Hagar (Sais), 13.
Saffi, island, 254.
Sagâdi, 157.
Saï, island, 266.
Saida, 394.
Salamât, Sanamât, 292.
Salame, 255.
Salhîeb, 405.
Samanub (Sebennyius), 389.
San, 389.
Saqara, 44, 51, 62, 67, 74, 77.

Sarbut el Châdem, 345, 353.
Shataui, 270.
Shendi, 162, 163, 213.
Sebastiêh, 392.
Sebûa, 125.
Sedeïnga, 266.
Selajîn, 88.
Selama, 163.
Selûn, 392.
Semneh, 268, 294.
Sennâr, 186, 189.
Serbâl, 334.
Sero, 155, 189.
Sêse, 265.
Sêsebi, 265.
Sin, desert, 335.
Sinai, 336.
Sinai, convent, 334.
Siut, 94, 112, 113.
Soba, 172, 205.
Soleb, 265.
Sorîba, 190, 192.
Suk el Barada, 405.
Sur (Tyre), 394.
Surarîeh, 93.
Surîe Abu Ramle, 211.

T.

Tabor, 393.
Taîba, 203.
Talmis, 124.
Tamaniât, 211.
Tamîeh, 86, 90.
Tanis, 389.
Tanqassi, 156, 256.
Tarablûs, 417.
Teirîeh, 14.

Tel Emdîeh. 397.
Thana, island, near Gorata, in
    Ethiopia, 91.
Thebes, 93, 114, 274, 277, 279.
Tiberias, 393.
Tifâr, 259.
Tombos, 264.
Tôr, 313, 319, 333.
Tripolis, 417.

U.

Um Shebah, 243.
Um Shômar, v. Gebel Um
    Shômar, 342.

W.

Wadi Auateb, 163, 164, 165.
Wadi Abu Dôm, 242.
Wadi Abu Harod, 240.
Wadi Aleyât, 340.
Wadi Bahr Hátab, 141.
Wadi Delah, 141.
Wadi el Arab, 271.
Wadi el Kirbegân, 113, 162,
    165, 167.
Wadi el Mehet, 240.
Wadi el Uêr, 240.
Wadi e' Sheikh, 338.
Wadi e' Sileha, 165.
Wadi e' Sofra, 160, 163.
Wadi e' Sufr, 141, 157.
Wadi Firân, 340.
Wadi Gazal, 243.
Wadi Gaqedûl, 240.
Wadi Gharandel, 354.
Wadi Gûah el âlem, 230.
Wadi Halfa, 100, 108, 134.

Wadi Hebrân, 333.
Wadi Ibrîm, 271.
Wadi Kalas, 242.
Wadi Kenus, 271.
Wadi Maghâra, 335, 353.
Wadi Mokatteb, 344.
Wadi Murhad, 144.
Wadi Nasb, 348, 353.
Wadi Nûba, 271.
Wadi Qeneh, 345.
Wadi Rim, 339.
Wadi Shebêkeh, 353.
Wadi Sebûa, 127.
Wadi Selâf, 339.
Wadi Sioh, 346.
Wadi Síqelji, 341.
Wadi Sittere, 346.

Wadi Taibe, 353.
Wadi Teresîb, 162.
Wed Mêdineh, 190, 194, 207.
Wed Negûdi, 183.
White River, 171.

Z.

Zachleh, 395.
Zahêra, 417.
Zani, 91.
Zauiet el Arrian, 35, 64.
Zauiet el Meitîn, 107.
Zebedêni, 398.
Zerîn, 393.
Zûma, 257.